HARVARD SOCIOLOGICAL STUDIES

VOLUME III

THIS STUDY HAS BEEN AIDED BY A GRANT FROM THE HARVARD UNIVERSITY COMMITTEE ON RESEARCH IN THE SOCIAL SCIENCES, AND ITS PUBLICATION HAS BEEN FINANCED BY THAT COMMITTEE

AN INTRODUCTION TO THE SOCIOLOGY OF LAW

BY

N. S. TIMASHEFF

GREENWOOD PRESS, PUBLISHERS
WESTPORT, CONNECTICUT

Library of Congress Cataloging in Publication Data

Timasheff, Nicholas Sergeyevitch, 1886-1970.
An introduction to the sociology of law.

Reprint of the 1939 ed. published by Harvard University Committee on Research in the Social Sciences, Cambridge, which was issued as v. 3 of Harvard sociological studies.
Bibliography: p.
1. Sociological jurisprudence. I. Title.
II. Series: Harvard sociological studies, v. 3.
Law 340.1'15 72-11238
ISBN 0-8371-6633-0

Originally published in 1939 by Harvard University Committee on Research in the Social Sciences, Cambridge, Mass.

Reprinted in 1974 by Greenwood Press, a division of Williamhouse-Regency Inc.

Library of Congress Catalog Card Number 72-11238

ISBN 0-8371-6633-0

Printed in the United States of America

PREFACE

THE first draft of this book was sketched in 1916–1920, in connection with lectures on sociological jurisprudence at the Polytechnical Institute in Petrograd. The manuscript was lost when I was forced to leave Russia in 1921. But in 1922 while in Berlin, I was able to publish (in Russian) an abstract of my lectures which comprised the basic ideas of the present work. Other scientific problems enforcedly engaged my attention mainly until 1935. Then in 1936 I was invited by the Department of Sociology of Harvard University to give a course on the Sociology of Law. This made available to me the riches of several Harvard libraries, and enabled me to give definite form to the work that I had planned many years before. The Harvard Committee on Research in the Social Sciences came to my aid with a grant for clerical assistance.

I am greatly indebted for many valuable suggestions to Professors P. A. Sorokin (Harvard University), J. Hall (Louisiana State University), H. E. Yntema (University of Michigan) and G. D. Gurvitch (University of Strassbourg, France) all of whom read my complete manuscript. I am grateful as well to Professors G. Allport (Harvard University), Read Bain (Miami University), F. H. Hankins (Smith College), L. J. Henderson (Harvard University), R. MacIver (Columbia University) and Max Rheinstein (University of Chicago) who have read and commented upon various parts of it. Also to Dr. E. Y. Hartshorne, Mr. Logan Wilson, and Mr. N. M. Oushakoff, who helped revise my manuscript for publication, and to Mrs. E. Y. Hartshorne and Mrs. Marjorie Noble, who put it into typescript, I am much in debt.

Several sections of the book have already appeared in Professor J. Hall's *Readings in Jurisprudence* (Indianapolis, 1938), and in the *American Journal of Sociology*,[1] in the *Journal of Criminal*

[1] "What Is the Sociology of Law," September, 1937; "The Sociological Place of Law," September, 1938.

Law,[2] in the *American Sociological Review*,[3] and, in French translation, in the *Archives de Philosophie de Droit et de Sociologie Juridique*. I wish to express my gratitude to the editors of the above journals, Professors Ernest W. Burgess, Robert E. Park, Read Bain, Robert H. Gault, and G. D. Gurvitch, as well as to the Chicago University Press, for their kind permission to include in my book the articles already published. The quotations are made with the kind permission of the following publishers: the Harvard University Press, the Houghton Mifflin Company, McGraw Hill Book Company, Harcourt, Brace and Company, and Harper and Brothers.

N. S. TIMASHEFF

Cambridge, Jan. 25, 1939

[2] "The Retributive Structure of Punishment," September–October, 1937.
[3] "The Power Phenomenon," August, 1938.

GENERAL EXPLANATION OF BIBLIOGRAPHY

For the sake of brevity, the works mentioned in the text and in the footnotes, and in the bibliographical notes attached to the chapters, are quoted only by the names of authors. Symbolic letters are added where two or more works of the same author are quoted. An exception is made in Chapter III, which can be considered as a kind of systematic bibliography of the works particularly relating to the field of the sociology of law.

The complete titles of the works are given in the general bibliography at the end of the book. Page numbers of quoted works are indicated only in cases where specific reference is made.

TABLE OF CONTENTS

PART I

SOCIOLOGY AND LAW

CHAPTER I

THE SOCIOLOGICAL PLACE OF LAW

§ 1. Law as a Social Phenomenon

When observing human behavior in society, we notice that it is often determined by its relation to an "X" called law. In some cases men act in a certain way and not in another, because law imposes upon them just this conduct. In other cases they carry out acts which they would be unable to accomplish had they to reckon only upon their own "natural" forces: law backs them up and endows them with additional power. In still other cases their behavior is determined by their concern for law. Finally, some acts are understood by their authors or by other people as transgressions of law, whereas many acts remain irrelevant or neutral from the legal point of view.[1]

The relation of acting individuals to the "X" representing law may be conscious or unconscious. If it is unconscious, there are other men who interpret the conduct of acting individuals in one of the above-described ways and sometimes, as a result of such interpretation, they themselves begin acting in a way related to law. However, in the majority of cases, individuals acting unconsciously are able to discover the relation of their behavior to law, sometimes by means of posterior introspection or interpretation of their conduct. This may be done either on their own initiative or as a result of suggestion or compulsion on the part of other individuals.

The "X" represented by law might seem to be merely a sum of subjective concepts or representations. This is not so, for law, to which acts of group-members are related in the above-described manners, is independent of individual opinions or concepts: within a certain social group identical patterns of conduct are considered to be legally imposed, to help one in one's actions, to

[1] The different aspects of the behavior related to law will be more amply treated in chap. XI, § 3.

be taken into account when acting, or to be transgressed. Not only have almost all group-members identical ideas concerning the law which is in force within the group,[2] but they know also that the law is truly "in force," that combined forces of men stand behind the law. The efficacy of law, i.e., its existence as a social force,[3] depends upon a stable disposition or attitude on the part of group-members toward helping law to be actualized in social life. This stable disposition is a product of a long-lasting social interaction. Such products form culture. Consequently, law is a part of culture, a cultural object or a cultural force.

The conformity of social life to law is, however, only a tendency, not a complete actuality. But, in conflicts with other forces (especially in conflicts with divergent individual wills) the triumph of the social force called law is the rule, the definite defeat of law merely an exception. How do we know this? Direct observation gives sufficient evidence. Everyone, observing his own life or the life of his relatives and acquaintances, notices that acts carried out in conformity with or out of regard for law are very numerous, whereas acts carried out against law, if any, are only exceptional. Try to represent yourselves acting against the law, and you will notice that a certain psychic resistance must be overcome in order to create a vivid representation of this kind; to continue the experiment and to act against the law in order to "prove its nonefficacy" would, generally speaking, be impossible.[4]

The value of such personal observation may be enlarged without difficulty: it is very easy to become aware that the efficacy of

[2] Of course, controversies frequently arise concerning what is "law in force" (judicial trials with the question of law as the point at issue; scientific polemics, et cetera). But (1) such controversies generally cover merely very small parts of the legal field; (2) the antagonists agree in every case that there can be only one "law in force" applicable to their case. Ideas of group-members diverge much more as regards law that ought to be; but this is another question.

[3] "The norms of law," says Rheinstein (*b*, 232), "exist in the same sense in which a poem, a symphony, or a singular proposition exist." This is correct, but perhaps insufficient: the norms of law are verbal formulas in which law is expressed. Law itself is a social force: i.e., something that exists in another plan of reality than mere verbal formulas. *Cf.* Kantorowicz and Patterson.

[4] Anticipating further explanations, it may be said that "experiments" of the kind discussed would be inhibited by large and strong complexes of acquired tendencies of behavior, the existence of which in individuals forms the social fact expressed in the term "the efficacy of law."

law is nothing specific to one's own city or country. Everything one knows about other cities and civilized countries testifies to the fact that there also people are adjusting their behavior to law and are taking part in the social process of securing its enforcement. Travelers give us (orally or in writing) sufficient evidence of this kind. Historians tell us that adjusting behavior to law already existed in ancient times; ethnologists that law already existed within many primitive tribes.

There is also "mass" evidence. Certain countries possess almost complete criminal statistics, showing the total number of cases of transgressions against law insofar as they have been tried by criminal courts. Of course, there have been many cases which do not pertain to the domain of crime; and also, of course, there are unknown and unreported cases. But even if we multiply by ten the figures of criminal statistics, the number of transgressions will remain very small as compared with the tremendous number of acts carried out in accordance with law.[5]

On the other hand, the number of habitual and professional criminals, in whose lives transgression of law is rather frequent and who are not normally motivated by law, is very small.[6] The conclusion is: the normal motivation by law is in force with regard to almost the totality of citizens in the large majority of life-situations in which the transgression of law is practically possible and would correspond to the resultant of natural (i.e., of nonsocialized) drives.

§ 2. Natural, Imitative and Imposed Uniformities

Individual observation, corroborated by introspective experiment and mass observation expressed in statistical data, shows

[5] According to *Criminal Statistics* (England and Wales: 1934) the number of known cases of indictable offenses was 223,359; but only 75,767 (or 32.4 per cent) could be prosecuted. The number of prosecuted nonindictable offenses was 634,226; the number of known cases has not been indicated. But, assuming that the proportion was the same as regards indictable offenses, the total number of known offenses (both indictable and nonindictable) must have been about 2.2 millions. The population of England and Wales (over 10 years of age) was 34.5 millions. Consequently, during one year only one inhabitant, over 10, out of 16 committed an offense.

[6] A very careful investigation of the number of habitual offenders in Germany by Heindl (p. 194) has shown that, in 1927, this number was 9.5 thousands for a population of about 65 millions, or 0.13 per cent.

that the triumph of law, i.e., the conformity of human behavior to legal precepts, is not a postulate, not a desire of well-intentioned individuals, but a fact of social life.[7] As conduct is generally adjusted to legal patterns and as legal patterns are relatively constant, the triumph of law means the shaping of human behavior in society in a constant direction. In other words, law produces similarity or uniformity in the behavior of individuals within a social group. Let us call such a uniformity a "socio-legal uniformity" and search for the place of this uniformity among social uniformities in general.

A social uniformity is a set of similar acts. Acts are never totally identical with each other in all their details. Similitude between two or more acts can be stated only by means of abstraction, by observing them from certain viewpoints and leaving others out of consideration. Every uniformity in human behavior can be reduced to the basic proposition: similar conditions acting on men of essentially similar nature produce similar effects. The classification of uniformities is to be based on the analysis of "similar conditions." Three main classes of uniformities may be distinguished from this viewpoint, for which the terms [8] natural, imitative and imposed will be used.

The uniformities of the first class (natural uniformities) can be contrasted with the regularities both of the second and the third class (imitative and imposed uniformities) in the following way. Acts belonging to the second and third classes are to be causally explained as reproductions of "original acts" [9] which are considered by men as "patterns of behavior;" whereas acts of the first class cannot be explained in this way.

[7] J. Hall says: "The basic hypothesis upon which a sociology of law rests is that rules are potent conditioning factors as regards the conduct both of lay population and officials — that rules make a difference that is 'sufficient' in degree and importance to engage serious intellectual interest" (*b*, 3). In actuality the proposition is more than a "basic hypothesis:" it is the statement of an observable fact.

[8] Every terminology is somewhat artificial; nothing should be deduced from the ordinary significance of the terms applied in addition to that contained in the definitions given in the text.

[9] In some cases the "original act" is replaced by a certain "ideal structure" indicating a pattern which is then actualized in a set of concrete and uniform acts (*cf.* below, under 3).

The uniformities of the second class (imitative uniformities) can be contrasted with the uniformities of the third class (imposed uniformities) in the following way. Acts belonging to the third class of uniformities are to be causally explained as determined by "the imposition of patterns of behavior," whereas acts of the second class are not. The imposition of a behavior pattern is given, if the adjustment of the behavior of *A* to the pattern *X* is influenced by the behavior of at least one other individual *B*, whose behavior tends toward the adjustment of the behavior of *A* to *X*. It is possible (but not necessary) that the behavior of *B* be adjusted to *X* too. But if there is no *B* influencing *A* in the adjustment of his behavior, this adjustment may originate only in *A* himself. In this sense it is free, and the adjustment seems necessarily to be based on imitation.

Let us make a cursory review of the uniformities of the three classes.

1. Uniformities of the first class are formed by sets of similar acts, insofar as every act is caused by something standing "outside" but not "above" the actors. There are neither preëstablished patterns to which single acts should conform, nor, within the set, acts selected as patterns which should be imitated by others. The observer is free to choose for description any act of the set, every act being neither more nor less typical than any other.

Statistical uniformities [10] belong, first of all, to this class. Within a certain social group, during a certain period, a rather constant number of crimes and suicides are committed, a certain number of marriages are concluded, et cetera. Furthermore, many of the uniformities described in general sociology or in political economy are also "natural uniformities;" cattle breeding is replaced by agriculture every time, when a certain density of the population is attained; every political society is destroyed by a revolution, if certain conditions are united; in countries with liberal economy men raise the prices every time, when the demand increases faster than the supply, et cetera.

[10] Such as the so-called tribute of humanity to crime and suicide discovered by Quetelet, I, 9, and II, 166–8.

Natural uniformities as such do not exert any pressure on the behavior of an individual. Pressure is exerted by many causative factors, the combined action of which forms the uniformity. Insofar as the behavior of the majority is determined, we may speak of typical acts. But conditions forming the social milieu necessarily do not determine the individual act: sometimes constellations of variable causes determine individual behavior in a way quite different from the typical one (atypical acts).

2. The second class of uniformities is formed by sets of similar acts, within which a certain type of behavior is "freely" chosen by an indeterminate number of individuals as a pattern for their behavior. In contrast to the first class, the sets of similar acts are formed as a result of a certain trend toward similarity; units in the series are not equal ones: there are, within the series, inventive or creative acts in the beginning and imitative acts in the other parts. Certain individuals introduce a new fashion of clothing, the others follow; a business man discovers an efficacious form of advertising, his competitors imitate him; a man preaches a new religious or philosophical doctrine, others are "converted."

In all these cases there is no compulsion, no imposition of patterns of conduct upon others. Sometimes the inventor would be glad to keep his invention for himself (our business man); sometimes the inventor is rather indifferent as to the success of his invention, or he may be imbued with the spirit of proselytism, but his manner of influencing action is only persuasion.

3. The third class of uniformities is formed by sets of similar acts within which a certain behavior is "imposed" on group-members as an obligatory pattern for their behavior.

An obligatory pattern for behavior might appear as (a) a concrete act or a series of similar acts, or (b) an ideal structure. In a primitive agrarian community everyone tills his allotment of soil just as his father and forefathers did; or, soldiers greet their superiors in the exact manner shown them by an officer; or again, grain merchants in a certain harbor, when settling their mutual accounts, take into consideration the manner in which this was generally done during previous years. An authoritative court decided that "the person who for his own purposes brings on his lands and collects and keeps there anything likely to do mischief if it escapes, must keep it at his peril, and if he does not do so, is *prima facie* answerable for all the damage which is the natural consequence of the escape" (*Rylands* v. *Fletcher*); other courts, in England and elsewhere, followed the same procedure when judging similar cases. Such might be examples of the first variety.

A law has been enacted ordering the declaration of income according to certain forms: persons concerned adjust their behavior to the "ideal" structure. A new rite has been established by a church council; priests and believers perform it. The chamber of commerce has decided that the rules concerning grain trade should be modified; the corresponding behavior replaces that which previously prevailed. Such would be examples of the second variety.[11]

The imposition of patterns, in accordance with our definition, depends on the display of energy on the part of certain individuals aiming at the adjustment of the behavior to patterns. Such individuals will be called "supporters of patterns."

If the number of the supporters of a pattern and the intensity of their attitudes are sufficient, individual behavior is generally adjusted to the pattern. Behavior modeled on a pattern in force (i.e., on a socially supported pattern) is normal behavior. Exceptions, cases of maladjustment, are always possible; they are considered to be "abnormal" behavior.

Normal behavior is coördinated behavior, for it is behavior in accordance with obligatory patterns. The process of imposing behavior patterns is social coördination, and the result of coördination is social order. Social order is, of course, composed not only of directly imposed acts, but also of acts performed with a "concern" for imposed patterns. At the periphery of social order are acts carried out with the intention of avoiding imposed pat-

[11] Of course, both varieties do not form two "species" of a "gender," so that every concrete case could be either of the first or of the second type. In actuality they overlap, for in many cases when an obligatory pattern appears as a concrete act, or as a series of concrete acts, an ideal pattern already underlies the act or acts. The presence or the absence of an abstract formulation of the pattern could be considered as the crucial symptom to be used by those who like precise classification.

terns; but acts incompatible with established patterns no longer belong to the social order.

§ 3. The Interdependence of Uniformities

What is the place of law in our classification of social uniformities? It is obvious that law is one of the instruments of social coordination and that therefore legal order is a part of social order, the social force called law always tending to mold individual behavior in accordance with preëstablished patterns imposed by individuals who play the rôle of "supporters of patterns." It is equally obvious that legal order does not form the totality of social order: for there are many cases in which the function of social coördination is carried out by instruments other than law, such as custom, morals and also naked power.

Before advancing further in our search for the precise position of law among social uniformities, especially among the instruments of social coördination, we must make the following additional statements.

In classifying social uniformities we must lay stress upon the *immediate cause* of similarity in behavior. Legal, moral or customary behavior, or behavior based upon obedience to power, develops uniformities immediately caused by the imposition of patterns of behavior. The imposition of patterns is, in its turn, a social phenomenon, determined socially. It might happen that this determination would belong to other classes of social uniformities. Let us choose examples related to law; it would of course be possible to give other ones referring to other domains of social coordination.

Legal patterns of conduct are very often similar in different countries, whereas their imposition is an activity confined to national borders. How is this similitude to be explained? First of all, by similarity of conditions. The "*sitting dharna*," i.e., the distraint of debtors by means of starvation on the part of creditors was known to the laws of Manu, to early Irish law, and, in vestige, to early Hebrew law (Maine, *c*, 40, 294–304; Tarde, *c*, 177). The constitutional law of the kingdom of Aragon in the fifteenth century and that of Poland in the seventeenth and eighteenth centuries present striking similarities: both know the "Privilege of Union" (of Confederation in Poland), by which noblemen were allowed to resist, collectively and by arms, the infringement of their liberties, and the *liberum veto* which gave to any member of the Cortes (in Aragon) or of the Seim (in Poland) the power to defeat the passage of a bill he did not approve of (Prescott, LXXXIX and XCVIII and Bobrzynski, II, 181–7). The law concerning the use of the "Almende" (common) is almost the same in Scandinavian countries and in the German Alps (Haff, *b*, 10). The administrative institutions created by Napoleon in France are assimilated by a great historian (Taine) to those of Diocletian (Tarde, *c*, 178). In the cases mentioned there was no imitation or imposition. The similitude of conditions resulted necessarily in a social uniformity of the first class: similar acts (in our case, acts imposing legal patterns) are carried out in various noninteracting social groups. This natural similitude of legal structures has been expressed in the idea of *jus gentium* by the Romans, and in that of natural law by the philosophers of the seventeenth and eighteenth centuries; the modern theory of "facts of the law" independent of positive law belongs to the same category.

The second factor is imitation. Roman law was reintroduced in the lands of the Holy Roman Empire during the later Middle Ages, by imitation. In Germany all municipal laws of the Rhine towns were derived from Cologne; while Lübeck served in the same way as model for the Baltic towns (Allen, 66). The municipal law of Magdeburg was imitated by the majority of Czech and Polish towns (Tarde, *c*, 178). The code of London was adopted by 49 English towns, that of Winchester by 24 (Allen, 67). The French Civil Code of 1804 has been imitated in many parts of Germany, Italy and Poland. The British jury was imitated, with modification, by France under the Revolution and the Empire, and later on the French law became a model for a number of European countries. Beginning with 1831 and until the Great War, the British parliamentary monarchy had become the model for European constitutional structure. Agrarian laws of the first years of the Russian Revolution have been imitated in Esthonia and in Bulgaria. Fascist legislation concerning national minorities has been imitated in recent dictatorships in the Baltic States. Of course, imitation is possible "because the fundamental institutions of civilized societies agree. If the two societies differed as largely as the uncivilized peoples or Bolshevist societies of modern civilized peoples, then a similar transfer of legal provisions would have become utterly impossible" (Ehrlich, *b*, 143).

The opposite relation between uniformities of different classes is possible. A natural uniformity is sometimes the function of imposed, especially legal uniformities. Many of the empiric laws stated by classic political economy belong to this category. These "laws" are uniformities of human behavior arising every time a specific legal regulation has taken place, particularly if the private ownership of the means of production, the freedom of contracts and of competition, and the principles of private profit and transmission of property to following generations by means of inheritance are guaranteed by law. The similar configuration of law in different countries forms those "similar conditions," which, without any preëstablished pattern, engender similar responses.[12]

When classifying social uniformities, the immediate cause of similar behavior should be painstakingly searched for; this was a necessary addition to the review of the main classes of the uniformities.

§ 4. The Forms of Social Coördination

Now we are able to advance further in our search for the sociological place of law. This advance presupposes a classification of the forms of social coördination, and such a classification might be made from either of two independent viewpoints.

1. The imposition of patterns of conduct on the individual wills may or may not be accepted by the ethical group-conviction.[13] Group-conviction is the converging conviction of the indi-

[12] The correlation is inevitably more complex: the existence of a legal guarantee of the "bourgeois-capitalist order" depends very much on the economic conditions of the countries where it has been introduced; but sometimes such guarantees are introduced by means of imitation, in order to display the forces which, almost necessarily, will produce the uniformities specific to the capitalist order.

[13] The proposition in text differs from that stated by me previously (*k*); *cf.* Rheinstein's remarks in his comment to my quoted article (*c*).

vidual group-members, insofar as similar conviction is based on social interaction, on the mutual induction of "belief," on "partaking in the belief of others." The conviction is an ethical one, insofar as its content is the evaluation of human behavior from a specific viewpoint, permitting the application of the term "duty" to the behavior which is in conformity with a certain pattern, and of the term "violation of duty" to the behavior nonconformable with it, in contradistinction to other evaluations, in which such terms as "truth," "beauty" or "usefulness" (and their opposites) are applied.

If the individual participates in ethical group-conviction he "recognizes" the corresponding patterns of behavior (ethical rules) and becomes very easily their supporter: he imposes them on others because everyone, according to his sentiment, ought to act in accordance with them. On the other hand, he considers himself to be tied by the ethical rules he recognizes. This is *ethical coördination.*

The other type could be formed correctly only by means of negation; it is social coördination not formed by imposed ethical norms. Motives such as fear, insofar as it is possible to sustain them, form the essence of social coördination in this case. When a tyrant, holding aloof from the ethical life of the group, issues general orders and secures obedience, there is social coördination of the second class. This is *nonethical coördination.*[14]

2. The imposition of patterns of conduct on individual wills may be effected in a centralized or a decentralized manner. In the first case there exists within the larger social group a smaller group which forms its active center, whereas other group-members form the passive periphery. This active center must be endowed with power; if not, it would be incapable of imposing patterns of conduct on group-members. The social interaction on which the adjustment of behavior to patterns is based is in this

[14] It might be assumed that habits ("folkways" in Sumner's terminology, as distinct from mores) also belonged to the realm of ethical coördination. Yet this would be an erroneous hypothesis; for habits lack any relation to the ideas of "duty," "ought to be," et cetera; they are beyond the limits of social coördination in the terminology of this work; the uniformity of behavior based on collective habits is an imitative (in some cases perhaps a "natural") uniformity.

case an unequal one, for the rôle of the active center is different from that of the passive periphery; this is *imperative coördination.*

The opposite type of coördination exists in social structures not endowed with active power centers. This is very much the case in primitive society. But it is very frequent in advanced society too. People have to greet acquaintances, address others in a polite way, rise during a religious ceremony when the congregation rises, keep silence during a concert, challenge an offender (if one belongs to a group within which this manner of procedure is considered obligatory). If, in such cases, social coördination actually takes place, it can rest only on equal interaction, i.e., upon an interaction in which all group-members play, as a rule, the same rôle — that of influencing the behavior of others and of being influenced in turn. There is no display of power in such cases; this is *nonimperative coördination.*

3. From the logical viewpoint four complex types of social coordination might be deduced from the existence of two pairs of independent primary types: (a) nonethical and nonimperative, (b) ethical but nonimperative, (c) imperative but nonethical, and (d) ethical and imperative.

In practice the first complex type would prove impossible: where there is neither group-conviction nor centralized power, there is nothing which could secure durable coördination. But the remaining three types exist actually as well as logically.

(a) The ethical but nonimperative (*purely ethical*) coördination is created by custom and social morals. Both custom and morals may be expressed in terms of "norms" of conduct. These norms are supported by the group-conviction and generally have sufficient force to shape individual behavior accordingly; but this is not the same as the force of centralized power. Social uniformities generally depend on such norms.

(b) The imperative but nonethical (*purely imperative*) coördination is created by despotic government; such governments often compel certain general regulations, as well as special decrees, which form patterns of conduct in spite of their not being sanctioned by the group-conviction. Such general orders are supported by a display of power sufficient to secure their enforcement, so that social uniformities also correspond to them.

(c) The *ethico-imperative* coördination is created by law. In law both the group-conviction and activity of centralized power combine to secure the realization of certain patterns of conduct. Legal rules are ethical rules or norms in the sense above described, for every legal pattern of conduct can be expressed in a proposition with the predicate "ought to be." At the same time legal patterns of conduct are supported by centralized power and its coördinating activity, and not merely by the mutual social interaction which produces and reinforces the ethical group-conviction.

These types of social coördination might also be distinguished by the degree of identification existing between the group of individuals subjected to an imposed pattern of behavior and the group of those who "support" it.

Imagine that a social group subjected to a behavior pattern consists of the individuals *a, b, c, d . . . n*. Logically the group of supporters may be (1) identical with the first one (*a, b, c, d . . . n*), (2) formed by a part of the subjected (*a, b, c, d*), (3) formed exclusively of "outsiders" (*p, q, r, s . . . x*), (4) formed by all the subjected plus outsiders (*a, b, c, d . . . n* + *p, q, r, s . . . x*), or (5) formed partly by the subjected and partly by outsiders (*a, b, c, d,* + *p, q, r, s . . . x*).

The first case presents the ideal type of purely ethical coördination; in actuality a certain discrepancy between the two groups is possible (an individual may be subjected to the rule but not support it; on the contrary, an outsider may add his efforts).

The second case (in which a minority sharing a group-conviction displays energy in order to exert its influence throughout the whole group) corresponds to legal coördination.

The third case presents the ideal type of purely imperative coordination: the persons imposing the patterns are themselves not subjected to them and do not share the group-conviction. Sometimes they may use as instruments that party among the group-members which has the conviction that behavior corresponding to the commands of the outsiders "ought to be;" this corresponds to the fifth case.

The fourth case seems to be theoretical: there are perhaps no real social groups which correspond to its pattern.

§ 5. Law as Ethico-imperative Coördination of Behavior

What is the logical value of the above assertions? Statements, in which natural, imitative and imposed uniformities have been distinguished and the classes of ethical, imperative and ethico-imperative coördination of behavior have been pointed out, mean the construction of a conceptual scheme. This scheme must and should be judged (1) from the viewpoint of its logical correctness and (2) from the viewpoint of its adequacy as an instrument of observation: for observation means the description of facts in the terms of a conceptual scheme.[15]

The assertion that the province of law coincides with that of ethico-imperative coördination is the statement of a working hypothesis. A proof is necessary to show that law is ethico-imperative coördination; in other words that (1) law does not contain elements other than those of ethico-imperative coördination and (2) that ethico-imperative coördination does not contain elements other than those of law.

Hypotheses of this kind are arrived at by means of the trial-and-error method. But is it not true that all hypotheses in the field of inductive sciences are of this type? When a group of phenomena is studied, an hypothesis is created; the influence of a certain factor is assumed. Hypotheses of this kind are necessarily constructed after a preliminary investigation of numerous facts; later on consequences are deduced and compared with the whole range of facts known. If one succeeds in explaining the uniformity of facts by the influence of the "force" or "factor" having the properties *a*, *b*, *c* . . . *n* ascribed to it, the hypothesis is retained; if not, the assumption is abandoned.

There have been so many trials and so many errors in searching for a basic hypothesis concerning law that now the situation seems to have become rather clear: under different verbal formulae the same idea — of the ethical and at the same time imperative character of law — is always expressed. It is highly probable that the

[15] Henderson, (*a*).

treatment of law as ethico-imperative coördination covers the cases of which most people think when speaking of law: legal order is constituted by patterns of conduct enforced by agents of centralized power (tribunals and administration) and simultaneously supported by a group-conviction that the corresponding conduct "ought to be." There are peripheral cases: the highest rules of constitutional law and the rules of international law seem to lack the support of centralized power; on the other hand, such rules as, for instance, those regulating traffic on highways or customary regulations seem to lack any relation to group-conviction. It must be reserved for further analysis to explain how these and similar cases could be interpreted from the viewpoint of ethico-imperative coördination.

BIBLIOGRAPHICAL NOTE

The idea of social order forms one of the central points in Max Weber's sociology of law (16); this author expresses the opinion that every order is based upon recognition (*cf.* below, Chapter V) and, on the other hand, considers transgressions as somehow related to the order. Social order as a complex of regularities in human behavior is studied by Lumley (5). The idea of controlling the behavior of individuals by their "concern" for others is expressed by Whitehead (9–10). The idea that law is only a sum of subjective representations forms the essence of Petrazhitsky's theory (*a*, *b*).

The lack of discrimination between uniformities of different classes is characteristic of Carter's theory of law: custom, which, in his opinion is the basis of law, is "the conformity of conduct of all persons under like circumstances" (122–3).

There have been in sociology certain tendencies to explain the total social process from the viewpoint of invention on the part of the élite and imitation on the part of the mass (Tarde, *a*). There is today in social psychology a tendency to deny the primary character and the social rôle of imitation (*cf.* Allport, *a*, 77, 239–40, 390; Brown, 91–2; LaPiere, 7–8, 124–5, 143). The first viewpoint was of course an exaggeration: social regularities based upon imitation form only one of the possible classes. The second viewpoint should not hinder us from seeing in imitation one of the basic social phenomena; a primary social phenomonon is not necessarily an irreducible primary socio-psychic phenomenon. "In any case," says Allport (*a*, 249), "we rise irresistibly when the congregation rises" (*Cf.* Murphy, 180–2).

The idea of "imposing" rules or patterns is discussed by MacIver (*b*, 248). The interdependence of uniformities of different classes is mentioned by Pareto (661).

The idea that legal rules might be understood as empirical propositions showing what generally happens is discussed by Michael and Adler (336). The concept of law from the viewpoint of regularity, probability and predictability is current in the modern sociology of law, *cf.* Max Weber (*c*, 23); Horvath (209); M. Cohen (198) and social psychology (*cf.* LaPiere, p. 98). Outstanding jurists agree *cf.* Holmes (173); Cardozo (*b*, 44); Harper (*a*, 316). Cardozo's statement is: "Law is the body of principles and dogma which with a reasonable measure of probability may be predicted as basis for judgment in pending or in future controversies."

For a further discussion of the essence of ethical coördination see below, Part II; of imperative coördination, Part III. Different types of definitions of law are indicated in chapter VII.

CHAPTER II

THE PLACE OF THE SOCIOLOGY OF LAW IN SCIENCE

§ 1. Sociology and Law

Sociology is a nomographic science. Its aim is to discover uniformities in society and to systematically describe them in the form of "natural laws," whereas the description of concrete or individual phenomena, insofar as they are at all scientifically relevant, belongs to the task of idiographic sciences. Consequently, the sociology of law is a nomographic science which aims to discover "laws" of a scientific nature concerning society in its relation to law. In this somewhat ambiguous formula, the term "law" is used with two different meanings: first, in the sense of a formula describing the causal connections between phenomena, and second, in the sense of socially imposed rules acting on human behavior.[1]

These statements are deductive and their verification presupposes an exact knowledge of the terms included in them. The term "law" has been defined, in a preliminary way, in chapter I, and the term "society" is to be accepted in the sense used in general sociology. Unfortunately, up to now sociological terminology is very far from being uniform, and it is necessary to introduce the following statements in order to avoid terminological misunderstandings.

The determination of human behavior by the specific social force called law takes place within social groups. A social group is an organic structure, a concrete system. In modern philosophy these

[1] A scientific law is a statement of uniformity based on observation and experiment. A legal rule is not a scientific law. Yet the existence of a legal rule, in connection with the experimental fact that human behavior in society is generally determined by legal rules in force, induces us to assume the existence of uniformities which would correspond to legal rules. In every concrete case this assumption is to be verified by observation, for (1) there are legal rules which do not demand direct obedience and only observation may show what the uniformities corresponding to them will be (chap. XI); (2) rules belonging to "written law" are sometimes followed with deviations and this again can be specified only by means of observation (chap. XV).

are terms applied to designate complex relations between individual things or beings, relations which create new complex units *sui generis* without destroying the individual existence of the members. Society is an example of such a concrete system or organic structure. Materially speaking, there are only individuals in a state of interaction, but this interaction creates a new unit, a social group. Society is therefore a relation among individuals, its members. This relation is of course necessary: being in society is an essential property of every individual.

This is a concept far removed from the so-called organismic theory of society. Instead of putting society and the living organism in the same series of concrete systems, having in common the general features described above, this theory has declared society to be an organism, possessing the qualities of a living organism, and has striven to give an adequate knowledge of society by using this analogy.

On the other hand, by describing social groups as concrete systems, the existence of society as such, or the fact that it is something more than a sum of individuals, is by no means denied: society is the sum of interacting individuals, and this interaction is what differentiates society from the mere aggregates of individuals. Sociological realism is frequently also sociological mysticism. In order to guard against the latter, the structure of the reality of social groups (in general, or of groups especially studied) is to be analyzed. Their reality can be reduced to the uniformity or similitude of the ideas and of the actions of group-members. How to explain similitude or uniformity is one of the problems to be solved by sociology, both general and special (limited to the study of certain social groups or of certain aspects of social interaction). Here the sociologists enter a field in which sociology and social psychology overlap.[2] Therefore, throughout this work socio-psychological facts will be carefully studied in which the reality of social groups is expressed, insofar as this reality pertains to law.

[2] Barnes and Becker call social psychology a "dangerous field;" of course it becomes dangerous only if sociologists and social psychologists lose touch with one another.

The property of every concrete system is to return to an original situation, if comparatively small disturbances have taken place. Disturbances may be considered as "small" if the forces creating the interdependence of the elements of the system are stronger than the forces causing the disturbance. This tendency of a social group to return to the original situation may be called "social equilibrium." In applying this term, one must be extremely cautious. To introduce into the investigation of social structures analogies based upon the equilibrium of a mechanical or biological character would be a mistake of the same kind as that made by the organismic theory in calling society an "organism." Scientists of this school tried to explain social phenomena as if society were actually an organism; terminology replaced true investigation. It would be preferable to replace the term of *equilibrium*, in its application to social phenomena, by some other, but, unfortunately, there is no other available.

Even in mechanics or biology the term "equilibrium" does not express a primary, irreducible phenomenon; equilibrium is the resultant of an interaction of forces, and in order to explain the phenomenon these forces are to be investigated and, if possible, measured. Social equilibrium is also not a primary property of social groups, but rather is the resultant of the interplay of social forces, i.e., of the forces resulting from the interaction of many individuals. These are to be investigated in order to replace the *term* equilibrium by the *knowledge* of actual facts.

§ 2. The Negative Approach

It seems that law is closely connected to social equilibrium and thus to basic social phenomena. Criminal law inhibits the urge to violate equilibrium and, if the inhibition is insufficient, reinforces the ethical group-conviction. Civil law secures and eventually restores that distribution of goods and services in which social equilibrium is expressed. Constitutional law secures the distribution of dominance and submission within the social systems. By many parts of modern "socialized law" [3] the degree of coöperation attained in a given society is secured, et cetera.

[3] To adopt a term used by Pound (*c*).

In spite of this, there are scientists who deny the very possibility of the causal-functional study of law. This negative approach is formulated by the legal philosophers of the neo-Kantian school and by the formalists in theoretical jurisprudence. According to them, sociology of law should not exist at all, for its very idea is erroneous. Law belongs to the world of values and this world is completely distinct from that of actuality; therefore, only the normative method is suited to the study of law, since application to it of the causal method would be an undertaking condemned in advance from the viewpoint of transcendental philosophy. H. Kelsen, a leader of this negative trend, denies the very possibility of creating a sociological concept of law. "A sociological concept of law," he writes, "is just as impossible as a mathematical concept of a biological phenomenon or an ethical concept of the physical phenomenon of the freely falling body. Hence every attempt to create sociology of law must result in simply speaking, in a general way, of social phenomena" (*c*, 876).

Kelsen's comparison is, to be sure, only a picturesque expression and not the source of his negative attitude; an analysis of it, however, would aid in understanding the essential error of his view. Law is a social phenomenon whereas biological phenomena lie outside the framework of mathematics. It is possible to accept the primordial difference between ontology (the science of actuality) and axiology (the science of values),[4] and in spite of this to recognize the possibility of causal studies of the type undertaken by the sociology of law. Values as such (the content of norms) might be studied only by the normative method (i.e., by means of constructing a hierarchy of values), yet values do act on the lives of mankind, determining their behavior; thus values are forces and forces are the main object of causal study. Law is an actuality. "The desire of men to regulate their mutual relations is just as brute an empirical fact as that water expands when cooling just above the freezing point" (M. Cohen, 178).

[4] From the philosophical viewpoint it is doubtful whether actuality and evaluation should necessarily be opposed. The axiological approach is truly incompatible with the approach from the viewpoint of causation or necessity. *Cf.* Kistiakovsky (253), Gurvitch (*f*, 31–3) and Morgenthau (4–6).

Another negative approach can be found in the works of some "positivists" who seem to deny the "reality" of law and the very possibility of its rôle in social equilibrium. One might be inclined to mention among them Pareto, the great theorist of equilibrium. Such an inference, however, would be false, for Pareto denies the influence on human behavior of "ideal things" which would exist independently of men and be imposed on them. Yet he is full of understanding as regards the sentiments manifested by the recognition of ethical and legal values. The point at issue between "positivists" (to whom Pareto belongs) and idealists is whether values are "projected" by individuals into an ideal world and then "recognized" by them, or whether they exist independently in the ideal world and are "introjected" into individual consciousnesses. This is a metaphysical problem, and the description of human behavior in its relation to values does not depend very much on its solution — admitted that one of the systems is true, human behavior can be correctly described *as if* the other were right.[5]

§ 3. The Sociology of Law and Jurisprudence

Theoretical reasons against the concept of the sociology of law are invalid. But is there not a good practical reason against it — the existence of jurisprudence which seems to make the sociology of law superfluous?

Since olden times, law has been the object of a science called jurisprudence. This science has had a glorious record, numbering in its annals many famous names and immortal treatises. It is a many-branched science, which has developed into a network of numerous special disciplines called civil law, criminal law, constitutional law and so forth. Is there room in this field for still another science, that of sociology of law? Or is "sociology of law" only a new name for a science known for hundreds of years?

Yes, there is room. No, it is not a new name for an old science. Law is the center of interest for all, but the points of view are quite different and, therefore, also the knowledge gained by them.

Law is a social force. Its social function is that of imposing

[5] This is the reason why quasi-idealistic interpretations of Pareto's approach to "ultimate ends" are possible. Such is, for instance, the approach of Parsons (*b*).

norms of conduct or patterns of social behavior on the individual will, and the aim of jurisprudence is to study these norms. This study may be carried out with regard to norms in force in a certain country at a given time. Each single norm has to be explained and elucidated, for very often it appears in forms far from clear. Different norms have to be brought into correlation with one another, as their true meaning appears only by comparison and contrast. Classifying them and working them into precise systems forms another task of jurisprudence. Finally, the norms of conduct included in law are sometimes not directly expressed, but only indirectly mentioned in other norms; therefore true juridical discoveries are possible. Such are the tasks of positive and analytical jurisprudence — arduous, to be sure, yet fascinating.

The concrete norms of conduct forming law may also be studied from the historical point of view. Instead of describing in detail the norms applied today in a certain country, we may analyze the gradual development of the principal norms within certain periods in a given country. Such a study is undertaken by historical jurisprudence.

In both analytical and historical jurisprudence the comparative method can be applied: legal norms are studied with regard to a group of countries the social structures of which present, or once presented, some degree of similitude. This is the task of comparative jurisprudence.

Finally, the structure of legal norms presents at all times and places certain unchangeable features which may be considered as belonging to the very essence of law. The study of this unchanging form of the fluctuating patterns, their "natural" elements, is the task of theoretical jurisprudence.[6]

[6] Observation shows that the content of legal regulation varies in time and space and that the constant elements are formal. Every legal rule comprises a hypothesis, a disposition and a link between both (*cf.* chap. IV); in every legal relation we may distinguish the subjects of the right and of the duty, the objects of the relation, and the link between its elements. This is the "form" in which legal values are embodied in facts. On this form depends the classification of legal phenomena and even their correct description. For jurisprudence, the study of such formal elements is analogous to general morphology for botany and zoology. It is a necessary part of jurisprudence carried out by German and Russian jurists under the title of "General Theory of Law," of which Korkunoff's well-known book is the most typical.

In all these cases the norms of conduct as such remain the object of study. This is, in spite of the opinion of some scientists, a study of actuality and not a study belonging merely to the domain of evaluation, since the social patterns of behavior included in law actually exist, forming a part of culture. Rules of evaluation are the objects of jurisprudence but considered in their relation to actuality.

Jurisprudence is the description of concrete systems of certain value — judgments which actually influence or are influenced by the behavior of men in society. It belongs therefore to the number of idiographic sciences. Yet the existence of an idiographic science does not hinder the existence of a nomographic science investigating the same field; for instance, the existence of botany and zoology does not prevent the existence of a biological science of the organic life within all the species studied by botany and zoology.

§ 4. Sociological Jurisprudence

In this way, the problem of the province of the sociology of law seems to be solved. Yet another idea still must be discussed before the scope, the material, and the methods of this science may be definitely stated. It is an idea which forms a logical contrast to the negative approach of Kelsen and of the normativists. It is the attempt to introduce the sociological viewpoint within jurisprudence; in its most radical aspect, this approach pursues the aim of replacing jurisprudence by the sociology of law. The most explicit example of this trend is, without any doubt, Ehrlich's book, *The Fundamental Principles of the Sociology of Law.*

"A group of human beings," says Ehrlich, "becomes an association through organization. Organization is the rule which assigns to each individual his position and his functions." We have to determine "the facts with which the human mind associates such rules." These facts which, in Ehrlich's book, are called "facts of the law," "may be traced to a very small number: usage, domination, possession, declaration of will." "The facts of the law, by their very existence, determine the rules of conduct for human associations. On the basis of norms of conduct 'norms of decision' are created; these are the rules studied in jurisprudence." But these rules are different from those of conduct: "for a relation as to which there is a dispute is something different from the same relation at peace." Norms of decision, the sanctions of which are punishment and compulsory execution, are "merely the extreme means of combat against those who have been excluded from their associations." "Human relations," says Ehrlich, "are independent of the legal propositions." It is possible to describe all these legal relations without reference to any system of positive law. "The first function of the social science of law is to present an exposition of the common elements in the legal relation . . . with reference to their causes and effects. We must know what kinds of marriages and families exist in the country, what kinds of contracts are being entered into, what their content is as a general rule, what kinds of declarations by testament are drawn up, how all these things ought to be adjudged according to the law that is in force in the courts, how they are actually being adjudged and to what extent these judgments are actually effective" (*a*, 74, 85, 118, 123, 478, 504–5).

Contrary to Ehrlich's opinion, human behavior related to law cannot be studied, even in the sociology of law, without reference to positive law. For the uniformities formed by human behavior conforming to law consist of facts which have in common only the property of being in conformity with law. To study legal acts without reference to law means to study biology, politics, economics, et cetera. Ehrlich is exasperated that no information can be gathered from juristic literature as to the systems of agriculture in Germany and Austria. Jurisprudence would truly become a substitute for the whole range of the social science if constructed according to this desire.

On the other hand, the unification of jurisprudence and of the sociology of law would be a big handicap for the advance of the latter. The sociological study of law cannot form merely a kind of adjunct to the analytical, historical, comparative or theoretical study of legal norms, because it is impossible to construct a system of knowledge which would in any accurate way combine the formal study of norms and the causal study of human behavior related to these norms. The latter type of study needs a place by the side of jurisprudence, but not within jurisprudence.

Very instructive, from this point of view, is the recent history of the science of criminal law. Lombroso's revolutionary accomplishments resulted in attempts to rebuild this science completely, to replace the formal study of patterns of prohibited behavior described in criminal statutes by a causal study of crime and of the effects of punishment, and later by attempts to combine both points of view in one system. All attempts of the latter kind were a complete failure, and today a resolute separation again prevails: there is a science of criminal law, studying in an analytical, historical and comparative way the patterns of prohibited behavior, and another science, called criminology, studying actual human behavior insofar as it is related to crime and punishment. Both should, of course, occupy definite and significant places on the general map of scientific knowledge.

The position of Ehrlich is untenable, but his statements raise a problem concerning the accurate delimitation between jurisprudence and the sociology of law, for there are intermediary fields, the adjudgment of which to jurisprudence or to the sociology of law is dubious.

In the first place, there is an actuality, closely related to the existence of legal rules, namely, human behavior in society insofar as it is determined by them. Should not the study of this actuality belong to the task of the sociology of law?

It should not. To the extent that this behavior conforms to norms — and this is usually the case — the study of such behavior can give no other results than the study of the norms themselves: there would be a difference only in the external form, in the mode of presenting the facts. As regards abnormal behavior, different from the normal, the separate study of these two would be extremely inconvenient as this would transform the object of jurisprudence into an incorporeal phantom of social relations and result in doubling the number of legal sciences; to every juridical science another "socio-juridical" would correspond. Both descriptions must be combined and compared within one system and the result explained. Concrete descriptions of this kind do not belong in the domain of the sociology of law. On the contrary, the combined study of the two fields corresponds to the best tradition in jurisprudence. Jurisprudence acknowledges cases of transforming or even repealing statute law by customary law or juridical practice. In such cases not only the primary, but also the transformed rules are to be studied by jurisprudence. On the other hand, jurisprudence applies, among others, the teleological method in interpreting legal norms; this method presupposes a careful study of the actual social relations and processes which are to be shaped by the corresponding norms. When jurisprudence proceeds in this way, it is truly "sociological jurisprudence." [7]

Finally, the correlation between the sociology of law and jurisprudence may be expressed in the following propositions:

1. The sociology of law is a science, the content of which depends only to a small extent on the changes in concrete legal regulations. If the generalizations effected by the sociology of law are correct, new regulations and configurations must be covered in advance by the framework of socio-juridical "laws." If generalizations must be changed, this proves that they were incorrect; they are to be modified in the same manner as new discoveries force physicists to restate their "laws." On the other hand, jurisprudence is a science with variable content: phenomena to be observed and classified come and go, and with them the statements of jurisprudence. This is a situation perhaps similar to the one in political geography; how different is a modern textbook from the one used a century ago, and this because of changes in phenomena to be described!

2. There can be only one sociology of law (with subdivision

[7] Sociological jurisprudence is not a new branch of jurisprudence which could be added to analytical, historical and comparative jurisprudence; it is rather a new method, or a new viewpoint, to be used within every branch. The term sociological jurisprudence is ambiguous and should be replaced by that of "the functional method in jurisprudence." The term "sociological" is frequently misused in jurisprudence, for instance: Fehr (168) calls "sociological interpretation" the method of interpretation introduced by the school of "Interessenjurisprudenz" (*cf.* chap. XIII). Cardozo (*a* 30–1 and 71) considers as sociological the method of filling gaps by placing emphasis on social welfare. Davy (*b*) identifies the sociological method with the "realistic" theory of juridical persons.

into criminology, the sociology of civil law, political sociology, et cetera — insofar as a sufficient number of valuable generalizations could be stated with respect to such subdivisions). On the contrary, there must be as many jurisprudences as there are social fields with diverging legal regulations, and this in the spatial and the temporal sense (modern civil law of France, Roman constitutional law, et cetera), with, in addition to this, a comparative branch (*cf.* Rheinstein, *b*, 232, footnote 2).

The difference between the nomographic science of the sociology of law and the idiographic science of jurisprudence imposes on scientists a separate treatment of the problems pertaining to both. It is the same necessity as the one which, on a higher level, imposes on us a separate treatment of history and of sociology and, on a lower level, a separate treatment of criminology and criminal law. Of course, a very definite delimitation is impossible — but is it possible anywhere in the entire field of scientific investigation? A close interaction between the workers in both scientific fields is desirable, but the principle of two distinct scientific fields should be maintained.

§ 5. The Sociology of Law and the Philosophy of Law

The philosophy of law could be assumed to form a third discipline. Yet the philosophy of law is, of course, an additional approach to the problems of law; it is, however, beyond the scope of science. The philosophy of law is the integration of legal phenomena into an entity assumed to be known, but the knowledge concerning the structure of this entity is gained by intuition and cannot be verified by scientific methods.

This delimitation between the philosophy of law, on the one hand, and jurisprudence and the sociology of law, on the other, is perhaps more a postulate than a proposition expressing historical truth. Historically the development of the philosophy of law, the sociology of law and jurisprudence were closely connected to each other, and many works entitled "Philosophy of law" contained valuable scientific propositions, and *vice versa*. Among recent authors Gurvitch (*e* and *f*) tried to define a special field for the scientific investigation of law and morals which would form the philosophy of law and of morals and appear as a kind of introduction to both jurisprudence and the sociology of law. He invokes radical empiricism as the basic method for such an investigation. Yet it is difficult to assume that on this basis any philosophy, distinct from science, could be built up. The question raised by Gurvitch seems to be one of scientific convenience. It could be put in the following way: is it or is it not convenient to create a special discipline which would investigate the "first problems" concerning law?

The philosophy of law was and will probably remain the preliminary investigation of problems which are not yet mature for scientific solution. Yet there is at least one field in which the philosophy of law will remain completely independent of any advance in science. This is the field of the evaluation of the ultimate ends to be attained by law. The sociology of law can formulate propositions in which the ends of positive legal regulations would be stated. But whether one or another of these ends should be pursued by law, whether within the competition of ultimate end systems (for instance, those of conservatism, liberalism, socialism, or fascism) [8] this or that system should be preferred, can never be decided by scientific methods, such questions being beyond the scope of science.

A corollary can be derived from the propositions stated above. If an "applied science of legislation" will ever be created, it will be based both on the philosophy of law and the sociology of law. The sociology of law will procure the best means to the ends; but ultimate ends will forever depend on philosophical, and not on scientific considerations.

§ 6. The Structure of the Sociology of Law

The determination and the coördination of human behavior in society by the existence of legal norms [9] is the object of the new science called the sociology of law. Causal-functional investiga-

[8] *Cf.* Mannheim.

[9] I am formulating my opinion in this way, in contradistinction to my statements in the article "What is the sociology of law" (*g*), recognizing the value of the remarks of Rheinstein in his excellent review of Ehrlich's book (*b*, 234–5, footnote 4).

tion is its chief method. This is the positive but moderate approach to the sociology of law which is now dominating and which makes it a science different from jurisprudence, with its selective, descriptive and classificatory methods.

The accomplishment of this task depends obviously on the structure of law described in Chapter I. Law is one of the forms of social coördination, perhaps the strongest of them. The structure of this form of coördination, i.e., the system of human actions and reactions composing this form, is the main object of study in the sociology of law. This study should explain how this force in general succeeds in molding human behavior in accordance with social patterns and what the conditions of its efficacy or nonefficacy are. This can be done only by recognizing that law belongs to the family of ethical forces, of which social morals and custom are the other members. On the other hand, law as a social force is closely related to specific social structures, namely, power systems. The place occupied by law in such structures and the difference between legal power and power not related to law are also topics to be studied in the sociology of law, as well as the conditions for establishing and destroying power.

On the basis of such knowledge a sociological theory of the determination of human behavior by law could be built up. The process of legal determination is, in its turn, a social one: the determination is socially set, depending as it does upon other elements of socio-cultural life. Therefore, abstract configurations of chains of human action and reaction must be searched for, chains in which legal norms and aspects of human behavior fulfill alternately the active or passive rôles.

In this way the study of the integration of law in culture could be prepared. Every act in any way related to law is simultaneously, from the viewpoint of its content, a biological, economic, political and cultural act. The relation of law to these aspects of human behavior forms a further field of investigation for the sociology of law. In every case the kind of correlation must be elucidated and the special character of correlation investigated. Searching for such correlations without an accurate knowledge of law as an actual social phenomenon would be a hopeless enterprise. The absence of precise causal knowledge of many social phenomena is one of the reasons why the study of social correlations results in rather negative or indeterminate statements. Especially in criminology, where knowledge of the factors correlated with crime is essential, the idea is sometimes expressed that, without a scientific knowledge of legal behavior and its factors, scientific statements concerning crime are almost impossible.

§ 7. The Sociology of Law and Psychology

The scope of the sociology of law once defined, a survey of the methods should follow. A general question arises at this point — that of the psychological basis of socio-juridical investigations.

The study of law in its relation to society must be primarily causal-functional. Causal-functional study is the study by means of observation and, if possible, of experiment. Of course, in this way we cannot study law directly. For law is a social force, and forces, whether social or natural, may be studied only through phenomena they produce: natural forces in the movement and transformation of matter, social forces in human behavior. Human behavior is one of the main objects of psychology (both individual and collective).

A discussion of the basic problems of psychology would, of course, be out of place. Yet the following statements are necessary for the same reasons as the statements concerning sociology (§ 1).[10]

1. Human behavior might become the object of scientific analysis from two different viewpoints. It might be considered (1) merely as a complex of outward movements or (2), in addition to this, as a complex of corresponding states of consciousness.[11]

The first viewpoint is that of behaviorism. After a certain vogue this trend has decreased in importance both in social psychology and in sociology. The use of purely behavioristic methods in the sociology of law, which is a part of cultural sociology,

[10] These statements might seem syncretistic or even eclectical. In the opinion of the author, in modern psychology different trends converge; in different terms and from different angles similar propositions are stated. *Cf.* the statements of P. Janet at the meeting of the French Society of Philosophy, May 17, 1928.

[11] A purely *introspective* study of human *behavior* is, of course, impossible.

seems to be impossible, for behavior determined by law is symbolic behavior. We understand by symbolic behavior "those actions of human beings which are effective and significant only because they have a socially designated meaning" (LaPiere, 77). "In the domain of law human actions and reactions are controlled by the *meaning* of the physical objects whose material stimulus-constituents are themselves irrelevant and ineffective save as vehicles and supports of the meanings" (Malan).

It is obviously impossible to find any external symptoms of bodily movements which would allow us to conclude with precision whether one or another movement was corresponding to law, was contrary to law or was irrelevant from the standpoint of law. The same bodily movements, let us say, for instance, those of detaining another man, may be conformable to law when performed by a policeman executing his commission, and contrary to law when performed by a private individual in order to avenge himself against his enemy. Not the bodily movements as such, but their social meaning belong to the essence of law.

2. Therefore, not the first, but the second method of analyzing human behavior should be used in the sociology of law. This method presents the following varieties.

(a) Behavioristic and introspective approaches might be used alternately in constructing chains of correlated human acts. This means that the hypothesis of psycho-physical interaction has been accepted. Physical phenomena are thought to "cause" psychic phenomena and *vice versa*. A causal chain beginning with the bodily movements of an individual might be pursued through the consciousness of another individual and be continued in the bodily movements of the latter.

(b) Behavioristic and introspective elements might be used to construct the causal chains of human behavior, the first bringing into correlation the bodily movements and the second the psychic states. This is the hypothesis of psycho-physical parallelism, according to which bodily and psychic phenomena form two parallel causal chains without being causally related to each other. This hypothesis is just as well suited to the facts as the previous one.

It is, of course, more cautious to study social phenomena by the second, rather than by the first method, for parallelism is an undeniable fact, and the point at issue is whether this parallelism is based on an internal link of the causal type, or not. But a certain additional step seems to be allowed by the nature of the case and to be very helpful in the solution of many problems. "The sequence of movement upon volition to move is an immediately observable and undeniable fact," just as "the familiar sequence of sensation upon the stimulation of a sense organ" (McDougall, 241). It is, of course, uncertain whether this sequence is causal or not; in any case, we are confronted with the following situation.

The volition *A* (observed by means of introspection) has been followed by a movement *b* (observed by behavioristic methods). A biological phenomenon *a* (excitement of the brain center and of the nerves) has necessarily corresponded to the volition, just as a psychic event *B* has to the movement *b*. There must be then: (1) a causal relation *A–B;* (2) a causal relation *a–b;* (3) at least a correlation of parallelism between *A–B* and *a–b*. Whereas only the elements *A* and *b* are immediately observable, the hypothetical elements *a* and *B* may be included in the chains studied with high degree of correspondence to actuality.

3. When describing the human behavior in society, the following three classes of actions will be distinguished: (1) inborn or instinctive behavior, or the sum of responses which practically all the individuals of a given species, irrespective of special environmental training, tend to exhibit;[12] (2) voluntary or centrally initiated behavior, in which the response is the result of the higher coördinative activity of the brain, and which takes place in "new situations," when neither inborn nor learned responses are possible, and (3) learned and fixed or acquired behavior, in which responses are almost as automatic as in instinctive behavior, but are based on the special environmental training of the given individual; conditioned reflexes seem to play a large part in the formation of the behavior of this type, but probably do not form the only way. In the following discussion the term "tendency" will be applied to designate fixed connections between stimuli

[12] A formula borrowed from Tolman, 305.

(situations) and responses (reactions), both in inborn and acquired behavior, with the addition of the terms "inborn" or "acquired" in cases when only one of these types is in question. The term "tendency" is introduced in order to stress the difference between the adjustment of the whole organism and partial or "molecular" adjustments, to which the term "reflex" is commonly applied.

(a) Inborn tendencies are always observable from the behavioristic viewpoint. From the introspective viewpoint they are more complex. Sometimes they are accompanied by consciousness: for example, when winking or sneezing we are very often aware of it and are sometimes displeased at doing so. This accompaniment may be vivid, in the center of attention, or blurred; the attention may be attracted by other objects; somewhere on the periphery of consciousness an idea of sneezing or yawning may appear and quickly pass. Yet in the majority of cases there is no conscious accompaniment at all. From the viewpoint of psycho-physical parallelism, we have to admit the existence of a corresponding current in the subconscious sphere. This assumption is corroborated by the fact that sometimes traces of subconscious currents of this kind become active in the consciousness. Here we enter the province of psychoanalysis. The more highly developed and compound reflexes of this type may be called *instincts*, a term unfortunately badly misused in science.

For our purpose the question of prime importance is whether an ethical or even a legal instinct exists. Earlier scientists were inclined to give a positive answer. In the year 1873 Maudsley asserted that a special brain apparatus of morality must exist; the German psychiatrist Kahlbaum advanced the hypothesis of a special system of "moral conductors in the brain" (Gruhle, 911).

Modern social psychology answers the question in the negative. Consequently, inborn reflexes and instincts *as such* are to be eliminated from our research, but this does not prevent our referring to them when searching for the primary basis of more complex phenomena.

(b) In contrast to actions based on "tendencies" (both inborn and acquired), voluntary behavior is a centrally initiated process.

It is coördination from above — the ability to *create* stimuli and to subordinate behavior to them. In voluntary acts the inner aspects can be described much more easily than the outer. From the introspective viewpoint a voluntary act is generally the result of a struggle of motives. A motive or incentive is the entertainment of an idea of a possible bodily act or set of such acts and their results, together with a feeling of satisfaction or dissatisfaction. The result of the struggle of motives is the decision to act or not to act in a given way; in voluntary actions in general the decision preceeds the adjustive effort.

What is the biological equivalent of the psychic phenomena just described? External or internal stimuli, when needing coördination, produce nervous currents which involve brain centers, the brain being the main organ of coördination or of higher adjustment. Nervous currents excite some of the brain centers and inhibit others. There is a kind of struggle among brain centers for nervous energy, since the quantity of potential nervous energy at a given moment is biologically limited; this struggle of brain centers runs parallel to the struggle of motives in consciousness. The struggle results in an efferent nervous current which produces the bodily movement.

Voluntary acts are very often related to ethics and especially to law. Introspection, corroborated by reliable statements about the psychic processes of other individuals, shows that very often a decision is taken because of its conformity with ethical patterns, but only after a struggle in which the conceptualization of nonconformity played a certain part. Rightly, but with exaggeration, Rolin (6 and 16–17) tried to construct a general scheme of motives in which the legal motive would play a central rôle.

(c) As regards "learned behavior," its behavioristic structure is very similar to that of actions based on inborn tendencies: certain phenomena in the outward world become "stimuli" which are necessarily followed by "responses," provided that some inhibitions are not present (among them voluntary acts may play a certain part). "One may be conditioned to a situation without knowing it; one may be negatively conditioned to situations" (Murphy, 162).

From the introspective viewpoint the situation is about the same as that stated with regard to inborn behavior: currents in the subconscious sphere must correspond to learned responses; the phenomena of the association of ideas and of memory are, of course, the psychic parallels to them. On the other hand, it is often possible to reconstruct in consciousness an automatic act, by using the method of subsequent introspection. Here again we reach the province of psychoanalysis.

The existence of learned responses forms, from the behavioristic viewpoint, a "tendency" (of behavior): behavior is structuralized in given patterns and other possible reactions are inhibited (Thomas, 28). From the introspective viewpoint, "dispositions" correspond to these "tendencies." The tendency or disposition to respond to a certain situation by certain behavior or by expressing a certain sentiment in action is recognized in the current discussion. "One may properly be said to love or to hate a man even at the times when he is not at all present in one's thought and when one is experiencing no emotion of any kind. Common speech recognizes that love and hate are not merely emotions, but enduring tendencies to experience certain emotions whenever the loved or hated objects come to mind" (McDougall, 23).

The following statements may serve to express the relationship between tendencies (dispositions) and single acts. Voluntary acts, when repeated under circumstances favorable to learning, engender tendencies (dispositions). Later on, when phenomena are occurring which correspond to stimuli, the tendency (disposition) is actualized in acts which may be completely unconscious or which may be accompanied by conscious processes.

Very often actions based on learned tendencies form true chains, in which the response of one serves as the stimulus for another, and so on; such, for instance, is the case in playing a piece of music by heart. Such chains are sometimes combined into higher units, according to the various needs of individual and of social life. A group of learned tendencies (sometimes concatenated with inborn ones), insofar as it tends toward a certain objective purpose, is a habit; a habit may be individual or social; it is social if similar groups of learned tendencies have been formed in many members of the social group. Anticipating further explanations, we may note that habits form the psychophysical basis of customs: customs are habits reinforced by the socio-ethical conviction that the corresponding behavior "ought to be."

As a habit may be reinforced by socio-ethical conviction, it is obvious that learned behavior plays a rôle in ethical coördination. Moreover, this rôle is very important in power structures, i.e., in imperative coördination. Consequently, learned behavior is related to law as a social phenomenon and must, therefore, be taken into consideration in the sociology of law.[13]

§ 8. The Materials and Methods of the Sociology of Law

After this long but unavoidable digression the following question should be answered: what are the materials to be used and the methods to be applied when constructing a scientific theory of law as an actual social phenomenon?

In the first place, important material may be collected by means of observation, which may be of two types. The first is introspection, i.e., accurate subsequent analysis of one's state of consciousness insofar as it is related to law (acting according to law; acting against the law; acting with intent to transform the law; reactions produced by another's acting in accordance with or against the law). Gurvitch insists on the necessity of studying the specific actuality presented by law and on beginning this study by the analysis of the "immediate juridical experience." This experience is given in the acts of legislators, of authorities, of electors, of persons contracting settlements, of persons taking part in the juridical life of corporate bodies. This type of experience is, in his

[13] "For sociology the concept of conditioned reflexes is of paramount importance; the phenomenon of associative transfer forms the basis of all acquired tendencies, of every progress in conduct" (Pieron, 35). On the contrary, some sociologists express the opinion that actions based on tendencies do not belong to the domain of sociology (e.g., Max Weber, *c*, 2, 3 and 11). This is an erroneous opinion. Sociology has to present the social process: i.e., the totality of human behavior in society, as an uninterrupted chain of human actions and reactions. But sometimes our voluntary actions result in the unconscious actions of the others; sometimes our unconscious actions produce the voluntary reactions of others; and sometimes our unconscious actions produce further reflex actions of others. Therefore, in a sociological theory which did not take reflex actions into consideration, many links would be missing and many breaks in continuity would exist.

opinion, veiled in the minds of the actors by too much reflection and conceptual formulation. Gradual reduction and "inversion" have to be applied in order to gain the needed insight into their dependence on law (*c*, 63–80).[14] This is, it might be added, a method analogous to that applied by psychoanalysts in the investigation of subconscious psychic tendencies.

The second type of observation studies overt human behavior in general as determined by law or relative to law. Material collected by those pursuing the sociological trend in jurisprudence may be very useful, insofar as it shows how the rigid legal formulae are transformed in actual life, or how (for example) unjust or antiquated laws are avoided. For jurisprudence with this sociological tendency the objects of study are the transformed norms replacing the dead rules included in written laws. For the sociology of law, not the transformed norms of conduct, themselves, but the fact of their transformation is of interest and creates an incentive for generally studying the process of modifying patterns of written law by means of conflicts with other social phenomena and structures. The sociology of law does not have to be limited by such type of data. Direct and special observation may also be applied in order to investigate such problems as, for instance, the rôle of conditioned reflexes in securing the triumph of law.

Experiment must be added to observation. Introspective experiments are proposed by Petrazhitsky (*a*, 228–37). According to him, juridical or, in general, ethical impulses may be successfully studied by applying the methods of contradiction or of teasing; impulse increase in force if attempts are made to hinder the running of their normal course, or if rapid changes of the situation occur, alternately decreasing and increasing the chances for realizing the impulses. In such cases these impulses, which are almost imperceptible when they develop in a normal way, assume a character of dominance within the consciousness and therefore may be described with great accuracy.

[14] In his newest book, Gurvitch stresses that actual moral (ethical) values are always unprecise and confused and that only subsequent reflection can purify and clarify them (*f*, 33), the necessity of "reduction and inversion" is once more stressed (*f*, 33, 127–8, 158 *ff*.).

Experiments by means of tests are also possible. Several authors (Piaget, Caruso, Mira) have applied an ingenious system of tests in order to study the growth of the retributive emotion in children or the moral attitudes of adults. Their point of view was rather that of morals than that of law; in spite of this, their results are of great help when studying the "immediate juridical experience." It would be very useful to apply the same method to the investigation of the juridical mentality. Such questions as the survival of the primitive revenge mentality, or the rôle of the retributive emotion, which is one of the roots of criminal law even today, or the relative force of norms of conduct belonging to the domains of law, morals and custom respectively, could be studied in a large number of different situations.

Just as pathology gives valuable data in biology, or psychopathology in psychology, so criminology, the study of abnormal behavior in human society, or the nonadaptation of the individual will to social patterns, may, together with the sociology of revolutions, give much valuable insight into the construction of a sociology of law. The sociology of law and criminology can thus be of mutual support.

Data, collected by observation and by experiments of the above-mentioned types and by using the results of criminological research, refer to the conduct of modern civilized men. In order to test the validity of the data thus obtained, the data on ethnology and on historical jurisprudence must be included, as well as the data on child psychology. To be sure, these data should not be given a disproportionate emphasis in the system: the sociology of law should not become a theory of primitive law, just as sociology in general should not be merely a science of primitive human behavior.

Material collected by comparative jurisprudence may be of great value. On its basis "ideal types" in the style of Max Weber can be created. For instance, many generalizations may be stated which would be valid as regards only primitive law or only mature law. Yet not these types but the correlation between them and their relations to social situations and processes must be studied in the sociology of law.

Last but not least, brilliant remarks on the sociological character of law have been made by philosophers of law, historians of law and students of positive law. But these remarks in their totality are not able to replace the sociology of law. Made without any connection to a general sociological system, sometimes without even knowing that sociology exists, or in conscious opposition to any sociology, especially to the sociology of law, these remarks have, almost without exception, been conjectures rather than scientific theories.

There is room for a new science of the sociology of law; there are sufficient materials and methods to help us gain new knowledge; and there exist already brilliant attempts to solve the problem of the sociology of law. Continuing those efforts is an important task, not only from the theoretical but also from the practical point of view, for the sociology of law might become a basis for an applied science of legislation. And, in opposition to the belief of Savigny and the other founders of the historical school of jurisprudence, our time calls for a more rational settlement of human relations by means of consciously elaborated legislation.

BIBLIOGRAPHICAL NOTE

The philosophical concept of the concrete system was developed by H. Cohen (280–338). The idea of society as a concrete system forms the central point in the doctrine of Gierke (*a*, *b*, *c*, *d*). The organismic theory of the State in his works means nothing more than the application of the idea of a "concrete system" to the problem of State (*cf.* *a*, 29–34, *c*, 110–16). In jurisprudence his chief followers were Preuss and Krabbe; among later authors Schinkler. Gierke's ideas have been systematized and developed further by Gurvitch (*a*). Pareto, whose sociological system is based upon the same idea, seems not to have known the works of Gierke. As regards the application of the concept of concrete system in natural science, *cf.* Henderson (*b*, 17); among social psychologists Brown (28) is inclined to accept it. A very vivid picture of an organization regarded as a system is that of Barnard (32–3). The organismic theory of society is criticized by Sorokin (*e*, 207–18).

The question whether the concept of equilibrium is applicable to social phenomena has been masterfully analyzed by Sorokin (*g*, 517–21); in his paper different meanings ascribed to the notion of equilibrium in social science are discussed. *Cf.* Duprat and Pareto (1433 *ff.*).

The importance of legal psychology for the sociology of law was stressed (and perhaps overstressed) by Kelsen (*b*, *c*), Kraft (*a*, *b*) and Robinson (22). The latter says: "The jurist will have to describe legal institutions and legal behavior in a manner congruous with psychology and other natural sciences." Special studies of legal psychology are those of Kornfeld (*b*), Riezler, Haff, Rümelin, Tripp and Hoche.

The impossibility of constructing the sociology of law on a behavioristic basis has been demonstrated by Malan. The symbolic character of social coördination is explained by Arnold, Allport (*a*, 55–6, 104), and LaPiere (77 *ff*.). A very good discussion of psychophysical causality or parallelism in its application to sociology is that of Sorokin (*e*, 646–59; *cf*. Holt, 254).

A general survey of the main trends in modern psychology is given by Müller-Freienfels. More complex classifications of human behavior than those proposed in text are sometimes given (*cf*. Thomas, 23).

Modern ideas concerning instincts are discussed by LaPiere (18–22); for earlier opinions see McDougall (19–31, 41–3). Among modern authors who acknowledge inborn ethics see Vierkandt (279).

Voluntary acts are characterized as "centrally imitiated acts" by Glueck (*b*, 100), Luriia (387) and Brown (26); as the "integration of disparate acts previously present" by Murphy (166); as "motor block" by Holt (231–51). His description of the reflex integration forms an exact counterpart of earlier descriptions of "the algebraic summation of motives" (*cf*. Windelbandt).

The theory of conditioned reflexes reached its full expression in the works of Pavlov (*a*, *b*, *c*). His works are very difficult for nonspecialists. A good interpretation is that by Hull. A survey of new studies in the same direction has been given by Drabovitch (90–1). Attempts to apply the theory to social phenomena: Malan, Humphrey and Boldyreff. The importance of conditioned reflexes for the study of social behavior is stressed by Thomas (26–33).

After a certain period when "all" seemed to be explained by conditioned reflexes, there arose in psychology and social psychology a certain tendency to deny the importance of the theory (Robinson, 102–6; LaPiere, 45; much more favorable, Holt and Murphy). Pavlov's school is partly responsible for the negative attitude. As Luriia writes, they have neglected the study of the "reactions . . . during the formation period and are losing the most interesting part of it" (395). This period of formation coincides with the voluntary act. Luriia's "psychologic reaction" (388) and LaPiere's "relatively undirected form of learning" are merely different terms for the voluntary act as the highest form of adjustive activity. On the other hand, recent investigations have shown that conditioned reflexes form only one (perhaps the most important) of the possible forms of learning (*cf*. especially Tolman,

319 *ff.*). Not enough stress is laid in modern science on the "fixation of learned behavior" (Tolman, 152–4 and 445).

The relationship between instincts and habits is discussed by Watson (*cf.* Malan). Habits are treated as post-conscious behavior by Brown (94). Collisions between tendencies and disorganized behavior form the main object of the excellent book of Luriia.

The creation of an "applied science of legislation" was one of the favorite ideas of Petrazhitsky. A number of excellent statements in the field of this science could be collected throughout the works of Pound (especially *f*, 724 and *h*, 150–65, where he speaks of "social engineering"). Among earlier authors Bentham is most important.

CHAPTER III

THE HISTORICAL DEVELOPMENT OF THE SOCIOLOGY OF LAW

§ 1. Introduction

STATEMENTS belonging to the domain of the sociology of law were made from the very beginning of the attempts to discover the essence of law. A good part of the history of legal philosophy, as well as a large number of doctrines expressed in theoretical jurisprudence, might be easily reinterpreted in terms of the sociology of law; the idea that law is causally determined by other social phenomena and in its turn causally determines them is an obvious one and has, therefore, been often expressed since remote times. Yet the idea of creating a special science of the sociology of law could appear only after general sociology had reached a certain stage of development and had overcome its "childhood disease" of being limited to discussions about aims and methods. The sociology of law is a creation of the twentieth century and has been until now rather in the stage of its infancy.

The history of the sociology of law cannot have for its aim the collection of all the statements which *could* be interpreted in socio-juridical terms, for such an objective would almost coincide with that of the history of legal philosophy.[1] A much more modest task will be attempted here: the selection from the history of legal and social thought of those statements which helped the terms of law and of sociology[2] to be brought into correlation.

If the history of an idea is to be something more than a collection of varying statements, it must stress "primary impulses" corresponding to invention in technology and show their influence on the further development. The more many-rooted and

[1] Kraft (*a*) discusses, from the viewpoint of the sociology of law, the theories of Aristotle, Montesquieu, Rousseau, Kant, Hegel, Savigny, Jhering and Gierke. Cairns does the same with respect to Montesquieu and Comte; Cress to Kant.

[2] Not society!

many-branched is the object of study, the more difficult is the task. As the sociology of law is an attempt to apply the concepts and the methods of one science, sociology, to objects traditionally studied by another science, jurisprudence, and as both sociology and jurisprudence are divided into many schools using different methods, the above-mentioned difficulty reaches a high degree indeed. It must be simply acknowledged that it is not always possible to discover the origin of some ideas and to discriminate between imitations (sometimes unconscious ones) and repeated "inventions" based on the similarity of situations.

§ 2. The Discovery of Law by Sociology

1. Sociology was born in the state of hostility to law. The father of sociology, A. Comte, believed that law was an emanation of the metaphysical spirit and would disappear when the positive stage of development would be reached: in future society "the vague and turbulent discussion of rights will be replaced by a calm and strict determination of duties," and law will definitely disappear (*a*, VI, 651–2; *b*, I, 361).

It is beyond doubt that this attitude of Comte was inspired by Saint-Simon, whom he followed in many ways and whose complete lack of understanding of law is well known.[3] There was, of course, another and deeper reason. Comte, like the majority of early sociologists, had only vague ideas on law and, just as a layman would do, identified law with written law or legislation. At the time he completed his system, the historical school dominated in jurisprudence, and its protagonists spread mistrust in legislation, accusing it of being arbitrary and disturbing to organic development; the misuse of legislation during the French Revolution certainly determined their position. There is some evidence for such genesis of Comte's hostility to law. Prophesying the disappearance of law, he expressed the opinion that law had played a useful part during the transitory period of revolution, because it helped to dissolve the previous social system.

That Comte's attitude was not accidental is corroborated by

[3] The statements of Saint-Simon concerning law have been collected and commented on by Gurvitch (*c*, 307–11).

the fact that another great sociological system, born almost simultaneously with his, comprised an analogous prophecy of the disappearance of law with the advance of society: for K. Marx, law was one of the "superstructures" characteristic of the "bourgeois" order and was to "wither away," together with the State, after the establishment of classless society.[4]

Comte never had true followers. Yet, if not his hostility to law, at least his lack of interest in law was inherited by sociology for many decades. The reason was probably the same as that which influenced Comte — the belief that law was something arbitrary, disturbing rather than expressing organic development. In addition to this, early sociology was very much the study of primitive society in which the germs of advanced society were seen; yet, it is dubious whether law is already present in the earliest stages of social development. Therefore, custom (and not law) was the main object of investigation, custom being considered *the* expression of social organization.

Such is the approach of H. Spencer. In Volume II of his *Principles of Sociology* (first published in 1882) he devotes a chapter not to law, but to *laws*, and this within a part dealing with "political institutions." Law is not given in his system as much place as ceremonies or ecclesiastical institutions; law is merely a subdivision of a greater entity. In his opinion law is nothing else than a "hardened form of custom" (III, 261), and as custom it "formulates the rule of the dead over the living" (II, 514). The treatment of the subject pursues the objective that the organismic concept of society is correct and that law develops according to the principle of differentiation and integration.

2. With Spencer, sociology finally became a reality, after having been rather a phantom. Immediately after having been created, sociology separated into many branches, and it was natural that this influenced the attempts to correlate law with sociology.[5]

[4] *Cf.* below, chap. XVI.

[5] A correlation between the main schools in sociology and different attempts to formulate a sociological theory of law has been stressed by Pound (*c*, 489–91); the term "stage" which he uses should be replaced by "trend," for the different approaches evolved practically simultaneously.

Spencer's sociology was biological and organismic. A subordinate place for law and the lack of active interest in it has been characteristic of the majority of authors of the same tendency.

A modification of the biological theory in sociology was the theory of social Darwinism. The first systematic attempt to apply that doctrine to the problem of law was made by M. Vaccaro's *Basi del diritto e dello stato* (Torino, 1893). The French translation of the book (Paris, 1898) amplified the title: "basis" became "sociological basis."[6] The main idea of the book as regards law is that law is the adaptation of men to the social milieu effected by the determination of the conditions of their existence, and that groups better organized by law survive in the struggle for life (452–3 of the French edition).

Economic determinism in sociology produced works in which law was considered an expression of the social relations of production. The earliest sociological work in which this idea was systematically developed was G. de Greef's *Introduction à la sociologie* (Bruxelles, 1886). Among later works A. Loria's *Basi economiche della costituzione sociale* (1893) should be mentioned.

Both social Darwinism and economic determinism in the sociology of law gradually lost their importance. Another fate was destined for the psychological approach to the problem. Developing Spencer's idea of the psychological basis of sociology, L. Ward published his *Dynamic Sociology* (New York, 1883) in which law, or more exactly, legislation, appeared as a series of inventions, of attempts to modify the results of "real laws" which exist in society (I, 36–8); the existing "compulsory legislation" was condemned and an "attractive legislation" was recommended which would use the natural drives of men.[7] The direct influence of Ward's socio-juridical ideas remained almost nil. The psychological approach was to be resumed independently by the Russian jurist, L. Petrazhitsky.

3. All the works mentioned were either preliminary programs

[6] This was probably inspired by the work of Anzilotti (*cf.* below).

[7] Did Ward, consciously or unconsciously, imitate Bentham and Fourier when making such recommendations? He repeated his early statements on law in his later works almost without modification. *Cf.* *c*, 306–11 and *d*, I, 275–6, 598–9; II, 540–1.

for the sociology of law or incidental discussions of law among various sociological subjects. General sociology could not prepare the elaboration of a special sociology of law until a conceptual scheme was discovered in which law would appear an essential element and no longer a disturbance. The decisive impulse was given by E. Ross, who, in a series of articles published after 1896 in the *American Journal of Sociology*,[8] coined the concept of "the means of social control" and described law as "the most specialized and highly finished engine of control employed by society" (106).

Another impulse was launched in W. Sumner's *Folkways* (Boston, 1906). This work combined the viewpoint of utilitarianism [9] with the ethnological approach of Spencer and of other early sociologists. In his introduction Sumner asserts that his intention was to write a book on sociology, and that this attempt necessarily deviated into the description of social life; the fact that not only primitive but also advanced peoples were studied adds to Sumner's merit. Legal phenomena were (partly and unsystematically) studied by him together with phenomena regulated by "folkways."

Analogous to Sumner's book were the works of E. Westermarck, *Origin and Development of Moral Ideas* (London, 1906–7) and of Hobhouse, *Morals in Evolution* (London, 1906). Both were devoted primarily to the study of moral phenomena, yet the term "morals" has been so broadly expanded by both authors that the scope of the described facts was not essentially different from that of Spencer or of Sumner. It included "the life of peoples," with a certain stress laid on the ethical element in custom (as compared with habit), but this element was also present in Sumner's book, where it was concealed to some extent by a reference of mores to *both* ethical and utilitarian considerations.

Fructifying the further development was another idea expressed in Sumner's book — that law is one of the "societal regulations." This viewpoint, however, was not very original, for the

[8] Later on collected into a volume entitled *Social Control* (N. Y., 1901).

[9] Applied to the problem of custom by W. Bagehot in *Physics and Politics* (London, 1873) and, simultaneously with Sumner, by E. Waxweiler (*Esquisse d'une sociologie*, Bruxelles, 1906).

same idea was incidentally advanced by many sociologists, for instance, F. H. Giddings (*a*), J. M. Baldwin and C. Cooley (*a*).

In Europe, from the viewpoint of preparing the way for the sociology of law, E. Durkheim's works (*a*, *c*) can be considered as the counterpart of the American development. Especially important was his discussion of solidarity as a basic social fact and his attempt to understand law as an expression of this fact, repressive (criminal) law corresponding to "mechanic solidarity" or to the similarity of group-members, and restitutive (civil) law corresponding to "organic solidarity" or to the differentiation of group-members and of their functions and to the interdependence of individuals created on this basis. L. Lévy-Bruhl's "science of moral facts" belongs of course in the same line.

As a completely independent impulse, V. Pareto's *Trattato di sociologia generale*, which was published in 1915, must be considered. Pareto tried to reduce law to a number of manifestations of basic "sentiments," these manifestations being the only observable juridical facts within the realm of reality in the narrow sense he gives to this term.[10]

§ 3. The Discovery of Sociology in Jurisprudence

1. Jurisprudence was perhaps better prepared to encounter with sociology than was sociology to encounter with the problems of law. Despite many misrepresentations, jurisprudence was never merely the study of the verbal formulas included in positive law or the art of their practical application. Formalism in jurisprudence is rather a new invention, perhaps a reaction against the lack of discrimination between normative statements and the facts to which they are related. C. F. Gerber, in 1865, introduced formalism into constitutional law, and was followed by P. Laband (in 1876). Binding (in 1872) represented the corresponding trend in criminal law, whereas Kelsen (*a*, published in 1911) sublimated the antisociological trend to a "normative theory of law" and postulated for it exclusiveness.[11]

[10] *Cf.* above, chap. II, § 2. The lack of continuity with the previous development (a kind of spontaneous creation) is stressed by House.

[11] Later on Kelsen developed his basic theory in numerous works. His conversion to sociologism in law was stressed during one of the last congresses of the Institut

But the main trend in jurisprudence was not hostile to the study of the facts lying beyond the words of which legal rules consist. In constitutional law it was usual to study not so much the letter of the constitution as its practical application, and, in addition to this, the nature of the body to which it was applied — the State; constitutional law was never strictly separated from political science.[12] It was a novelty in form, but not in content, that G. Jellinek introduced into his famous *Allgemeine Staatslehre* (I, Berlin, 1900) a "sociological part." Almost simultaneously L. Duguit (*b*), applying E. Durkheim's sociological concepts, tried to explain legal phenomena by the natural fact of solidarity.

In criminal law the hypothesis of free will simplified the task of earlier scholars, for it made the concrete offense the only relevant fact to be studied. Yet, since the second quarter of the nineteenth century, there has existed a remarkable literature concerning the facts regulated by criminal law.[13] After C. Lombroso, biological and, very soon, sociological considerations made their appearance in the field of criminology. In 1884 E. Ferri published a book entitled *Sociologia criminale.* This was not yet sociology of law (or of criminal law), but it was already a sociological study of the phenomena regulated by one of the branches of law.

In civil law, B. W. Leist (in 1877) insisted on the necessity of studying the actually existing rules which forerun legal rules. R. Jhering's works (especially *b*, published in 1877–83) introduced a new spirit, fructifying the analysis of legal formulas by the concept of the interest protected by law.[14] O. Gierke (espe-

International de Philosophie de Droit et de Sociologie Juridique. *Cf.* Kelsen (*h*), in *Annuaire de l'Institut International de Philosophie de Droit et de Sociologie Juridique* (1935), 60–80; "Discussion du rapport de H. Kelsen," *ibid.*, 81–2.

[12] The most typical work of this trend was perhaps that of J. C. Blüntchli, *Allgemeine Staatslehre* (München, 1852).

[13] The competent article of A. Lindesmith and Y. Levin, "The Lombrosian Myth in Criminology," *Amer. Journ. Sociol.*, March, 1937, gives a good review of the corresponding works, but overlooks the fact that it was C. Lombroso's merit to have destroyed the barrier of "free will" which hindered the causal-functional study of crime from penetrating into the domain of criminal law and accordingly influencing legislation.

[14] This was the source of the ideas developed much later by F. Gény (the "given" and the "constructed" in law, in *a*), by E. Ehrlich ("Rechtseinrichtungen" in *a*) and by M. Hauriou (juridical institutions as actual situations, in *a*). The genealogy of ideas has been traced by H. Sinzheimer (*b*, 134).

cially in *b*) studied the "real" structure of corporations and of other juridical persons.

Yet even before Gierke and Jhering, "realistic" considerations were never absent from the minds of scientists. The study of civil law in continental Europe was always the study of the rules found in statutes or in customs, but as they were applied by juridical practice. As practical cases were necessarily a part of actual life, contact with life was never broken.

2. Only theoretical jurisprudence, which, in continental Europe, was commonly assimilated to the philosophy of law, seemed to be confined to discussions concerning verbal formulas and to ignore observable facts. It was in the year 1880 that it was touched by the advance of sociology.

The dominance of the ethnological approach in early sociology suffices to show that the first attempts to apply sociological viewpoints to law were effected on the ethnological basis also. In 1880, A. H. Post published a work entitled *Bausteine für eine Rechtswissenschaft auf vergleichend ethnologischer Basis* (*b*), in which an attempt was made to replace traditional jurisprudence, based on the study of legal norms, by a new science of law based on the methods applied in natural science and on the data of ethnology. Four years later, in 1884, he published another work, entitled *Die Grunlagen des Rechts, Leitfaden für den Aufhau einer allgemeinen Rechtswissenschaft auf soziologischer Basis* (*c*), in which the sociological works of Spencer, Schäffle and Lilienfeld were quoted. For the first time the terms sociology and law were combined in one unit. This was, of course, not yet the creation of the sociology of law, for sociology, in Post's opinion, is identical with ethnology. Collecting exhaustive material on legal life, past and present, he hoped to solve the problem of what is (legally) right or wrong, and the idea of unilinear evolution led him to assume that a definite solution could so be reached. Two years later F. Störk, in an excellent review of Post's work, demonstrated the fallacy of his hopes — there is no way from Post's material to the essence of law. A little later Tarde, in *Les transformations du droit* (Paris, 1894) began to undermine the belief in unilinear evolution, at least in the legal field. The total destruction of the hypothesis which had dominated early sociology, was, of course, the deed of F. Ratzel.[15]

3. A new impulse toward the application of sociological viewpoints to the problems of law was given in Italy. In 1885 G. P. Chironi, professor in Turin, delivered a lecture which was published the next year under the title *Sociologia a diritto civile*. Explicitly quoting Comte and Spencer, the Italian scholar discussed the possibility of enriching both civil law and sociology by mutual knowledge and understanding. Unfortunately, throughout his discussion he accepted as definitely proved some of the basic propositions of Spencer (especially the law of the decreasing interference of the State in economic affairs).

His work was continued by the Italian philosopher of law, D. Anzilotti, who was also directly influenced by Post. In a book *La filosofia del diritto e la sociologia* (Firenze, 1892) he coined the term "sociology of law" (*sociologia juridica*) and attributed to it the task of studying the empirical manifestations of juridical facts. The discussion was continued by L. Ratto, *Sociologia a filosofia del diritto* (Milano, 1894), and an attempt literally to apply the program was made by R. de la Grasserie, whose books (*a*, *b*) are examples of how not to proceed when creating the sociology of law. These treatments duplicate already existing juridical sciences (especially those of constitutional and of civil law), by means of transforming legal rules into empirical propositions.

4. A further impulse toward the creation of the sociology of law was given by the school of "free law" which was started [16] in 1906, by H. Kantorowicz, his brilliant book having been published under the pseudonym Gnaeus Flavius.[17] Stressing the necessity of studying law as a sum of "vital relations" and not as

[15] Tarde (pp. 162 *ff*. of the 8th edition of the quoted book, Paris, 1922) attacked the theory of unilinear evolution from the viewpoint of his general sociological theory stressing invention and imitation. F. Ratzel (*a*, *b*) created the basis for the later positive development.

[16] In conscious opposition to formalism in jurisprudence.

[17] This book was entitled *Der Kampf um die Rechtswissenschaft* (Heidelberg, 1906). For the earlier history of the idea of "free law" see H. U. Kantorowicz (*c*). A summarized study of the development in France and Germany is given by G. Gurvitch (*d*, 213–78).

that of preëstablished rules, H. Sinzheimer (*a*), L. Spiegel, I. Kornfeld (*a*) and E. Ehrlich (*a*), in contradistinction to de la Grasserie, pointed out the difference between "written law" and "living law." Ehrlich's book was the first monograph entitled "Sociology of Law," although the term "descriptive sociological jurisprudence" would have been more appropriate, for the lack of discrimination between the concrete description of legal configurations and the nomographic study of law was characteristic of Ehrlich's work.

5. In the meanwhile, the first treatise which actually made law the object of a systematic nomographic study was published by Petrazhitsky who continued in the first decade of the twentieth century the task undertaken about the end of the nineteenth.[18] This treatise consists of *An Introduction to the Study of Law and Morals* (1905) and of the two volumes of *The Theory of Law and State* (1907). In this work he tried to reduce all legal phenomena to certain basic psychological regularities. These elements being present in everyone's mind, the regularity of legal conduct was explained, provided that the psychological premises were correct. Before the war only a part of the Introduction had been translated into German; the rest remained inaccessible for non-Russians; hence the little influence his work has had in the development of universal science.[19]

Without any connection with Petrazhitsky, a Belgian jurist, H. Rolin, undertook a similar task in a book entitled *Les prolégomènes à la science du droit*, published in Brussels in 1911. His main idea was to analyze the motives of legal behavior and to

[18] *Die Lehre vom Einkommen*, II (Berlin, 1895), comprises, in rudimentary form, the essential elements of the "psychological theory of law." The necessity of the causal-functional approach to law was stressed in Russian science very early. In 1879 S. H. Muromtseff, in *The Concept and the Basic Division of Law*, expressed the opinion that law should be studied causally. N. Korkunoff's *General Theory of Law* applies many actually sociological concepts without using the corresponding terms. *Cf.* Babb (*b*, 511–13).

[19] The German translation was entitled *Über die Motive des Handelns und über das Wesen der Moral und des Rechts* (Berlin, 1907). The interest in Petrazhitsky has grown in later years, as is testified by the publication of excellent essays by G. Gurvitch (*d*, 279–95; *e*, 153–69) and by H. Babb. A completely inadequate treatment of Petrazhitsky's theory is that of Meyendorf. Among Russian presentations the best is that of Guins (*a*).

describe the constant elements it contains. This work cannot be compared with that of Petrazhitsky as regards originality of ideas and profundity of analysis. Of still less value is the book of R. Brugeilles, who, under the promising title *Le droit et la sociologie* (Paris, 1910) gave merely an additional "philosophical" treatise on law, in which some sociological terms were very loosely used.

6. For further advance it was very important that the internal unity of the various attempts be stressed. This step was made by R. Pound, in 1911–12, in a remarkable article "The Scope and Purpose of Sociological Jurisprudence," (*b*). The unity of sociological jurisprudence was found by Pound in that its adepts "look more for the working of law than for its abstract content," and "lay stress upon the social purposes which law subserves rather than upon sanctions;" yet with good reason he also pointed out the great divergences in their philosophical views (516). A kind of preliminary unification was undertaken about the same time (in 1915) by B. A. Kistiakovsky, *The Social Sciences and Law.* This attempt was based on the "pluralistic" approach to law, in the style of the neo-Kantian philosophy. According to Kistiakovsky, the sociological concept (and the sociological study) of law must be added to the normative and the authoritative concepts.

The same years brought the first scientific attack against the very idea of the sociology of law. This attack was made by H. Kelsen (*b*, *c*) and proved to be very stimulating for the further advance of the new science.[20]

§ 4. The Classification of Science and the Sociology of Law

Within both sociology and jurisprudence, but outside the main trends studied until now, an idea, which just like the ethnological approach had been characteristic for early sociology, was applied in the early discussions concerning the sociology of law. This idea was that of the classification of science. Comte and Spencer worked on it and had many followers. Law did not commonly appear in such classifications, and this for a good reason: from the

[20] Ehrlich (*d*) replied to Kelsen. Kelsen (*d*) rejoined and, later on, systematized his attacks against the very idea of the sociological study of law and of the State (*f*).

viewpoint of sociologists, science coincided with theoretical science, and the science of law is very much a practical science, the theory of a practical art, i.e., how to apply specific rules in determined situations.

In 1895 R. Worms published an article (*a*) in which, operating with the idea of the rational classification of sciences, he assimilated the science of law to the comparative history of legal phenomena and denied the possibility of a juridical *science* of another type.[21]

This was an idea to be developed in different directions: (1) some jurists assimilated the sociology of law with comparative jurisprudence, (2) other scientists tried to deduce, from the classificatory viewpoint, what the most appropriate field for the sociology of law could be. Prepared by Post, Worms and E. Durkheim [22] the identification of sociology of law with comparative jurisprudence was effected by Sir P. Vinogradoff in his article on "Comparative Jurisprudence," (*e*) published in the 11th edition of the *Encyclopedia Britannica*. The study of this article shows that, under comparative jurisprudence, Vinogradoff understood also what is called ethnological jurisprudence.[23]

The most important attempt to develop the classificatory viewpoint in the second manner was made in H. Kantorowicz's paper read at the first meeting of German sociologists in 1911 (*a*). Sociology being for Kantorowicz the science of correlation be-

[21] He repeated his statements, with many amplifications, in *b*, I, 194.

[22] In "La sociologia e il suo dominio scientifico," (*Rivista italiana di sociologia*, 4, 127 *ff.*), Durkheim discussed the close relation of sociology to the comparative history of law, religion, et cetera.

[23] This article has been reprinted, with some additions by H. Goithein, in the 14th edition of the *Encyclopedia* (vol. XIII). Actually, with the decline of the theory of unilinear evolution, the identification of comparative law and of the sociology of law becomes less and less possible. It is symptomatic that the identification was made by one of the last representatives of the theory, C. Nardi-Greco, in *La sociologia giuridica* (Torino, 1907). The title is misleading, for the book comprises merely an old-fashioned description of the unilinear development of law. Simultaneously, G. Mazzarella, in *Les types sociaux et le droit* (Paris, 1908), a French condensation of many articles published in Italian, showed the way to a "typological" comparative jurisprudence. Of value also were the works of S. R. Steinmetz (*a*) and of J. Makariewicz in the special field of criminal law, whereas the works of the prolific J. Kohler (*a, b*) still maintained the unilinear tradition. To the same tradition belongs also W. Wundt's volume on law in the monumental *Völkerpsychologie* (vol. IX, Berlin, 1918).

tween factors in culture, the corresponding task as regards law [24] was ascribed by him to the sociology of law.

§ 5. THE FURTHER ADVANCE

About 1914 the foundation for the construction of the sociology of law was sufficiently prepared. The term itself was coined in 1892; later on, several works entitled "sociological jurisprudence" or "sociology of law" appeared. The first systematic treatises were published — the most important of them, unfortunately, in a language inaccessible for universal science — and the internal unity of the movement had been now realized. In the history of almost every theoretical science the Great War and the first years of the post-war period naturally form a period of stagnation; if important works appeared during that period, they could not be sufficiently appreciated and produce their full effect. Such, for instance, was the fate of Pareto's treatise. When the theoretical movement was resumed, the trends described above continued. They were: (1) a trend in ethnological and comparative jurisprudence directed towards a precise determination of the correlation of these sciences with the sociology of law; (2) a trend for which the name of "descriptive sociological jurisprudence" is appropriated, and (3) a trend formed by the theoretical sociology of law. Within every trend may be distinguished works (a) that advance programs, and (b) that represent attempts to realize the program comprised in the term "the sociology of law." Of course, within this framework many of the works must be placed more than once.[25]

1. Comparative and ethnological jurisprudence was of course affected by the definite disappearance of the theory of unilinear evolution. Insofar as comparative jurisprudence remains historical, the doctrine of "cultural areas" has grown to dominate. According to this theory, similarities in legal configurations are

[24] In 1923 Kantorowicz repeated his statements, in somewhat modified and very much abbreviated form (*b*).

[25] Another classification is given by H. Sinzheimer, *De Taak*. He distinguishes descriptive, critical, genetic and theoretical sociology of law, yet it is extremely difficult to realize why Max Weber's work should be considered critical and not theoretical and that of B. Horvath theoretical and not critical.

ordinarily based on common origin and on the expansion of patterns by means of imitation, whereas parallel creation, based on the similarity of human nature and of the environment, is given only a secondary rôle. Such an approach necessarily separates comparative jurisprudence from the sociology of law, this latter being a nomographic science, as uniformities in legal configurations appear to be historically conditioned and limited to special cultural areas.[26]

(a) Among works devoted to the discussion of programs of scientific activity in this field, H. Trimborn's substantial article (published in 1928) brilliantly expounds the manner in which the technique of "cultural areas" should be applied in the field of law.[27] Warning against the exaggeration of the new technique has been given by K. Haff (*b*), who pointed out that the concrete possibilities of legal regulation were limited, and that this produced parallel lines of development in legal systems not genetically connected with each other.

If the sociology of law cannot be identified with the comparative history of legal institutions, it could be a theoretical introduction to it and to its epistemology. Such was the idea expressed by Schönfeld in 1927.

Moreover, comparative jurisprudence does not necessarily have to be historical; modern development makes it somewhat functional, striving towards the understanding of how one or another social function can be and actually is realized by various legal configurations. Functional comparative jurisprudence has been subsumed under the sociology of law by M. Rheinstein (*a*, *b*). The kind of study effected in functional comparative jurisprudence not being nomographic, it would probably be more correct to say that this discipline can provide the sociology of law with valuable material; perhaps Rheinstein's statements are to be understood in this sense.

[26] The movement discussed in the text was a continuation of the destructive process directed against the theory of unilinear evolution. The "typological approach" of Mazzarella (*cf.* above, § 3) proved to be an insufficient compromise.

[27] The author also gives a good review of the achievements gained by means of the new technique. Valuable, but now somewhat out of date, are also the statements of G. Davy in the introductory chapters of *La foi jurée* (Paris, 1922).

(b) As regards "realizations," ethnological jurisprudence produced some works of importance for the sociology of law. Malinowski (*a, b*) made several attempts to create a particular "ethnographic" concept of law and to prove its existence in primitive society (*cf.* below, chap. XII). Thurnwald (*b*) selected, among the innumerable data collected by ethnology, those which seem to be actually related to law and ordered them in accordance with the new technique in a way which makes them appear the function of particular cultural situations. Another excellent selection of relevant material has been made by W. I. Thomas.

2. (a) In Europe, descriptive sociological jurisprudence has not made great advance.[28] The discussion of its purpose was almost limited to an article of M. Rumpf, who insisted on the necessity of studying, in jurisprudence, both written law and its realization, but did not stress their frequent divergence. This was a return to the position of descriptive jurisprudence of before Ehrlich, and it was only natural that his program did not find any followers. On the contrary, J. H. Fürth thought that the basic aims of the sociology of law should be to investigate whether, in various fields of legal life, "subjects" actually behaved in accordance with written law and whether governmental agencies enforced sanctions against transgressors.

(b) As regards realizations, E. Jung (*b*) made a new and good contribution to the problem of the divergence between "written" and "living" law. G. Davy (in 1922) gave a sociologically colored pre-history of contract in his already mentioned book. Cornil (in 1926) made an attempt to write a "simplified" sociology of civil law. A great contribution to descriptive sociological jurisprudence has been that of G. Mazzarella in the fifteen (sic!) volumes of *Studi di etnologia guiridica* (Catania 1903–37), devoted to the study of legal life in India.

The American "realism in jurisprudence" forms another variety of the same type. It is not easy to give an accurate definition of this movement, which certainly does not form any school.

[28] In German science Jhering's and not Ehrlich's ideas have prevailed and engendered, in jurisprudence, a school called "Interessenjurisprudenz;" the outstanding representative of the school is Ph. Heck (*a, b*). *Cf.* M. Rheinstein (*b*).

R. Pound (*n*) formulated the specific attitude of the members of the movement in the following terms: (1) they assume that every nonpsychological jurisprudence is unscientific and illusory; (2) they insist more on single cases than on the uniform course of judicial behavior; (3) they conceive law as a body of devices for business and not as a body of means towards general social ends.

However, one of the leaders of the movement, K. Llewellyn, contests every one of R. Pound's characterizations and considers as expressive of the movement: (1) the conception of law in flux; (2) the conception of law as a means to social ends; (3) the conception of society in flux, faster than law; (4) the temporary divorce of "is" and "ought" for purposes of study; (5) the distrust of legal rules as they purport to describe what courts or people are actually doing; (6) the distrust of the fact that the traditional rule formulations are the heavily operative factor in producing court decisions; (7) the insistence on the evaluation of every part of law in terms of its effects. Here again, as within comparative jurisprudence, one of the impulses towards the creation of the sociology of law has deviated from that end.[29]

3. (a) As regards the scope and the purpose of the theoretical sociology of law, the following statements are important: J. Kraft (*a*, *b*) expressed the opinion that the sociology of law should be based on the study of the "legal mentality" of mankind; furthermore, Kantorowicz's idea (*cf.* above) of the sociology of law as the study of the correlation between law and other factors in culture has been once more stressed by him. The Hungarian, B. Horvath, devoted a large part of his *Rechtssoziologie* (published in 1934, in German) to the discussion of the problem of the relation of the sociology of law to other sciences, especially to jurispru-

[29] When specialists disagree as regards the essence of a phenomenon to be observed in their own country, the opinion of outsiders may be of value. See A. L. Goodhardt, A. Auburtin, Kantorowicz (*d*), and G. Radbruch (*b*). In the author's view, the movement negatively continues Ehrlich's theory of the destruction of the dogma of abstract law as regulating in advance all possible legal conflicts. Positively it is largely an attempt to create a new science of law on a psychological basis, psychology being applied first of all to the genesis of judicial decisions. Unfortunately, as there is no "common opinion" in psychology, the efforts diverge very much. J. Frank seems to follow the doctrine of psychoanalysis; other members of the movement have not so well expressed predilections.

dence in its various aspects. The Dutchman, H. Sinzheimer, in *De Taak der Rechtssoziologie* (Haarlem, 1935) assimilated the sociology of law to the science of legislation; in other words, he interpreted it as a practical science showing the lawmakers the better way to proceed in their task. A thoughtful article by J. Hall (*b*) gives a correct definition of the sociology of law as a theoretical science consisting of generalizations regarding social phenomena, insofar as they refer to the contents, purposes, applications, and effects of legal rules.[30]

"Realizations" concern either the sociological place of law, the mechanism of law, or the correlation between law and other elements in culture.

The first task has been carried out primarily by sociologists. Three of the earlier acquired concepts of law were used; law as means of social control, law as one of the "ways" of behavior, law as "societal regulation." The idea of social control was furthered by C. Cooley (*b*), L. T. Hobhouse (*b*), C. Ellwood and E. Lindemann.[31]

As regards the second concept, in 1922, Giddings (*b*), who in his earlier works did not pay much attention to law, made an attempt to express law in terms correlated to folkways: if the latter are the ways of unorganized masses, laws are the ways imposed by the State, stateways.[32]

The idea that regulative principles form a necessary part of the social structure was introduced by R. M. MacIver in *Society* (1930).[33] The general concept of societal regulation as well as the difference between its kinds (especially between law and custom) has been amply studied in sociological terms, partly with the application of the concepts of social control and of folkways

[30] J. Hall's book, *Crime, Theft and Society* (Boston, 1935) gave an example of how the study of concrete legal configurations could lead to statements of the nomographic type.

[31] F. Lumley does not especially study law; his approach to the problem is more socio-psychological than sociological.

[32] A similar idea was expressed by Post as early as 1880, but remained outside the threshold of scientific consciousness. According to Post, law is state custom in contradistinction to tribal custom (*b*, 49).

[33] Not yet in *Community* (1917) and in *The Modern State* (1926). In the second edition of *Society* (New York, 1937) the problem is treated under the title "sustaining forces."

and mores, the legal codes being identified by the author with state codes.[34] In this manner a new possibility for the incorporation of law into the objects of accurate sociological study was created and was used by many authors, for instance by M. Ginsberg (*Sociology*, London, 1934) and by R. Linton, whose *Study of Man* (New York, 1936) gives an excellent chapter on the patterns of behavior.

The study of the mechanism of law was advanced both by jurists and sociologists. In 1921, appeared Max Weber's *Wirtschaft und Gesellschaft.* Extremely important for the sociology of law is his discussion of the ways in which social actions may be determined, of the modes of orientation of the actions, of the modes in which the legitimacy of an order may be guaranteed and of the reasons why binding legitimacy is attributed to the order by the actors.[35] Great also is his contribution to the problem of power, the relation of which to the problem of law he completely realizes, while among his somewhat erratic statements concerning particular problems of the sociology of law perhaps those concerning the connection of law and religion are the most valuable.

In 1922 the author of this book published (in Russian) a paper (*b*) in which he made an attempt to orient the sociology of law on social psychology rather than on individual psychology, as had been done by Petrazhitsky and Rolin; in this study Pavlov's theory of conditioned reflexes was applied to the explanation of the fixation and automatism of legal behavior.[36] In the same year G. Humphrey and C. H. Malan (from South Africa) published papers in which Pavlov's theory was used in the same sense.

In 1925 a work of F. W. Jerusalem appeared, entitled *Soziologie des Rechts*. It was disappointing however; only Volume I was published, and this contains little more than the discussion of the problems of causality and of collectivity.

In 1931 G. Gurvitch published a book on social law (*c*), the

[34] Continuing Giddings' idea of "stateways" and the "state theory of law" in jurisprudence.

[35] These statements are unfortunately very short and somewhat contradictory. An excellent interpretation is given by Parsons (*b*, 640 *ff.*).

[36] Later on the author published further essays of the same trend (*e*, *f*, *g*).

first part of which is truly an introduction to the sociology of law. The author tries to discover the essence of law by means of an accurate analysis of "legal experience."[37]

The study of correlation, emphasized in 1911 by Kantorowicz and in 1930 by Kraft, was advanced by the Swiss jurist, D. Schinkler, in a book entitled *Verfassungsrecht und soziale Struktur* (Zurich, 1932), in which the problem of the relation between legal and extra-legal phenomena was submitted to a stimulating study. The problem of correlation also forms the main object of the mentioned book by B. Horvath. The author analyzes the correlation between law, on the one hand, and economics, combat, power, knowledge and procedure (ceremonial institutions), on the other hand. His exposition is handicapped by a highly artificial philosophical scheme which forces him to treat every problem from the viewpoint of historical evolution, social correlation, juridico-logical fluctuation and axiological limitation. The rather philosophical work of H. Morgenthau, *De la réalité des normes* (published in 1934) throws new light upon the sociologically important problems of the efficacy of norms (especially of legal norms) and of the correlation of law, morals and custom. The monumental work of P. A. Sorokin (*h*) contains several chapters in which the correlation between law and other elements in culture is treated from the dynamic viewpoint, and changes in law are shown as a function of general cultural fluctuations.

Throughout all the years covered in this section, Pound (*f–r*) continued to make valuable contributions to the sociological study of law.[38] More than once he has shown the various stages of this study[39] and what theoretical and practical aims could and should

[37] *Cf.* above chap. II, § 7. Gurvitch continued his contribution to the sociology of law in further works (*e*, *f*, *g*).

[38] His own approach to the problems studied is similar to that of the German "Interessenjurisprudenz": a careful analysis of what law does and how it works, with the idea of the social evaluation of interests as guidance. See especially *m* (710–11). Valuable contributions of the same trend were made by Justice Holmes and Justice Cardozo. About them see F. Frankfurter, *Justice Holmes and the Supreme Court*, Cambridge, Mass., 1938, and M. Aronson, "Cardozo's Doctrine of Sociological Jurisprudence," *J. Soc. Phil.*, 4 (1938).

[39] See especially "Fifty Years of Jurisprudence," *Harv. Law Review*, 51–2 (1937–38).

be pursued, but as yet he has not fulfilled the promise made in 1911 to publish a book entitled *Sociological Jurisprudence!* [40]

This cursory review shows that the sociology of law has become an internationally recognized field of scientific work. Another expression of the same fact was the creation of an "International Institute of the Philosophy of Law and the Sociology of Law" (in 1933) and of a special journal, *Archives de philosophie du droit et de sociologie juridique* (in 1931), the contributors to which are recruited throughout the world.

The sociology of law has gradually grown from a mere program to a body of knowledge. Many scholars belonging to different nations contributed to this growth, and only by combined efforts of still more numerous students, representing different legal areas and different trends of human thought, can the knowledge already gained be advanced and fructified. The next task is to unify the trends, so that general sociology can discuss law on the basis of the knowledge gained by the special science represented by the sociology of law, and that the sociology of law can directly use and apply the principles developed by general sociology.

[40] *Cf.* the first footnote to his *Scope and Purpose of Sociological Jurisprudence.*

PART II

ETHICS

CHAPTER IV

THE ETHICAL GROUP-CONVICTION

§ 1. Values

THE ethical coördination of behavior forms one of the main classes of social coördination (chap. I, § 5) and the legal coördination of behavior comprises one of the subclasses of the ethical category (*ibid.*).

Behavior is ethically coördinated, insofar as the imposition of patterns is related to ethical values. Therefore every study of ethics is a study of values. Is such a study possible in sociology, this science being a nomographic and not a normative one, and the normative method being the normal method of studying values? This problem has already been discussed (chap. II) in connection with the negative approach to the sociology of law. Values are embodied in human behavior, determine it, give it a precise meaning and a specific force to produce results. Insofar as values are embodied and play a part in causally determined processes, they can and are to be studied by nomographic sciences.

In values primary relations of an individual to everything in the world (himself not excluded) are expressed. They are truly primary and irreducible. "Values," says Sherif (137), "are products of the contacts of individuals who have a temporary place in the history of the group; but they cease to be private properties . . . once formed. As standardized fixations values are sociological realities." [1]

Values can be classified and grouped into hierarchies. There are, among values, such values which obviously may be considered as supreme or highest; ethical values belong to their number. Together with the ideas of the True and of the Beautiful, the ethical idea of the Good forms the summit in the realm of the

[1] In another place the same author says: "Social values are standardized affective fixations. They serve as more or less stable frames of reference" (195).

axiology (evaluation). Human behavior is often incompatible with the Good, the True and the Beautiful; but no man can seriously assert that he is striving toward the Evil, the False or the Ugly.[2]

The conformity of a certain behavior to higher values is expressed in the words "ought to be" (in the words "ought not to be" — their nonconformity with such values).

"Ought to be" is a primary, irreducible content of consciousness. A person who does not understand the meaning of the words "ought to be" is incapable of social conduct and is considered to be outside the pale of society. This is a state especially studied in psychopathology under the name of moral insanity. It is an insidious disease, for the corresponding person shows no signs of intellectual defects; his ideas seem to be clear; but one conception is completely lacking, namely, that of right and wrong; therefore the determination of the will becomes quite abnormal and horrible acts are sometimes committed. The relation of the morally sick to ethical ideas is just the same as that of a Daltonist, of a colorblind person to colors: as the latter is unable to distinguish red from green, so the moral idiot cannot distinguish acts which ought to be from those which ought not. Ethics and law appear in his consciousness only as external hindrances, without any internal meaning. According to the specialists in psychopathology (especially Krafft-Ebbing), the disease is based upon poor inheritance or degeneration.

The essence of the behavior which ought to be or ought not to be varies with time and place. Of course, there are a few ethical rules which seem to be common to every society (for instance, the prohibition of murder or of high treason); there are certain rules which, once originated, seem to become stable and to resist every change in social conditions.[3] Yet muta-

[2] The three highest values tend toward unification. It is noteworthy that several peoples have created notions combining two of the three cardinal values. Thus, the ancient Greeks expressed their ideal of men in the terms *καλοσκἀγαθοs* (beautiful and good); the Slavic languages possess a term (pravda) which means both true and good or right; it corresponds to the English notion of righteousness: a righteous man loves truth and strives for what is good.

[3] Examples in Sorokin, *h*, II, 576 *ff*.

tions in the interpretation of basic rules, the introduction or the abolition of exceptions, and, still more, changes in the evaluation of the relative importance of different rules are so large that it is quite impossible to construct a universal "socio-ethical minimum" or to determine immutable trends in the development of social ethics.

Today we consider parricide as one of the most horrible crimes; but not long ago primitive tribes in Northeastern Asia considered it the duty of a good son to kill his parents when their strength began to decline; and in several tribes living in Central Africa the King's son is obliged to kill his father, during a solemn ceremony, for the sake of the kingdom. Until recent time in India a widow had to be burnt, together with the corpse of her husband; great efforts on the part of the British government were necessary to uproot this custom.

Today the variability of ethical rules is a commonly recognized fact.[4] Frequently the variability is stressed as regards law. "Hardly a rule of to-day" says Cardozo (*a*, 26), "but may be matched by its opposite of yesterday" — "Most general propositions in law," says Harper (*b*, 327), "can be matched by general propositions of equal weight and authority of the very opposite trend."

The contents of the "ought to be" are various, but we do not know of any tribe, however rudimentary its cultural development may have been, which did not possess in its culture a system of formulas marked by the words "ought to be" or "ought not to be."

§ 2. Justice

Within the realm of the Good the idea of justice appears. The opinion is often expressed that the idea of the Good is the culminating point in morals, whereas for law the culminating point is represented by the idea of justice. Were it so, the general concept of ethics and of ethical rules would be void of precise meaning. But it is not so. Of course, the first attempts to formulate the

[4] Earlier scholars hoped to discover regularities in the content of ethical rules. This was, for instance, the basis of Post's hope to be able to discriminate the right and the wrong by mass observation of the life of peoples (*cf.* chap. III).

idea of justice were undertaken in the realm of law, especially in the domain of criminal law, which is in general the oldest part of every system of law. When studying various sources of primitive law, men of science determine their relative age by the relative number of rules referring to criminal law: the larger their percentage, the more ancient is the corresponding source (*cf.* Maine, *a*, 355–7). But older codes did not create new ethical convictions; they were only the expression of already existing beliefs. Therefore we must admit that the idea of justice, already expressed in the oldest criminal laws, was implicit in the undifferentiated ethical conviction which ruled society before law originated. "In every society," writes Bergson, "the idea of justice covers all relations between men" (68). It is obvious that not all relations between men are covered by law, so that, according to the great French philosopher, justice is to be recognized as corresponding to a domain larger than that of legal coördination; this can only be that of ethical coördination in general.

The idea of justice is a general ethical idea. In the hierarchy of ethical values (i.e., of values related to the idea of the Good) it is inferior only to the general idea of the Good. The Just is what is (or should be) recognized as good by society.

The idea of justice was "discovered" by mankind very early. But, in any case, it is an idea which has once been discovered. Does this not mean that justice is merely one of the creations of human phantasy?

We are not obliged to think so. The properties of the inanimate world have existed throughout all history and yet have been discovered by the human mind at certain historical times. Gravitation, chemical affinity, the tendency of energy toward dispersion existed in spite of their being unknown to men. But how is it with the complex combinations of these properties, which are applied in constructing machines? Did they exist before the invention of such machines, or were they created by men when the new possibilities were discovered? Of course they existed potentially and became actually existent when practically applied. The properties of inorganic matter, as well as those of living organisms, are, of course, only abstractions carried out by the human mind. And philosophy teaches us as regards abstract notions that the question of time and place is irrelevant. Abstract notions belong to the ideal world, separate parts of which may form the content of human thought at a given time and in certain places, but which themselves do not belong to any specific time or place.

Such is also the notion of justice. It may have been "discovered" by human beings at a certain time and in a certain place; today it may be one of the most efficacious ideas. But its existence, in the ideal world, is independent of such discoveries and of such efficacy. On the other hand, the assertion that justice existed before its discovery would also be wrong, because any proposition including the notion of time is incompatible with abstract notions.

Are such statements not beyond the limits of sociology, of science in general? No, they are just on the periphery. The sociology of law has to explain the efficacy of a system of rules, and these rules are correlated with the idea of justice. It might be difficult to explain this efficacy without any knowledge of this idea and of its place in the ideal world.

Justice is, of course, not a "thing" or a "person" which could be observed and measured; in this sense it does not "exist" in the experimental world (Pareto, 731). But justice is a term applied for the manifestation of a particular bio-psychic state which is able to determine human behavior in society. The conditions under which this state plays its part in the determination can be observed. As a first approximation the following propositions may be offered.

Men say that a situation expresses justice and may act correspondingly, if this situation is considered by them as a concrete embodiment of a recognized system of values. An act is called just if it increases the conformity between actual situations and the ideal situation which would be the complete embodiment of a value system. A man is called just if his acts are commonly just.

The system of values applied may be individual, i.e., not fixed by society. In such cases nobody is the judge if two or more evaluations conflict. This is the reason why no practical question can be decided by an appeal to justice as such.

But, in addition to individual values, there are also socially recognized systems of values. The term of justice is applied when evaluating concrete situations, acts or persons in terms of such value systems. In such cases there might be agencies which authoritatively decide what does and what does not conform with one or another value system. A court decides it, when legal values are referred to; a prophet, a saint or a clergyman, when a system of religious ethics is involved; arbiters of different designations, when business ethics, a dueling code or rules of a game are to be applied.

In all the cases mentioned, the term "justice" could be dropped. A decision in accordance with law, social ethics, et cetera, can be made without reference to justice. Yet the term designates the element which these decisions have in common, i.e., the property of being based on social ethics (on the social recognition of value systems).

§ 3. The Emotional Character of Ethical Conviction

Ethical values are embodied in human attitudes and human behavior. In this way ethics become a social force. This is possible because (1) the relation of men to values (especially ethical ones) is not only intellectual, but also to a larger extent emotional, and (2) the ethical convictions of group-members are generally similar. Let us study both elements separately.

Conviction is a specific attitude of men toward certain mental objects (contents of consciousness): ideas concerning the structure of the universe, of society, of a certain social group; rules of conduct; aesthetic ideals.

Conviction is, of course, irrational; it forms a part of the emotional life. Of course, the object of conviction may be investigated by means of the intellect; but the result of this investigation is not decisive for the specific attitude of conviction. Conviction may persist in spite of the intellectual rejection of its content ("*credo quia absurdum*"); on the contrary, sometimes conviction does not appear in spite of overwhelming evidence (many individuals do not "believe" in the modern physical theories concerning the nature of electrical phenomena or the structure of atoms). Even if there is agreement between the results of intellectual investigation and the content of conviction, a causal connection between them is not always there; scientific conviction is the attainment of very few.

Conviction is one of the forces playing a part in voluntary actions; conformity with conviction colors the idea of a possible action with a positive affective tone of some intensity. Only in exceptional cases is conviction present in the struggle of motives as a precise element clearly distinguished from others. Very often conviction acts as a subconscious element, as an element in the "character" of the acting individuals: the sum of convictions forms one of the most important elements in a person's character. For every individual to act according to his conviction has become habitual; there is, perhaps, a general habit of acting according to conviction; but to every distinct element of conviction a certain habit corresponds as well. From the behavioristic viewpoint it might be said that certain words, gestures, symbols or signals concerned with the object of conviction have become stimuli in learned tendencies of behavior. Insofar as voluntary acts related to the content of conviction are concerned, a multitude of stimuli are given, so that an automatic response is impossible and the coördinating activity of the brain (the struggle for power among brain centers) becomes a physiological necessity.

Habitual behavior is commonly post-conscious behavior: there must have been at least once a case when the coördinating activity of the brain (to which consciousness is the psychic equivalent) strove to find the solution which is now carried out almost automatically. Behavior of this type is subconscious; but the possibility is given to interpret it, to actualize its intellectual content. This must be done by the method of "inversion," i.e., of returning from the posterior subconscious to the primary conscious conduct.

There is in these statements no contradiction with the assertion that conviction is irrational: the relation of the individual to the object of his conviction cannot be reduced to a logical form; but this does not hinder the object of his conviction from being expressed in the form of propositions susceptible to logical analysis.

§ 4. The Convergence of Individual Convictions

Conviction becomes a social force insofar as it is group-conviction. A group-conviction cannot be anything other than the converging convictions of the individual group-members: ascribing the conviction to the group, or to society in general, would be an illicit personification, incompatible with the idea of society as a concrete system. The existence of parallel convictions in a certain number of group-members does not form a group-conviction. Society is a sum of interacting individuals; group-conviction is therefore the similar conviction of group-members insofar as this conformity is based upon social interaction. Group-conviction is based upon mutual induction of "belief:" every (or almost every) group-member "partakes" in the belief of "others." His belief is, in great part, based upon the fact that others are also believers; on the other hand, his belief induces the "others" (or at least many of them) to continue believing.

The identity of group-conviction seems to be contradicted by everyday observation. Superficial introspection often results in a proud assertion: I feel myself free, in the sense that I behave according to ethical rules which I freely recognize, which I have freely chosen as patterns for my conduct. Such statements occur not only in daily life.

A completely individualistic theory of ethics has been formulated with great brilliancy and in much detail by Petrazhitsky (*b*, 38–45). According to him, the efficacy of ethics is nothing more than a subjective phenomenon parallel in the consciousnesses of all group-members; there is, in the objective world, nothing to correspond to these phenomena. The objective validity of ethics (i.e., of morals and law) is no more than an illusion of men; Petrazhitsky often speaks of the "phantasms" represented by law. For him the uniformity of group behavior is merely a "natural" similarity (chap. I, § 2).[5]

[5] I maintain these propositions despite the arguments of Babb (*b*, 555 s. s.) for a socio-psychological interpretation of Petrazhitsky's theory. Of course, Petrazhitsky

This individualistic theory is, of course, completely erroneous. Men are social beings and the content of their consciousness is mostly determined socially. Therefore the list of recognized ethical rules is practically the same for all the members of a certain social group. To be a group-member means, first of all, to share in the group-conviction and to behave in accordance with it. "Communities," says Allport, "are small groups, whose members are governed by modes of conduct they recognize" (*a*, 384). Therefore "the essence of moral (ethical) conduct is the performance of social duty, duty prescribed by society, as opposed to the mere following of the promptings of egoistic impulses" (MacDougall, 313). There exists, of course, an emotional solidarity of group-members (Mead, 541) and a contagiousness of emotional expression (Stearns, 228) which helps the ethical convictions of group-members to tend toward similarity.

In order to prove the collective (in contradistinction to the individual) character of ethical conviction, the following small experiment is very conclusive: try to think of an ethical rule which you would recognize in contrast to the other members of your own group. You will find it difficult, because every rule truly recognized by you will be a rule which you received from your family, your community, your professional associates, the Church, the fraternity or the club to which you belong, or from the State. There may be exceptions: an individual of a very high moral standard may recognize rules imposing special duties not accepted by the average man; or a social reformer may try to impose new rules of behavior. But such individual rules are diverse, and, when acting on human behavior, they often come into conflict with one another just like sound waves or even ripples produced by stones thrown into a pond: interfering waves destroy one another. The same happens with private ethics, with ethical rules recognized only by single individuals: they may sometimes determine individual behavior but have no serious influence on the social proc-

frequently speaks of law as of a product of successful *mass* adaptation. Yet this is, for Petrazhitsky, merely a natural, not an essential element in law; many phenomena in which this element is lacking are considered legal. The restriction of Petrazhitsky's concepts by introducing into them socio-psychological concepts would produce a completely different theory.

ess, on human behavior in society. "There is no such thing as individual ethics;" writes Makariewicz (64); "there are of course individual opinions as to what is good, but they are also acquired."

The essence of ethics does not pertain to the individual's but to the society's interpretation. It does not matter whether Mr. A. or Mr. B. interprets the situation in this or in that manner; whether the one or the other considers an act good or bad, a line of conduct right or wrong. What is important is that their social environment considers certain actions as necessary or "expected." To be sure, the collective interpretation of human behavior is worked out from a multitude of uniform and simultaneous individual interpretations, but uniformity and simultaneity of interpretation is essential to social ethics, and accidental and quite original interpretations remain beyond its limits.

The social origin of ethical rules creating their uniformity within social groups may be again corroborated by the study of the mentality of an ethical nonconformist. Westermarck states (I, 123): "Though persecuted by his own people as an outcast, the moral dissenter does not regard himself as the advocate of a mere private opinion. Even when standing alone he feels that his conviction is shared at least by an ideal society, by all those who see the matter as clearly as he does himself and who are animated with equally wide sympathies and an equally broad sense of justice."

Is therefore the sentiment of ethical freedom entirely a mistaken one? A primitive man does not possess this sentiment; all his behavior is unambiguously determined by the ethical rules of his group. Since the early stages of social development are characterized by lack of social differentiation, he belongs to only one group and has practically no choice or freedom at all. For a modern man the situation is somewhat different. Everybody belongs to more than one social group: the State has been created and between the family and the State there are numerous social groups of various types. Membership in many of these groups is voluntary, optional. An individual may become a member of a club, or of a student fraternity or of a community of commissioned officers of a regiment. One who freely joins such a group is also free not to join it; if he joins, he is obliged to recognize the corresponding ethical rules; but the idea of having been free to join or not produces a sentiment of freedom even after having joined the group and having submitted oneself to its rules.

Secondly, there are many alternative groups; in contemporary society the most adequate example is that of occupational groups. An individual may become a physician, a lawyer, a shopkeeper, a mason, a farmer, et cetera. Each of these groups has its special ethical rules, binding only for its members and not for others. The possibility of belonging to one and not to another group, and the consequent knowledge that there *are* ethical rules which are not obligatory for one, give rise to the sentiment of freedom.

The diversity of social groups is the main cause of the differentiated behavior of men in modern society in contrast to their more uniform behavior in primitive groups. This diversity may be as great as possible, but still the behavior of every individual is subject to a multitude of ethical rules corresponding to the social groups to which he belongs. As a social being, every individual is bound by socio-cultural, especially by ethical tradition.

Finally, the social group is not a mystical superhuman being, but a sum total of interacting individuals; the creation and imposition of ethical rules is effected by interacting individuals, and in the interplay of forces forming the process of imposition almost everybody takes a greater or lesser part. The individual who could not devise an ethical rule of his own possibly played a part in such a process. Yet even in this case not the fact that he, the individual, gave a new impulse was socially important, but the fact that this impulse was followed by group-members and became a factor in the formation of new uniformities in their behavior. Were he not followed, his newly gained ethical conviction would have remained on the level of inefficient private ethics.

§ 5. The Structure of Ethical Rules

It is possible (*cf.* above, § 3) to express the objects of ethical conviction in the form of propositions susceptible to logical analysis. Applying the method of inversion, we are able to discover that ethical group-conviction is the acceptance, the recognition of statements of a uniform type: if the situation *A* is given, behavior *B* ought to be (or ought not to be). There are three elements in this formula: (1) the reference to a certain condition, the description of a certain situation; (2) demanded behavior and (3) the link represented by the words "ought to be" or "ought not to be." The formula is always a general one: every ethical rule is combined with the idea that acting in conformity with it is the duty not of one person, but of every person whom it concerns. We may say: Mr. A has to pay his debt to Mr. B. But the true meaning of the sentence is that every person (among them A), having contracted a debt, ought to pay the corresponding sum at the stipulated time. We may say: A should have greeted B when he met him; but we may say so only because we recognize the general rule admonishing us to greet acquaintances when we meet them.

1. The if-clause (condition) is obviously present in the majority of ethical rules. Legal and customary rules always refer to certain situations; they indicate how to act when buying an object or declaring income or joining a club or meeting acquaintances. There are, of course, some negative legal and customary rules (thou shalt not kill; thou shalt not steal) and also some positive moral rules (help your neighbors), which seem to have an "absolute" validity not bound to any conditions. But in actuality even these rules are limited by a general clause: "in relation with other group members" (sometimes also in especially stated relations with members of other groups). For legal rules there is no exception possible as they are tied to precise social groups (first of all States) and are not "in force" outside their limits. With regard to moral rules, the following "natural law" may be stated: the efficacy of a rule is in inverse ratio to the dimensions of the group to which it refers; universal rules are almost always inefficient rules. Actually, every time when the existence of a universal rule is asserted, it is not actual rules (i.e., rules actually determining human behavior) that are expressed, but merely the representation by men of what rules of conduct ought to be (see below, chap. VII, § 3).

There are, of course, several rules (do not kill, et cetera) which are included in the group-conviction of almost every social group; practically speaking, they are almost universal. But their universality is based not upon imposition (social coördination), but upon similarity of conditions (natural uniformity). Theoretically each of them is not a universal rule, but a set of similar rules spread throughout the social universe. Up to the present, exceptions to almost every rule have been discovered: savage tribes exist who do not "recognize" the most "sacred" objects of the common conviction of civilized men. The ethical uniformity of mankind is *Zukunftsmusik* (*cf.* above, § 1).

2. To the condition must correspond an effect. The effect to which ethical rules correspond is always human behavior, practical behavior related to other group-members. By means of this element an ethical rule may be distinguished (a) from a logical rule in which the postulated effect refers not to practical behavior, but to intellectual processes; (b) from an aesthetic rule in which the postulated effect refers not to practical behavior, but to creative acts in art, or to the application of art in life.

3. The link between the condition and the effect is represented by the formula "ought to be" (or "ought not to be"). It must be stressed that such is the logical link between condition and effect. The sociological link (to be studied in Chapter V) is a corporate, mutually induced will disposition of group-members to actualize the contents of ethical rules.

The "ought to be" element of the ethical formula is the intellectual equivalent of its emotional basis. This basis is nothing more than the relation of every ethical formula to the realm of higher values, especially to that of the Good. If condition *A* is given, behavior *B* ought to be, for it is good or just — such might be a more extended formula of the general structure of an ethical rule. Therefore ethical rules, just like logical or aesthetic ones, are not only rules demanding in advance a certain conduct, but also rules helping us to evaluate behavior which has already taken place.

§ 6. Ethical Rules and Technical Rules

Ethical rules do not form the only category of general regulations tending to impose themselves on the practical behavior of men in society. Another category is formed by technical rules. The notion of technical rules has a wider application than merely to the field of technology. Technical rules exist in every applied science, such as medicine or scientific agriculture, and in every art, high or low — architecture, music, poetry, et cetera — but also in such occupations as those of cooks, tailors, et cetera. These rules designate the conduct a man has to choose when aiming at a definite goal. Medicine gives the rules for preserving or restoring health; architecture those for building solid houses and beautiful palaces; the rules applied by tailors or cooks show how to proceed in order to produce good clothes or savory dishes. Like ethical rules, technical rules are rules of conduct; in a certain manner they influence human behavior. What is the difference between the two?

The essential difference is that technical rules refer not to absolute, but to relative values. The formula "ought to be" is inapplicable to technical rules. It is replaced by the notion of conduct which is necessary to attain a specific aim. Every technical rule is merely an application of natural laws to our practical needs. A natural law expresses a necessary link between certain conditions and certain effects. Therefore, when we are aiming at a certain goal, we must satisfy (if we are able) the appropriate conditions; nature will then do its part and produce the situation corresponding to our wishes. The study of the human body and of its functions resulted in the formulation of a multitude of "laws"; the science of medicine is a system of practical precepts based on this knowledge. And as natural laws work with surety, in technical rules the link between condition and result is that of natural necessity.

Like natural laws, technical rules refer to the order of nature; but they have to do with an order of nature applied to the needs of culture, while ethical rules belong entirely to the order of culture. As in ethical rules, so also in technical rules the human will plays a rôle, but not the same rôle. In ethical rules the link between condition and effect is realized by the human will; efforts of men are needed to transform the condition into its effect, to actualize the pattern of behavior (see below, chap. V). In technical rules this link is realized by nature; the human will does its part only in bringing together all the conditions necessary to produce the effect.

There is another difference between ethical and technical rules. A technical rule shows us how we have to proceed in order to attain a certain aim, general or special; but it never indicates whether or not this aim ought to be attained. On the contrary, an ethical rule tells us which aims ought to exist for us and which ought not, but it never indicates the means to be adopted in order to attain them. The technical rules of applied political economy show us how wealth may be increased; but they do not answer the question whether, in a certain case, the aim of gaining profit ought to be pursued or ought to be given up in favor of other aims. Ethical rules will show, on the contrary, whether the aim of gaining profit may be, in certain circumstances, considered a "right" one, or not, but will never show the technical means to be used in order to increase our wealth. Therefore a technical rule may be applied in pursuing aims incompatible with the commands of ethical rules. Many detective novels are based upon the idea of a criminal using modern techniques in order to attain his ends. In such cases he is acting according to technical rules, but transgressing ethical rules. The same happens daily in actual life. How often, when attending a criminal trial or reading the report of such a trial, we involuntarily admire the technical skill of a criminal who succeeded in forging bank notes so perfectly that they could not be distinguished from real ones or who succeeded in making an experienced businessman his dupe.

There is a third difference closely related to both the preceding ones. When I pronounce with conviction a sentence expressing an ethical rule, my will aims at effecting the realization of this rule, not only in my own conduct, but also in that of others. When I say "do not lie," or "help your neighbors" or "vote for the man you think will be the best candidate," I would like to see everybody acting according to these rules and, if I suspect that many people do not know or do not recognize my rule, I am inclined to resort to propaganda in order to help in making it universal. On the contrary, when I formulate a technical rule, I express, of course, the idea that everyone who intends to achieve a certain aim has to behave in a corresponding way. But it may happen that I shall not be at all pleased when I see that other people know my rule and act according to it. Imagine the case of an inventor or that of a businessman who has acquired a patent; they do all they can to keep their technical rules secret. Ethical rules belong to the common domain of culture; they tend to spread, to convert new proselytes through the agency of persons already knowing and recognizing them. Technical rules may also belong to the common domain of culture, but for them this qualification is not essential; there may be private, even secret technical rules.

The differences between ethical and technical rules may be summed up in the following way. Ethical rules show the aims to be pursued, technical rules the means of pursuing them. Ethical rules show the conduct that ought to be or ought not to be; technical rules the conduct that is necessary, if a certain aim is to be attained. Ethical rules have a tendency toward proselytism; technical rules may be associated with a tendency toward secrecy.

It might be argued that there is a kind of "technical conviction." There might even be a technical conviction of many group-members. But in technical conviction the rational element is much stronger than the emotional, therefore it is subjected to the influence of "enlightenment" and is much more changeable than ethical group-conviction with its primarily emotional roots.

BIBLIOGRAPHICAL NOTE

A good general study of ethics is presented by Bunge. In his opinion ethics represent a criterion, more or less relative and constant, for the qualification of human behavior (XII). Excellent statements concerning the correlation of higher values are to be found in Kistiakovsky (197–206). The ideas of ethical values and of the hierarchy of values has been studied by Meinong, Durkheim (*a*, *b*). Max Scheler, Hartmann, Gurvitch (*f*), Perry, Murphy (198–205), Parsons (*a*), Folsom. A very good study of the concept of ethical duty is that of Le Senne.

As regards moral insanity, a hundred years ago Grohman in Germany and Prichard in England gave its first scientific description; later on the French scientist Morel described it in some detail. The statements in text are based on the famous work of Krafft-Ebbing. In modern literature the very existence of moral insanity is sometimes denied; *cf.* Glueck (*b*, 337, footnote) and Healy (*a*, 788).

The idea that justice is the legal principle (and not that of ethics in general) has been once more expressed by Radbruch (*a*). A similar statement is implicitly comprised in the following words of Hall: "the ought that is relevant (in law) is not a purely ethical ought, nor is it any logical ought. It is instead the correct solution of existing social problems" (*b*, 9). Of the earlier literature see Gierke (*d*, 244). A good criticism is that of Gurvitch (*a*, 113–4): "If the idea of law," he says, "forms one of the elements in a hierarchy of values, there is no reason to deny the possibility of deducing it from above." As regards Hall, his proposition refers obviously to problems *de lege ferenda*. A somewhat simplified view on justice is contained in Carter's work: justice is what is customarily done (162). That justice is an ethical and not a specifically legal notion is stressed by Schinkler (39). Justice's conformity with a system of (ethical) values is analyzed by Morgenthau (35). The relation of the concepts of duty and of ideal is discussed by Stoop (159).

The importance of criminal law in ancient law forms one of the major parts of the doctrine of Sir Henry Maine (*a*). His doctrine is attacked by Diamond whose arguments are, however, unsatisfactory.

Petrazhitsky gave the first consistent theory of the emotional character of ethical motivation. Yet the terms "emotions" or "impulses" (he uses both without distinction) are applied by him in a specific sense: they designate two-sided psychic phenomena (in contradistinction from the one-sided intellectual, emotional or conative elements in psychic life) and roughly correspond to "reflexes" in Pavlov's terminology or to "tendencies" in this book. In any case, the fallacy of the intellectual explanation of ethical phenomena was brilliantly proved by Petrazhitsky. The emotional (irrational) elements in moral (ethical) conviction are shown by McDougall (215–19). The idea of mutual induction of group-conviction is stressed by Gurvitch (*e*, 73–5), Makariewicz (64), Steinmetz (*a*, I, 289), Tönnies (*d*, 240–2), Vierkandt (384–5), Ehrlich (*a*, 28–38, 79), Jerusalem (176), Delos (98–9), Brown (254–6), Ginsberg (141). The uniformity of standards in primitive society is contested by Malinowski (*a*, 9–16); *contra* Brown (253). The problem of personal selection of "moral codes" in modern society, in correlation with the multiformity of groups, is discussed by MacIver (*b*, 284, 295–302). Tufts (3) distinguishes between "personal or individual morals" (decision of an individual) and "social morality" (group standards). It is obvious that what he calls individual morals are not morals at all, but behavior partly determined by morals. Collective and individual moral experience is contrasted by Gurvitch (*f*, 178–82).

The study of the general content of an ethical rule is commonly carried out as regards legal rules only; it is one of the commonest elements in every "Outline of Jurisprudence" (*cf.* Kocourek, *a*, 143–4). The idea that these achievements of jurisprudence should be used when studying ethics in general has been maintained by H. Cohen. Petrazhitsky (*b*, 25–30) expands the concept of aesthetic rules much more widely than is generally accepted and includes rules of decency in this category.

The concept of technical rules in their relation to ethical rules is explained by Korkunoff (*b*), Duguit (*a*, I, 36), Fehr (29), M. Cohen (243–4) and del Vecchio (*d*). Odum studies the technical rules as "technicways" which he contrasts to folkways. The rôle of human will in the realization of ethical rules (norms) is excellently described by Morgenthau (22–3, 34); *cf.* his study of the relation between ethical rules and natural laws (39–43).

CHAPTER V

SOCIO-ETHICAL EQUILIBRIUM

§ 1. Introduction

Almost every social group has a complex of ethical rules; their influence in shaping the behavior of group-members produces a special equilibrium which might be called "socio-ethical equilibrium." This equilibrium is a property of social groups, whereas the activities producing it form one of the types of social coördination, and the result of coördination forms social order (chap. I, §§ 2 and 5).

In the concrete system presented by a social group, characterized by socio-ethical equilibrium, there are both objective and subjective elements: the subjective elements are the individuals imbued with ethical group-conviction and ready to act according to the precepts of ethical rules, and the objective elements are the rules followed by them. Actually the behavior of group-members is not in complete conformity with the precepts of ethical rules. Abnormal behavior creates disturbances which, according to the very essence of a concrete system, must be overcome in order to restore its original condition.

The disturbances of this kind are generally "small," for the forces of group-cohesion are able to restore the situation. On the other hand, these disturbances are internal ones, in contrast to external disturbances created by the influence of other groups (for instance, war) or even emanating from sources of energy outside social groups altogether (changes in climate, epidemics, et cetera). Socio-ethical equilibrium concerns only small infra-group disturbances. Single violations of ethical rules are of course merely small disturbances, but as they would not necessarily counterbalance each other, they might, added together, transform the system. Insofar as the group is truly a system (in other words: insofar as the group is truly safeguarding its identity), it must display activity in order to restore the original situation.

What situation should be restored? This is generally one of the most difficult questions in applying the term *equilibrium* to social phenomena. In our case there is no difficulty; the original situation, the restoration of which is desired, is of course the "normal" situation, that determined by the objective elements of the system; in other words, social order.

The reaction of the social group to disturbances seems to be just as natural as the response of a living organism to a stimulus. We might therefore speak of a "socio-cultural reflex." Of course, the similarity is only superficial. In a sequence of the type studied, neither stimuli nor responses are established by nature, but are socially determined — coördinate dispositions of human wills must exist in order to effectuate the social response. The socio-cultural reflex consists of a multitude of individual attitudes and activities; socio-ethical equilibrium is the sum of activities of group-members accepting ethical rules and acting according to their content, with the conviction that these rules ought to be followed.

It is not the intellectual, but the emotional element in the relation of men to rules which creates socio-ethical equilibrium. A purely intellectual relation to an ethical rule remains without force. Very often general propositions lack all relation to emotional life. Every formula stating a causal connection between phenomena is of this kind, as well as every universal proposition of the type: all men are mortal; all Negroes are black. We may also scientifically analyze an ethical rule without considering it emotionally; in other cases people may consider an ethical rule even with repulsion, with the precise aim of acting against it. For a revolutionary the ethical rule of obeying authorities is hateful, whereas an ordinary criminal does not always act with the intention of transgressing an ethical rule, but only, perhaps, in spite of his knowledge of it. Such cases are exceptional, for the triumph of ethics is the rule, and this presupposes a positive emotional attitude on the part of the greater number of group-members.

§ 2. The Recognition of Ethical Rules

Ethical rules are social rules in the sense that they are created by social interaction and therefore are practically the same for all group-members. But these rules become a social force only through recognition on the part of the individuals; the sum of these individual recognitions forms the socio-ethical conviction. This recognition contains a double tendency: (1) toward bringing one's own behavior into accord with the pattern of the rule and (2) toward doing the same with the behavior of others.

The first tendency, related to one's own conduct, to the behavior of the person recognizing the rule, is essential for ethical rules. Recognition, insofar as it is directed toward one's own behavior, is not so much the ethical "profession" of an individual (verbal statements of his principles of conduct), as his actual ethical attitude, i.e., his readiness to act in accordance with certain ethical rules. Discrepancies between these two are not at all rare.

On the other hand, recognition does not necessarily imply internal conviction as to the excellency of a certain rule. Such a relationship between one's mentality and a rule might exist, but other forms are much more frequent. According to Max Weber (*c*, 19), there are four ways of ascribing "legitimate validity" to an order (and, of course, to the separate elements of the order, i.e., to rules). The recognition of validity may be based on tradition, on affective faith (for instance, new revelation), on evaluating faith (absolute validity) or on positive institution. In any case the rule must be accepted by the individual as a guide in the situations it covers. In the earlier juridical literature this external relationship of men to rules was expressed by the term *opinio necessitatis*, which was stressed especially when speaking of customary law. This *opinio necessitatis* is nothing more than the acceptance by an individual of the fact that the rule has been imposed by a social group to which the individual belongs. Of course, *opinio necessitatis* exists not only in the domain of law, but also in those of morals and custom; in other words, in the total domain of ethics; by this qualification custom is distinguished from habit.

The first element of recognition is sometimes absent from the relations of men to rules. A despotic ruler imposes a complex of patterns of behavior on his subjects but does not recognize them as compulsory for himself. This is not merely a fictitious case:

many rulers of the so-called "patrimonial type" consider ethical rules, especially rules imposed by Christian or other religious ethics, as excellent instruments of domination and therefore demand that their subjects behave in accordance with them, but are convinced that for themselves, in their high position, no rules exist. Such an attitude toward a rule of conduct cannot be considered "recognition." The interaction between ruler and subjects is quite different from ethical coördination.

The second element in recognition, that directed toward the behavior of others, was already mentioned when speaking of the tendency of ethical rules toward proselytism in contrast to technical rules which may often be kept secret (chap. IV, § 6). This tendency toward proselytism is nothing more than the sum of the second parts of individual recognitions. And as the same rules are recognized by a large majority of group-members, the individual tendency toward proselytism results in a corporate tendency, which could, in a metaphorical way, be ascribed to the rule itself.

Both parts of the recognition are closely related to one another. If someone recognizes an ethical rule, this means not only that he endeavors to act in conformity with it, but also that, when he evaluates the behavior of others, he applies this rule and behaves socially in accordance with this evaluation; he approves others when their behavior is molded by ethical rules and disapproves when it is contrary to them. On the other hand, when one is taught by experience that a rule one recognizes is not carried out or is no longer carried out by others, one gradually loses the impulse to act in accordance with it oneself. Obviously it could not be otherwise. The recognition of ethical rules is closely related to the idea of justice. Everyone feels that it is contrary to justice that others act freely when he is bound, that duties are imposed upon him and not upon others. Therefore when he observes that others are no longer bound by an ethical rule which they formerly recognized together with him, he begins to feel it unjust to be bound any longer. The feeling of satisfaction arising from the consciousness of carrying out the rule is transformed into its opposite — dissatisfaction; and the general urge toward adjusting his behavior to the rule will no longer exist.

§ 3. Direct and Indirect Recognition

The recognition of a certain rule on the part of an individual may be of two kinds: direct or indirect. In the case of direct recognition, the object is a separate, clearly definite rule: I know the rules forbidding one to lie or to enter a foreign country without permission of the competent authorities. I recognize them and act in accordance with them. In cases of direct recognition, the knowledge of the abstract rule is not necessary. Such knowledge is possible only in highly developed societies and only for their intellectual élite. In the majority of cases the rule is present in the minds of persons directly recognizing it, but in the indefinite form of typical instances of its application. This is the general situation with regard to children, primitive tribes or backward classes in civilized society. A boy knows that he is forbidden to steal apples from the neighboring orchard. A member of a primitive group knows that it is forbidden to strike another, to blind him, to break his legs; but he is not able to conceive the abstract rule: "Do not cause any bodily harm to others." (*Cf.* especially Lévy-Bruhl's works.) Sufficient evidence is comprised in primitive codes: the laws of the barbarian German tribes of the fifth to the eighth centuries or of the Slavic peoples several centuries later were no more than catalogues of concrete offenses.

If the recognition is indirect, its object is not a definite rule, but an indefinite complex of rules. The link uniting the separate rules has nothing to do with their content: I do not recognize indirectly all the rules of civil law or all the rules concerning railway traffic. But I recognize the rules which are recognized by "others": by my relatives, by my friends, by my partners, by all persons whose judgment is important to me, by all persons whose anger I fear, by the holders of power and, finally, by "everybody," by the impersonal "they." Persons whose recognition of ethical rules is decisive for the attitude of others may be called "ethical leaders"; their recognition of ethical rules may be, in its turn, direct or indirect (if they are following other persons who represent ethical leaders for them).

Students who lay stress on the logical elements in law and ethics try to explain this indirect recognition as a logical consequence of the direct recognition. Their argument is as follows: if I recognize a rule directly, I have, as a logical being, to recognize all the derived rules which may be deducted from it. But man is not at all a completely logical being and may sometimes act against the precepts of logic as well as against those of ethics; besides, observation shows that men often recognize indirectly complexes of rules which are not at all the logical consequents of rules recognized directly. The main method of creating indirect recognition is that of cultural inheritance. The cultural tradition of every group is self-imposed upon each of its members. According to Sorokin's three types of social relationship the familistic, the contractual and the compulsory (*h*, III, 23 *ff.*), membership may be natural, voluntarily acquired or compulsorily imposed. The forms of adjusting individual behavior to the cultural tradition vary with each of these types, but this does not prevent their essential character from remaining the same in all.

It is obvious that, from the quantitative point of view, indirect recognition is more important than the direct. Lawyers and students of law are supposed to know the totality of legal rules, but even they would be unable to enumerate the ethical rules of other categories, though recognized by themselves. The knowledge of an average man is still more restricted, and this in spite of his being ready to act according to every ethical rule established in the social groups to which he belongs.

Nevertheless, the direct recognition is the basic one. First of all, an individual is unable to recognize ethical rules indirectly if he does not recognize at least one directly: for his relation to indirectly recognized rules is based upon the analogy of directly recognized rules. On the other hand, the indirect recognition of ethical rules by indeterminate masses of individuals is impossible, if nobody recognizes these rules directly; to recognize rules means to recognize rules which are recognized by our parents (familistic adaptation), by older members (voluntary adaptation) or by superiors (compulsory adaptation). If such "ethical leaders" no longer recognize the rules, the indirect recognition may last a certain time; the law of inertia plays an important rôle in social life and acquired ethical dispositions are therefore not destroyed at once, when their bases have disappeared. But somewhat later the evident loss of the ethical conviction on the part of the ethical leaders results in extinguishing the conviction of the average members of the group, for both parts of the recognition, that for oneself and that for others, are closely interrelated.

§ 4. The Influence of the Recognition on One's Own Behavior

We must now study more precisely the influence of the recognition of ethical rules on human behavior and, to begin with, the first part of the recognition. What is the nature of this influence?

In juridical literature the opinion has often been expressed that the relationship between a rule and the behavior determined by it is a causal one. The situation, however, is much more complex. The content of a rule belongs to the "ideal realm" (see above, chap. IV, § 2) and therefore cannot be brought into causal relationship with bio-psychic events; the content is the logical ground for evaluating human acts. On the other hand, an ethical rule may become an object of conviction and the psychic state designated by this term may cause decisions. Finally, certain symbols related to the ethical rule and expressed in words, gestures, et cetera, become stimuli in systems of conditioned reflexes and therefore cause the responses. In any case, if one recognizes a rule "for oneself," one's behavior is influenced by this attitude. The recognition plays an important rôle both in voluntary acts and in conditioned reflexes.

In the beginning, acting according to ethical rules is voluntary.[1] "In the beginning" means in the beginning of every individual life (childhood and youth), in the early stages of a new situation (after the general milieu has been changed or after having entered a new social group), in the early stages of the introduction of new ethical rules (see below, chap. VI). In these cases behavior must be voluntary, for there is as yet no automatic mechanism to carry through the precepts of the rule; *inborn* ethical reflexes do not exist.

[1] In the sense given to this term in chap. II, § 7.

Within the struggle of motives forming the essence of a voluntary act the thought of an ethical rule often plays an important part; this representation may, of course, be concrete or abstract (according to the different forms of direct recognition); it may be clear or confused; it may be present in the form of the general idea of "ought to be" or as the representation of the "sanction" of the ethical rule, the punishment resulting from its transgression or the reward following upon its fulfillment; or in the form of revulsion, because of the disapproval and the reproaches of one's parents, friends, superiors, et cetera. In any case, the idea of the rule introduces into the struggle of motives a positive impulse toward the commanded act or a revulsion from the prohibited one.

There may be a "temptation" not to carry out the commands or to commit a prohibited act. A temptation means the existence of "natural" motives inclining one toward an act incompatible with ethical precepts. In such cases general ethical conviction (i.e., the decision to act in conformity with ethical rules) will be reinforced by the idea that everybody (i.e., all members of the social group) recognizes these rules, tries to impose them upon everyone else — among others, upon the individual in question. The knowledge of such an attitude of the others will, of course, be of considerable weight in the decision of the individual. It is possible that even this idea would not prevent him from acting against the rule, but it would be possible only in exceptional situations, when anti-ethical motives are extremely strong. In ordinary cases the consideration of the attitude of others is not at all necessary; the idea of "others" standing behind the ethical rule is one of the constant impulses and thus influences the decisions without being clearly represented in every single case.

The ethical motive (the representation of an ethical rule) joins the group of motives opposed to the "temptation." Insofar as ethical motives are social rules, they tend to socialize natural drives. The influence of these motives upon individual behavior is that of a "censor"; the metaphor of censorship is useful in showing the close relation between the conscience of the individual and the ethical code common to the group (Allport, *a*, 377, footnote 3). Another good metaphor is that of a "barrier" (Brown, 54 and Luriia, 331, 394).

Some authors (e.g., McDougall, 229 *ff.*) raise the question: How is it possible that the "higher" but weaker ethical motive gains victory over the "lower" but stronger motives? The question seems to be improperly phrased, for there is no reason to suppose that the ethical motive (that of acting in accordance with a socially imposed pattern of conduct) is always "weaker," i.e., endowed with a feebler affective tone; and secondly it is impossible, without leaving the domain of causal knowledge, to assert that the ethical motive is "higher." "Higher" and "lower" are formulas of evaluation which can be studied only from the normative point of view. The proper question would be: What are the conditions which help ethical motives generally to gain victory in the struggle of motives? It should be answered in the following way: When we examine a motive which has acted in our consciousness, but which did not belong to the realm of law or of any other ethical force, we feel that the affective tone of the conceived action is something born within us, arising from our personal, "free" relation to objects and acts. When a legal or, in general, an ethical motive is present in our consciousness, we feel that the affective tone is emanating from something external to us, from something to which we belong as parts of a totality.[2] The affective tone has its origin in social interaction; it is a result of culture.

Voluntary acts in harmony with ethical rules are needed in the "beginning" and later on in complex cases for which no automatic mechanism of behavior is ready. But in the majority of cases the adjustment of behavior to ethical rules is carried out by means of this automatic mechanism, created already in the early years of childhood. "The love of a child is early conditioned by the signs of approval or disapproval of the parents; the deepest affective cravings are satisfied through continual *rapport* with father and mother. This *rapport* can be maintained only if the child performs certain acts and inhibits others, according to the parents'

[2] This is an idea studied in its broader aspects by Petrazhitsky (*b*, 34–6); *cf.* Durkheim (*b*, 32). *Contra*, McDougall, 240.

wishes" (Allport, *a*, 337). And these wishes of the parents are likely to correspond to ethical rules expressed in abstract or concrete form. Certain words, gestures or other symbols become stimuli in acquired tendencies in which behavior in accordance with these wishes is the response secured by the natural tendency toward maintaining the friendly *rapport*. For instance, conditioned reflexes of this type are created: the word *lying* is applied to a projected action; it is "not to be done" (negative reflex or inhibition); the symbol of a closed door to father's room comes to mean, "not to enter"; or the hand of the watch approaching a certain point means, "begin to prepare lessons."

Later on, adjustment to the wishes and indications of other persons begins to play a part, first of all to those of ethical leaders. New symbols are introduced into the acquired behavior tendencies of an individual; the appearance of these symbols is followed by positive acts or forbearances, according to the structure of the tendencies. It must be noticed that the acquired responses of an individual, insofar as they create a drive to act in accordance with ethical rules, are closely related to similar responses of other individuals: for A every case of carrying out an ethical rule on the part of B, C or D is a stimulus to which corresponds the response of doing likewise.

When the content of a number of ethical rules has become incorporated into the behavior tendencies of an individual, he is acting according to the rules without noticing it. "To the outsiders a rule is a restriction and nothing more; to the native it has become the right way to behave and it implies no conscious restriction to his initiative; people are doing what they like, but they like to do things in an accustomed manner" (Whitehead, 217).

Later influences may change and increase the content of the tendencies acquired in childhood and in youth. But modern criminological research has proved that the general tendency to follow ethical rules must be formed in youth. If an individual has not acquired the habit of acting in accordance with ethical rules, such a habit cannot be created in him by later educational influences, or at least this can be done only in exceptional cases.

On the other hand, it must be acknowledged that not every familistic initiation to ethics is adequate to the task of socializing natural drives. There must be, even in childhood, a certain balance between voluntary acting in accordance with ethical rules and acting automatically.[3] If a child is endowed with a number of acquired tendencies securing ethical behavior, but not endowed with the faculty of easily forming new tendencies of the same type by consciously adjusting his behavior to the precepts of ethics, later on the young man will be unable to adjust himself ethically to new situations, and temptations, unavoidable in everyone's life, will gain victory over ethical impulses.

§ 5. Retributive Emotions and Tendencies

The second aspect of the recognition of ethical rules is the inclination they inspire to perform acts influencing the behavior of others. First of all, there may be acts of proselytism, using all the various means of persuasion or enlightenment. This tendency lies outside the limits of socio-ethical equilibrium for the existence of which it is prerequisite that a hostile social attitude appear when a transgression of an ethical rule is threatening or has become actual.[4] This hostile attitude of group-members toward potential or actual transgressors of ethical rules is nothing extraneous to socio-ethical conviction; it is one of its aspects.

An actual hostile attitude is a response within a specific behavior system, which might be called "the retributive tendency." From the introspective viewpoint, a "retributive emotion" or "retributive disposition" corresponds to a "retributive tendency."

Ordinarily retributive emotions are subconscious. According to the general rule (chap. II, § 7) every act corresponding to the response in an acquired tendency may, by posterior introspection,

[3] Barnard says: "The task seems to be one of 'conditioning' the mind and to let nature do what it then can. The conditioning will consist of stocking the mind properly and in exercising the non-logical properties" (38).

[4] The following study of the hostile attitudes and of their rôle in securing the efficacy of ethics should not be misunderstood as the assertion that ethics is based on hostile attitude. It is obvious that ethics possesses at least two roots. The other is described as the sentiment of solidarity (Kropotkin, *b*) or of sympathy (Soloview, Max Scheler, *b*).

be made susceptible to rational investigation. Therefore those less frequent cases when the retributive emotion is conscious may be utilized in order to clarify the general structure.

The retributive emotion, in its developed form, has the following structure. We concentrate our attention upon the act of an individual, find it good or evil, i.e., in conformity or nonconformity with ethical rules which we recognize. Then we transfer our attention toward the later history of the same individual to see whether his fortunes improved or became worse. If we are able to say that after an act which we consider to be good the fortunes of its author improved, or that after an act which we considered to be bad the fortunes of its perpetrator became worse, we state that retribution has taken place. We shall call such sequences of facts "retributive sequences." If, on the contrary, there is a discrepancy between our judgment of the acts of an individual and his later fate, we say that retribution has not taken place. Every time a retributive sequence takes place, an average man feels satisfaction; when a sequence of facts contrary to the principle of retribution transpires, and a reversal of the situation is out of the question, the average man feels dissatisfaction. An intermediate case is imaginable, when retribution has not yet taken place but still remains possible. In such cases the retributive emotion becomes a drive for action: the idea of acting so as to complete the retributive sequence is endowed with a positive affective tone, and thus enters, sometimes with great power, into the struggle of motives.

Examples might be useful. You read in your paper that a brute has violated a little girl and then killed her and that he has thus far remained undiscovered. You have, of course, a strong sense of dissatisfaction because the fate of the criminal, who continues to enjoy the life of a free man, is incompatible with the "horrible" act performed by him. On the other hand, you are of course enthusiastic, have a strong sense of satisfaction, when the performer of a brilliant feat is crowned as a national hero. Think of Lindbergh after his glorious performance and think of Lindbergh again, after the crime perpetrated against his little son: the discrepancy between Lindbergh's pain and his heroic deed was a most pregnant case of nonretribution; it may be cited in order to illustrate the feelings arising when retribution fails to take place. Alexander and Staub (211) describe this same phenomenon in another case: "Everybody demanded the head of the mass murderer Haarmann. . . . Capital punishment in such case is but the expression of the demand for retaliation which insists that blood be paid by blood." In a more general form Hall (*b*, 11) says: "History, anthropology . . . and observation of contemporary phenomena all support the thesis that socially dangerous behavior sets off deeply rooted emotional responses that tend towards overt actions against the offenders."

It is sometimes stressed (*cf*. Hall, *a*, 289) that retributive emotions exist only in more serious cases. This is true as regards overt action; but retributive dispositions are potentially present in every case of violation of ethical rules. They may be strengthened by the method of "teasing" (chap. II, § 8).

Now we are able to explain more precisely the relationship of ethical rules, on the one hand, and of hostile attitudes and retributive emotions, on the other. Every case of actual retributive emotion is first of all an evaluation of a certain manifestation of human behavior from the point of view of ethical rules. These ethical rules remain the same in all cases where by definition they "apply." In all our ethical judgments ethical rules are constant, whereas the concrete conduct compared with them is variable. It is obvious that this constant part of ethical judgments forms also a part of the constant retributive tendency. To be endowed with retributive tendencies signifies therefore: to recognize ethical rules. Or *vice versa:* the recognition of ethical rules signifies the acquisition of corresponding retributive tendencies.

The satisfaction which one feels from one's desire for retribution is independent of single causes of achieved retribution. A believer thinks it is God's hand which rewards good or evil deeds. A philosopher may assert that retribution is immanent, inherent in our acts; that a good deed contains in itself its reward and an evil act its punishment. A sceptical scientist may prove that in every case the carrying out of the retributive sequence is merely the result of a casual combination of natural forces. An average man will express his satisfaction when a retributive sequence has taken place, without analyzing the causes of the phenomenon.[5]

§ 6. The Roots of Retributive Emotions

How can the existence of hostile attitudes based upon retributive tendencies be explained? Very often the explanations proposed are merely statements of the fact. Thus, according to Bergson: "Violation of social order appears as something unnatural; even if it is frequently repeated, it seems to be an exception which is related to Society as a monster is to Nature" (5). According to Pareto: "The masses . . . are satisfied as long as society has rules that are accepted and obeyed. In the opposition that is aroused by any violation of them the sentiment chiefly manifested is hostile to any disturbance of social equilibrium" (1343). "Individuals manifest a dominant antipathy to those variations from type which attract attention" (Giddings, 203).

A very ingenious explanation has been given by Humphrey. According to him, an act which is a "breach of habit" tends to produce in individuals two incompatible responses: (1) the response suited to the habit and (2) the response based upon the tendency to imitate the acts of others, in our case those of the breaker of a habit. This conflict in systems of conditioned reflexes results in an "unpleasant thwarted feeling and a struggle to prohibit the disturbing suggestion" (117–19). However, a desire to imitate another's behavior is not necessarily present in every case; therefore a hostile attitude based upon a dissatisfaction of the kind stressed by Humphrey is not a necessary accompaniment of every breach of habit.

But something really is broken; not the tendency of imitating the behavior of *A* (*A* being the transgressor of the ethical rule), but the internal harmony of one's responses to the behavior of group-members: commonly, the behavior of everyone forms a

[5] The following recent case shows how unsophisticated ideas concerning retributive sequences may be present even in our day. In Ireland two old bachelors, living alone, had been fired upon in the night. The country people had their suspicions directed against the kin of the old men. A week later a young man, one of the suspected kinsmen, lost his eye in a purely accidental way. In the loss of his eye the community felt he had paid his penalty: his crime had met its just punishment (Arensberg, 28–33).

stimulus to ethical behavior on one's part; all stimuli of this kind are ordinarily harmonious, tend to the same response. In our case the behavior of *A* does not any longer form a stimulus of the normal type, whereas the behavior of others continues to do so. There is a certain contradiction within the impulses acting upon an individual — a disharmony; and disharmony produces dissatisfaction.

From the genetic viewpoint the phenomena studied may be expressed in the following way: the hostile attitude related to violations of ethical rules is an element of acquired tendencies based upon revenge, which, in its turn, is based upon certain inborn tendencies and may, therefore, be considered as an instinct. The revenge attitude is primarily provoked by damage caused to one's personal interests; but in primitive society a precise limit between personal and group interests is lacking; revenge attitudes are provoked also by an injury to the interests of group-members and of collective interests. Such attitudes arise not in one, but in many group-members; they interfere with and reinforce each other. By means of this interaction they are somewhat modified, for a total expression of every hostile attitude is inhibited by the existence and, eventually, the realization of parallel attitudes in others.

On the other hand, injury to group interests (i.e., interests considered as relevant by many group-members) is the object of the earliest ethical rules of the prohibitive type. The prohibited situations must therefore have gradually become stimuli in acquired tendencies in which the response was the same as in the system of inborn tendencies of revenge: namely, a hostile attitude.

In the psychic realm the sentiment of injustice corresponds to a "breach of custom." The injured sentiment of justice produces the retributive emotion. How do we know this? First of all, because the sentiments related to the retributive sequence are subjected to the law of adequacy, according to which there must be a certain qualitative proportion between acts and one's subsequent fortunes. If such a proportion does not exist men feel dissatisfaction. For a developed consciousness there would, for example, be no retributive sequence, if a man who had stolen a worthless thing were sentenced to death, or if he succumbed to a painful illness. On the contrary, we should recognize as illustrating a retributive sequence the story of a man who, having neglected his parental duties, suffered in his later years from the lack of love and support of his own children. This we would feel to be a "just" retribution.

Rules defining adequacy may vary and supplant one another, but the general law of adequacy remains. It is a kind of natural law; attempts to avoid it result in socio-pathological phenomena. If, in general, repression does not follow crime, or if punishment is too obviously below the degree indicated by the rule of adequacy (with regard to the socio-ethical evaluations of the epoch), a tendency toward the restoration of the private, individual revenge-reaction arises; this is the root of "lynch justice." If the repression becomes obviously too severe, as compared with that demanded by the socio-ethical evaluations, punishment does not result in reinforcing socio-ethical conviction, but, on the contrary, it produces collective sentiments which rather undermine it; offenders are considered "victims" and governmental agents applying the punishment "tyrants."

For instance, in Russia, where until the middle of the nineteenth century the criminal law remained extremely severe, the common name for convicts was "unfortunates." In the same country the punishment for stealing horses and cattle was considered by the peasants as too mild; this resulted in attempts to inflict "collective revenge" of quite the same type as "lynch justice" in the southern United States. In 1911 a law was enacted in Russia increasing the punishment of these crimes, in order to restore the balance. In England, in the eighteenth century, larceny laws were considered unjust. "The effect of this . . . upon the public sense of Justice was disturbing and harmful" (Hall, *a*, 55–6).[6]

[6] Psychoanalytical considerations of the good style (devoid of any kind of pansexualism) give an additional explanation of the "law of adequacy." In the case of miscarriage of justice (when the punishment is too severe) the individuals feel that the remnants of their personal freedom are endangered. In the case of the escape from justice every member of the community feels that he is wronged by a man who violated the law and escaped punishment. In both cases a struggle for the freedom on one's instinctive drives takes place; desire for "adequate" punishment is a protest against the restriction of these drives (Alexander and Staub, 212).

In a more general and objective manner the law of adequacy may be corroborated by the study of criminal codes from the earliest times down to our own. All such codes are constructed in the form of catalogues of possible crimes and the social reactions against them; the higher the socio-ethical value injured by a crime, the stronger the social reaction. Some modern criminologists deny the universality of this structure; but in so doing they are confusing two viewpoints: that of what really exists in positive law and that of what should exist. When antagonists of the traditional retributive structure of punishment proceed fairly, they must agree that this structure plays at least a very important part in modern criminal law. In modern criminology the idea is widespread that the retributive structure of punishment should be replaced by another, which might be called "the teleological structure." But the very possibility of altogether overcoming the retributive structure of punishment is doubtful, although the concrete rules of adequacy are changeable, and a new teleological retaliation is imaginable, realizing, to a certain extent, the aspirations of reformers. For example, recent events in Italy and Russia have shown that even the boldest reformers dare not break with the tradition based upon retaliation: the Italian Draft Code of 1921, produced by the leaders of the "positive school," was constructed in accordance with the normal pattern of criminal codes, and the revolutionary Russian Draft Code of 1930 was never enacted.

Furthermore, the basic importance of the law of adequacy is corroborated by the fact that its influence is not at all limited to hostile attitudes. Specialists in ethnology, such as Thurnwald and Malinowski, see in the adequate retribution of human acts the root of that part of primitive ethics which later developed into civil law. They stress the principle of give and take and the expectation of an adequate recompense; they assert that if this expectation is not realized, a strong retributive emotion arises, not only on the part of the interested parties, but also in other members of the group.

In modern society the idea of adequate recompense is very well expressed in the differentiation of wages. "Wages," writes Whitehead (16), "are an expression of the social function. . . . The wage differential is one of the numerous mechanisms by which sentiments, accompanying the differentiation of social activities, find their expression."

The retributive structure is clearly expressed in law. It is not improbable that it forms also the backbone of ethics in general. Justice is an element in every higher moral system. Sanctions are present in morals and custom as well (see below, § 8); in more highly developed moral systems these sanctions are always related somehow to the principle of adequacy. Morals and custom very often contain certain elements of reward for "good behavior," and proportion or adequacy is always the principle of retaliation *in bonam partem*.

§ 7. Retributive Tendencies and the Triumph of Ethics

How does this retributive tendency secure the efficacy of ethics? The transgression of recognized ethical rules results in natural hostile attitudes. This sequence may be understood as a cluster of individual tendencies of behavior in which a single act (violation of a rule) forms the stimulus, and the hostile attitude of an indeterminate number of group-members is the response. The hostile attitude may result in a purely individual hostile act; this is revenge, not to be confused with socio-ethical retribution, and often a hindrance to the latter.

The interdependence of the hostile attitudes of group-members often results (especially in the higher levels of social development) in an inhibition of individual responses, because of the expectation of a response on the part of "others" or by the group (in its unorganized or organized form). But the excitation which has not been allowed to run along its natural course creates a state of dissatisfaction, or rather, reinforces the dissatisfaction created by the original violation of the rule. The socially controlled response may then be carried out (1) by unorganized individuals, though designated by ethical rules, generally from among the number of direct "victims" (organized blood revenge is one of the forms of such reaction); or (2) by social organization (punishment and other social "sanctions"). The knowledge of the activity of "others" performing the socially controlled response of both types, and still more the knowledge that the desired end has been completely carried out, produces a state of relaxation or satisfaction among the group-members whose initial hostile attitude has thus been inhibited by the expectation of corporate action. These hostile attitudes have been extinguished as well as if they had resulted in individual hostile acts. We might speak of a further cluster of individual tendencies of behavior, in which the knowledge of the punitive acts of the officials forms the stimulus, and the conduct signifying the recovery of confidence, peace and quiet, the response.

All these tendencies are to a larger degree acquired than inborn, for there is no inborn tendency of retaliation. Yet, like every acquired tendency, they must be finally based on some inborn tendencies of behavior, described in psychology under the terms of self-preservation, anger, fear, et cetera (*cf.* below, chap. VI, § 2). According to the laws of learned behavior, a complete expression of the tendency implies its reinforcement, whereas non-expression means inhibition or even destruction. One of the links in our chain has been a hostile attitude toward the author of the transgression; but the hostile attitude is nothing more than one of the elements of the recognition, which, from the individual point of view, means the same as the ethical group-conviction from the social. Therefore the activation of the complex system of tendencies results in reinforcing the ethical group-conviction. The ethical group-conviction forms here the alpha and omega. We are in the presence of a system of socio-cultural "circular tendencies" analogous to the individual circular reflexes studied in social psychology.

In this way, the retributive disposition plays an important part in social life, in spite of its being a natural phenomenon which does not include any consciously purposive tendency. One feels a drive toward retribution, independently of any advantage or profit for oneself, for one's neighbors or for the community. One may of course utilize it for the advantage of individuals and of society; criminal law is merely a utilitarian adaptation of the acquired retributive disposition; but it would be an inversion of the true relation between the facts if we should say that men are endowed with the retributive disposition because it is useful, because it serves the interests of individuals or of society. There is, perhaps, an instinct of investigation, and it is skillfully used in the course of the educational process; but it would be erroneous to suppose that men were endowed with this instinct in order to help their learning. In both cases this would be a kind of naïve utilitarianism.

This helps us to analyze and take exception to the view that the retributive disposition is "immoral" and therefore could not be considered as the basis for the efficacy of ethical rules.

According to McDougall (188, 252 *ff.*, 313) the highest level of moral conduct is attained when men act out of respect for certain abstract rules; to act because one fears punishment or expects a reward is immoral; and as, in his opinion, Christian ethics are based on the incentive of rewards and punishments (not in this, but in the other world), this system of ethics is to a certain extent immoral.

These statements must be contested. Modern moral philosophy seems to incline towards the idea that the highest type of moral conduct is that incited by pure love, without any regard for preestablished rules. In a society where everybody acted under such an impulse, every kind of ethics would become superfluous. This is also the true interpretation of Christian ethics, which seem to be completely misunderstood by McDougall (*cf.* Allport, *a*, 605).

There is and there has been no society in which this degree of perfection was ever attained. Rules of social conduct are therefore needed, and these rules must be constructed in such a way as to allow them to exert actual influence on human behavior, which may be permanently influenced only by using inborn instincts or by creating suitable habits. The retributive tendency developed from the primitive tendency of revenge, itself based upon inborn instincts, has served successfully in many human societies for the subordination of individual conduct to social patterns (*cf.* Allport, *a*, 392). The utilization of retributive tendencies in this sense (and not of the instinct of revenge) is a social necessity.[7]

§ 8. Social Pressure

The second part of the recognition of ethical rules must be also studied from another standpoint: how is the behavior of other group-members influenced by my recognition, by the tendency to mold the behavior of all group-members in accordance with the ethical rules recognized by any one? The second part of individual recognition insures that every group-member is bound by common ethical rules. Let us suppose that an individual denies that he is bound by the ethical rules of the group. For him the proposition "Everyone is bound by the ethical rules of his group" represents only a distortion of the true proposition "Everybody is supposed to be bound by ethical rules." This is an extreme case, imaginary rather than actual. This individual begins to act "freely," without any regard for the ethical rules. He may be lucky and accomplish one, two or more deeds without being disturbed; but finally his "free" conduct will be discovered, and then he will find out how erroneous was his interpretation of the generally accepted postulate of ethical universality. The social reaction to his misdeed will depend upon the kind of the rule transgressed, upon the stage of social evolution, upon the concrete circumstances. But a social reaction there will be, based upon the retributive disposition of the individuals and on their common recognition of ethical rules. In many cases the idea of being bound by ethical rules, which was previously lacking in his consciousness, will thus be introduced and will influence his subsequent behavior.

In normal cases there is no denial of the validity of ethical rules on the part of group-members; they are inclined to act in accordance with them.[8] This does not prevent "temptations" from sometimes becoming very strong. In such cases the individual

[7] It is therefore erroneous to oppose retributive justice and the protection of society (for instance, Michael and Adler, 344): retributive justice is one of the instruments of social self-defense.

[8] From the behavioristic point of view: the individuals have become receptive to the symbols by means of which behavior is socially controlled.

feels that the rule to be transgressed inhibits his drive to act. "If he resists to this resistance, he will feel a certain tension . . ." (Bergson, 15–16).

We may represent a social group, from the viewpoint of securing the efficacy of ethical rules, as a complex of energy centers sending out waves of a specific quality — suggestive waves tending to secure the triumph of ethical rules. Every group-member represents one such center. The waves are sent in all possible directions; therefore the waves emitted by center *A* are "received" by all other centers — *B*, *C*, *D*, et cetera. But center *A* is in its turn receiving waves from all directions, those emitted by the other centers — *B*, *C*, *D*, et cetera. The social pressure of the kind studied is an extremely obvious case of mutual social interaction: every group-member influences all the others and every group-member is influenced by all the others. The mysterious "social pressure" may be reduced to a phenomenon which everybody can observe within his own consciousness.

As long as the situation is "normal," i.e., as long as no transgression threatens, the social pressure remains latent, potential, concealed; for the behavior of the individuals forming the social group and having to display pressure when needed remains determined by the retributive disposition only, and not by actualized retributive emotion. The waves sent out by them are dispersed in social space; there is no occasion for them to be concentrated at certain points.

The situation changes when a transgression is imminent. The retributive dispositions of the individuals are actualized, becoming retributive emotions, and brain processes corresponding to these emotions compel the individuals to act in such a way as to prevent the transgression. To be sure, only a small part of the group-members may be aware of the danger; only within *their* consciousnesses does such an actualization of latent possibilities, such a transformation of dispositions into emotions, take place. But their speech reactions to the danger, and still more their actions, have displayed their psychic state; knowledge of the threatened transgression spreads to a larger number of group-members, and with every step the process of transforming the retributive disposition into retributive emotion becomes quantitatively larger. The ideal limit of the process coincides with the limits of the social group; but in the majority of cases it does not extend thus far. In some cases the social pressure of a number of group-members may have already become sufficient to prevent the transgression; in other cases it may not have been strong enough, and the transgression has actually taken place. As social groups may be very large — a State and even "civilized humanity" are social groups, though, of course, of very different degrees of cohesion — the number of energy centers sending suggestive waves may become immense. Imagine the case when a *coup d'état* threatens a democratic country — actual retributive emotions may become dominant in the consciousness of the majority of citizens.

If retributive emotions are actualized by the threat of a transgression of ethical rules, the corresponding waves are no longer "dispersed" in space; they are concentrated on the right spot. The emission of waves, which, in normal cases, occurs in all possible directions, becomes focused toward the threatening transgression. The individual representing the threat becomes the object of unusually strong pressure, and this may prevent him from actualizing his antisocial intention. But if transgressions are imminent at the same time, at many points in the social field, the pressure emitted by energy centers sending out "suggestive waves" has to be divided into many parts and may become insufficient; the intended transgressions then become actual — as also in cases when the antisocial purpose remains hidden until the moment of its execution.

An actual transgression is the third case we have to consider. The retributive emotion is, of course, evoked not only by threatening transgressions but also by those actually achieved, and in the latter case the emotion is generally stronger. This is an application of the general psychological law, according to which a representation of an actual situation or of changes in the environment occasions a stronger affective tone than representations of merely possible situations or changes. If a transgression has taken place, the retributive emotions of the individuals become stronger than they were when the transgression was merely threatening; these emotions spread with more force and intensity, and the "suggestive waves" are concentrated with more vigor on the ethically weak point. An intense social trend arises, striving to restore the "proper" situation.

Social sanctions form the expression of this restorative trend. The forms of sanctions are many and varied. Insofar as social response has been organized, a scale of punishments is at the disposal of the social agents. To the gamut of official punishments corresponds a gamut of unorganized sanctions. They may be classified as social ostracism, face-to-face ridicule, destruction of property and the infliction of bodily pain up to death.

First of all, we may take an example of social ostracism from primitive society. Among the Caribs the breaker of a custom and his family become social outcasts: they are not invited to drinking parties, the head of the household will get no help in hunting, et cetera (Thomas, 518). In modern society, according to Pareto, "an individual who is barred from a group finds that his integrity has been altered . . . and the alteration may be felt so keenly as to serve as a very heavy penalty indeed (801)." Breaking the rules of a club is sanctioned by the loss of membership or of esteem. The workman who transgresses the regulations of the factory may lose his job. The believer may be excommunicated; the doctor or lawyer may lose his right to practice (MacIver, *b*, 250; Merriam, 11).

Face-to-face ridicule often appears in primitive as well as in civilized society. In Groenland the sanction of *Katzenmusik*, or of singing satirical songs in front of the house of the offender, is used. In old Russia the gates of a house were smeared with tar in order to punish a girl who had transgressed the rules of decency. A Negro tribe uses general spitting as a sanction against the transgressor of a customary rule. In modern society "the regular organs of the public — the pulpit, the press, the caricature, the topical song, the poster, the lampoon, the resolutions of societies and public bodies — help give vent to its indignation" (Ross, 91).

As regards direct bodily attacks, to the blood revenge custom of olden times there corresponds in modern society "occasional resort to egging, whipping, branding, riding on a rail, running out of the town, tarring and feathering, or lynching" (Ross, 92).

The very meaning of an ethical rule is the molding of behavior in accordance with it. Therefore the idea of reinforcing the rule with a sanction, with a proviso indicating how to proceed when the rule has been transgressed, belongs to the very nature of ethical rules. Therefore ethical rules form sequences in which further links become actual in case the preceding ones prove too weak. It is by virtue of this structure that the triumph of ethics may be secured.

Ethical rules are like chameleons, being in general invisible and inaudible until they have been transgressed. The rule "do not lie" is but a whisper in our conscience. But if somebody is convicted of having lied publicly, he may become an object of repulsion on the part of his fellowmen, and this repulsion will be expressed in sanctions.

As in the case of mere threatened transgression there may be exceptions. Sometimes a transgressor succeeds in avoiding the normal social reaction, if he is so shrewd that his guilt or even his deed remains unknown. If the misdeed is discovered, but men are unable to discover its author or to hold him in custody in order to concentrate the social pressure upon him, a certain uneasiness, a collective dissatisfaction is felt; every excitation without its corresponding relaxation produces this effect. If such cases become numerous, the social order is weakening; and statements to this effect by many group-members result in its further weakening: the personal vector ("first part") of the recognition of ethical rules tends to disappear if experience shows that the social vector ("second part") remains ineffective. This is one of the symptoms of a threatening ethical revolution (see below, chap. VI)

The notion of social pressure is commonly used when speaking of the efficacy of ethical rules, but in general this phenomenon remains unanalyzed. The pressure is ascribed to "society," but it remains mysterious how society can exercise pressure upon its members. Our previous study enables us to give the necessary explanation. The social pressure supporting ethical rules is nothing other than the sum of the individual recognitions of these rules, or, more exactly, of their social vectors. "All the time group members are occupied in forging chains which they have to wear themselves" (Vierkandt, 407). The specific social pressure, which we call socio-ethical pressure, is the mechanism of socio-ethical equilibrium for which we were searching. It results in the "triumph of ethics," one of the major manifestations of social order.[9]

BIBLIOGRAPHICAL NOTE

The basic importance of recognition, as regards the efficacy of legal rules (not of ethical rules in general) has been discovered by Bierling (I, 40–8). The weak point of his work is the lack of understanding of the mutual interdependence of individual recognitions. This mistake has been corrected by Kistiakovsky (357–68) and Gurvitch (*e*, 73–5). Both parts of the recognition and their correlation are studied by Allport (*a*).

The concrete character of direct recognition in the earlier stages of social development was one of the most important objects studied by the historical school in jurisprudence. The theory of the logical character of indirect recognition is developed by Bierling (I, 46). The gamut of affective tones united with recognition is described by Tönnies (*d*, 200).

The idea of causal relationship between a rule and the behavior determined by it was expressed for the first time by Schützenberger (40). In more recent times the theory was once more accepted by Zitelman (210–25), but in later works the author admitted he was wrong.

The best studies of the rôle of ethical rules in individual consciousness are those of McDougall (229, 237), Allport (*a*, 310–18, 337, 375), MacIver (*b*, 249–50).

The almost definite formation of habit systems in childhood and youth has been studied by Healy (*a*, 215–16), Glueck (*c*, 229–30) and Healy-Bronner (184–215).

The question of retribution in its relation to the reinforcement of ethical rules has been extensively studied in modern German science. (*Cf.* R. Schmidt, Günther, Beling, Nagler, Baumgarten, Drost, Mezger and Hoche.) The modern pedagogical doctrine admits the retributive element in familistic and school punishment; *cf.* Förster and Hessen.

[9] This is, of course, a "formal" concept of socio-ethical equilibrium. It is entirely different from every attempt to create a material concept of "moral equilibrium." *Cf.* Duprat (469), for whom moral equilibrium of a larger group is merely a contrast to disturbances resulting from the opposition of habits, customs, traditions and desires of various minor groups.

In American literature this factor is generally misunderstood and reduced to a mere remnant of the revenge attitude; *cf.*, for instance, MacIver (*b*, 40). The statements on this subject of Lisle, Mead, Margolin and Stearns are of value; *cf.* Bradley, Michael and Adler, Glueck (*a*), Ewing, Stoop (188–9), Timasheff (*h*). A concrete study of retributive attitudes, based upon a set of tests, is contained in the papers of Sharp and Otto. Concerning the notion of circular reflexes (or circuitous reactions) Allport (*a*, 39) and Luriia (419).

As regards failures in attempts of a radical reform of criminal law in Russia, *cf.* Timasheff (*d*, *h*).

The importance of the reciprocity principle in primitive society is stressed by Thurnwald (*a*, *b*, *c*), Malinowski (*a*, 22–3, 37, 39–50, 68) and Ehrlich (*a*, 105–6).

The close connection between ethical rules and punishment (sanctions in general) is recognized by Durkheim (*b*, 184), Pareto (II, 792), Stephen (II, 79–81), LaPiere (122), and MacIver (*b*, 249). For sanctions in primitive society, *cf.* Thomas (518–28).

Excellent statements on social pressure are given by Tönnies (*a*, 14), Ehrlich (*a*, 77–8), Allport (*a*, 375, 395), and Robson (307).

CHAPTER VI

CHANGES IN ETHICS

§ 1. Introduction

In the previous chapter society was described as a system in socio-ethical equilibrium, within which small disturbances are always overcome by means of socio-ethical pressure. This was, of course, only an abstract way of treating the problem, for society is much more complex.

Socio-ethical equilibrium did not arise simultaneously with society: it is the result of a gradual cultural development and is constantly subjected to further change. The changes within the system of equilibrium are of three kinds: (1) the system of equilibrium develops in its totality; (2) the objective elements of the system (the rules by means of which group-members are held in a state of coördination) change; and (3) the subjective elements of the system (the individuals bound by the rules) change their attitudes toward the rules. These elements will now be studied one by one.

§ 2. From Revenge to Retribution

The socio-ethical equilibrium secured by means of socio-ethical pressure is a creation of culture. In other words, there was a time when this equilibrium did not exist. This does not mean that ethics as such were also absent: a common conviction of the group-members concerning practical behavior in society, developed by means of mutual "induction," must have preceded the creation of the system of equilibrium; [1] but the social mechanism to stabi-

[1] Vinogradoff says: "Neither succession, nor property, nor possession, nor contract started . . . from direct conflict. Succession has its roots in the necessary arrangement of the household on the death of its manager, property began with occupation, the origins of contract go back to the customs of barter" (*b*, I, 368). Whether ethical coördination of behavior is as old as society is sometimes doubted. According to Mannheim (72) "morality and ethics are conditioned by certain definite situations. Concepts of duty, transgression, etc., have not always existed, but have made their appearance in correlation to distinct social situations."

lize it was lacking, and the predictability of "normal behavior" (chap. I, § 2) was therefore very small indeed.

Social equilibrium was built on the basis of revenge. Social interaction based upon revenge is very different from that based upon retributive tendencies (dispositions). When revenge attitudes were dominant, true notions of causal relationships were still imperfectly developed and the idea of personal responsibility had not yet been born. Finally there was no idea of proportion between the damage caused by the transgression and the wrong to be inflicted on its author.

Revenge is a purely instinctive reaction of men against damages caused by other beings, living or imagined (gods or the shades of the dead). There is no regularity in revenge, there is no definite order to be followed in the execution of the acts demanded. In its most primitive form it may not even be directed against the author of the injury. This is the case in the well-known "running amok" of the Malay. "The man who has suffered injury or insult does not deliberately plan out and execute his vengeance on those who have injured him. He broods for a time . . . and then suddenly takes his 'kris' and runs through the village, cutting down every living being he encounters, until he himself is slain" (McDougall, 141–2). Obviously this is a case when the radiation of the excitation studied by Pavlov is exceptionally strong and long lasting.

Later on, this instinctive reaction of revenge changed its character. Our knowledge refers only to the history of law and not to that of ethics in general, but in these early stages of human evolution the division of ethics into its subclasses was not yet clear; it would not be too bold to express the opinion that the differentiation of ethics took place parallel with the transformation of the primitive instinct of revenge into the more complex retributive tendency (disposition).

The principal steps were the following: The individual instinct of revenge produced the social habit of blood feud. On the basis of this habit, a corresponding custom arose (see below, § 4): a man who had been offended, personally or indirectly through injury to his relatives (in the larger sense of the word), *had* to perform the "retributive sequence," i.e., to kill or to wound the offender or his relatives, to set fire to their property or otherwise destroy it. An act of "blood-vengeance" tended to produce retroactive feelings and attitudes within the family of the victim and thus generally gave rise to a perpetuation of the struggle (blood feud).

The custom of blood vengeance resulted in decreasing the number of men belonging to the group and therefore in decreasing its fighting force in the struggle among groups. Some groups began to organize blood vengeance and to reduce the evil deed and the reaction toward it. This was a decisive step: individual revenge became a social action performed, in the beginning, by the offended individual himself, and later by representatives of the social group. The mechanism of social retribution was thus definitely created. Tribes where such changes had taken place became victorious in the struggle against others, because they were more populous than the latter. The idea of replacing individual vengeance by social retribution was a discovery of many separate tribes. For some time it was only a minority idea; later it became a majority idea, and still later a common idea — the idea of all nations whose activities and convictions form the basis of modern culture.

The transformation of the primitive revenge pattern into that of socio-ethical pressure was gradual. In the beginning, there was the notion of material retaliation expressed in the Old Testament formula: an eye for an eye, a tooth for a tooth. The codes strove to balance every wrong by causing equal wrong to the evil-doer.

Later on, the idea of material retaliation was replaced by that of ideal retaliation, of an ideal proportionality between the deed and the recompense or punishment. Furthermore there gradually arose the idea of individual responsibility for one's fault. It appeared in the moral philosophy of ancient Greece and in Roman law, and after having been once again forgotten during the barbarous centuries of the early Middle Ages, it reappeared and gradually triumphed in modern times.

But its triumph is not yet assured. Even now the old sentiments of revenge are still alive. When the retributive emotion is very strong, behavior shows that the old instinct of revenge is not yet dead. It is well known that people acting in crowds fall in their actions to a lower level of cultural development. One of the clearest evidences of this "low" social level is the substitution for the culturally acquired mechanism of social retribution of its predecessor, the primitive instinct of revenge. Terrible scenes can be described of people acting under the influence of this instinct in, say, the early years of the Russian Revolution or during the recent events in Spain. Suddenly liberated from all the restrictions imposed by modern ethics, people killed, wounded and robbed actual or imaginary enemies without any regard for the rule of proportion between the individual deed and the collective response, or for the principle of personal responsibility.

On the other hand, the custom of "vendetta" was practiced up to the most recent times in Corsica and Italy and exists even today in Albania. Earlier cases of lynching were obviously a revival of primitive revenge tendencies caused by unsatisfactory social repression; in our day cases of lynching seem to arise from other causes.[2]

§ 3. The Evidence of Child Psychology

The structure and the evolution of socio-ethical pressure is so very important that we should use every means to elucidate the question. The evidence of child psychology tempts one to apply the general law of evolution, stating that ontogeny (development of the individual organism) recapitulates philogeny (development of the species) in this connection. The species *homo sapiens* outgrew the primary instinct of revenge and acquired the complex retributive tendency; therefore a recapitulation of the same development should be expected in the life-history of every representative of the species. To be sure, it would be too dangerous to apply this parallel literally. The child's consciousness is, to a great extent, a mirror of the adult's. If we find a definite trend in

[2] There exists, among the white population of the Southern States, a sentiment of superiority as regards Negroes. This sentiment is not and, of course, cannot be expressed in law. Therefore the legal reaction against the crimes of Negroes does not form a true equivalent of the hostile attitudes created by these crimes. The surplus of hostile attitudes results in direct attacks, as also commonly happened in primitive society, prior to the creation of the socialized and organized reaction.

the psychic development of the child with regard to retribution, it will merely show which are the simpler and which the more complex elements in the adult's psychic structure, insofar as they are reflected by children; but this would also be helpful for our purpose.

Very interesting assertions have been made by the Swiss scholar Piaget, according to whom there are two definite stages in the development of a child's judgment concerning responsibility. Up to the age of eight the child's state of mind is that of "ethical realism": it is the extent of the damage which furnishes the basis for the judgment; the idea of personal fault is completely lacking. Then an ethical revolution takes place and the child begins to take into consideration both the intention of the offender and the relation of the act to social needs.

Piaget's statements are based upon a certain number of experiments in the form of questionnaires and tests. Unfortunately, the tests were of such a kind as to render the answers given not entirely free from the possibility of prior prejudice. A new series of experiments has been carried out in Brussels by Caruso, who applied some of the methods of American character studies. Three hundred and forty school children, six to fifteen years old, were given very simple questions to answer. The results were somewhat different from those of Piaget. No ethical "revolution" was observed by Caruso, but rather a gradual change of mind. Before the age of eight "ethical realism" prevails (95.5 per cent of the cases); but only after the age of thirteen could more than half of the children be said to have "ethical idealism." The idea of immanent retribution was present in 67.4 per cent of the answers of children under eight and in only 9.3 per cent of children of thirteen years and older.

The results of the experiments of Piaget and Caruso corroborate the idea that socio-ethical pressure is a complex, evolved structure, bearing even now many remnants of earlier forms. Further changes will undoubtedly occur, but very gradually and slowly. The substitution of a purely teleological treatment of offenders for traditional convictions deeply rooted in the retributive disposition would be a revolution of the same caliber as that which replaced revenge by social retribution. This early revolution lasted thousands, if not tens of thousands of years.

§ 4. The Selection of Best Ways

The socio-ethical equilibrium is continuous. This does not prevent the concrete ethical rules in which the interdependence of group-members is expressed from constantly changing. New patterns of behavior may be imposed: (a) in the form of concrete examples to be followed or (b) in the form of "ideal structures," i.e., of abstract descriptions of behavior to which individuals should adjust their conduct (chap. I, § 2). This is a distinction correlated with the two forms of "direct recognition" (chap. V, § 3). Let us call these "concrete" and "abstract" imposition. Within the concrete imposition of patterns two main forms might be distinguished: that of "selection of the best way" and that of "radiation and concentration."

Within the process of selection two steps must be distinguished: the creation of a collective habit and its transformation into custom, the earliest form of ethics.

A collective habit is a system of tendencies acquired simultaneously by a certain number of group-members. Collective habits are social regularities of either of the first two classes (chap. I, § 2): similar conditions induce men to act in the same way; or an imitation of the same pattern of behavior may produce the same result.

In general, not one but many modes of action were objectively possible; only one of them was chosen. In general, not one but many behavior patterns could have been imitated; only one of them was. How and why was this one way selected?

The historical school of jurisprudence answered the question in a somewhat mystical way. It declared that law (the doctrine of the school could be reinterpreted with regard to ethics in general) was a product of the national spirit (*Volksgeist*). Every nation possesses its specific spirit, living in the souls of its members. This spirit points out to them the line of conduct they should adopt in doubtful cases, and as the spirit is one and the same in all members, their conduct is always similar in similar cases. This spirit is submitted to an organic development, and this development is manifested in a parallel and simultaneous change of the line of the conduct of group-members.

This explanation is not acceptable for later generations of scientists: the "national spirit" is a fiction and a reference to it explains nothing. The doctrine tried to find another explanation and seemed to have found it in the idea of social utility: out of many possible ways that one prevails which is the most profitable to the social group. It is repeated, and repetition produces a habit in the individual and a custom in the group. Later on it becomes an innate trait by transmission and reinforcement from generation to generation.[3]

This theory is not altogether satisfactory either. The old national mysticism is simply replaced by the assumption that society possesses the power to discover the ways of individual conduct which would be in conformity with the interests of the social group. Secondly, the theory was created when biologists still believed, with Darwin, Lamarck and Spencer, in the inheritance of acquired characters; that such inheritance is possible we can no longer assume. Thirdly, the utilitarian theory does not explain the existence of harmful customs, the existence of which induces Sorokin (*e*, 699, note 70) to say that selection is not always to the good or that sometimes there is no selection at all.

The theory of selection must be restated in order to free it from these unsatisfactory elements. In order to do this, we must distinguish between two stages: (a) the formation of habit systems in empty "social fields" [4] and (b) their further development.

(a) A social field is ethically empty if there is no preëstablished regulation for a life-situation demanding the social coördination

[3] As an instance, the ideas of Vaccaro should be mentioned. Within a certain group a nucleus is created by men who react in a solidary way against aggressions. Every single individual is weaker than this nucleus. Repeated experience of this superior force creates a rule of conduct. After the rule has been in force a certain length of time, the idea of the illegitimacy of contrary conduct arises (447). Modern representatives of utilitarianism (for instance, Le Henaff) try to prove that the way chosen was the only one possible.

[4] By the term "social field" indeterminate masses of individuals will be understood, insofar as these masses form the objects of potential or actual display of social forces.

of behavior. Such situations may be studied (1) in primitive society, where in some cases they may be found in a rather "pure" form and in others are absent,[5] and (2) in modern society — in those rather exceptional situations when no social regulation exists, but where it is objectively needed. Experimental study is also possible.[6]

In empty social fields individual responses to situations are necessarily at random.[7] Yet experiments show that, if the same individual is to face the same situation more than once, an average, almost constant response [8] is created.

Individual responses do not yet form any basis for ethical rules. But in addition to this, further experiments show that men, being within ethically empty fields, coming into contact with each other and having to face the same situation, form responses with a convergent tendency (Sherif, 105).

This is a primary, irreducible phenomenon. Its importance is very high, for it explains the necessary correlation between living in groups and being submitted to common rules. The relationship is obvious, but an explanation is generally lacking. For Gurvitch, the community forms the "normative fact"; in other words, the community is intuitively recognized by group-members as the basis of (legal) value, from which all legal norms are derived (*c*, 113). Parsons (*a*, 295) sees in the existence of common systems of ultimate values a factor of social stability, whereas a random variation would make social life impossible. This seems to presuppose something like social Darwinism.

Convergent responses become collective habits; in other words, they are standardized and fixed (Sherif, 126, 137).

(b) When a system of habits is already in existence in a social

[5] There is then a possibility of comparing the cases of presence and absence, such comparisons in sociology to a certain extent taking the place of experiment in the natural sciences.

[6] *Cf.* the very interesting experiments of Sherif (104 *ff.*).

[7] The selection is "at random" from the social viewpoint; nothing in the structure of social fields can, at these early stages, predetermine the response; but, for every individual, the response is determined by his character structure.

[8] Sherif (104) already here speaks of "norms," whereas this term should be reserved for the following step, corresponding to the transformation of habits into customs; the lack of insight concerning this further process is the main defect in Sherif's brilliant contribution to the subject.

field, it is transmitted by means of cultural inheritance to later generations (see below, § 8), but not without changes: "A human society cannot perpetuate its behavior patterns completely unchanged as animal reactions are perpetuated, because the human habits are not based on unlearned organic reactions, but are learned and must be communicated from generation to generation, and an inevitable and undesigned direction of change is introduced by the inability of individuals to reproduce precisely the prevailing stereotypes" (Thomas, 612; *cf.* Sumner, 86).

The analogy of language is very useful in order to explain the development of habits. "Language is a living organism even to-day. . . . In remote ages language developed freely like trees in a virgin forest. . . . There is no reason for believing that the situation is, or has been, different with other similar products of human activity" (Pareto, 283–4).

The developmental process, both in language and in habit-systems, is generally as follows: Individuals make slight changes in the pronunciation of words, in their meaning, et cetera, or in their responses to life situations for which habitual responses already exist. These "suggest" new ways. The majority of suggestions are rejected; in other words, people continue to behave in the accustomed way, but some of the suggestions are "accepted" and become patterns of human conduct.[9]

How does this selection take place? Here, a certain qualification in Pareto's statements is necessary. The development of a language is never completely free; new elements are introduced and changes effected according to the principle of compatibility; not every proposed change is commonly accepted, but only that one which is more compatible than the others with the total system. The same is, of course, true as regards habits; out of the possible additions and modifications those are chosen which are *emotionally* more compatible with the existing system.[10] The

[9] Cruet says (73): "The neologisms in law, just as those in language, are not accepted at once; the period of agreement is preceded by a period of fluctuations."

[10] The principle of emotional compatibility is clearly expressed when, fortuitously, social fields are created which are "empty" from the standpoint of ethical coördination, while the men composing them are imbued with ethical convictions formed under other conditions. Such was, for instance, the situation in California in 1848 and in certain goldfields in Eastern Siberia (studied by Ross, 42–9 and 58–9). In

development of habits by means of selection is not logical at all.

Selection is therefore more subjective than objective; the ways chosen are not necessarily those suited in an objective way to social needs, but rather those which are more in harmony with the emotional attitudes of the group-members, both leaders and followers — for the followers would imitate the leaders only if the new ways were felt by them also to be emotionally compatible with the established system of behavior.[11]

Such are the ways of creating collective habits. How are these habits transformed into customs, sanctioned with the formula "ought to be" and thus related to the highest values of morality and law?

There is an irreducible phenomenon called by Jellinek "the normative tendency of the actual" (*Normative Kraft des Faktischen*, *d*, 307–14). Every time a certain situation or practice seems to have become permanently established, the idea arises that it is just as it "ought to be." It is well known that logically there is no transition possible from *is* to *ought*. Yet men are not entirely — perhaps not essentially — rational beings, and the logically impossible transition is daily effected with great facility.[12]

It would be very important to give an accurate description of the life-situations which favor the "normative tendency of the actual." Many attempts have been made in science to discover such situations, frequently without any reference to the special problem we are just studying. Duguit (*b*, *c*) sees the basic situation in solidarity, i.e., in the interdependence of group-members, and asserts that the *fact* of solidarity creates the *duty* to act in accordance with the demands of solidarity.[13] For Ehrlich there

both cases men created new habit-systems based upon "imported" convictions, i.e., upon the emotional relationship of the men to the rules.

[11] There is no reason to accept the statement of Allen (50) that "customs establish themselves because they fit to the economic convenience of the most powerful cast." Thurnwald (*b*, 4) stresses the acceptance of new ways by leading personalities.

[12] Morgenthau (92) speaks of an "original and inborn" tendency of human mind to deduce, from the stability of a situation, its necessity or even "oughtness."

[13] Pareto frequently derides the *idea* of solidarity, insofar as scientists and philosophers use it, to explain human behavior in society. But the *fact* of solidarity plays an outstanding part in his system.

are facts with which the human mind associates rules, assigning to each individual his position and his functions. These are reducible to usage, domination, possession, declaration of will (*a*, 85).[14]

Gurvitch (*g*) expresses the idea that social interaction is able to produce law if the group is an "active" one; in other words, if men have a common work to accomplish. Modern ethnologists (Malinowski *a*, *b;* Thurnwald *a*, *b*, *c*) stress the importance of the situation termed "reciprocity."

A systematic and consistent classification of basic situations does not yet exist. As a first approximation, the idea could be expressed that the situation demanding the distribution of goods or services, the situation demanding coöperation and the face-to-face situation of people with different degrees of dominance feeling (*cf.* chap. VIII) are basic. The combination of the situations of distribution and coöperation gives rise to the more complex situation designated by the term reciprocity. Furthermore, some relations of men to things (primarily to land) produce a situation called possession or occupation; this occupation may be collective and then be nearer to coöperation, or individual — nearer to distribution. Every primary situation, when threatened by any kind of disturbance on the part of human beings, engenders a new situation — that of conflict.

Why do such situations play a part in the formation of ethical group-conviction? Because in these and similar situations, relations of men to men or to things are emotionally colored; for instance, the occupation of a certain piece of land or the reciprocity situation is not only coldly perceived by men, but also creates emotional currents in them. This is, of course, the essence of Pareto's remarks (173 *ff.*) concerning the views of Fustel de Coulanges and of Sir Henry Maine (*a*). Pareto says that the fact of occupation is in all probability antecedent to any abstract concept, legal or religious, concerning the occupation. Developing his ideas in his own manner, one could say that there are cer-

[14] Ehrlich's catalogue is faulty at many points: for instance, usage is not so much a situation as it is the result of situations; usage or habit, as has already been shown, is the first step toward the creation of ethical rules regulating some situations.

tain psychic states ("residues") which are expressed (1) in a definite behavior signifying occupation and (2) in religious, legal (or generally ethical) "theories."

Examples used by Pareto belong to the type of primitive behavior. But the "normative tendency of the actual" is not at all limited to it. The following instances may be observed in advanced societies.

After a successful revolution, the new situation is at first considered as merely "actual," or as it is sometimes expressed, *de facto;* there is not yet any group conviction (with the exception of the group formed by the revolutionary leaders) that it ought to be so. On the contrary, there are in the society many attitudes continuing the older currents destroyed by the revolution: it is no longer thus and so, but it ought to be just as it was. Gradually these *ci-devant* currents decline in force and the experience that the older ethical rules are no longer obligatory for some group-members destroys the conviction that they still are obligatory for any. Gradually an opposite current begins to develop; repeated actions, corresponding with the new, *de facto* order, begin to acquire an ethical tinge; the idea arises, today in one, tomorrow in another group-member, that perhaps things are "best" as they are. By mutual induction this idea is reinforced, and after some time the general attitude of group-members towards the new situation becomes just the same as it was before the revolution with regard to the old order: the new order has been accepted and "sanctified" by ethical group-conviction. It is not only "actual," it is "right."

A second case is that of despotical rule, where the relation between ruler and subject is based not upon ethical rules but on naked display of power (see below, chap. IX, § 6). But since this is rather an "unnatural" situation on the part of the rulers, as well as on the part of the subjects, the tendency arises to sanctify the general orders of power, to transform them from naked commands into ethical rules supported by group-conviction. "Men cannot be happy in the acceptance of limitations simply imposed by force; they must recognize them to be just; the discipline must carry moral authority" (Parsons, *b*, 336).

Therefore, being sometimes unable to change the rules imposed on them by force, they endow such rules with the superior authority of ethics.

The third case is that of an "ethical vacuum" (already mentioned). First of all, a certain collective habit is formed, generally by the trial-and-error method. Very soon the conviction arises that acting in accordance with this habit is obligatory; habit is transformed into custom. Such was, for instance, the history of the creation of rules concerning checks and *conto-currenti*, as well as those concerning "three days of grace on bills of exchange." [15]

These few cases, all easily observable, display a general tendency, which constitutes the mechanism by which habits are transformed into customs, thus introducing changes into the complex of socio-ethical conviction. A rather definite line differentiates a habit from a custom. Insofar as an individual has no fear of a hostile reaction in case of a transgression, or if he fears the hostile reactions of only a few, then habit has not yet been transformed into custom; only when group-members begin to consider this hostile reaction to be "just," only when they begin to feel that they themselves, in the others' places, would take the same attitude, does the habit become the object of group-conviction, and an ethical rule arises which is recognized by group-members for themselves and for others.

Not every habit is transformed into a custom. In many cases there are inhibitions of different types which hinder the process of "normalizing the actual." The essential factor giving rise to the inhibition is that many diverse social groups coexist within every social field. New habits may arise which might be compatible with certain group-convictions existing within the field, but incompatible with others; the compatibility allows the formation of habit systems, but the incompatibility hinders their elevation to the level of custom. In certain cases a kind of competition between groups arises, and its very existence constitutes an intense inhibition of the process of normalizing the actual.

From the sociological viewpoint there is nothing mysterious in this normative tendency of the actual; but for social philos-

[15] *Cf.* Gray (282). Other examples in Robson (300 *ff.*).

ophers, insofar as they are inclined to separate completely the world of actuality from the world of values, the problem is much more difficult, for through the normative tendency a fact becomes a value, or, more exactly, the embodiment of a value. In general facts *are* evaluated (by history, public opinion, et cetera) and values *are* actualized (in scientific discoveries, heroic acts, creations of art). The human mind is, of course, the point where the physical, the psychic and the ideal worlds (values belong to the last of these) meet.

§ 5. The Radiation

The second way of creating ethical rules is radiation, i.e., the tendency for ethical rules to spread out into larger behavior complexes than those they primarily referred to. The mechanism of radiation is obviously dependent on individual attitudes.

From the introspective viewpoint, the tendency of radiation is a case of applying the laws of the association of ideas. Every ethical rule is a general proposition forming an object of conviction. Very often a convinced individual is not only inclined toward proselytism (toward winning new disciples), but also toward enlarging the behavior field to which the ethical rule originally had reference.

A very good instance is that of rules concerning incest. The primary rule referred only to kin in the biological sense of the word. Later on, habits of speech and attitudes, which were used with regard to relatives, were applied to persons who were not relatives in the direct sense: to the relatives of the marriage partner, to people called "spiritual relatives," et cetera. This resulted in an expansion of the ethical rule prohibiting incest. Many centuries later the circle of relatives was restored to its natural limits; in a parallel way a "concentration" of the ethical rule thus took place, abolishing the earlier expansion.

Another example (Jerusalem, 264): the rules for determining sovereignty in international relations have derived by means of extension from those determining the relations between "cavaliers" at the court of Versailles. Furthermore, in France, under Napoleon, the rules directed against the Protestants, after the revocation of the Edict of Nantes, were applied to political *emigrés*.

In the domain of law the term *fiction* is applied to the phenomenon of a rule being applied to situations for which it was not primarily intended. One of the most interesting examples is that of the development of the "benefit of clergy" in England (*cf.* bibl. note).

Development by means of extension of meaning can completely transform the objective aims (the social function) of whole sets of ethical rules. For such cases the term of "heterogeneity of aims" created by Wundt (*b*, 279), should be applied.

§ 6. Harmful Customs

Now the problem of harmful customs may be attacked. It is well known that such customs are not very rare. Blood revenge, which has been mentioned above; killing one's aged parents; dueling, which did so much harm in upper European society in the fifteenth to seventeenth centuries; drinking habits at festivals, those remnants of ancient ceremonies; taboos concerning food (Bushmen do not eat goat flesh in spite of the fact that goats are the most frequent game in their territory); taboos against the killing of harmful animals (crocodiles, snakes, et cetera); child marriages — such are familiar examples found throughout the world.

The instance of human sacrifices among the Carthaginians and the Aztecs is the most unambiguous case. This custom was harmful not only for the neighboring tribes, whose members were immolated, but also for the sacrificing tribes, whose antisocial instincts were favored and negative biological selection introduced.

The existence of harmful customs is incompatible with the theory of the objective selection of socially useful ways as the unique mode of the concrete creation of ethical rules. Modifications, introduced above, especially the recognition of radiation as a second way of creating ethical rules, parallel to selection, seem to overcome some of the difficulties.

In the second place, customs which seem harmful in later times perhaps seemed useful at the time of their adoption — useful from the viewpoint of special groups which imposed them. Harmful drinking habits have degenerated from religious festivals at which they increased the strength of one of the social forces, that of religion. Dueling has degenerated from the tournaments of knights which, of course, reinforced the military efficiency of the upper classes of medieval society.

Last but not least, groups with harmful customs of secondary origin have been defeated and destroyed in the course of history. Where are the Carthaginians or the Aztecs? And have not groups among which drinking to excess was a social custom also been destroyed?

Therefore we may end the analysis of harmful customs on an optimistic note. Not only the earlier, but also the later stages of evolution seem to give the victory to those social groups whose members succeeded before others in creating and making obligatory ethical rules compatible with the true interests of the community, or, in other words, with the general welfare.

§ 7. Abstract Changes in Ethical Rules

Abstract change in the content of ethical rules is first of all effected by legislation, a process studied in jurisprudence (see chap. XII, § 7). But ascribing the abstract way of changing the content of ethical rules to law is merely one of the numerous examples of the logically inadequate theories so frequent in social science, especially in the domain of legal and ethical studies. These abstract changes may occur not only in legal rules but in ethical rules in general.

When the Gospel or the Koran were preached, there were tremendous changes in the content of recognized ethical *rules* of nonlegal types. When a "social leader" introduces new rules of behavior and "imposes" the new patterns on other group members, "abstract" changes in recognized ethical rules take place. When people join together in order to form a private society (of a type not recognized and not protected by law) they create new *rules* of behavior.

Changes in abstract rules may be not only creative but also destructive; they may result in abolishing the efficacy of rules belonging to the ethical tradition. This is well known with regard to legislation: how many laws, especially in revolutionary times, tend merely to abolish previously imposed patterns of behavior without setting up new ones.

It is less obvious that conscious destruction is possible also within the nonlegal parts of ethics. The following example is very instructive. In 1866 and 1879 the Ossets (a tribe in the Caucasus), at a general tribal meeting convoked by the Russian Government, repealed a number of customs recognized as harmful. These were: (1) paying high bride-prices (sums so large that their payment sometimes resulted in the complete ruin of the family, and which were impossible without selling a part of the landed estate or of the livestock); (2) compelling the widows to marry one of the brothers of the deceased husband; (3) allowing child marriage and (4) arranging obligatory festivals in honor of the deceased (such festivals took place eight to ten times a year and the expenses were often terribly high) (Kovalevsky, I, 241–8, 268).

§ 8. Changes in the Ethical Behavior

Changes in the objective elements of the socio-ethical equilibrium commonly produce changes in the behavior of the individuals who form the subjective elements of the system. But changes in individual behavior with regard to ethical rules which remain in force may take place independently of the changes in the objective framework.

According to contemporary doctrines, learning and appropriating the ethical rules in force in a certain social field are the first changes in the ethical attitude of an individual. "The child is at first amoral and only begins to exhibit a moral behavior to the extent that prohibitions and commands from the elders work upon him" (Mira, 861).

"The child learns to accept many current maxims through suggestion; his parents and teachers repeatedly assert various moral propositions: it is wrong to tell a lie, to steal, to deceive, to be cruel; it is right to be honest, kind or generous. The child accepts these and many other propositions and will apply them to the conduct of himself or of another, before he can understand the ground of them, and before actions of the kind to which they are applicable have evoked in him any emotion that could determine the appropriate moral judgment" (McDougall, 215–16).

The cultural tradition of a family is never something peculiar only to this one family; families belong to larger social groups and are imbued with their cultural tradition. Therefore, acquiring (by cultural inheritance) the family tradition, the child or youth becomes also attached to the cultural tradition of larger (religious, professional, political, et cetera) groups. A part of their stock of rules is learned individually; other parts are recognized *en bloc*.

Let us now suppose that an individual becomes a voluntary member of an "artificial" social group — a commissioned officer in a regiment, a member of a club or fraternity, a monk in a certain order. Generally his chief desire is to become as soon as possible a member like the others; in order to obtain this result he makes an effort to learn the specific rules of conduct imposed by the group and to adapt his conduct to them; but before knowing each separate rule he accepts them as a whole; he is ready to act according to them in every instance. His willingness to adapt himself to the specific tradition of the group is favorably accepted by the older members and is made use of in teaching him as a new member how to act according to the rules.[16] But in this case, the case of a "contractual" or voluntary membership, the continuous efforts of new members toward conformity are more characteristic than deliberate inculcation by old members.

The third case is that of compulsory membership. Its most conspicuous example is that of entering the army if military service is compulsory; a less striking example is that of a boy or girl entering primary school. Commissioned and noncommissioned officers in the first case, teachers in the second, apply a great number of methods which vary in the course of time and from place to place, but all tend toward the same goal: to imbue the

[16] On Sorokin's suggestion Timofeevsky has found forty-four different methods of modification of human conduct practiced in medieval ascetic orders (Sorokin, *e*, 602, footnote 5).

new conscript or the new pupil with the cultural tradition of the regiment or of the school. They explain the principal rules of conduct, develop the sense of obedience (see below, chap. VIII, § 3) and endeavor to inspire in the new members a general willingness to accept and recognize all the rules of the group, so that in every case, when a new rule not yet applied appears before the consciousness of the individual, he will immediately accept it, without making any attempt to analyze it, or decide whether this rule is clever or stupid, or compatible or incompatible with his general ethical conviction.

The acceptance or recognition in a block of all the rules in force in a given social group is the essence of the indirect recognition. Thus indirect recognition is the basis of social conservatism, of transmitting the cultural tradition from generation to generation. It may also sometimes be applied as a method for changing or reforming the cultural tradition, of which ethics forms a part.

The example of training a conscript in the army is very useful when analyzing this possibility. The training is carried out, perhaps, with the help of soldiers who one year earlier were themselves objects of the same process. Therefore it is possible, when acting carefully and rationally dividing the process into several stages, to incorporate within a social group and to imbue with its specific tradition numerous individuals who, if subjected simultaneously to the same process, would resist defiantly. Such is the technique of training and developing the "ruling" or "monopolist" parties in modern dictatorships. Their leaders proceed by gradual steps, separated by shorter or longer intervals; during these intervals previously incorporated elements are molded, transformed into true and loyal members endowed with the corresponding acquired tendencies, thus to become appropriate instruments for molding conscripts of the next grade.

Generally speaking, changes in ethical convictions and attitudes are gradual. The ethical conviction of an individual is not quite the same during his whole conscious life; some parts of the ethical systems recognized in childhood fade out in later years, and the experience of mature years adds new elements. But, in general, the bulk of ethical convictions remains a constant part of the individual's conscious life. The great expert in concrete psychology, Dostoievsky, said that the second half of a human life generally consisted of habits acquired during the first half (*The Possessed*, part II, chap. 2).

There may be exceptions: ethical revolutions, individual or collective. For a young man, the critical years of physical maturity are sometimes combined with a radical change in his ethical conviction; for instance, he may lose his faith and become an atheist. Consequently he loses the basis of an important part of his ethical belief and becomes an adherent of another ethical system. On the contrary, it sometimes happens that an individual of a more advanced age suddenly feels the inanity of his "positive" convictions and of his utilitarian ethics; he becomes a believer and begins to recognize a much more complex ethical system than that of his younger years. Such cases are called "conversions."

There may also be minor ethical revolutions. Take a young man who has grown up in a rather secluded family, entering a public school, or a youth coming from a rural district to a great city; the ethical rules recognized in his new environment are not at all the same as those of his upbringing. If his ethical conviction was very strong, this change will perhaps only reinforce it; but if it was not so intense, the fact of seeing his conviction not recognized by others, perhaps by people whom he now admires, may result in breaking up his previous ethical conceptions and in his becoming a follower of another ethical system.

Insofar as ethical revolutions remain individual, they do not perceptibly influence the efficacy of ethical rules in force in a certain group. But under certain circumstances such individual revolutions may become more frequent and therefore present a specific social process. We are living in an epoch of collective ethical revolution or, more exactly, of a complex of such revolutions. The symptom of such a revolution is the repeated demonstration of the loss of ethical convictions on the part of persons who previously recognized them directly. Such demonstrations result in a change in the attitudes of those who looked toward these rules for guidance. Such was the preparation of the great ethical revolutions represented by the victory of Christian ethics in the later Roman Empire, of Protestant ethics in the transition period between medieval and modern times, of utilitarian ethics in the nineteenth century and of Communist ethics in contemporary Russia.[17] Collective ethical revolutions destroy direct and indirect recognition of ethical rules: first of all various directly recognized rules and then the whole bulk of indirectly recognized ones. Former ethical rules finally remain without supporters and cease to exist as actual social forces, as objective elements of the socio-ethical equilibrium. In this way a link between changes in subjective attitudes and in objectively imposed patterns is created.

BIBLIOGRAPHICAL NOTE

The elementary bodily reactions to disturbances are studied by Cannon. — The best general history of the transformation of primitive revenge into social retribution is that of Makariewicz (*cf.* Post, *d*, I, 226–61). The special question of indirected revenge is studied by Steinmetz (*a*, 318 *ff.*) and Westermarck (I, 23–38). See examples of old laws based upon material retribution in Diamond (30–1, 116, 122, 140, 321).

The behavior of crowds as return to primitive standards is stressed by Allport. Modern "vendetta" and lynching are discussed by Pareto (1519–21); *cf.* a note of the translator; Adams (114–16), LaPiere (68–9), Chadbourn, Coker and Raper.

The doctrine of the historical school concerning the development of legal rules is presented in the works of Savigny (*a*, *b*), Puchta (*a*, *b*, *c*) and Beseler. A brilliant account is that of Ehrlich (*a*, 443 *ff.*). A partial

[17] During the first years of the Communist revolution in Russia the author had an opportunity to observe the following events. In the beginning the abolition of laws corresponding to general ethical conviction, for instance those concerning marriage, had no actual influence on behavior; only monogamic marriages consecrated in church (such was the law of pre-revolutionary Russia) were considered valid, and the new opportunities for divorce were not acknowledged. Very soon several individuals changed their minds and took advantage of the new opportunities; others followed suit, and after some time many families which had seemed to be firmly united were disunited. When I asked people concerning this, they answered me: "Why should I continue living with a woman I do not love any more, when A, B, and C have already accepted the new law?" The same happened with many rules concerning private ownership.

In order to show how important the amplitude of this revolution was, one single example may be offered. If you asked a modern Russian youth, completely trained in the new ethical tradition, what, in his opinion, was the greatest sin, he would undoubtedly answer: "To possess individually instruments of production."

revival of the doctrine is characteristic of some recent German works (e.g., Nicolai).

The utilitarian theory of the development of ethics has been represented by Bagehot, Sumner and Waxweiler. Not very different are the views of Carter (123, 132), Wallas (69–83) and Ehrlich (*a*, 341).

Attempts to adapt this theory to the results of biological study were made by Atkinson and Lang and by Westermarck. These authors investigated especially the development of the rules concerning sexual intercourse; this made their task rather easy, for in that domain the biological substructure is evident. McDougall (*a*, 282 *ff.*) introduced valuable corrections in the theory of Atkinson and Lang. Westermarck's incest theory was attacked by Havelock Ellis (*a*), without sufficient arguments; but recently Thomas (196) has shown that the *horror incesti* is not stronger than the horror of violating other taboos. Good modern studies of the mechanism of habit formation are those of Brown (94), MacIver (*b*, 246, 293) and Sherif.

The principle of the normalizing tendency of actuality has been investigated by Jellinek (*c*, 307–14). It is acknowledged (without reference to Jellinek) by Max Weber (*c*, 13–16), Tönnies (*d*, 248) and Le Henaff (39); for a criticism see Stoop (244). The gradual adjustment of attitudes to post-revolutionary situations is described by Sorokin (*a*, 168–9).

The nonlogical character of ethical development is stressed by Pareto (especially 247). Excellent studies of the content of ethical development, in its nonlegal aspect, are contained in the works of Friedländer for Rome and of Rudeck for Germany. For the contents of legal development see Kocourek and Wigmore.

The phenomenon of radiation has been studied, under different names, by many authors, for instance Pareto (949), Ehrlich (*a*, 350, 402–3), Rolin (6), Bergson (128), Robinson (227–33), Thomas (9). The development of the incest taboo has been thoroughly studied by Westermarck; additional examples are given by Thomas (190–7). The evolution of the "benefit of clergy" in England is studied by Maine (*b*), Pound (131 *ff.*) and Hall (*a*, 74–83).

Harmful habits have been studied by Sumner (25–6, 34, 44, 61, 66–71), Kovalevsky (I, 241–3, 268–70), Thomas (293–7, 303–8, 668 *ff.*) and many others. On the survival of old rules see M. Cohen (192).

The original amorality of children is stressed by Freud and his school; *cf.* Healy (*c*). The general question of individuals being molded by groups is excellently treated by Brown (65–6); that of the introduction of children into legal mentality by Rolin (80–4).

The question of ethical revolution is studied by Vierkandt (389). A marvelous description of an individual ethical revolution is contained in Tolstoi's *Anna Karenina* (part IV, chap. 18). A study of collective ethical revolutions in this country has been made by Tufts, especially as regards sex, marriage and family (92–121 and 313–24) and business (122–181).

For the origin of the duel see Below (6 *ff.*). Very interesting statements concerning modern drinking habits in Sweden, a country which has done a great deal to combat them, are to be found in Childs (113–15).

CHAPTER VII

DIFFERENTIATION OF ETHICS

§ 1. The Branches of Ethics

The idea that ethics forms a complex but uniform system of social coördination is not generally recognized. Generally the different types of ethical coördination are thought to be in opposition to each other: law *versus* morals, law *versus* custom, et cetera, and "ethics" is very often identified with "morals." Yet to think of objects as being in opposition to each other means to compare them, and though when we compare two or more objects we search for differences between them, we are also convinced, from the beginning, that the compared objects have something in common, for comparable objects always fall under a higher category which includes them all. The higher category including law, morals and custom is that of ethics.[1]

Ethics as a genus has only very seldom been studied in a scientific way, whereas law is the object of study in jurisprudence, morals in moral philosophy, custom (primitive much more than contemporary, and in general without clearly distinguishing it from collective habits) in ethnology.

Insofar as the genus of ethics is recognized in science, it is divided into branches or species. The ordinary division is that followed in this work: three species — law, morals and custom — are recognized. There are also divergent opinions: (1) that of introducing religion, or, more exactly ethics based on religion as a fourth class; (2) that of denying the independent existence of custom and therefore dividing ethics into law and morals only, and (3) that of replacing custom by an indeterminate number of ill-defined branches called folkways, mores, fashion, etiquette, custom (in a narrow sense), et cetera.

[1] The proposition that law is a branch of ethics is not at all identical with the statement that "every legal duty is founded on a moral obligation" (Lord Coleridge, *Queen* v. *Instnam*, 1893, 1 Q. B., 450). The correlation is much more complex than expressed in the quoted formula.

1. It is, of course, wrong to introduce religion as one of the species of ethics. First of all, religion contains more than ethics: the conviction of a believer is not only a practical (ethical), but also a theoretical one. The doctrinal side of religion is commonly an explanation of the structure of the universe and of the rôle of human beings in it. A complex of ethical rules is "derived" from this theoretical belief; but this is no property peculiar to religion. Developed philosophical systems possess the same property. Consequently, if we include religion under ethics, we should do the same with philosophy.

In actuality, religion and philosophy are not parts of ethics but possible supports of ethics (see below, § 3). The influence of religion can exist in all the different spheres of ethics: there is canon law, but also religious morals, and custom consecrated by religion. Philosophy seems to engender moral rules only.

2. The opposite theory is that of denying the existence of custom. Nobody has professed this opinion with greater tenacity than Petrazhitsky.[2] According to him, the efficacy of ethics is based upon the existence of primary "ethical impulsions," subdivided into moral and legal ones. The general function of ethical impulsions is to produce the "sentiment" of being bound by a duty. This sentiment may or may not be combined with "ascribing" the corresponding "right" to another person. In the first case there is a two-sided, "attributive-imperative" impulsion; we are in the domain of law. In the second case there is only a one-sided, "imperative" impulsion; we are in the domain of morals.

Petrazhitsky is not afraid of any consequence of this theory; according to him the so-called rules of politeness belong to the category of law, as well as rules in force between two lovers or among friends; whereas many rules of decency should be included in the realm of morals, or even aesthetics.

Terminological conflicts of opinion are always lamentable, especially in the social sciences which have to deal with phenomena lacking precise boundaries. It is rather a matter of convenience

[2] Another author, Radbruch, who denies the independent existence of custom, is forced to call custom "an absurd mixture of legal and moral evaluation" (*d*, 78).

than of scientific necessity to classify these phenomena in one or another way, and it is of course possible to divide ethical phenomena into the two classes proposed by Petrazhitsky. The point at issue is whether his classification does justice to the main feature of the genus itself. As has already been shown (chap. IV, § 4), Petrazhitsky's individualistic theory is inadequate to the very essence of the generic notion (ethics). Almost necessarily his classification must be inadequate too. And truly the elements introduced by Petrazhitsky into his notion of law form a completely disparate group. They are dissimilar because they belong partly to the system of social interaction centralized by power and partly to that of decentralized interaction. Behavior systems belonging to these two groups have very little in common; there is, perhaps, from the sociological viewpoint, no contradistinction more important than this.[3]

3. Authors recognizing the existence of a number of branches of ethics besides law and morals disagree completely in enumerating them. A study of their enumerations would not be very useful, for their catalogues are almost never based upon a scientific analysis of the branches and of their interrelations; it seems that every author was rather trying to show that there were a multitude of minor branches than attempting to analyze them.

For instance, Sumner introduces the term "folkways" for the total field of habit and custom and subdivides it into "usages" (containing no reference to common welfare) and "mores" (containing such reference) (30, 57).[4] Vinogradoff speaks of fashion, manners and customs, conventional standards (19–23); Ehrlich of decency, tact, etiquette, fashion (165). LaPiere recognizes folkways, custom and mores. "The term folkways," he writes, "has been applied to those [behavior patterns] which are the least vital and are therefore most susceptible to change. . . ." They "are

[3] Petrazhitsky's dichotomy is followed by Sorokin (*h*, II, 525–6). This seems to be incompatible with Sorokin's recognition of the basic importance of the contradistinction between organized and nonorganized groups (*ibid.*, III, 18–22), which almost corresponds to that between centralized and decentralized coördination discussed in the text. Del Vecchio (*c*) repeats Petrazhitsky's dichotomy, without knowing his works.

[4] Giddings (*b*, 191–3) accepts the term folkways and contrasts it to "stateways" — a new term for law.

the proper ways of doing things, they are not however the 'only' ways. When the members of a society consider that there is only one possible way of accomplishing a given end, we speak of that way as a custom. . . . Standing high above . . . are a number of precepts for the guidance of individual behavior, which must be . . . carefully followed; these are mores."

Tönnies distinguishes between (1) "*Eintracht*," i.e., "concord," rules based upon relations of the community type and considered as "natural" or "necessary," (2) "*Sitte*," i.e., mores, based upon common habits and (3) "*Konvention*," i.e., rules formed by explicit or implicit agreement based upon common aims for which the rules are considered to be the right means (*b*, 10–11).

It cannot be denied that custom forms a complex category. But all the elements of the category are internally united by the fact that their efficacy is based only upon socio-ethical pressure, whereas the efficacy of law and of morals is assured, in addition to this, by other means. This is a very important point, combining, for scientific purposes, all the elements of ethics beyond law and morals under one general concept, for which the term "custom" is of course only partly adequate.

§ 2. The Gamut of Definitions

That ethics should be divided into three types is a rather common opinion. But there is no common opinion with regard to the "principle of division," or, more exactly, to the specific properties of law as compared with the other ethical branches; for this is, in general, the aspect under which the question is treated.[5]

[5] It is not always easy to correctly classify the definitions of law. For instance, Gierke says: "The State does not say in Law that the behavior prescribed by legal rules should be obligatory, but says that it (the State) insists upon the validity of these rules because they seem to be just" (*a*, 76). Gurvitch understands this statement as a negation of the theory, according to which the support of power is essential to law (*a*, 136). Actually it is nothing more than the recognition of the double root of law (*cf.* chap. XI); the State insists upon the validity of legal rules (this means: displays power in order to secure their efficacy), because they seem to be just (this means: because they are in conformity with the ethical group-conviction).

On the other hand, there are definitions of law which seem to be quite original without being so. For instance, Commons (p. 6) tries to explain law and some other parts of ethics (business ethics and "norms of conduct") as "working rules of going concerns." But working rules are nothing more than rules in force; and

These theories will be briefly described and commented on and the place of our working hypothesis within their gamut will be established. This cursory review should by no means be considered as an argument in favor of the hypothesis; it is only a second approximation developing the first one (chap. I, § 5); the hypothesis can be definitely verified only after the study of the imperative coördination of behavior will be completed (Part III).

1. Attempts to discover a specific legal content of rules were frequent in the beginning of the nineteenth century. They continue to this day. Thus for Kistiakovsky (680) law always tends toward the embodiment of liberty and justice. For Radbruch law is a specific part of the actuality meant to serve the idea of justice.[6]

Every attempt to classify ethical rules from the viewpoint of their content must prove unsatisfactory, for the same rule may belong at once to two or even to all three branches of ethics; it is immoral to steal, but it is also illegal and indecent (*cf.* § 7).

On the other hand, the content of ethical rules varies so immensely that there is scarcely a behavior pattern recognized by a certain social group which has not been repudiated and replaced by the opposite pattern in other groups. This is, of course, the most general impression created in everyone by the comparative study of ethical rules in force in primitive society.

2. Classification according to the social functions of the ethical rules is also unsatisfactory; if the function of protecting freedom or interests is ascribed to legal rules, it is obvious that such are also the social functions of many rules belonging to other branches of ethics: for instance, many moral rules protect the sexual integrity of women and children in cases when legal rules have left

going concerns can be understood as nothing more or less than social organizations.

An extremely complex concept of law (in the Neo-Hegelian style) has been recently given by Schinkler. According to him, we have to distinguish between formal and material elements in law; the formal elements are order and authority (of the State), the material elements refer to ethics and to vital interests. Law is always endowed with all the four elements, but their distribution and relative importance fluctuate and can be accurately described only when using the dialectic method. Yet it is evident that order is not an element in, but a function of law, and that the reference to "vital interests" (extra-legal factors in culture) cannot be introduced in the concept of law.

[6] Concerning the true relationship between law and justice, *cf.* chap. IV, § 2.

attacks "free"; or many rules of politeness gratify the desire to be "honored" by one's neighbors. Quantitative, but not qualitative differences might be discovered, and these quantitative differences cannot be measured; limits of such a sort are necessarily too imprecise.[7]

3. The psychological function of ethical rules of different types is stressed by Petrazhitsky and Ehrlich.[8] We have already had an opportunity to discuss Petrazhitsky's theory; the limit proposed by him is precise, but cuts ethics into two classes, each of which unites heterogeneous phenomena.

On the other hand, Ehrlich's theory is a remarkable assemblage of completely vague statements. "Compare," says Ehrlich, "the feeling of revolt that follows a violation of law with the indignation at a violation of a law of morality, with the feeling of disgust occasioned by an indecency, with the disapproval of tactlessness, the ridiculousness of an offence against etiquette, and lastly with the critical feeling of superiority with which a votary of fashion looks down upon those who have not attained the heights he has scaled" (*a*, 165).

In his review of Ehrlich's book, Kelsen justly mocks this completely mistaken statement. He compares sentiments which accompany the transgression of the legal rule prescribing the payment of interest on commercial loans and the sentiments produced by a violation of a moral rule, say, that prescribing charity. "Is it possible," asks Kelsen, "to distinguish between the revolt following the first offence and the indignation following the second? Would it not be possible to call the sentiment in the first case 'indignation' and that in the second case 'revolt?' Would not many people agree that they felt revolt when in the presence of a breach of tact, or even indignation, and that their sentiment with regard to a violation of legal rules was disapproval?" (*c*, 861)

4. The doctrine which searches for the specific properties of

[7] A general attempt to study the social functions of ethics has never been made; the author is aware that such a study should follow this chapter, but in spite of this he is able to offer only a partial study in Chapter XIV.

[8] Of the same type is the theory of Kraft, for whom law is the expression of "legal sentiment" (*a*, 9). The legal sentiment should be defined before such a definition could become of any use.

law in its origin is of course the most influential in jurisprudence. Its simplest expression is that law is a complex of rules created by the State; frequently this viewpoint is combined with that of sanctions, and legal rules are defined as rules created by the State and protected by State sanctions.

The idea that law is a complex of rules created (or recognized or protected) by the State is refuted by historical evidence: law is older than the State — it existed when the State had not yet appeared on the scene; there was also a period when both existed without there being any connection between them (see below, chap. XII). On the other hand, rules of conduct may exist in and be protected by a despotical State, but these rules would not be legal rules (in general not ethical rules at all; see chap. IX). The connection between State and law is only natural, not necessary.[9]

5. The theory according to which the specific properties of law are to be searched for in the realm of sanctions was expressed with much vigor by Austin, who gave it the form of the "constraint theory." Austin says: "Every law is a command which obliges a person or persons . . . 'I am bound or obliged by your command, or I lie under duty to obey it' signifies that I am 'liable to evil from you if I comply not with a wish you signify.' . . , Command and duty are correlative terms" (88–91).

This is a very crude expression of the "constraint" theory; it does justice only to the second (imperative) and not to the first (ethical) root of the efficacy of law. Therefore, the truth of this theory could be and actually was successfully contested. Yet the theory could be and actually was improved: not every constraint but only organized constraint is declared to be the specific sanction of law.[10] A good instance of the modernized re-

[9] In Anglo-American jurisprudence the State theory of law was transformed into a theory according to which law is that which is applied by the courts. *Cf.* the well-known dictum of Justice Holmes: "Law is a prophecy of what courts will do in fact" (173). The Anglo-American theory is shared by Tönnies, who expressed the opinion that not the factual application, but the ideal applicability by courts was decisive (*b*, 10–11).

[10] The Austinian command theory is now sometimes considered to be not the correct expression of the nature of law, but "a moderately accurate portrayal of the public attitude towards law" (J. Frank, 194).

straint theory can be found in Thurnwald's book: "The recognized constraint makes custom to law" (*b*, 4). Another example is Morgenthau's theory (70 *ff*.). In his opinion, customary and legal rules are to be distinguished in that the sanctions of the former are not predetermined by rules, whereas the sanctions of the latter are; a rule is legal if there is another rule determining in advance who is to apply the sanction, or of what kind the sanction should be, or both. This transformation of the constraint theory is not yet satisfactory. Morgenthau is forced to recognize that (1) some rules are legal only because they are imposed by power and (2) that a rule imposing the duty of being polite to one's host must be considered legal if there is another rule which imposes the application of sanctions (boycott) on everybody present, and is customary if there is no such secondary rule; he is also forced to recognize that such results diverge from facts—a sufficient negative test of the validity of the theory.

A further modification of the sanction theory is necessary. But its kernel is correct: the essence of law must be searched for in the manner of imposing patterns of behavior.[11] The general structure of ethics prescribes this. Ethics is the imposition of social behavior patterns. Therefore, different species of the genus ethics must be related to the different means of imposing patterns or securing their efficacy. The decisive point is whether socio-ethical pressure is supported by some other force or not.

Social retribution is one factor in the system of ethical coördination; if, simultaneously, imperative coördination plays a part in securing the efficacy of an ethical rule, we are in the presence of the more complex phenomenon of ethico-imperative coördination, that is, of law. If simultaneously, modes of persuasion derived

[11] This view is contested by Pareto in the following terms: "It does not have the slightest scientific value, since it assumes as criteria elements which are secondary and changeable. An action passes from law to morality (or *vice versa*) according to the will or caprice of the legislator" (243). This is a rather surprising error on the part of the great Italian scholar. The imposition of patterns by legislators is not mere caprice, but a socially determined act which can be and actually is scientifically studied in comparative jurisprudence. In the second place, it is obvious that the situation within a social field changes every time a certain behavior pattern is included in, or excluded from the number of patterns imposed on group-members by law.

from religious or philosophical systems aid in securing the triumph of ethical rules, we are in the presence of another complex phenomenon, that of morals. If neither power nor persuasion are active, and socio-ethical pressure alone has to restore the socio-ethical equilibrium, we are in the presence of custom.

This classification is correct not only from the systematic, but also from the genetic viewpoint. The three branches of ethics appeared on the scene by means of differentiation. In the beginning there was only undifferentiated ethics secured by means of social retribution in its early very primitive forms. Law could only appear when organized power (not necessarily the State) was created and became interested in supporting certain of the ethical rules (*cf.* chap. XII). Morals could only appear when higher religious and philosophical theories had been created.

The possibility to improve the sanction theory in the described manner depends on the possibility to create a scientifically correct theory of power and to make this theory independent of any knowledge concerning ethics. This possibility will be studied in Part III of this work.

§ 3. Morals

Law will be the object of a special study in Part IV of this book. At this point we must give more precision to our discussion of morals and custom.

Morals form a part of ethics and are, therefore, enforced by socio-ethical pressure. Moral rules are obligatory for adult members of a society, insofar as there is a group-conviction concerning these rules. These are assertions which most authors who have dealt with the question would probably contest. Their contention is that morals are autonomous and individual; they consist of rules which an individual freely creates or accepts; he acts according to them not because others consider these rules obligatory, but because he himself considers that they truly express the idea of what is good.

Such opinions are erroneous. Moral rules are obligatory. Social groups consider these rules not as "recommended" statements, which may be recognized or not recognized by group-members, but as social commands which must be carried out, even if they run counter to individual interests or desires. The moral rule, "Do not lie," is imposed upon all group-members; social groups whose members recognize this rule aim toward a possible complete elimination of falsehood in all relations among group-members; if this rule is transgressed, a social reaction generally takes place.

Of course it is easy to transgress a moral rule. But a legal rule may also be transgressed. Stronger motives hinder the transgression of legal rules than that of ethical rules of the other categories. But this is only a quantitative, not a qualitative difference.

What is the specific characteristic of a moral rule? A moral rule demands not only that one act in accordance with it, but demands also a direct recognition on the part of the actor that corresponding acts ought to be, i.e., an internal conviction of the excellency of the rule.

Let us analyze a rule belonging to every highly developed system of social morals: Help the poor according to your means. Insofar as this rule is a moral one, it demands not only the accomplishment of concrete acts of giving help, when the corresponding situation is presented, i.e., when you are in the presence of persons actually needing material help and when you are able to extend such help, but it also demands that you act with positive conviction and with an active love for your neighbors. Let us now suppose that material help to the poor has been widely given by some rich person, but that this person acted not because he was moved by active love toward his neighbors or because of internal conviction that helping the poor was the duty of everyone, but, on the contrary, in order to hear his name praised by his associates or even in wider social circles, or because he hoped thereby to win rank and title (in many countries the practice existed of granting honors to liberal donors). Such an individual has gained no merit from the point of view of morals, for the moral rule has not been carried out.

This is an important distinction between morals on the one hand and custom or law on the other. A man who wears a dress coat when going to an official ball has followed the corresponding rule of custom, even if he considers such a garment ridiculous. A man who challenges an individual who has given him offense, has complied with the rules of the dueling code, even if he considers a duel an immoral action. On the contrary, a man who abstains from challenging his offender, not because of moral feeling, but because he fears the possible consequences (death, wounds, judicial trial, censure of persons whose opinion he holds in esteem), cannot be considered to have acted in accordance with a moral rule.

Recognition is an element necessary to the efficacy of every ethical rule, but in general a recognition by the average, by the majority of group-members is sufficient. Recognition on the part of everyone, especially on the part of the acting individual, is unnecessary — an indirect recognition may be sufficient; no more than readiness to act according to the rule, because it is recognized by others, is demanded. In morals the element of personal, direct, internal recognition is especially stressed.

The necessity of direct recognition, of acting according to personal conviction, is the source of the erroneous doctrine ascribing "autonomy" to morals in contrast with the "heteronomy" of custom and law. The meaning of this theory is that morals are entirely individual; they are supposed to be a complex of rules imposed on an individual's will by his own free decision. But every rule of social behavior is of social origin; in this sense all rules, including those of morals, are heteronomous. In other words, the autonomy of morals is merely a designation for the second root of its efficacy, for the "voice of conscience," whereas the social pressure represents the first root, common to all branches of ethics. This voice of conscience plays in morals, therefore, a rôle analogous to that of power in law: the rôle of a "second root."

The source of the erroneous opinion ascribing autonomy to morals is to be found in the circumstance that individual moral convictions, having no connection with social rules of behavior, are also termed "moral" convictions. We have to distinguish between (1) true moral rules, rules of behavior imposed by social groups and (2) individual ideas of what moral (or generally ethical) rules should be (*cf.* Tönnies, *c*, 205).

Individual moral convictions, which may play a certain rôle in personal life, do not play an essential part in the determination of social life, because of their multiformity, their divergent tendencies. Their existence must, of course, be studied if we search for a complete explanation of human behavior.

As regards true social morals, they are always connected with great religious or philosophical movements, or at least with attempts to create them. There are sacred morals connected with Buddhism, Judaism, Christianity, Mohammedanism, et cetera. There are secular morals connected with the ancient Greek philosophers, or with the victorious ascent of the State idea in ancient Rome. There has been an attempt to create a *morale civique* in France, connected with the a-religious trend of her ruling class; there has been another attempt to construct "Communist morals" in Soviet Russia. In all these cases a direct appeal to conscience is made, even if the existence of the "soul" is denied.

In the majority of cases morals, in the form of sets of behavior patterns, insofar as they are truly in force in a certain social field, are connected with the appearance of ideal men or of ideal structures as examples to be imitated. "At different times," writes Bergson, "exceptional men appear, in whom absolute morality seems to be embodied." Its universality is based "upon the common imitation of a pattern" (29).

It is noteworthy that even in less highly developed societies (where higher types of religion are still impossible) a similar means of "moralizing" people has been tried. The Maoris, for instance, instituted a "selection of girls to be trained as examples of conduct" (Thomas, 489–90).

The specific sanction of moral rules, added to social retribution (which is also applied), is *remorse*. This appears to be a purely internal sanction, but is not so. "It is more likely . . . that conscience is the reflection of public opinion rather than public opinion the reflection of conscience" (Ross, 64). "Conscience is an inner mirror of public opinion, an anticipated feeling of what would be the experience if secret sins were made public." It is a "consciousness of separation between the group and self-censure as a group-member" (Thomas, 599). "In this connection confession is the first step toward reconciliation" (Thomas, *ibid.*).

§ 4. Custom

Customary rules form another part of ethics and are obligatory in the same sense as legal or moral rules. This is again a statement contested in certain scientific circles. For instance, Stammler (*c*) contends that customary rules leave every individual free from their pressure by admitting the possibility that he can forsake the corresponding social group. Customs, in his opinion, are merely a complex of conventional rules of conduct valid within specified groups. Sometimes the idea that custom is not obligatory is expressed only implicitly. When, for instance, Fehr (26) asserts that "custom becomes law when it gains the power to be actualized in the community," he actually says that custom does not possess such power.

The opinion of Stammler is not in accordance with reality. An individual is, of course, able to set himself free from the rules of a club by leaving it; but, on the other hand, sometimes social groups organized by specific customary rules are so closely related with the total life of an individual that his freedom to leave is theoretical rather than practical. Many professions — medicine, the law, et cetera — have developed far-reaching systems of professional ethics; a member of one of these groups may "free" himself from the pressure of these specific ethical codes, but only by abandoning his profession and thereby his means of earning a livelihood.

On the other hand, sometimes it *is* possible to free oneself from the pressure of a certain complex of legal rules by forsaking the corresponding social group. Churches of ancient origin are governed by canon law; every member is supposed to obey the commands of this law; but in the modern State he is able to separate himself from his church and in this way emancipate himself from the corresponding restraint. Many corporations and associations have statutes belonging to the domain of law; if membership has been voluntarily accepted, retiring from the corporation or association means at the same time liberation from the statute, a part of law. There is almost no difference between this case and that of withdrawing from an association the corporate life of which is regulated merely by "conventional rules" (in Stammler's terminology).

As a matter of fact, customary rules are not at all optional. The sentiments of the individual subjected to custom sustain this proposition. "An average Englishman could no more be induced to wear his hair long than the average Chinese mandarin could be induced to wear his fingernails short" (Allen): both consider their way obligatory. The customary rule — "Greet acquaintances when meeting them" — is imposed upon group-members willy-nilly; everyone is supposed to act according to it. If it is transgressed, a social reaction may occur, initiated by the "victim" (the person who has not been greeted); later on, the reaction may spread through the social group and sometimes result in a kind of boycott or ostracism.

The manner in which social pressure is displayed is varied. All the sanctions of ethical rules described above (chap. V, § 8), with the exception of organized punishment, may be applied. There is sometimes a kind of formal procedure: "courts of honor" (Pareto, 801) in modern society, tribal assemblies in primitive society. "In Samoa there are organized assemblies whose judgments are executed by a kind of mob action, either by the destruction of the property of the offender and his family, or by the injury, death or banishment of the individual offender" (Thomas, 62). But commonly there is no organized action: sanctions are carried out by individuals acting according to the common conviction of group-members.

§ 5. The Rôle of Custom in Modern Life

For a long time, custom played a very great rôle in social life. This is sufficiently proven by ethnological studies of the life of savage tribes. Later on, with the rise and growth of law, custom was relegated to a place of minor importance, a large part of earlier custom becoming a part of law under the name of customary law.

It is often supposed that in modern society custom no longer plays any rôle at all. This is incorrect. "Our highly developed societies are just as replete with social customs as the primitive societies of the past or the backward societies of to-day" (Allen, 26).[12] In order to refute the opposite opinion the following survey of present-day customs may be useful; this survey is based upon the brilliant description by Jhering (*b*, vol. II) supplemented by several elements taken from other sources.

In order to classify the very complex network of customary rules, we might separate them into two main classes: (1) rules of a transitive, attributive character [13] and (2) rules of a non-attributive, intransitive character.[14] Let us begin with the latter class.

Rules of this class are often negative: they do not oblige you to follow a certain type of conduct, but prohibit certain acts. For instance, it is indecent to make superfluous noise, especially when sitting at dinner or in the theater; it is indecent to sneeze or blow your nose in an ostentatious manner. The obligatory use of a handkerchief is now a positive rule of decency, whereas in a book dealing with decency published two hundred years ago in Germany only a negative rule was to be found: Do not use for this purpose the skirt of the lady with whom you are sitting at table.

A long series of rules of decency deals with eating and drinking; their main sense is to make these acts as imperceptible as possible. Now we are no longer aware of the rules of decency which abolished primitive communism — all the rules prohibiting the use of another's fork and knife or taking food from another's plate. There are, in addition to this, many positive rules connected with eating and drinking, and these rules vary from country to

[12] Yet the rôle of custom should not be overstressed, as done by Carter who says: "While all law is custom, all custom is not necessarily law. Law differs from custom as a part differs from the whole" (120). In his terminology custom takes the place of ethics in this book; in addition to this a specific theory concerning the correlation between law and other factors in culture is contained in his quoted words (*cf.* below, chap. XIV).

[13] Rules of politeness according to Jhering; rules of unofficial law according to Petrazhitsky.

[14] Rules of decency according to Jhering; aesthetic rules according to Petrazhitsky.

country. In Great Britain there is a set way of laying down the fork and knife after having finished eating. In the middle and lower classes of pre-revolutionary Russia there was a custom of turning over the cup after having finished drinking tea.

Another long series of rules prohibits rough or "low" expressions in conversation. Concrete rules vary extremely, not only from country to country, but also from class to class: expressions considered quite decent in a company of stevedores would be impossible in a company of "gentlemen."

A number of rules prohibit too frank an expression of sentiments. When in company a gentleman must not express joy by laughing too loudly or by making gestures which are too "natural," or by crying out when feeling moral or bodily pain. Bad humor must not give vent to disagreeable remarks or looks. Finally, a number of negative rules are connected with sexual instinct. Permissible manifestations of this instinct belong to the most variable class of rules of decency.

A large number of positive rules of decency concern the ceremonies adapted to special occasions. One of the most curious groups is that of ceremonies adapted to the commemoration of the dead.

The rules concerning clothing are also of a rather positive kind. In earlier times the manner of clothing was prescribed in detail by customary rules which varied with regard to sex, age, social position, et cetera. Today a general difference in clothes for men and women reflects that original obligatory character of the custom: it is indecent for a man to be clothed like a woman or for a woman to be clothed like a man. Another series of obligatory (but now rapidly changing) rules indicates what parts of the body may be left uncovered and on what occasions. There are, in addition, definite prescriptions of custom for festival and mourning clothes. It is indecent to appear at a wedding or at a ball dressed in business clothes. It is, on the contrary, indecent to appear at a burial ceremony without showing marks of mourning in your clothes.

There is a specific set of rules of decency primarily concerning clothes known as "fashion." Fashion is a complex of changing patterns for clothes, imposed by special leaders and leading families, obligatory for all members of "fashionable" society, and, in a smaller degree, for all the members of social groups where imitation of the social élite is considered to be obligatory. Jhering supposes that fashion is an invention of modern times. This opinion is not quite correct: a cursory review of illustrated works on the history of clothing proves with sufficient clearness that fashion already existed in the Middle Ages (*cf.* Tönnies, *d*). Of course the velocity of the changes was then not the same as it is in our times; we have to take half or even a whole century as a unit in order to notice changes; today a "season" or a quarter of one year represents the unit. But this is only a concrete application of the general phenomenon of the acceleration of the speed of social change during the last few centuries.

Fashion is not restricted to clothing. Personal posture (especially the manner of walking), furniture, literary and artistic tastes are also subject to the dictates of fashion. However, the rate of these changes is much less than in the domain of clothing.

To follow the patterns imposed by fashion is a kind of ethical rule obligatory only in certain social groups; a person violating this rule, wearing unfashionable clothes, may be rejected by the circle of fashionable people — though he may succeed in imposing his own pattern of clothing on others, which would mean that he had become a "leader in fashion." [15]

Jhering gives an ingenious explanation of the social rôle played by fashion. By imposing on its members constantly changing patterns of clothing, the higher circles try to seclude themselves, to put a definite barrier between themselves and the others. These others, imitating the higher circles, try to break down the boundary. But, as fashion is ever changing, they do not attain their aim; they adapt external appearance not to the fashion accepted today by the higher circles, but to the fashion which was accepted yesterday.

[15] Do therefore the concrete prescriptions of fashion belong to the number of ethical rules? Not at all, for economic, aesthetical and undetermined "vital" values which, as such, are not related to ethics, may become "Strahlwerte" (term created by W. Stern), illuminated by ethical values, when they accidentally come in touch with them.

Jhering's ideas may be corroborated by two further proofs. In the first place, at times when authorities found it necessary to separate the different social classes, the type of clothing was not left to the free will of the individual, more exactly to the separate social groups, but was imposed by law. In such cases the social function of clothing styles was obvious. Secondly, the acceleration in the succession of fashions coincided with the destruction of a multitude of former barriers between the social classes; as long as these barriers existed and social ascent was very difficult, there was no need for adding the additional difficulty of keeping up with the fashion. Later on, when artificial barriers were broken down, the higher circles found a new and very efficient manner of separating themselves from others by changing the fashion every season.

Let us now pass to the second main class of customary rules, those of politeness. According to Jhering, their very essence is public recognition of another's honor and dignity. Transgression of such a rule, therefore, means a lack of recognition of the personal value of another person; this person is the primary "victim." However, the social group is also offended, for it imposed the general rule which was not followed in this concrete case.

The first rule of politeness is that of greeting when meeting an acquaintance. In more primitive societies (and in rural districts in many parts of Europe even today) you have to greet every person you meet. The manner of greeting depends sometimes on the social relationship of the persons involved. When the person you greet is a superior, the greeting should show respect or reverence. The Asiatic manner would be in this case to prostrate yourself. In ancient Rome the clients had to kneel before their patron; in the Middle Ages the vassal had to do the same before his sovereign during the ceremony of investiture. Today a deep bow is sufficient, even in the presence of a monarch.

Other rules prescribe what you must do when you meet on a narrow path: the younger must make way for the older, the gentleman for the lady, et cetera. When a guest arrives at your house you must go out to meet him. When a person asks you a question you must answer. When a person is speaking you have to listen silently. When people sit down together at a meal, different rules decide how they should be placed, especially to whom the first place belongs and which it is. When courses are served, rules impose a definite behavior as regards the order in which the persons present are to be served (guests before hosts, ladies before gentlemen, older people before younger, et cetera), and also the kind of small services which the gentlemen have to perform for the ladies.

A complex series of rules determines the manner of addressing another person in speech or in letter. Everywhere there are formulas of respect. We have to say "Dear Sir" to persons who have not been knighted. The French use the word "Monsieur," the Germans "Herr." In both cases they designate as "lords" persons who have nothing to do with domination. Long and complicated titles are used when addressing persons of higher social rank. In Germany, before the War, you had to know exactly the official rank of the person with whom you were in conversation or correspondence, for you had to address him by his official title: "Herr Geheimrat," "Herr Ministerialdirektor," et cetera. In France today a person who has been Minister or President of the Council for perhaps only three days has the right to be addressed for the rest of his life as "Monsieur le Ministre" or "Monsieur le Président." In English the terms of addressing a person are simpler and less varied than in other languages; but in French, German or Russian these formulas are manifold and their correct usage is sometimes not at all easy. An extremely complex technique of addressing people prevails in Sweden (Thomas, 96).

A number of rules of politeness determines human behavior with respect to events taking place in the life of one's acquaintances. You have to congratulate persons on the occasion of a wedding, of the birth of a child (in very intimate circles even on minor occasions such as birthdays); you have to express your sympathy on the occasion of a death in your friend's family and attend the funeral. These obligations on your part are correlated with the duty on the part of others to let you know of the events which give rise to your obligations.

When a person takes his leave you have to wish him a happy journey or good health (Latin *salve*). You must pick up an object another lets fall; you must open a door when certain classes of persons approach it; you must bring a chair for a lady or an elderly man.

Rules closely related to those of politeness (because they are also transitive) must be followed in small and private groups. Petrazhitsky draws our attention to various rules entering into force after a "formal declaration of love," as well as to rules of friendship (*b*, 192–5). In earlier times friendship was formally sealed by shaking hands, by clasping hands, or even by shedding some drops of blood. A remnant of this latter custom is the German pledge of *Bruderschaft:* drinking wine while keeping arms interlocked.

Customary rules in force, even today, are so numerous that an exhaustive list could not be prepared. But even an incomplete enumeration seems to prove that, contrary to current opinion, custom continues to play a large rôle in modern life. Perhaps a greater number of our acts is determined by custom than by law.[16]

§ 6. The Rules of Games

Might not the domain of custom be enlarged still more? Petrazhitsky (*b*, 88–9) considers the rules of games, both children's and adults', to be a part of ethics. This is an attractive idea. It is one of the insights of modern psychology that the play of young animals and of children is a useful preparation for the serious business of life, perfecting by practice the most specialized and difficult kinds of activity on the successful performance of which their survival in the struggle for existence must depend.

Play is a preparation for serious life. Developing this idea further, it might be said that games combined with rules (and social games are always of this kind) are a preparation for serious life, insofar as this life is also determined by rules, and that the

[16] Their content is sometimes not so important as their mere existence (Makariewicz, 62), for the existence of rules deciding how one should behave in many situations (1) saves energy which would have to be spent in order to find the right "voluntary decision" and (2) prevents many conflicts.

study of the rules of games, of their origin, development and decline would be of great help when analyzing ethical rules.

Unfortunately, this line of thinking is not correct. In the first place, adult games form a kind of collateral development; the direct development goes from children's games to serious business, whereas the collateral development tends to give adults the illusion of youth or, perhaps, the possibility of displaying the still retained youthful features of their psychic structure. Deductions from adult games to serious life would therefore be without a solid basis.

Secondly, the very essence of the rules of a game does not permit us to regard them as ethical rules. Every game consists in the ascription of conventional properties to men or things. Take, for instance, a game of cards. The partners use colored pieces of cardboard, giving to each of them a certain "value," varying from one game to another; these conventional properties are superimposed on the natural properties of the objects. The rules of the game occupy here the place of technical rules in serious business; the rules of the game are deduced from imaginary ascribed properties of the things used in the game. They are technical rules of a hedonistic cast; they help give entertainment of a certain kind. The term "conventional rules" would fit them, which Stammler wrongly applied to the rules of custom.

Game rules are not at all like those of ethics; but nevertheless the players are supposed to adhere to them strictly, to be "honest." Here is the ethical element of the game, often referred to as "fair play."

Therefore a study of the conventions forming the basis of games cannot be used as an introduction to the study of ethics. But the mentality of games plays an important part in what is called business life. The institution of money, with all its ramifications (credit, stock exchange, et cetera), forms a curious adaptation of the mentality needed for games to more serious purposes.

§ 7. Negative Ethical Conflicts

It would be an error to suppose that an ethical rule must necessarily be *either* a customary *or* a moral *or* a legal rule. On the contrary, the same rule, determining the same pattern of behavior, may be at the same time a customary, a moral and a legal rule. It is immoral to steal; but it is also illegal and indecent. What is the exact meaning of this statement? That three kinds of sanctions, corresponding to three kinds of pressure upon the individual, may be put in force in case the rule is violated. The voice of conscience will be heard by the thief, if he belongs to a group where the corresponding moral rule is in force; if it is not heard, this in itself will be an object for censure, a new motive for blame on the part of group-members. The unorganized reaction of the social group will be displayed: the thief will be censored, will not be greeted, will be submitted to boycott or ostracism. State authorities will display activity imposed on them in such cases by law: the police will search for the offender; the courts of law will try him; officers belonging to the prison administration will take care that the sentence is executed.

This similarity of content is the result of the common origin of all three branches, which once formed a homogeneous whole. On the other hand it is reinforced by their constant interaction and their mutual support. "Not a single one of the jural associations," wrote Ehrlich (*a*, 56), "could maintain its existence solely by means of legal norms; all of them, at all times, require the aid of extra-legal norms which increase or eke out their force."

It is obvious that the case of complete unison as regards the three branches of ethics may be exceptional. If the three branches were generally in concord, two of them would be superfluous, and everything that is superfluous is sooner or later eliminated in the course of social development.

There are, therefore, many rules which belong to only one of the three branches of ethics. In Section 5, many special rules of decency and of politeness (i.e., custom) were studied. Every higher moral system, for instance the Christian moral code, consists in part of a certain number of rules recognized as obligatory by the members of the corresponding group, but having no counterpart in custom or law. Finally, the greater part of legal rules of a modern State are related to its organization and to the functions of its authorities; these rules have no counterpart in morals or custom.

Even if a rule seems to belong simultaneously to two or three of the branches of ethics, its exact meaning is frequently not identical in each of them. A good instance is represented by the above-discussed rule against stealing. In custom this rule presents no exceptions: it is always indecent to steal. Generally it is also illegal; however, the ordinary legal sanctions against theft are in some countries omitted, if the offender is a near relative of the victim. But in morals the situation may be judged in a different manner. Saint Francis of Assisi stole in order to help the poor. And who of us would accuse him from the moral point of view?

The analysis of some other rules results in further interesting conclusions. Take, for instance, the rule, "Do not lie." In morals the rule seems to be quite general, but there is at least one exception: the "saving" lie is not only not prohibited, but even imposed on individuals by some moral systems. For instance, a physician, in his relation to a dying patient, has to maintain hope in the latter's consciousness. In custom lying is generally prohibited, but in some cases directly imposed, as in the case of the so-called conventional lie. You have to use the ordinary formula of politeness testifying your respect even toward persons you do not respect, whom you even despise. You have to express indifference at the loss of large sums of money in a game. You have to express sympathy with the joy or with the pain of another, even if you do not care at all for him or his fate.

As regards law, there is no general rule prohibiting lying. Only special cases have been selected from the mass of possible lies and covered by legal sanctions. A lie which results in bringing the prevaricator a certain material profit is illegal; it is punishable and, on the other hand, it gives the "victim" the right to claim an indemnity in court. A false statement before the court, especially if made under oath, is severely punished. A false statement before an officer as regards marriage results in the marriage being nullified and the offender punished. A false declaration of income is punished by the increase of the sum the offender is to pay to the State. The last example is very important, for it shows that State authorities not only select special categories of lies already reproved by morals and custom, but, in addition to this, create behavior types in which telling the truth is directly demanded.

Outside the limits traced by different statutes, lies are irrelevant from the legal point of view. Consequently, there may be cases in which the reaction of different ethical branches will be of a different kind. Lying about one's social relations, wealth or noble origin is immoral and indecent, but not illegal. But an understatement of income is hardly considered indecent by many social groups. On the other hand, acting according to the moral rule permitting "saving" lies, a physician may enter into conflict with the law, if the law orders him to ask the consent of the patient before a dangerous operation.

A kind of "empiric law" may be stated with regard to the sanctions of nonconcordant ethical rules: the sanctions of ethical rules, belonging only to one of the three systems are, other things being equal, more severe than the sanctions of rules acknowledged by two or three systems.

For instance, failure to pay debts is always not only illegal but also indecent. Generally the social, customary sanction of this transgression is not very severe: people having difficulties with their tailors, restaurant owners, et cetera, still remain in the best society and may be considered as leaders of fashion. Why is it so? Because it is a function of the State authorities to secure payment of debts and the help of social groups is hardly needed. There are cases, however, when debts are not recognized by law and their payment is, therefore, not secured in the ordinary manner. For instance, debts resulting from card-playing are nonexistent from the legal viewpoint and their payment cannot be claimed in court. On the contrary, the social sanction, at least in higher circles, becomes more rigid: a gentleman who fails to pay such a debt is no longer considered to be a gentleman; he will be excluded from the clubs to which he belongs; his friends will not speak to him when they meet him in the street; he will not be invited to parties where before he would have been welcomed. Before the War, in the German and Russian armies, a commissioned officer would have been immediately discharged for such an offense, for his fellow officers would not have approved of him any longer as a member of their narrow social group. Thus, the very minimum of legal sanctions corresponds to the very maximum of unorganized social sanctions.

Another example: smuggling, i.e., the bringing of foreign commodities into a country without paying duty, is an act against the law, but almost nowhere is this an act reproved by custom. It is done by some ladies of the best society who even boast about the quantity and quality of dresses imported by means of fraud. As regards morals, it is, of course, a case of violation of the general rule demanding obedience to legal authorities, but this is one of the moral rules endowed with only very mild sanctions, and one hardly ever hears of a case of remorse ensuing from disobedience to the law prohibiting smuggling. Consequently, law has no allies in this case and it has to reckon merely upon its own force. Therefore, the legal sanctions for smuggling are relatively high; sometimes corresponding, in the general scale, to those of misdeeds which dishonor their perpetrators for life.

§ 8. Positive Ethical Conflicts

In the cases studied there is of course no conformity among the rules belonging to the different ethical categories, but their conflicts are on the whole negative: behavior which is exacted by one is not exacted by the others and is considered irrelevant. No conflicts arise, therefore, in the consciousnesses and habit systems of individuals subjected to different rules; behavior which should be compatible with the ethical rules of all branches is possible, because the branch which considers a certain behavior irrelevant does not hinder an individual from acting in a manner which would satisfy the commands of other branches.

More difficult cases are possible, creating positive conflicts between the various ethical branches: behavior "A" demanded by one of the branches is prohibited by another which demands behavior "non-A." The following examples may serve as illustrations.

Denunciations are strictly disapproved of by higher moral systems; but denunciation is demanded by law in many countries as regards more important crimes; the only concession to morals, in some countries, is that denunciation is not obligatory as regards one's own relatives.

Law may introduce compulsory military service; but some moral systems closely related to certain religious denominations prohibit any kind of bloodshed, even though the very existence of the national State might be endangered; members of these groups refuse to enlist for military service and they are severely punished by the State. Sometimes they have to leave their country and look for a new fatherland where compulsory military service does not exist. The majority of the so-called Dukhobortsy left Russia for this reason during the last decades of the nineteenth century and founded flourishing colonies in America. During recent years many trials against so-called "*objecteurs de conscience*" (conscientious objecters) took place in France.

Roman law established public worship to be performed before the traditional gods and statues of emperors and every citizen had to participate. Christian morals, as well as Judaic, emphatically prohibited such acts. Persecutions followed which nevertheless failed to break the moral strength of the Christians.

Even today conflicts of the same type take place in most civilized countries. In the years 1905–6 many officers of the French army had a difficult problem before them when they were commanded to carry out expulsions of monks and confiscations of church property according to the law concerning the separation of Church and State. But religious morals ordered them to venerate cloisters and churches and to protect them against the incursions of secular authorities. Generally they personally solved the conflict by resigning from the army. Analogous and sometimes much deeper conflicts arise in modern dictatorships.

Other series of conflicts have arisen between custom and law. One of the most difficult is that connected with dueling. Under certain circumstances custom compels citizens of certain classes to challenge offenders and to accept a challenge to fight, thus putting human lives into direct jeopardy. The State prohibits such private fighting.[17] The State does so for the same reasons as those which, a thousand years ago, led to the limitation and then to the abolition of the blood feud. Private wars are incompatible with order and peace and with the monopoly of coercive power which, in modern societies, belongs to the State alone; and furthermore, the loss of human lives or the damage caused to human bodies decreases the forces of the State as a whole. The conflict is an unfortunate one. Dueling is so deeply rooted in certain circles that individuals who have transgressed the rules imposed by it are expelled from the corresponding groups. Such, for instance, before the War, was the situation in the German and the Russian armies and in the German student corporations. The State used to proceed in a merciless manner. In some countries, until recent times, taking part in a duel was punishable by death. Up to the present time the punishment for dueling, especially if death or serious wounds result, is very severe.[18]

Examples of the same category of conflicts are presented by the activity of European States in their colonies. In India there was a custom requiring the widow to follow her husband in death by mounting the funeral pyre and allowing herself to be burned. Such proceedings were prohibited by the British Government, but it was a long time before the custom was definitely uprooted. On January 11, 1907, the governor of the former German colony of Togo enacted a decree prohibiting abortion (which was allowed by custom), immoral conduct related to the ceremonies of the cult, and judicial duels (directly imposed by custom). This meant complete revolution of the habit-systems of the natives and resulted in much disturbance (Rolin, 13).

[17] In a certain degree dueling is endowed with the same social function as fashion: people who "defend their honor" by means of dueling are selected out of the mass of common people who apply to tribunals or who attack their offenders. This element of selection obviously prevailed in the "Mensur" of German students, who contrasted themselves with the "*philisters*" or townfolk who had no recourse to dueling. In appreciation of this situation, Hitler has tried to transform the duel custom into a general one: every German will be allowed (eventually compelled) to act as "a man of honor," or, in the German phrase, to be *satisfaktionsfähig*.

[18] Of the American States three (Alabama, Louisiana and Virginia) make dueling punishable by death (Kohlrausch, 179).

Sometimes, when a law remains unchanged while the social conditions regulated by it have changed, new customary rules arise counter to the law. A good example is the breach of the inferior legal status of women in France and pre-revolutionary Russia. In France nobody any longer asks the husband's consent when concluding a legal agreement with a married woman (with the exception of those concerning real estate). Custom has supplanted law (Binet, 36). In pre-revolutionary Russia the legal right of the husband to have his wife compulsorily brought back to the common dwelling she had left could no longer be carried out because of the resistance of custom.

Finally, conflicts are possible between morals and custom. Custom commands us to pay a debt contracted at cards. If, however, by paying such a debt the head of a family destroys the means of livelihood of the members of his family, he acts against a moral precept; he ought to take upon himself the dishonor of leaving such a debt unpaid and fulfill his duty of supporting his family. It is a very curious case, for each one of the three ethical branches gives a different solution to the problem. Paying or not paying is irrelevant from the point of view of the law, obligatory from the viewpoint of custom and prohibited from that of morals. Many drinking habits imposed by custom are in direct conflict with the moral systems recognized by the same individuals.

§ 9. The Settlement of Ethical Conflicts

Real conflicts between ethical rules belonging to different branches sometimes result in tragedies for the person concerned: he has to make a decision and to act; yet whatever his decision may be, he will inevitably be acting against one or more of the rules. And each one of the rules points, or seems to point, the way toward justice. Of course, there must be, among the ways indicated by the rules, deviations from the "right" path, for there can be only one "right" path. But who is to decide which of the ethical systems is the right one in a concrete case? And who will give the individual the heroic force which is sometimes necessary in order to carry out the "higher" duty, without regard to the evil consequences of disobeying the command of another rule?

The difficulty lies in the absence of an authority who might solve the conflict impartially. Law has physical power on its side; but morals sometimes have on theirs the irresistible force of inner conviction; and custom is supported by secular tradition, by everybody's "natural" tendency to act according to it. Historical evidence shows that in ethical conflicts victory is not decided beforehand in favor of either one or the other branch.[19] Law abolished the custom of burning widows in India and, after a long struggle, the dueling custom in modern Europe; but many laws have remained dead letters because of the resistance of the subjects, a resistance based upon custom and morals. For instance, the Austrian Civil Code was unable to break the custom according to which, in certain provinces, the earnings of children (even adults) were appropriated by parents who appeared punctually every month at the employer's place of business and collected the wages (Ehrlich, *a*, 370). Further instances are the failure of the laws creating the equality of Negroes in the Southern States, or of the Anti-Trust laws (Carter, 212 *ff.*) In other cases, changes in custom attempted by law are carried out only gradually. This was, for instance, the case in regard to divorcées in England, who, in spite of the law's recognition of the legality of divorce in certain cases, were punished by social ostracism (Whitehead, 204). Morals gained the upper hand in the conflict between the Roman Empire and the Church. Traditional morals as regards the family have survived in wide masses of the Russian population, despite the intentional attempts at their destruction by means of law. Evidence of this is now given by the concessions made by the Communist Government, concessions which may be explained only by the fact that the ethical group-conviction has not been overcome by the "new morals" officially imposed.

It would be of very great interest to make an inquiry, throughout all ages and nations, concerning ethical conflicts and their results, and to discover the reasons why one or the other ethical

[19] Sumner (56) is wrong when he says that "legislation . . . must be consistent with the mores," as are also Sutherland and Woodsworth (3) who assert that "mores win at the end."

branch had gained victory. This, however, is a scientific task, which has not yet been attempted.

Ethical conflicts, when they last for a certain time, have an unfavorable influence upon social life and must therefore be avoided. This is a task for which law, especially "abstractly created" law, is better suited than the other ethical branches, for law is the most adaptable of them. There are quite definite ways of changing a law, of shaping legislation according to certain aims, while there exist only indirect means of influencing a custom or a moral practice or belief. Therefore it greatly depends upon the wisdom of legislators whether ethical conflicts shall or shall not be avoided.

Of course, there are cases when law is obliged to attack custom or morals; sometimes there are moral usages or customs which are incompatible with further progress of society. The morals of "lower" races which have been included in the sphere of domination of "higher" races, or customs rooted in social conditions now obsolete because of the further advance of culture, have to be repealed. This task, however, may be accomplished in a ruthless or in a gentle manner. In the first case, failure, or at least much trouble, are the only result. In the second case, the social operation is sometimes carried out painlessly.

One of the striking examples of the latter method was the abolition of the dueling custom in England under the reign of Queen Victoria, which was provoked by a *cause célèbre*. In 1843 Lieut. Colonel A. L. Fawcett was killed in a duel by his brother-in-law, Lieutenant Munro. Queen Victoria addressed the officers of the army in the following way. "We hereby declare our approbation of the conduct of all those who having had the misfortune of giving offense to, or injured or insulted others, shall frankly explain, apologize, or offer redress for the same; or who, having had the misfortune of receiving offense . . . from another, shall cordially accept frank explanations, apology or redress for the same. . . . We accordingly acquit you of disgrace, or of opinion of disadvantage . . . who, being willing to make or except such redress, refuse to accept challenges, as they will only have acted as is suitable to the character of honorable men" (Hansard's Parliamentary Debates, vol. 73 [1844] col. 812). After this, only one more duel took place in England: the ethical group-conviction of English officers followed the royal injunction, and as the attitude of officers is decisive in the duel problem, the custom was definitely uprooted.[20] The action of Queen Victoria was successful, for it combatted the social roots of a harmful habit. Generally, conflicts between the ethical branches are based upon the resistance of minor groups to the ethical systems of larger ones. Social roots of moral or customary rules to be abolished should, therefore, be studied and then rationally combatted.

BIBLIOGRAPHICAL NOTE

Petrazhitsky mocks jurists for their failure to discover a valid definition of law (*a*, 11–12). The same is also done by Pareto (231–2, 243–6), and Arnold. According to the latter, "Law can never be defined. . . . There can be no objective reality behind the law. . . . Law is the most mysterious and the most occult of all branches of learning" (*b*, 31, 36–7).

A good survey of different definitions of law is given by Korkunoff (*b*, 57–84). For some modern theories see "Modern Theories of Law." *Cf.* Kocourek, Vinogradoff (*a*, 28–48), Stoop.

The most typical definitions of law are: (1) from the viewpoint of content, that of Kant; *contra*, Jhering (*a*, *b*, *c*); (2) from the viewpoint of social function, that of Jhering (*ibid.*); (3) from the psychological viewpoint, that of Petrazhitsky (*cf.* the text): *contra*, Kistiakovsky (250–68) and Taranovsky (*a*, 65–71, 157–62), whose statements have been partly followed in the text; (4) from the viewpoint of origin, again that of Jhering (*ibid.*); *contra*, Korkunoff (*b*, 65–7), Ehrlich (*a*, 24, 61, 366–90 and *passim*), Duguit (*d*), Gurvitch (*e*, 145–7); in another form Kelsen (*g*); and (5) from the viewpoint of sanctions, that of Austin (88–92); *contra*, Petrazhitsky (268–85); the Austinian theory in mitigated form: Rolin, Max Weber (*c*, 17–18), and Horvath (207–16). Thomas gives to the term "law" obviously too large a scope: according to him law is the complex of all means of preserving group-habits (515).

The best modern studies of morals as an object of scientific investigation have been written in French. After Lévy-Bruhl denied the possibility of a science of morals, Bayet and Gurvitch expressed the con-

[20] It is noteworthy that an attempt by the Austrian Emperor Joseph II, made in the year 1771, and in its main features identical with the method of Queen Victoria, was a complete failure (*cf. Der Gerichtsaal*, X [1858] 423). Obviously social conditions were not yet sufficiently mature for such a "gentle" transformation of custom.

trary opinion. The conclusions of Gurvitch are, *mutatis mutandis*, analogous to those included in this book as regards the sociology of law: the sociology of morals is to be created and should distinguish, within social actuality, moral facts, describe them and correlate them with the totality of social facts.

In modern philosophy the opposition between law and morals as complexes of autonomous and heteronomous rules by Christian Thomasius. Later on, the theory was developed by Kant and Fichte (in his earlier works). For Hegel, ethics (*Sittlichkeit*) form the "synthesis" in a dialectical development in which law is the "thesis" and "formal morals" the antithesis. The separation between law and morals continues to dominate in French science (*cf.* Delos, 89–90); but it is also often expressed in German science; for instance, by Gierke (*d*). Among recent authors, Morgenthau (23, 53–6) gives perhaps the strongest arguments in favor of the traditional theory; yet he is forced to recognize that, from its point of view (1) a value judgment concerning the behavior of another cannot be moral; (2) a legal norm cannot create a duty. Both propositions are refuted by facts; this is, of course, a sufficient test, forcing us to reject the hypothesis.

Concerning the relation between law and morals see Jellinek (*a*), Soloview, Petrazhitsky (49–61), Pound (*j*), Laun (*a*), Dunan and Baumgarten. The impossibility of distinguishing law and morals from the viewpoint of external or internal behavior was once more proved by Radbruch (*a*, 54–9) and Gurvitch (*f*, 163). The ideas expressed in the text are derived from those of Tönnies; for him moral rules are rules to be applied by an "ideal judge" (God or an abstract being, or Mind). Very near to him Ginsberg (149 and 198 *ff.*). Conscience is recognized as the second root of the efficacy of morals by Morgenthau (55); for a special study of the problem see Jankélévitch.

Among modern authors Merkel, Gény and Hippel make attempts to introduce religion into the series: morals — custom — law. The relation between law and religion is studied by Wundt (*a*, 27–36).

Concerning the relation of law and custom see Vinogradoff (*a*, 148–68) and Stammler (*c*, 116–125). The theory of the latter is accepted by Max Weber (*c*) and MacIver (*b*, 273).

Different classifications of custom (in addition to those indicated in the text): Durkheim (*a*, 193), MacIver (*b*, 288–94), Allport (*a*, 392–5), Brown (169) and Ginsberg (150 *ff.*).

As an example of the common assertion that custom no longer plays an important rôle in modern life, *cf.* Tufts (198); more correctly Pareto (176).

Jhering's brilliant study of modern custom forms the second volume of his "End in Law"; unfortunately this volume has not been translated into English. It is amazing that Jhering's study has not provoked analogous studies for different epochs or social circles. The book of Weigelin does not add anything new. The books of Tufts and Drake do not investigate the *concrete* structure of custom in the United States. Several good remarks are to be found in LaPiere (282, 286). Brilliant additions to Jhering were made by Petrazhitsky (*b*). Among older studies that of Spencer should be mentioned; in his opinion "ceremonious institutions were engendered by submission." A good criticism is that of Tönnies (*a*, 64–6).

For the subject of fashion *cf.* Simmel, de Barr (*b*) and Kellett. Rules concerning love affairs are studied by Petrazhitsky (*b*, 91–5) and Brown (232); some indication of rules united with occupational groups is given by MacIver (*b*, 252).

The theory of children's play was inaugurated by the great German poet Schiller. Modern views are based upon the classic work of Gross. *Cf.* J. Baldwin, and Carr. The element of play in business life is stressed by Simmel (*c*). There is no better way to understand the element of play in business than to read E. Zola's "*L'Argent.*" Concerning the rules of games, see Piaget and Sherif.

Conflicts between custom and law are studied by MacIver (*b*, 275–7) and Tufts (5 and 261); between morals and law by Tufts (264–8, concerning conscientious objectors). The natural law of inverse ratio between the sanctions of different branches of ethics is stated by Tönnies (*a*, 41). *Cf.* Giddings (*b*, 195), Ginsberg (166–7) and Schinkler (76–9).

PART III

POWER

CHAPTER VIII

POWER EQUILIBRIUM

§ 1. Introduction

The imperative coördination of behavior forms one of the main classes of social coördination (chap. I, § 4), and legal coördination comprises one of the subclasses of the imperative category (*ibid.*). This is the reason for studying imperative coördination in the sociology of law.

Imperative coördination exists insofar as the behavior of some group-members is determined by submission to other group-members whose behavior expresses the attitude of dominance. Both basic attitudes are in close interdependence, a fact which may be observed in individual consciousness and behavior. The tendency toward dominance among some remains meaningless, if the others are not inclined to obey: how many pseudo-*Führers* we have seen in Europe since the War. On the other hand, to the tendency to obey must respond the will to dominate. When actually correlated, both attitudes give rise to the phenomenon of power.

The existence of power, like the efficacy of ethical rules, is a species of social interaction: individuals influence others and are influenced by others, and the combination of various influences produces the phenomenon we are studying. But in the two cases the interaction is of different types. The interaction resulting in giving force to ethical rules is an equal one: in this process everyone plays the same part, imposing the common will on others and feeling this will imposed upon him. Within power-structures, the social interaction is an unequal one—the waves of influence run only in one direction. Of course, the rulers are influenced by the attitudes of the subjects, but not in the same manner as they influence them: they proclaim commands but receive none; they are obeyed but do not have to obey; they are sometimes begged to act in one or another manner but they do not beg in their turn.

The existence of power influences the determination of human behavior in society; the behavior of the "submitted" is frequently determined not so much by themselves as by individuals in "dominating position." Some kind of a somewhat mysterious unity seems to be created between them.[1]

The phenomenon of power is very complex and a special terminology is necessary to accurately describe it. Hereafter the term "power relationship" will be applied to face-to-face situations uniting dominators and subjects, the term "power structure" to social groups molded by this relationship, and the term "power system" to larger groups consisting of a number of power structures.

§ 2. Polarization

A social group in which the power phenomenon appears is a polarized group consisting of two correlated elements: the active (dominators) and the passive (subjects). Its twofold character is clearly expressed by the term "dominance-submission." The polarization is a kind of "law of nature" which is observable whenever individuals of certain types come in contact. This law applies to animals as well as to men.

As regards human beings, the relationship of dominance-submission may be observed even in the simplest social groups composed of two persons: a married couple, in case either the husband or the wife dominates (of course not every married couple stands in a power relation); two friends, one of whom is the leader and the other his satellite; two playmates in a like relationship; a master and a servant, et cetera.

The same structure remains in force if the number of group-members is increased. In a family the husband may dominate over his wife and children; leadership may of course belong also to the wife or even to the child or to any two members in relation

[1] Tönnies (*d*, 194) expresses analogous ideas: "Power creates a relationship not far distant from that of identity." Allport (*a*, 252) gives a description of suggestion in terms similar to those used in the text as regards power: "The nature of suggestion is that one who gives the stimulus controls the behavior and the consciousness of the recipient in an immediate manner, relatively uninfluenced by thought." About the relationship of power and suggestion see below, § 5.

to the third.[2] Often a child becomes the leader of a group formed by his brothers and sisters, playmates, schoolmates, et cetera.

In the Middle Ages, armies of mercenaries were dominated by their captains. Power is displayed in the relationship of the "chief" and the rank and file—gangsters or racketeers. Domination is sometimes exerted within modern economic or professional organizations; one individual or a group of individuals determine the behavior of others; the same may happen within political parties (especially in the "ruling parties" of modern dictatorships). A Church may also be a power structure, as is so obvious in the Roman Catholic Church, with the Pope as spiritual monarch. The most highly developed of all social groups, the State, obviously belongs to the number of power structures.

The polarization of social groups which forms the essence of power structures is primarily based upon the natural division of individuals into two classes: those of high and low dominance feeling, with an intermediary group in between (Maslov). Stress must be laid upon the word *primarily*, as with development, other types of differentiation are superimposed upon the basic one (chap. X, § 2); but the very possibility of this development and of the existence of such superstructures cannot be explained otherwise than with reference to the basic phenomenon.

The existence of individuals of active and of passive nature and the correlation of this fact with the phenomenon of polarization is beyond any doubt. According to Laski (32), "the tendency of men to accept leadership is vital." "Creatures tend as rapidly as is practicable to assume either the active or the passive rôle," says Allport (160); we may speak with him of a "law of polarity in social contact." [3]

There are individuals with a clearly expressed "will for power," individuals with a strong will dominating their other psychic

[2] *Cf.* the "filiarchic family" (Brown, 223).

[3] This natural law is sometimes treated as an ethical rule. "There is no act more moral," says Carlyle, "than that of rule and obedience. Woe to him that claims obedience when it is not due; woe to him that refuses it when it is." ("On Heroes," lect. VI.) An interesting example of the application of the "law of polarization" is told by Leopold (13). In 1210 the order of *fratres minores* was created on the basis of perfect equality. Seven years later aristocratic tendency set in and its democratic character began to fade.

capacities. Their ability for making decisions and for not vacillating when they have to be acted upon is above the average. Ordinarily they are deficient in the sentiment of pity as regards pain given to others, or at least this sentiment is below the average. They are sometimes endowed with a steel-like glance, with a metallic voice penetrating deep into the consciousness of the listeners. Sometimes they have great bodily strength, sometimes great skill in the art of persuasion, sometimes both.

Such or similar traits are recognized by almost all investigators of the dominator type; these traits may be present in smaller or greater degree. The following descriptions are apposite only to the higher degrees of the phenomenon.

"Ascendance of manner is usually combined with physical power. High motility (rapid and energetic reactions), tonus shown in gesture and ring of voice, erect, aggressive carriage, tenacity, face-to-face mode of address. . . . The air of inscrutability increases submission of attitude through the awe of the unknown and the veneration of genius" (Allport, *a*, 422–3).

According to Merriam (40–4) the following are the domination traits: (1) a high degree of social sensitivity; (2) a high degree of facility in personal contact; (3) great facility in group contact; (4) facility of dramatic expression; (5) facility in inventing formulas, policies, ideologies; and (6) a high degree of courage.

On the contrary, there are individuals whose psychic constitution is more intellectual or emotional than volitional; they are inclined toward indecision; their sympathy with the pain of others often prevents them from acting; they fear failure and its possible results for themselves; they doubt their strength and in this way decrease it; their glance and their voice are average. They may be endowed with bodily strength, but what is bodily strength without a corresponding strength of will to direct it in action? Their attempts to persuade are timid and sometimes too honest; therefore they often remain ineffective.

Is the separation of individuals into those of high and low dominance feeling, into those of "dominator type" and of "subject type" based upon inborn or acquired qualities? It is obvious that the quality of a dominator is but seldom inherited. A cursory review of general history shows that sequences of true dominators on thrones are only of exceptional occurrence.[4]

But the amazingly low number of dominator sequences, of dominant dynasties, does not definitely refute the idea that inheritance plays a part in separating individuals into "dominators" and "subjects."

Dominance and submission are already present in the animal kingdom. Speaking of the attitude of small dogs before big ones, Pavlov wrote: "There is a submission to the will of the stronger, analogous to the prostration of human beings before dominators. This instinct of submission is of course useful from the biological point of view. The passive attitude of the weaker results in the decrease of the aggressive attitude on the part of the stronger, whereas resistance would only reinforce this aggressive attitude and increase its destructive effects" (*a*, 308; *cf.* McDougall, 65).

A number of investigators have shown that the domination and submission attitudes exist at various levels of the animal kingdom; among ants, bees, hens and higher animals of the gregarious type. The appearance of dominance-submission in early childhood (see below, chap. X, § 2) corroborates the idea that these attitudes are based upon groups of inborn tendencies transformed into instincts.

We are perhaps in the presence of two contrary instincts, that of dominance and that of submission. Every individual seems to be endowed, in some proportion, with both, but the distribution of them among individuals is not equal: in the minority the first prevails over the second, in the majority the second prevails over the first. This seems to be a rather contradictory state of affairs. But we possess antagonistic muscles and use them alternately; this means that we give, alternately, opposite impulses to our limbs.[5]

It is probable that a certain inborn distribution of the two in-

[4] The grandfather and the father of Charlemagne were strong dominators like himself; there was, in the history of Russia, a succession of strong grand dukes of Moscow who built up the national Russian State.

[5] Weininger constructed a theory based upon the assumption that the male and female are both endowed with both male and female traits, but in different distribution.

stincts within an individual is not the only decisive factor in his development towards the "dominator type" or the "subject type." The social environment is also of great importance. The practical nonexistence of dominant dynasties may be explained by the fact that strong dominators do not permit strong persons in their environment; if they have male descendants they give them no opportunity for developing the qualities of domination. Their relation to their sons is generally of a kind favorable for creating an "inferiority complex" in the latter. On the other hand, a kind of negative selection plays a destructive rôle with regard to offspring; history is full of revolts of sons against ruling fathers and of pitiless destruction of the progeny in such cases.

This is a process not at all limited to political power. Strong fathers generally fear rivalry of their sons and use their natural power in order to prevent them from becoming dominators. On the contrary, when young men have to grow up without the guidance of strong leadership, in the atmosphere of a merciless struggle for life, the development of a strong character is favored.

We may suppose that a large number of "potential dominators" remain undeveloped as the result of unfavorable circumstances which check the actualization of the inborn instinct of dominance. The vocation of leadership or domination often remains unapplied, like a talent for art, literature, et cetera. Vocations of all kinds are born in quantities superior to the actual need, and a rigorous selection decides whether this or that individual will be given the chance to develop his faculties. This excessive supply of potential dominators explains the somewhat mysterious fact that a dominator is always on the spot when he is needed. Washingtons and Napoleons were probably much more numerous than is known to history. But only to one Washington and to one Napoleon did "fate" give the opportunity to develop their gifts of leadership.

A natural law (almost without exception) might be stated at this place: the number of individuals forming the active center is much smaller than that forming the passive periphery. Nature seems to create individuals of the first type in smaller numbers. Industrialists complain that they are not always able to select the "dominators" (technicians, foremen, officials) they need in their enterprises: they simply do not find enough individuals with the necessary traits. However, the social function of domination demands only a minority of individuals and the social molding of individuals into dominators or subjects naturally results in preparing rather adequate numbers of individuals of both types.

Special studies have just begun to explain why individuals are so unequally distributed between the active and the passive groups. Pavlov's experiments with dogs have shown that it was possible to overcome the reflex of liberty; but it was very difficult, almost impossible, to overcome the instinct of submission and to transform an "obedient dog" into a "free citizen," to create "free conduct." According to certain pupils of Pavlov, free conduct necessitates the application of all the higher psychic functions; it is high-tension work for the brain, whereas, from the biological viewpoint, obedience is much simpler (Drabovitch, 57–60).

§ 3. The Introspective Aspect of Power

From the introspective viewpoint, the basic factor in the consciousness of individuals in a power structure is a disposition to carry out suggestions coming from (willed by) the dominators. This disposition is the very essence of every power relationship. It will become clearer if we analyze a situation in which this disposition is lacking.

If an individual is "free," i.e., stands outside the limits of a power structure, if he is not subjected to some dominator and exercises no domination over others, he himself determines all his acts. Of course, he is influenced by suggestions emanating from others, by their actual words or gestures or his memory of them, and his own suggestions influence others, not only when he actually speaks and moves, but also when his previous words or movements are remembered by others or influence them subconsciously. If there is no power relationship, these suggestions affect the consciousness of our individual just as all other outward actions perceived by him or as other ideas arising in his consciousness according to the laws of association. The general character of the individual and the momentary content of his consciousness will determine whether an introduced or aroused idea will have a positive or a negative affective tone, i.e., whether it will produce a positive or a negative impulse, how intense the affective tone will be, and therefore how strong the motivation. This will determine the rôle of this motive in the everlasting "struggle of motives." An idea suggested by a man to whom one is not bound by a power relationship may be accepted or rejected. In such a case, one feels "free."

The situation changes completely if a power relationship unites the individuals. In this case waves of influence may be observed only in one direction. Volitional acts directed toward the determination of the conduct of others arise only within the active center of the group; they are received only in the passive periphery.[6]

A wave emanating from the active center and represented by words or gestures enters the consciousness of the members of the passive periphery. It is endowed with a specific psychic force: the affective tone of the corresponding motive is determined in advance and also its intensity, its capacity to determine behavior. If *A* (one of the dominators) gives a command or authoritative direction to *B* (one of the subjects) the motive arising in the consciousness of *B* does not become the object of the ordinary elaboration; the character of *B* i.e., his constant motives, and the momentary content of his consciousness play little part in the further psychic process. On the contrary, the imperative motive emanating from *A* has a positive affective tone and is a positive impulse to action. The usual process is, of course, not *entirely* eliminated in a situation of this type, but the motive emanating from *A* has an intense positive coloration just because it emanates from *A*. An order from a dominator may not be carried out, but this happens only when very strong opposed motives are present in the consciousness of the subjected persons. In other words, motives emanating from dominators are very powerful when they

[6] Of course, the passive periphery to a certain extent influences the active power center; but this is persuasion, not imperative determination. The existence of this influence is frequently misinterpreted by theories which consider the behavior of rulers or of leaders merely as the expression of group sentiments or volitions.

enter the consciousness of subjects, *just because they come from dominators.*

The relationship between dominators and subjects forms true dispositions in the consciousness of both. Not only when parents and children are together in one room does a power relationship exist, but also when they are separated by great distances, children retain the disposition to obey commands emanating from parents. The power relationship exists between officers and soldiers not only at the moments when military drill is being performed and the officers determine the behavior of the soldiers by certain preëstablished words representing commands, or when, during a war, the officers send the soldiers to certain death and are obeyed by them, but also during inactive periods, as long as the readiness to obey remains untouched. These are typical cases for the power phenomenon in its latent, potential stage; it is a psychic structure characterized by the tendency to transform itself into an active expression of dominance — submission under proper conditions. An individual may be unaware of being in a latent power relationship but this does not prevent his acting several minutes or even years later according to the "natural laws" of this relationship.

The situation can be summarized in the following way. The power phenomenon may exist as an active process or as a latent disposition. When a command is given by the dominators and acts of obedience are performed by the subjects, the phenomenon is in its active stage. If such a sequence of overt events is not repeated, we cannot yet speak of a power relationship. Only when repeated, perhaps many times, can the power relationship arise. Repetition creates in the consciousness of the subjects a disposition to obey and the corresponding disposition to command on the part of the dominators. Only under such conditions does a power relationship unite group-members.

§ 4. The Behavioristic Aspect of Power

Now let us study the same phenomena from the behavioristic viewpoint. Here the main proposition will be as follows: in a true power relationship (i.e., insofar as a personal relationship between individuals has become an interdependence on the basis of power) acts of submission, which are voluntary in the beginning, have been transformed into habitual, automatic ones, belonging to the category of learned and fixed behavior.

Here are some examples. When you see a "stop sign" you stop without reflection, without being conscious of performing an act belonging in the sphere of a power structure. Members of athletic teams carry out the necessary movements without being aware of the power relationship. The same is true of parent-child, officer-soldier, priest-penitent, teacher-pupil, and numberless other power relationships — muscles work automatically just as a motor works when the proper levers have been manipulated.

How may these facts be brought under the "natural laws of acquired tendencies?" In their rudimentary form, both dominance and submission are inborn or instinctive. On the basis of inborn tendencies, a multitude of acquired tendencies can be and in fact are created. Whenever a power relationship is established by a "powerful" act of the dominator, imperative speech or gesture stimulus, or even bodily domination over the subject, the inborn tendency of submission or already existing acquired tendencies are activated. This happens in a certain set of circumstances, and, according to the laws of learning, every external excitation which coincides with the manifestation of an existing tendency may become a stimulus in an acquired tendency of the same trend. The dominator was seen and heard when an experience of domination took place; seeing and hearing the dominator may become the stimulus in the newly formed tendency. The domination of the master over the serf was often established by a single act of subjection. It may seem strange that the effects of such an act could be felt for many years after, but there is no mystery whatever — an acquired tendency had been established and lasts as long as inhibitory conditions do not appear.

Further tendencies may be created on the basis of already existing ones — inborn or acquired. Even the name of the dominator may become a stimulus in the tendency of submission. This is often used in official formulas. Other symbols of dominance, present when an act of domination occurred, form another group of stimuli; among them "words of command" play an important part.

Returning to one of our examples, that of the soldier almost unconsciously obeying words of command, we may say that the movements of his arms, legs, et cetera, are determined immediately by sound waves, which in ordinary conditions do not possess this stimulating effect; e.g., a person not involved in a power relationship will not obey at all when receiving the same waves. A "beginner" in a power relationship will possibly act after a difficult mental coördination of the excitations perceived by his brain.[7] Obedience will follow much later and usually will be incomplete, the movements not corresponding entirely to the true meaning of the sounds expressing the command.

Why does the soldier behave "correctly?" Because during a certain length of time certain sounds accompanied the display of an already existing tendency of submission (inborn or acquired). In the beginning, our soldier was impressed by the meaning of the words he heard and by the sounds as such; these meanings, through the complex mechanism of voluntary action, resulted in the corresponding bodily movements, which were, of course, carried out quite inaccurately; later on, the nervous current engendered in the sense organ by sound was directed immediately toward the centers ruling the commanded movements,[8] and these movements were performed automatically and, therefore, with more accuracy.

The situation is quite clear if the content of the tendency of submission is simple; certain words of command become the stimulus to a tendency in which the response consists of a series of well-established bodily movements. Usually, however, the content of a concrete power relationship is much more complex. The stimulus expressed in the commanding words, gestures or symbols produces a response which is not determined in advance;

[7] In this case the behavior is voluntary.

[8] This does not necessarily presuppose the localization of acquired behavior systems in specific arcs. Against such localization, Lashley presents good reasons (163); but in any case, some simplified mechanism is obviously present in cases of acquired tendencies as compared with voluntary actions; a sufficient proof seems to be given in the relative speed of both reactions, *cf.* Luriia, 267 *ff.*

it is determined, in the concrete case, by the specific content of the separate stimulus or, more exactly, by something accompanying this stimulus. This determination is, therefore, an "indefinite" one; the response action has to be adapted to the specific form assumed in each case by the stimulating action.

A too simple application of conditioned response theory to the problem seems unsatisfactory; therefore the following ideas are advanced. An act in which the dominance attitude is clearly expressed becomes, in the brain activity of the subject, a generalized inhibition. This inhibition may be also learned and fixed by means of conditioned reflexes or in other ways.[9] In other words, various overt behavior patterns (words, gestures, symbols) which existed simultaneously with the display of dominance, may become stimuli in newly created inhibitions. The attitude of dominance is not only an inhibition of many brain processes, but is also the introduction of a positive cue for a determinate type of behavior; this is generally performed by means of already existing conditioned reflexes or other tendencies associating words (combination of sounds) with determinate speech or gesture responses. Thus the "cue for an outward movement" becomes the unique or almost unique excitation in the brain, because other excitations have been inhibited. This excitation, on its way to the motor center, does not encounter any resistance, which always takes place when other excitations are present, and has of necessity to be carried out.

The situation is somewhat simplified if the dominator stimulus is aimed at inhibiting rather than eliciting a positive act. In this case, the inhibition need not be diffused throughout the whole of the brain. A number of centers remain "free" from inhibition and their relative excitation will decide what the positive activity of an individual dominated by a "negative command" of the dominator will be.

A true power relationship, after obedience has become automatic, is merely a system of acquired tendencies in which the stimuli are represented by words, gestures or symbols of the dominators, and the responses consist of an inhibition of the excita-

[9] By the trial-and-error method or by "inventive learning," *cf.* Tolman, 371 *ff.*

tions which otherwise would prevent the execution of the "indicated" action.

This analysis corroborates the often expressed similarity between power phenomena and hypnosis. Hypnosis also, first of all, inhibits all processes in the brain which might impede the influence of the hypnotist and, in addition, introduces an indication for a certain activity which is necessarily carried out. Most assuredly, the means of establishing a hypnotic *rapport* and a power relationship are somewhat different, and different also are the extents of brain activity inhibited in the two cases — this being larger in the case of hypnosis — but the essence of both processes is the same. The affinity between conditioned reflexes of the submission type and hypnosis has been corroborated by experiments of one of Pavlov's pupils, Professor Platonov (42–3).[10] These experiments prove that individuals who submit easily to hypnotic influence are those whose suggestibility to dominance-submission, i.e., the creation of conditioned reflexes by attitudes of domination, is higher than the average.

Many reflexes tend toward inhibition and, later on, toward extinction, if their stimuli have not been followed often by the response of the inborn tendency, or of the previously established, learned tendency. Acts of command represent the stimulus in our tendency; executing the will of the dominators is the response. Furthermore, for individual *A*, the fact that other individuals — *B*, *C*, et cetera — are also obeying, stimulates a secondary tendency of submission, i.e., acts of command addressed to *B*, *C*, et cetera, and their resultant obedience also become stimuli of obedience for *A*. If *A* notices that *B* or *C*, for whatever reason, no longer obey, the corresponding tendency in *A* is weakened and finally destroyed, and with it the primary submission-reflex of *A*. This is because tendencies form groups and the inhibition of large parts in such groups is diffused to the remainder.[11]

Without being acquainted with the theory of acquired tend-

[10] The contrary physiological evidence of Bass (382–399) is not definitely persuasive, for it is not asserted that hypnosis means the inhibition of every system of reflexes.

[11] Lashley says: "The activation of a habit involves a partial activation of all closely related habit-systems, with the possibility of mutual facilitation" (170).

encies, every ruler uses these principles in practice. This explains what is called the policy of prestige, viz., having once commanded something, the rulers insist on the performance of the orders even though they may realize the command was inexpedient. The nonperformance of *B* would cause decreasing obedience on the part of *A*, and thus would threaten the very existence of the power relationship; therefore rulers strive to prevent any case of disobedience. Such prestige policy may sometimes cost heavily in lives and goods, but rulers frequently regard their prestige, authority and dominant position as more important than such sacrifices.

The prestige policy of rulers is similar to what everyone must do when he automatizes his behavior. As William James (56) put it, "Never suffer an exception to occur till the new habit is securely rooted in your life." Analysis of the methods used by all kinds of dominators reinforces this conclusion. Military drill furnishes a good example. The system consists of everlasting repetition of the same exercises, with a display of force by the dominators (corporal punishment and imprisonment) and with an effort to make the whole conduct of the soldiers automatic. Historically, and to some extent now, pedagogical methods illustrate the same principle. Ritual is another means of creating and reinforcing automatic obedience. Ritual is merely the creation of large systems of acquired and fixed behavior, in which the ritualistic words, robes, utensils, gestures and other symbols have become stimuli to obedience.

Nowadays more elaborate techniques are used. Among these are gigantic military and quasi-military ceremonies, speeches before hundreds of thousands of people, memorial days and periods, dedication of public squares and monuments; the use of flags, decorations, uniforms, et cetera. Such are the methods of inculcating and reinforcing submission today (Merriam, 105). Automatic submission is thought to be the best support of totalitarian governments but to some extent all governments are dependent upon it.

§ 5. The Reality of Power

Every power structure is a complex of behavior tendencies and corresponding psychic dispositions in many interrelated individuals. This interrelation gives to the power phenomenon that quality which makes it so "mysterious"; it also gives it what may be called its "objectivity."

There is no better way to understand the objectivity of power than to imagine or observe an absurd power structure such as an active center composed of nullities acting for obviously egoistic purposes, representing only a small minority, but with the large majority obeying blindly and suffering continual injury. This sounds absurd. Would the subjects not revolt and overthrow the hated and contemptible power and create a new power structure, based upon greater "Justice" and "Welfare?" Sometimes they might, but more often they do not. The above description closely approximates many observed past and present power structures. However, surprise at the passive behavior of the dominated periphery is diminished when we analyze more completely the nature of a power structure.

Every power structure is a historical fact. It arises under certain circumstances as the result of forces which completely explain its structure in the early stage. It continues to exist until other forces arise which are strong enough to overthrow it. The dissatisfaction of individuals with a concrete power structure, their feeling that it is "unjust," "absurd," et cetera, is generally not a sufficient force to destroy it.

What is the exact meaning of the statement that the subjects within a power structure are dissatisfied with their lot and with the rule of the dominators? The answer to such a question frequently assumes that if the subjects were free from all domination, if they had a free opportunity to create a new power structure, they would create one quite unlike the existing one. The content of the if-clause is never realized, however, for being under domination, the subjects are not "free" and have to create a new power system not in a social field where no power is exerted, but in one where they first have to overthrow an existing power system. The holders of power are generally aware of the situation and use their force to prevent upheavals. Their strength is based upon the fact that in the previous period a multitude of tendencies of submission were created and that the commands of the dominators became stimuli for eliciting acts of submission. Every power structure, once established, continues because of social inertia, and "social inertia" in this case is merely the existence of these dominance-submission tendencies.

The difficulty of transforming subjective attitudes of dissatisfaction into a social force strong enough to overthrow a power structure increases with the dimensions of the system. In a small system (or social field) it is obvious to every member that the power relationship consists merely of the dispositions of the partners; but even within a group of two (husband — wife, father — child, master — slave, the dominating playmate and the subjected one), there is a certain tendency to see not two, but three elements, viz., the dominator, the dominated and the power relation itself. Such an idea is often unconscious and, of course, not very permanent, since an effort on the part of the subject or negligence on the part of the dominator, such as his failure to use his power, are sometimes sufficient to destroy the illusion of this third element, of the objective relation uniting the two, and even to destroy the power relationship itself.

As has been observed by Simmel (*a*, 92 *ff.*) and further analyzed by S. Frank, the situation changes completely when the group is increased and consists no longer of two, but of three members. In a system of three elements, *A*, *B*, *C*, there are three links, *AB*, *AC* and *BC*, and for every member one of the links is independent of his will, is "objective," e.g., *BC* for *A*, *AC* for *B* and *AB* for *C*. Imagine that the illusion of the "chain of power" has been destroyed in one of the members, say *A*. The links *AB* and *AC* cease to exist, but the link *BC* continues to exist, and the corporate influence of *B* and *C* upon *A* may be strong enough to withhold *A* from acting in a manner corresponding to complete freedom. *A* learns from experience that the idea of objective links or chains of power may be an illusion, but that notwithstanding he must perforce behave *as if* they were real.

Imagine now that the number of group-members is larger. With every new member the number of links which are "objective" for each one increases very fast. The speed of this increase could be accurately calculated. Let us speak of the number of group-members N. Then the number of individual links within the group is equal to $\frac{N(N-1)}{2}$ because every member is related to every other except himself, and, on the other hand, because every link is a double-sided one. Of these links, $N - 1$ are personal for member A in the sense that he personally takes part in them. The number of transpersonal links for every member, will therefore be equal to $\frac{N(N-1)}{2} - (N-1) = \frac{(N-1)(N-2)}{2}$. Applying this formula to a group of a hundred members, we arrive at the result of 4,851 "objective links" for every member. Now almost every "objective" link means for A a reinforcement of the necessity of submission, because in every group-member the submission reflexes are reinforced by the submissive attitudes of the others.

Vaguely feeling such a situation, A will, of course, be inclined to consider the power system as "objective," and of course it is transpersonal for him, as also for every other group-member, whereas it is not transpersonal for their totality. The mistake of A will therefore consist in transforming a situation which is transpersonal *for him* into a situation absolutely transpersonal. The mistake is intelligible and excusable. Moreover, everyone acts as if it were not a mistake but an actuality.

This is a new argument showing that a power system is not a mere sum of the submissive attitude of the subjects (Korkunoff's theory). The sentiments (subjective attitudes) of others are objective facts. One has to submit even if one is disgusted and rebellious; and every group-member has to do the same.

§ 6. The Power Defense System

For every concrete system a tendency to restore the initial or the "normal" situation in the case of minor disturbances is essential. Imperative coördination truly exists only if minor disturbances (cases of disobedience, of acting without regard for the structure of domination-submission) are counterbalanced by social activity which tends toward — and generally succeeds — in securing the general readiness of group-members to behave in accordance with the power structure of the group.

Minor disturbances, when repeated, generate social resistance to power. The greater the tendency to resist, the stronger the power waves emanating from the active center must be. If conditions are in other respects unchanged, the resistance will be stronger if the power structure is based upon brute force in contrast to a structure based on consent; resistance will be stronger if the dominators use their power to satisfy their egoistic instincts, rather than in the interest of general welfare; resistance will be stronger if the dominators try to break the given order and to replace it by a new one, rather than to aim at maintaining the old order; resistance will be stronger if the dominators strive to achieve aims not supported by public opinion as contrasted with a policy supported by the latter, et cetera. In any case, to the latent force of resistance on the passive periphery a certain intensity of combined will on the part of the dominators must correspond.

Social activity displayed in order to maintain the integrity of the power structure might be called the "power defense system." This may be of different types. If there is imperative coördination in its "pure" form (without connection with ethics) dominators will simply display force in order to maintain the situation and to instill new inhibitions in their subjects (by means of fear). Considerations of a purely utilitarian type will determine what measures will be taken in a concrete case; no definite manner of imposing the will of dominators, no limit for their intervention, will be fixed in advance. Such methods as violence, deceit, corruption and abuse of privilege will be ordinarily applied.

If imperative coördination is united with ethical coördination, power display is submitted to ethical rules. The power defense system is transformed into a system of legal sanctions (chap. XI, § 7).

The tendency for a polarized social group to restore itself to its initial situation might be called imperative equilibrium. The sum of the activities which actualize the relationship between dominators and subjects forms imperative coördination. This actualization is carried out by means of commands on the part of dominators and acts of obedience on the part of subjects.

The instrument of dominance, command, may be opposed to persuasion which is the instrument of influence outside power structures. Persuasion may create imitation; if this is so, a certain interdependence in the behavior of individuals is created: the successful persuader has become a "leader," the imitators his "followers." But persuasion is never more than a suggestion of ideas, whereas domination is an imposition of will.[12]

Commands may be general or special. The first embrace whole categories of cases; they express the will of the dominators as regards the behavior of the subjects, if a certain situation occurs. Special commands take into consideration only concrete cases; they express temporary injunctions of the dominators. Austin, the great authority on the notion of command, illustrates the difference in the following way. If someone orders his servant to rise at such and such an hour on such and such a day, this is a special command; but if the injunction is given to repeat the same act every day, the command becomes a general one (93).

Another example: a despot may order a certain tribute to be raised in this or that town only this once — a special command. On the other hand, an organized State must order the collection of definite taxes every year in certain amounts — a general command.

It is theoretically possible that a power structure could be actualized only by means of special commands. In practice this does not happen, if the power structure is stable and consists of a group larger than the family. The tendency to conserve energy, which plays a large part in the behavior of everyone, induces the dominators to actualize the power relationship by means of general commands more frequently than by special commands. These latter are commonly applied in addition to the former ones, in order to specialize or reinforce them.

[12] The boundary between *domination* and *leadership* is not always completely precise. Leadership may gradually evolve into domination; domination is sometimes transformed into leadership. In many cases true domination is called leadership.

Of course, a concrete order given to a single individual does not create the coördination of behavior in the true sense of the word; but concrete orders addressed to many result in similarity of their behavior; general orders always create such a similarity, assuming they are obeyed. This is the means whereby imperative coördination is created: patterns of behavior are imposed both by similar special commands and by general commands.

Whether such commands actually will create imperative coordination depends on the relation between the force of the active center and the latent force of resistance. This relation may be called "the potential" of a power structure. It would be an error to suppose that every type of power structure was endowed with a constant potential. On the contrary, the potential may vary within each type.

It is generally supposed that in slavery the potential is always very high. Such an opinion is not corroborated by the facts. According to Westermarck, (678 *ff.*), the slavery prevailing among the Malays is generally mild. Travelers have related that they had difficulty in distinguishing the servile portion of a household from the freeborn. Intra-tribal slaves are generally better treated than extra-tribal or purchased slaves. In ancient Mexico there were various classes of slaves, but it was a rather mild subjection. According to the laws of Manu, there were slaves of seven kinds.

In the second place, there are enormous differences in the power potential in the various types of States, beginning with high values in despotic States, and falling almost to zero in democratic States, so long as no acute social conflicts exist.

If the potential is near zero, it sometimes becomes dubious whether there is a power relationship at all. For instance, when people begin to follow an ethical leader, a transitional situation may arise. Then, at a certain moment, the ethical leader may become a ruler or dominator. The line between situations where this has not yet taken place and others where it has already happened will not be very precise. But this is a familiar situation to students of social phenomena.

§ 7. The Social Function of Power

Concluding this chapter we might ask the question whether we are able to ascribe to imperative coördination a precise social function? The idea has been expressed that within power structures men are ordered to take a share in an historic destiny (Ortega), or that the function of power is to assist the group in maintaining its customs, its purposes and its attitudes undamaged by the chance ineptitude of less experienced or less skillful members (Whitehead, 69), or that the function of power is to secure mutual advantages to both sides (Ehrlich, *a*, 90).

Imperative coördination is so common in social life that it is hard to believe it could possess *definite* social functions. In juxtaposition to every one of the quoted opinions cases could be indicated in which the corresponding phenomena do not take place: no "historical fate" is carried out by African tribal despots; the maintenance of group custom is not the aim of modern dictatorships; mutual advantage is not the aim of slavery.

The social functions of power structures are as many as there are types of dominators and of dominations. This does not prevent the following statement from probably being correct: "As long as there is any doubt as to who commands and who obeys, all the rest will be imperfect and ineffective. Even the very conscience of men, apart from special exceptions, will be disturbed and falsified" (Ortega, 155).

BIBLIOGRAPHICAL NOTE

Power is a basic social phenomenon which has interested humanity from Homer and the Greek tragedies until our day. The struggle for political power is one of the main features of history and dominant themes of literature. Statesmanship is the art of using political power adequately. Revolutionists sometimes devote their whole lives to the "gaining of power," i.e., to attaining the dominant positions within a large social group.

The phenomenon of power has been analyzed many times, but usually in only one of its aspects and from some specific point of view, such as the power of the State, and, as this is power in its most complex form, students have not succeeded in finding suitable explanations. The power phenomenon in its totality has received little scientific study. Generally it has been studied from the legal point of view. Students have tried and still try to describe what human behavior "ought to be," within a power structure, according to legal rules. This is, of course, useful, but it does not explain adequately how the State and personal or collective dominators exercise their power in actual life.

In this connection, only the will to dominate has been studied; the readiness to obey has been neglected. This will was frequently conceived as similar to individual will; such procedure was necessarily valueless for causal explanation of the actual power phenomenon.

Developing an idea already expressed by Hume, the Russian jurist Korkunoff (*a*, 22–4) made an attempt to explain the phenomenon of power from the opposite side. For him, the domination ascribed to the monarch or to the State is an illusion. What actually exists is the sentiment of submission common to all citizens, their feeling of dependence on leaders. This was an important but insufficient step toward explaining the power phenomenon. If the sentiment of dependence does not correspond to any actuality, Korkunoff's theory is like explaining religion as an invention of priests. If the sentiment of dependence corresponds to something really existing, the problem remains unsolved; further research is needed to discover this "something."

At the end of the nineteenth century, the power phenomenon became an object of sociological study. Early sociological studies are those of Simmel (*a*), Tarde (*b*), Mumford, Havelock Ellis (*b*) and Leopold. Of modern works those of Bogardus, Pigors, Merriam and Russell are especially devoted to the study of this phenomenon. Excellent chapters on the same subject are contained in the socio-psychological works of Allport (*a*, 398–402), Brown (329–80) and LaPiere (403–65). The best applications of the sociological viewpoint to constitutional law are those of Jellinek (*d*) and Duguit (*a*, *b*, *c*).

Definitions of social power, similar to that given in the text, are to be found in the works of Max Weber (*c*, 28) and Horvath (213–14); other definitions in Tarde (*b*, 117 *ff.*) and Darmstaedter (*a*). The difference between domination and leadership is especially studied by Pigors (81–2, 101–26); the author traces the limit between them in a somewhat different way, expanding the notion of leadership.

The empiric law of polarization was mentioned by Chapin, Laski (32), Bogardus (8), Allport, LaPiere (291) and Delos (97). Traits of dominators have been collected by many authors, for instance, by Rolin (97), Vierkandt (82–3, 87), Bogardus (207–13), LaPiere (293), and Merriam (40–4). Important are the statements of Thomas (420–3) based upon the study of primitive behavior. Modern literature suffers from overstressing the personalities of Lenin, Mussolini and Hitler. An interesting study of Latin-American dictators is contained in the paper of Rippy; the traits noted by this author corroborate common opinion.

The status of the problem of heredity in domination is discussed in the book of Bogardus (32–48); *cf.* Sorokin (*b*, *c*) and Sherif (184–5). The study of the heredity of character traits is now one of the major objects of investigation in Pavlov's Institute near Petrograd (*cf. Izvestia*, February 22 and 24, 1937).

Dominance-submission in the animal kingdom is studied by Schjeldrupp-Ebbe and Zuckermann. The genesis of the instinct of dominance is discussed by Kotliarevsky (16–17) and Post (*b*, I, 356 and II, 87). The latter's study is based upon concrete investigation of primitive behavior.

The rôle of social environment in forming individuals of the dominator type is stressed by Merriam (35), Bogardus (53–61); Brown (356) seems to recognize only social influences.

A good study of obedience from the behavioristic viewpoint is that of Malan. Petrazhitsky's theory concerning "indeterminate emotions" is expressed in *b* (13–14); *cf.* Pavlov's statements (*a*, 395–6).

The correlation of hypnosis and power was studied by Sidis (308); *cf.* Allport (*a*, 249), Brown (338). Very important is the work of Platonoff.

Concerning the practice of domination: Pew (52), Pigors (131–41), MacIver (*a*, 25–8), Merriam (105), Leopold (303–9).

The terms *potential*, as regards power, has been introduced by Brown (344). A good study of the conditions which necessitate a tension in power is that of Ross (342).

CHAPTER IX

DIFFERENTIATION AND INTEGRATION OF POWER

§ 1. The Spatial Identity of Power Structures

Imperative coördination is the result of the fact that a certain social group has been polarized, has become a power structure: within such a group men act in accordance with orders issued by the active center.

It would be an ideally simple situation, if power structures corresponded to clearly delimited "social fields," or in other words: (1) if every individual were influenced by one power center only and (2) if the barriers between power structures were so insurmountable that no efforts could be reasonably displayed in order to enlarge the dimension of a structure. If such were the case imperative coördination would be a relatively simple object for study.

The actual situation is completely different. Within every social field many power structures coexist. Their active centers struggle for dominance, i.e., for priority before other centers sending waves of influence into the same social field, and for expansion, i.e., for the possibility of determining the behavior of more and more individuals.

Humanity represents the largest possible social field. This field can be considered as being under the influence of as many power centers as there are independent States. The situation seems to approximate the "ideal case" mentioned above, for there are precise limits for the exertion of power by every active center, these limits corresponding to political frontiers. But (1) existing power centers are, commonly, involved in an interplay tending to establish dependency relations among States (great powers and satellites); (2) these centers struggle against one another more frequently than they remain in peaceful relations.

On the other hand, the social field represented by humanity is subjected to the influence of non-State power centers aiming at universality. Oecumenical churches are one example. International labor organizations (especially the "Comintern") are another.

Let us now observe a comparatively small social field, for instance a small town or a rural district (in a civilized country). Individuals belonging to this field form (1) a number of complete power structures and, in addition to this, (2) parts of power structures extending beyond the limits of the social field we are examining. Complete power structures would be: (1) families of the patriarchal type; (2) parishes of different denominations, insofar as real power is exerted by religious groups; (3) some local economic enterprises of the authoritative type; (4) local schools; (5) sundry athletic teams; (6) possibly one or more criminal gang, et cetera. Our social field would, of course, be part of an area with political subdivisions, of an area where large economic enterprises or professional organizations display power, where oecumenical churches or parties endowed with the character of dominance have adherents or are in search of new ones, et cetera. The relationship between these power structures might be peaceful, but might also correspond to the picture given above as regards the "total" social field.

Every power structure is a specific coördination of human behavior. But the coexistence of many systems of coördination within the same social field, especially if active power centers are struggling against each other, means disorganization of behavior. Nevertheless complex coördination of behavior in the basis of power is possible because of (1) the differentiation of power structures, making them dissimilar and helping them to become permeable to each other, and (2) the integration of power structures, based upon the principle of hierarchy.

Before beginning the study of such aspects of power, we have to define more precisely the type of unit which we are to take into consideration when speaking of possible correlations between power structures. In other words, it is the problem of identity as regards social groups molded according to the power principle.

This problem presents two aspects, the spatial and the temporal. The second aspect belongs to dynamics and will be discussed in the next chapter. From the spatial viewpoint, the identity both of the groups imposing patterns and the groups submitted to the patterns is decisive: if, within a given social field, either the groups imposing patterns (the active center) are not the same or the groups subjected to the patterns (the passive periphery) are diverse, the existence of two or more power structures must be admitted, which of course may be integrated into some higher unit.

There is only one principle of integration and that is hierarchy. But there are many principles of differentiation. From this viewpoint power structures may be classified by taking into consideration (1) the volume of social activity coördinated, (2) the relative dimensions of the active center and of the passive periphery, (3) the personal or the institutionalized character of the domination, and (4) its legal or despotic character.[1]

§ 2. Specialized and Generalized Power Structures

From the viewpoint of social activity determined by power structures, the latter may be divided into two main classes, specialized and generalized.

In a specialized power structure, dominance-submission is limited to definite domains of human activity. For instance, a school may be considered as a power structure: the directors and teachers are dominators, the pupils subjects; but the domination concerns only one part of the lives of the dominators and pupils, that bearing on education; outside the school organization schoolteachers are not dominators, nor pupils subjects. As another example, we may consider an athletic team; an unfaltering obedience to the leader is required of all members, but only as regards sport and the preparation for it. Further examples of specialized power structures are economic firms, labor organizations, et cetera (*cf.* Merriam, 66–71).

The clearest type of generalized domination is that of the State. The State potentially dominates its members in all respects; there

[1] The dimensions of a power system, as has already been remarked, influence its internal structure and may therefore be used for purposes of classification; on the other hand, differences in the "potential" could be used for another classification if they could be measured.

is no realm of human life which might not be dominated or regulated by the State. Of course, it is not actually necessary that the State should fully use this faculty; the modern democratic State (especially in the liberal variety which prevailed during the second half of the nineteenth century) is characterized by relatively large "areas of freedom." Subdivisions of the State (provinces, et cetera) are also generalized types of domination. Together with the State they form what is called "political domination."

There are certain power structures which may sometimes belong to the one, sometimes to the other category. In former times the family was something of a generalized type of domination, influencing group-members in all kinds of activity. At present, in most civilized societies, it is rather a specialized power structure, limited to the domestic order. During certain epochs the Church, especially the Roman Catholic Church, claimed a right to determine human behavior in its totality; at other periods, the Church was limited to determine only the spiritual life of its group-members.

The distinction between generalized and specialized power structures is of the greatest importance from the viewpoint of the higher imperative coördination of human behavior.

A peaceful coexistence of power structures within society is possible as long as the structures do not claim universality, but remain "specialized." A political party, based upon strong discipline (and forming therefore a power structure) but limited to political affairs, does not enter into any conflict with a sport organization or a church or an educational institution, even if these organizations are coexisting power structures. The same individual may take part in many power structures of the specialized type; he may be a dominator in one (leader of an athletic team) and a subject in another (ordinary layman in a church).

Specialized power structures may peacefully coexist even if they pursue similar aims. Insofar as families bear the character of power structures they do not enter into conflict with each other, for membership in more than one is impossible from the start. Different political parties or professional organizations may also have an aspect of power structures but nevertheless coexist without conflict: these are "alternative power systems." The existence of one political party is conditioned by the existence of another or several others, the existence of one professional organization by the existence of another. The competition between alternative power structures *may* grow into a true conflict; but such conflicts do not generally destroy the power structures; on the contrary, such conflicts sometimes give them new vigor.

Quite different is the situation if two or more generalized power structures struggle for domination within one social field. If, in such a case, the claims of all the active centers were to be satisfied, the bulk of the group-members would have to form at the same time the passive peripheries of two or more power structures. The behavior of every group-member would be determined by commands emanating from two or more active centers. It might happen that for a certain time no concrete conflicts would arise: commands emanating from active center *A* would be compatible with those emanating from center *B*. But such a fortunate harmony might not last forever. At a certain moment two commands emanating from different centers would come into conflict, putting the subjects into a difficult situation: they would have to choose between obeying *A* but disobeying *B*, or obeying *B* but disobeying *A*. In either case the center whose command remained unfulfilled would insist: for insisting on the careful fulfillment of commands belongs to the very essence of the prestige policy, in conformity with the general technique of reinforcing acquired tendencies of behavior. In our case the individual is not able to behave simultaneously in accordance with the commands of *A* and *B*. Disobedience toward at least one of the competing centers is thus a necessary consequence of the conflict-situation. And disobedience decreases the force of domination and later on destroys the tendency of submission. Therefore every attempt to introduce two or more generalized power structures within the same social field results in destroying all but one structure, or even all structures without any exception — if the structures, that is, are not coördinated in hierarchical formation.

The best historical example of a destructive conflict of two generalized power structures is that between the emperors and the popes during the later Middle Ages. The theory of the "two swords," the spiritual belonging to the pope and the temporal to the emperor, was based upon the fiction that both State and Church were specialized power structures compatible within the same social field. In fact each structure claimed to have the priority, to be more generalized — a claim which, if true, should have resulted in the subjection of the other.

The other possible issue of a conflict between general power structures which arise within the same social field is the creation of a hierarchy: one of the structures becomes the "superior," the other or the others the "inferior."

Hierarchy is the usual manner of coördinating the relationship between generalized and specialized power structures. Insofar as a generalized power structure is supposed to determine all spheres of human activity, it also potentially determines those of specialized power structures. Under such circumstances the normal development of these latter is possible only if they form parts of a hierarchical system headed by the generalized power structure.

No difficulty arises if the State (i.e., the typical generalized power structure) is democratic, inclined to "self-limitation"; it leaves free or not regulated areas for the activity of individuals and social groups, and this "free" space may be occupied by special power structures. But historically the modern democratic State is an exception. The democratic State of ancient times was a total or unlimited domination of the collectivity over the individuals. Such are also the autocratic States, sometimes only potentially, sometimes even actually: the theocratic State of the ancient Orient and of medieval Europe, and again the modern totalitarian State, both in its Communist or Fascist variety.

Within the modern totalitarian State there is no free space left for individual or group activity, and specialized power structures have to be transformed into subordinated branches of the generalized power structure or to enter into a conflict with it. Both in Russia and in Germany the continuous conflict between the new State and the various churches is based upon the internal incompatibility of these specialized power structures with the totalitarian State: in such a State even the churches have to become branches of the state administration, and this, on the other hand, is incompatible with the very essence of the churches.

§ 3. The Relative Size of the Center and the Periphery

A differentiation of power structures, from the viewpoint of the relative dimensions of the active center and the passive periphery, seems to conform to the well-known Aristotelian classification of States into three groups, based on whether the rule was of the One, of the Few or of the Many.

Within every larger power structure supreme power may belong to only one person, in the sense that his commands determine the behavior of all other group-members. Such were and are (1) despotic and autocratic monarchies; (2) modern dictatorships of the "leader type" (Russia, Italy, Germany) and (3) the Roman Catholic Church, especially after the Vatican Council of 1870, which definitely gave to the Pope the supremacy over the Oecumenical Council. But one person cannot really dominate over a large mass. If a power structure is large, it is generally subdivided into a number of smaller ones. A large State is divided into provinces, provinces into minor districts, these districts into urban and rural communes. A large army is divided into corps, divisions, regiments, battalions, et cetera. A large school is divided into classes. Insofar as the Church becomes a specialized power structure, its organization presents another example of hierarchy. Even in large families of the primitive type, when they were headed by patriarchs and were formed by a number of married couples with their children, a certain hierarchy could be observed: all had to obey the patriarch; but the wives and the children had also to obey their husbands and fathers.

This phenomenon is a quite general one, based upon the experience that a dominating will is unable to determine directly the behavior of too large a number of subjects. Specialists in military affairs assert that a commander ought never to direct immediately more than five subordinates; this rule is rigidly observed in the structure of modern armies.

On the contrary, what is the exact meaning of the assertion

that in power-structures of the opposite type power belongs to the "many," this assertion being in our day transformed into the assertion that, in democracy, power belongs to all, i.e., is shared by everyone? Such a statement would mean that within democratic societies everyone is dominator and nobody subject. This is, of course, impossible. The meaning of democracy is not at all that of a group composed only of dominators without subjects. The true essence of democracy is twofold: (1) the dominators are not "one," not "a few," but "many" (but, of course, even in democracy forming only a minority) and (2) the dominators receive their positions with the consent of the others; their power is not imposed by force, but founded "on the consent of the governed."

The difficulty of classifying States (and large social groups in general) in accordance with the Aristotelian scheme was realized by Montesquieu. His ideal State, which he called the "moderate government" and which he wrongly thought had been achieved in the political system of Great Britain, was a combination of monarchic, aristocratic and democratic elements. In modern times an obvious mixture of the three elements constituting the basis of the Aristotelian classification is realized in power structures very different from Montesquieu's ideal type, namely, in modern dictatorships, where the "leaders" (dominators) are the monarchic, the "ruling party" the aristocratic, and the "representative" institutions (soviets in Russia, parliament in Italy, Reichstag and plebiscite in Germany) the democratic element.

A modern investigator, Horvath (199–206), made an attempt to replace the Aristotelian scheme by another. According to him, we should distinguish between synarchy, monarchy and polyarchy. Synarchy is the primitive power organization, or rather *lack* of power structure, with a strong socio-ethical coördination of life. Monarchy is characterized by concentration of power and its pyramidal structure. Finally, polyarchy is a structure characteristic of the age of the decline of power. In a polyarchy power is distributed according to a skillful plan, so that a single power no longer exists, but nevertheless anonymous powers are able to carry out the general plan. This is, of course, not a successful solution of the problem. Synarchy is rather anarchy, the contrary of power. Polyarchy corresponds to democracy in its misinterpretation (see above) and in addition makes power a kind of mystery. Monarchy remains in this scheme the only realistic form of power.

In actuality it is not monarchy but oligarchy (rule of a minority) that is the actual arrangement of every power structure. Monarchy forms merely a particular case of oligarchy: in very small groups the minority is reduced to one. Democracy, as has already been said, refers not so much to the structure of the active center, as to the manner of selecting leaders.

Very often in larger and more developed power structures the power center as such becomes structuralized. In accordance to the specific Constitution of a State, the monarch, the president, the premier, et cetera, may be considered as the head of the administration or as its supreme ruler. He has at his command a certain number of immediate helpers called ministers, and these in turn a certain number of higher officials. All are members of the same active center; the activity of each of them refers to the same passive periphery in its totality. Therefore it would be erroneous to describe the structure formed by them as a system of power structures: no, they form together the active center of one structure. But this active center is, in its turn, differentiated and organized.[2]

In a modern democratic State further complications are possible. Individual dominators have to act in accordance with the will of a body of individuals known as "the electorate" who represent the "public opinion," or the "sovereign nation," according to the formula used in continental Europe.

Works of specialists in constitutional law have shown that the term "representation," in this connection, is somewhat misused: the representatives are not supposed to act according to the mandates of the voters but according to their own insight. A representative body is merely a collective dominator, included in

[2] In integrated power systems there are immediate power relationships at least between the supreme ruler and secondary rulers, between secondary rulers and tertiary ones heading their sections or clans, between tertiary rulers and the corresponding groups of members of the passive periphery. Generals have to be in touch with the commander-in-chief, officers with generals, soldiers with the officers. A ministry is in touch with the higher representatives of power in the provinces, and these representatives with officers of inferior categories, et cetera.

the complex structure of the active center. If this kind of structuralization is carried out, the will of the active center, determining the conduct of the passive periphery, has then to be formed as a result of a complex series of interactions among certain individuals.

The structuralization of the active center is not at all limited to the State. Large churches possess similar structures in their active centers. Insofar as economic powers exist in the specific form of joint-stock companies, a similar phenomenon is possible. According to many continental European laws a board of directors (an oligarchy, with the chairman or managing director representing the element of monarchy) is supervised by a "Council" elected by the shareholders and having to take part in the most important decisions.

§ 4. Personal and Transpersonal Domination

A very important variation within the complex of power structures might be expressed by the contrast of the terms *personal* and *institutionalized* or *transpersonal* domination.

In a personal power structure dominance-submission is a sum of the face-to-face relations of individuals. The relationship may be direct if the group is small or, in modern times, even if it is large, as the means of communication (radio) have become so excellent that millions can be frequently put in immediate contact with one (or a few). In this case men obey other men, and men command other men.

There are, on the contrary, power structures in which dominance-submission seems to be primarily related to supernatural beings or to abstract ideas: men obey not the concrete dominators, but the beings or forces which the dominators are thought to represent: God, or the State, or the principle of justice, et cetera; other men command not as individuals, but as representatives of these beings or forces. Domination is transpersonal, the power structure is transformed into a social institution.

There is, of course, a certain element of illusion in such attitudes. Not superhuman beings or abstract ideas are social forces, but only individuals imbued with such ideas or endowed with the prestige of representing them as superhuman beings. But it is an illusion that cannot be uprooted and which determines human behavior as much as if it corresponded to actuality.

This illusion is closely related to the "objectivity" of every larger power structure (chap. VIII). An individual "feels" that the power structure to which he belongs is something much higher and stronger than himself. There is, moreover, a general tendency to personify relationships. Generally people are inclined to see new emergent entities in the relation between two "substances" or in the qualities of substances. In this way primitive men created an imaginary world of gods, genii and ghosts: the forces of Nature — i.e., properties of material things — were personified; and until recently remnants of such beliefs could be observed in the ideas of the less cultivated classes of advanced societies.

This tendency played and continues to play a large part in science and in the current ideas on nature. Warmth was, until the end of the eighteenth century, considered to be an imponderable fluid, exuded by wood, paper, et cetera, when they were burned. The same happened with electricity: the theory of two imponderable fluids, corresponding to positive and negative electricity, seemed to be a sufficient explanation fifty years ago. Now we know that electricity is a specific relationship between the particles of atoms. But the tendency to hypostatize substances is so strong that even now many people, when the modern theory of electricity is explained to them, shake their heads and declare, "Still, you do not know what electricity *is*." For the average man explanation means finding a substance.

Very strong was the same trend in sociology. National and, later on, social mysticism have already been mentioned when discussing the origin of ethical rules. Social mysticism, ascribing a personality, a super-individual existence to social groups, remains even now the basis of more than one sociological doctrine.

This is the way in which the belief comes to prevail that a concrete domination is the display of God's will, of the State's will, of class will, et cetera. These transpersonal dominations are, in the common belief, considered to act in the name of general ideas: God or the gods are imposing justice, or the State is tending toward a condition of common welfare, or the class is securing its historical mission. Such general ideas or tendencies, ascribed to the transpersonal dominators, might be called "principles of domination." It is possible that many principles of domination would be simultaneously ascribed by group-members to one particular domination. This may happen in two ways: either many compatible principles are ascribed to the domination by common opinion; or several incompatible principles (for instance, common welfare and egoistic class interests) are ascribed by fractions of a divided opinion.

The preceding statements should not be understood as implying the negation of the real existence of the State or as an attempt to discuss the theological problem of the existence of God. The idea is rather merely to stress the fact that power is always a relationship between individuals. The State is such a relationship. This relationship is an actuality, but is not a transpersonal entity endowed with individual will; the will displayed in power structures is always human will, the will of individuals. Ruling in the name of God remains the rule of men over men; within a theocracy, just as in every other power structure, the relationship to be studied is that between individuals.

Of course, personal and transpersonal domination do not completely exclude each other. There may be an intermediary type: domination may be ascribed to an abstract idea and the actual dominator considered as its instrument; but, in addition to this, the actual dominator may be supposed to be the true and unique incarnation of the dominating idea. This seems to be the essence of "charismatic domination," a rather obscure notion used by Max Weber (*c*, 140 *ff.*). Modern dictatorships obviously belong to this type.

There is no doubt that an institutionalized power structure differs in many aspects from a personal one. First of all, in a purely personal power relationship the death of the dominator or of the principal one among several dominators, even the decline of his bodily or psychic forces, very often result in a weakening of the power structure and finally in its total suppression.[3]

[3] A good example is that of Primo de Rivera's dictatorship in Spain (1923–29).

The modern family is, more than the primitive one, a personal relationship. With the death of the head of the family the old "home" generally comes to an end. On the contrary, the primitive family was, to a certain extent, a transpersonal domination, based upon the principle of worshiping one's ancestors or cultivating the soil in common. In such a family the death of the head of the family did not signify the destruction of the power structure: the eldest son or the eldest brother took the place of the deceased, and the structure continued almost unchanged.

The same also happens in larger power structures, if they are institutionalized. The death of the usurper generally means the end of the concrete power structure founded by him; unrest, upheavals, civil war, et cetera ordinarily follow. The weakest point in the structure of modern dictatorships (in Russia, Italy, Germany, Poland, et cetera) is just this: the power of the ruler is essentially personal (based on specific personal properties of the ruler, in spite of the fact that he is considered to be the incarnation of the dominating idea) and no one knows who will be capable of succeeding him.

But the death of a monarch, of a president, of a prime minister or of a director of a corporation does not have the same effect. *Le roi est mort, vive le roi!* The personal element in the power structure is reinforced by an "abstract" one, and at moments when changes of persons might endanger the further existence of a power structure, the "principle" is there in order to render the transition quiet and peaceful.

Secondly, the transformation of a power structure into a transpersonal one results in important modifications in the process of polarization. When the power-structure is personal, the polarization takes place by individuals of high dominance feeling being naturally attracted to the active center and those of low dominance feeling toward the passive periphery: the distribution of individuals between the two poles of the group is completely natural. If the power structure becomes transpersonal, the distribution of individuals between the poles comes to be dependent not only on their characters, but also on the influence of the principle. We may observe this phenomenon already within the family: the power in the family is generally based upon the principle of seniority; this principle generally corresponds to the natural relationship of group-members if the family is a small one; but in large families (formed not by two, but by three or more generations) individuals of an active nature, at a disadvantage according to the principle of seniority, may belong to the passive periphery, and individuals of passive nature favored by the principle, to the active center. Tensions, conflicts, struggle for power, sometimes destruction of the concrete power structure are possible consequences.

This is also the weak point in monarchy and aristocracy in States or in other large groups: the principle of birth decides who has to occupy the first place in a concrete power structure, but Nature is not at all inclined to adapt herself to human institutions. Those designated to be rulers may be weak persons; strong personalities may arise within the social circles destined to form the passive periphery. The result is the rise of potential active centers of dominance within the passive periphery and a struggle for power between them and the already existing traditional centers.

A somewhat artificial distribution of individuals between the active center and the passive periphery is not limited to monarchy and aristocracy. Every transpersonal power structure is exposed to the same dangers if social stratification becomes too rigid, if social advancement is not easily enough secured for individuals of an active nature born within the passive periphery. Such is, for instance, the danger inherent in plutocracy, a type of power structure widely spread in modern times under the guise of democracy.

Thirdly, the mode of action of the dominators is very different in transpersonal power structures from what it is in personal ones. In a power structure the will of the dominators determines the behavior of the subjects. But this does not mean that the will of the dominators itself is not determined by something in turn. In a transpersonal power structure the rulers have to act in a manner adapted to its "principle." In some cases they themselves believe in the principle and act in conformity with this belief; in other cases they do not believe in the principle, but nevertheless have to act as if they did believe, because if they acted otherwise they would gradually destroy the principle upon which their power is based and at the same time their own situation as dominators.

In a transpersonal power structure are the dominators themselves dominated by ideas or by other individuals? A domination of an idea is only a metaphorical formula. As regards domination on the part of other individuals, in our case only a domination by "all," or by the totality of group-members could be taken into consideration. But a domination by all is a domination by none: for domination is conditioned by polarizing a social group, by separating it into an active center and a passive periphery.

In a democracy, "all" have to take part in the formation of the representative body and, sometimes, in the selection of supreme rulers also. Insofar as "all" are divided in opinion, the majority has to replace them. According to common opinion, democratic government is an instrument giving the majority the rule over the minority. And as 51 per cent constitute a majority and 49 per cent a minority, a democratic structure would allow 51 per cent of the citizens to impose their wills on the other 49 per cent, even if the occasion for disagreement concerned internal conviction (imposition of a religion or official philosophy), or even if, in the nature of the case, no similarity were necessary at all.

Democratic government may be of this kind, but may be of another also. A sublimated theory of democracy is expressed by Kelsen (*h*). According to him, democracy is the rule of the majority, but with a consideration for the minority interests; not the will of the majority is to be imposed, but the will corresponding to the resultant of the forces represented by the majority and minority wills taken together. It is another question whether a democratic structure of this type ever existed.

In any case, even in a democracy the "majority" only help to select and to inspire the ruling minority. Therefore we can assert that the submission of dominators to an abstract principle is quite another social phenomenon than the submission of the subjects to the will of dominators. The transformation of a domination into a transpersonal one results in far-reaching changes in the situation, but it does not destroy the position of the dominators. Their will is molded in conformity with the principle of domination, but it is *their* will that continues to determine the behavior of the subjects.

The situation we are discussing is characterized by the institutionalization of the power structure as such, but not necessarily of the total behavior of the individuals subjected to the structure. The attitude of dominance on the one hand, that of submission on the other, have become socially determined (this is the true meaning of institutionalization), but within the concrete power structure acts of the dominators may remain free from every institutionalization, i.e., from any subjection to definite patterns. Their inspiration will decide in any concrete case what behavior corresponds to the principle of domination. Insofar as their behavior is not necessarily institutionalized, that of subjects cannot be subjected to precise patterns, with the exception of the formal pattern of obedience.

The institutionalization of power is of course very helpful from the viewpoint of the higher imperative coördination of behavior. An institutionalized power structure is endowed with a principle of domination. Every principle of domination is a value, actual, hypothetical or false. Values, according to their nature, tend to form themselves, in the human mind, into hierarchies. Hierarchies of values naturally open the way for the creation of a hierarchy of power structures.

§ 5. Legal and Despotical Power

Closely correlated to the distinction between personal and transpersonal power is that between legal and despotical power. For the transpersonalization of power structures opens the way for combinations of power display with the efficacy of ethics. Justice may become one of the principles of domination and justice is *the* ethical principle. Where it is one of the principles of domination, the general commands of the dominators take on the features of ethical rules.

A purely personal domination can scarcely be "legalized;" but within the intermediary class of "charismatic domination" this is already possible. In any case, the institutionalization of behavior goes one step further: not only the general attitude of domination-submission becomes institutionalized, but also the single manifestations, at least in the majority of cases.

This process is not at all a necessary one: Sometimes power structures may be institutionalized, but not legalized. Therefore we might distinguish between legal domination and illegal or despotic domination.

Two problems must be discussed in this place: (1) Is integral legal domination possible and (2) is integral despotic domination possible?

1. The first problem can be stated as follows: Insofar as power has not transformed all its general commands into ethical (legal) rules, a certain sphere of activity remains where special commands may be given freely, without rupturing the legal order. But if all general commands have become ethical (legal) rules, such space no longer exists. The question arises: Does not this mean a complete elimination of all personal elements in the legal power structure? In other words: Can a legal order possibly exist in which the dominators only carry out the abstract principle of domination?

In modern science the idea has been more than once expressed that this is the true meaning of democracy. According to the opinion of the Dutch jurist Krabbe, democracy implies the sovereignty of law in which the will of the nation is expressed. Democratic rulers must hence strip themselves of everything personal, since their task is only to execute the common will. Is this theory correct?

It is obvious that no democracy, ancient or modern, has been able altogether to eliminate the personal element in domination. Of course, democratic rulers have to adhere strictly to the law, but this limitation is rather negative than positive. Ethical rules, including laws, can never completely determine the conduct of men. Even in tribunals, which are rightly considered to be the instruments for the actualization of law, a complete predetermination of human activity is impossible. Judges have to search for the historical truth in order to apply the appropriate rules; but no law, no general rule can indicate in advance every step which may be expedient in a concrete situation. Therefore even judges are granted "discretionary powers:" within the limits set down by law, they have to use their own intelligence in order to attain the chief aim of judicial procedure, namely, to secure the triumph of law.

This personal element is quite obvious in the administrative activity. Every individual belonging to administration is bound by law. But it is only a very superficial view which regards the activity of an official as "the execution of law" only. Law cannot foresee the concrete needs of the community at a given time and has to give discretionary powers to the administration.

According to the British constitution, the prime minister possesses the right of legislative initiative; he has to propose bills to parliament calculated to secure the general welfare at all times. But we cannot imagine a law that would indicate under what circumstances the prime minister was to use this right. Even less readily can we imagine what the substance of the bills to be introduced by him should be. In introducing a bill for a certain purpose, the prime minister displays the personal element in domination, but without transgressing the principle of legality.

No one would deny that the United States is a democracy; but neither could any one deny the personal rôle of President Wilson in involving the United States in the Great War or of President Roosevelt in combating the economic depression.

This personal element is not by any means limited to the top of the power structure. Officers of administrative boards have much more to do than simply to apply law: their activity is frequently of a creative sort, within the limits imposed by legal rules.

In continental jurisprudence the view prevails that in such cases law grants certain individuals with a discretionary, personal power. From the sociological viewpoint we must judge somewhat differently. The discretionary power of judges and of officials is that part of social power which has not been limited by ethical rules. The lack of limitation is, of course, only partial, as there is no positive, only a negative restriction. This is the difference between discretionary power compatible with law and arbitrary power incompatible with it.

Naturally the question could be raised as to whether we are not in the middle of an evolution leading toward the complete elimination of the personal element from legal power structures. We are unable to foresee the future; but it may safely be asserted that a complete elimination of every personal element from domination would be a rather dangerous experiment. For the impulse towards dominance is deeply rooted in human nature and becomes sometimes the dominating passion. In a society without any personal element in domination, persons endowed with highly developed tendencies of the active type would be inclined to create a type of domination more suited to their preferences. Such, for instance, was the history of the establishment of Communist rule in Russia in 1917. The Provisional Government consisted of persons inclined toward ultrademocratic theories. To show personal domination and to make use of force seemed to them to violate the principles of democracy. This might have been harmless in a country where everybody held the same views; but this was not the case. There were people there with clearly articulated inclinations toward becoming rulers of the personal type, namely the Communist leaders. And almost without struggle they became dominators of the country and proceeded to rule it in an absolutely undemocratic way.

From these remarks we may conclude that as long as the inclination toward commanding others is not uprooted from human nature, to eliminate every personal element from domination is a danger for democracy. The problem of democracy as a legal order is not at all that of abolishing the personal elements in domination. The real problem is that of securing a steady ascent of leaders whose mentality will be in conformity with the prevailing principles of domination in their most sublimated form.

2. The second problem could be posed in the following way. Is integral despotic domination possible? Is not every power structure necessarily also an ethical system? [4] This opinion is expressed with great vigor by the outstanding German jurist, Kel-

[4] The term "ethical" is applied in its generic sense (*cf.* chap. VII); the substitu-

sen (*g*, 44, 91). For him the highest of all power structures, that of the State, is merely a personification of the order of law. In other words, State and law are the same; law is social order and the conception of the State is a superfluous repetition of this order, due to the tendency of the human mind to personify abstract notions. This is a theory parallel, and yet standing in contrast to that of Petrazhitsky. For Petrazhitsky law was a phantasma, an erroneous projection of individual psychic phenomena into the trans-subjective world; for Kelsen law has a very positive existence, but the State is a projection into the world of fictitious personalities of the abstract conception of legal order. The logical consequence of Kelsen's theory is that every act of State domination is at the same time a display of law and that every act in any way related to law is an act of the State; therefore, according to Kelsen, when somebody buys a package of tobacco in a shop, he acts as an organ of the State; his act should be attributed to the State.

It is not necessary to share Kelsen's theory in order to contest the validity of the idea of a distinction between domination of a legal and a despotic type. Many authors who are rather conservative as regards the correlation between State and law express the same opinion. "Arbitrary rule is not in contradiction to law. It is either unrighteous law or illegal behavior," says Radbruch (*a*, 43, footnote).

There is, of course, very much of the purely terminological in this conflict of opinions. Observation shows that there are two "ideal" types of domination, with a gradual transition between them: a type characterized by the limitation of power display by ethical rules and another type characterized by the absence of such limitation.

A lack of ethical limits is typical for the early instances of power. In its early stages of development the power of the head of the family was unlimited; this is so well known as regards the Roman family that arguments would be superfluous. Less well known is the large scope of paternal power among the nations of the ancient Orient and among barbaric nations of pre-Columbian America.

tion of "moral" instead of "ethical" would completely vitiate the proposition in the text.

The early State was also unlimited in its power. The great oriental despotisms (Egypt, Assyria, Babylon, Persia) were ruled on the basis of the "good pleasure" of the monarch; there were no limitations of any kind. The power of the early German kings was of the same type, at least during war. A good example is that of the Empire of Runjeet Singh in Punjab (*cf.* Maine, *c*, 381–2 and Carter, 197). In the world of savages despotic rules is widespread; especially typical are or, perhaps, were the conditions in Africa described in the interesting book by Post (*a*).[5]

In our days a serious attempt to construct State domination without any connection with ethics has been made in Soviet Russia. We are often told of Soviet law. A law of revolutionary origin may exist as well as a law of traditional origin. But what is called Soviet law is sometimes not law at all, especially as regards the period of War Communism (1917–21) and that of the Second Socialist Offensive (1929–34). Lenin, the creator of the new State, often acknowledged that a decree (the name given to a general command issued by the new government) was not a rule binding the revolutionary power itself; it was, first of all, a means of propaganda. The principle of legality, which dominates in countries where power is governed by ethics, was replaced by the principle of revolutionary expediency, for the welfare of the revolution had become the supreme principle of domination in Soviet Russia. According to this principle, every local authority had to act in conformity with the general orders issued by the central authority, but only insofar as this would not run counter to the

[5] According to him, the heads of the families and of the tribes often possess despotic power over their subjects, who are considered to be their slaves. All the Kasembes are regarded as slaves of the king. The king decides about the marriages of the young people without any possibility of appeal. The kings of the Gold Coast do anything they please. In the tribe of Amazulu, the king is a true despot. The Damel of Cayor has the power of life and death over his subjects as well as full power over their estates; the same is true as regards the king of Kimbunda. In Dahomey, even tribal chiefs are regarded as slaves of the king. The king of Matiamvos once entered his capital, killing everyone he met on his way, in order to increase his authority; similar events take place among the Niamniam. Another author says: "The system of government of Jukun is of a highly despotic character. The King is supreme. There is no appeal. He has the power of life and death. He could order the deposition or the execution of chiefs. He could take as wife not merely every unmarried girl, but the wife of every one of his subjects" (*cf.* Thomas, 437).

interest of the proletarian revolution. If these interests commanded an act contrary to general orders contained in the decrees, the contrary or illegal act had to be carried out, since revolutionary expediency was to prevail over legality. According to this general principle, executions took place even when capital punishment was abrogated by decree. During the curious period called the "New Economic Policy" (1921–29), these ideas were clothed in the external form of law. Codes were promulgated; but in every one of them a "safeguard clause" was introduced in order to secure the further domination of the expediency principle.

How do we distinguish despotic rule from legal order? The best distinction was given by Stammler. According to him, the characteristic feature of legal power is that the commands of the rulers remain obligatory for the rulers themselves as long as they are obligatory for subjects. This does not mean that the contents of the commands should be identical for both, but merely that such commands bind both sides as partners, whereas within despotic rule the commands of the rulers do not bind the rulers (Stammler, *a* and *c*, especially 483–500). Developing Stammler's ideas one could say that, within despotic power structures, general commands of the dominators are technical rules showing the best means of profiting by the situation; for subjects, obedience to these rules is the best means of avoiding the anger of the dominators and of acquiring their favor.

There must be a specific mentality underlying a despotic rule. This is what in Europe is popularly called "Hottentot morals." Such mentality is not at all confined to lower types of civilization; Tolstoi, in *Anna Karenina*, gives a marvelous description of a personality of a high social level who views rules as binding only for others, but not for himself (part I, chap. 36).

This peculiar mentality influences the behavior of rulers when decreeing "rules of conduct" (general commands). If one decrees rules which are applicable only to others and not to oneself, one may act in an entirely egoistic way: one's personal welfare may determine the content of the rules and the welfare of others may be left without any consideration at all.

Quite different is the situation if one decrees rules which are applicable not only to others, but also to oneself. In this case the ruler tries to consider the situation from a higher viewpoint. This need not necessarily be altruistic, but at any rate it will be social: he will give the problem which arises the solution which seems to him most compatible with the interests of all, including himself. His personal egoism, his consideration of his own interests, will incite him to act according to the rules which Kant thought to be the supreme principle of morals: "Act in such a manner that the rule of your conduct may be accepted as a rule for the conduct of everyone."

It is decisive, for the behavior of the subjects within a despotic power structure—, that they cannot count on the behavior of the dominators as being in conformity with the general commands; for these commands do not bind their authors, and strict obedience to a general order issued yesterday may, today or tomorrow, call forth anger and revenge on the part of the dominators. Every individual must be aware of the passing whims of the dominators and try to adjust his conduct to them. Troubled and insecure must be the ordinary state of mind of the subjects in a power structure of this type; and this refers not only to the States, but to tyrannous or arbitrary domination in the family as well.

The existence of these two types of power structures, depending on their relation to ethical rules, is so obvious that one wonders how it is possible to deny it. The basic ground for repudiating this theory is the over-logical character of thought of many writers, for instance of Kelsen. Kelsen identified every order with *legal* order and then "successfully" proved that a personalization of order was superfluous. Actually there are many types of order not related to law.

Kelsen's theory (as well as similar theories of other authors) is incompatible with history. If State and law are the same thing looked at from different points of view, then the historical struggle of European nations to endow their political life with the principle of legality lacked meaning and sense. For, according to the theory discussed, there is no fundamental difference between the rule of the Stuarts and parliamentary government in modern England: tyrants acted as representatives of law in just the same manner as did righteous rulers, for whom justice was the supreme ideal. Every State, as such, is justified from the viewpoint of law. On the contrary, the value of law becomes doubtful; for any domination is related to law, the most tyrannical as well as the most benevolent.

The importance of the contradistinction between legal and despotic rule for the problem of higher imperative coördination is obvious. If institutionalized power structures are more easily built into hierarchies than personal structures, then legal power structures, where the degree of institutionalization is much higher, must be still more adapted thereto.

§ 6. Hierarchies of Power Structures

The general form for the higher imperative coördination of behavior is the integration of power structures by means of hierarchy. What are the peculiarities of human behavior within such complex structures?

In a nonhierarchical power structure, every individual takes part either in the active center or in the passive periphery. In hierarchical power structures, a certain number of individuals stand in an intermediate position; they belong to the active center of the lower power structures and are dominators there, but at the same time they belong to the passive periphery of the higher power structure where they are subjects. Their will determines the behavior of subjects in the lower structure but their will is, in turn, determined by commands emanating from the active center of the higher structure. If this higher center is inclined to determine in detail all the processes in the lower structure, then the members of the lower active centers become merely distributors or conductors of the higher will. In other cases, the rulers of the higher structure allow a certain degree of freedom to those of the lower, and within this free space the latter act just as if there were no hierarchy. The situation of intermediate persons may be dual in attitude. How can this be brought into conformity with the fundamental difference between high-dominance and low-dominance people?

Both types are expressions of the relative predominance of the tendencies of dominance or of submission, but both tendencies, insofar as they are inborn, are present in everyone, as well as acquired tendencies based upon the inborn ones. Everyone is able in some degree both to obey and to command. In a simple power structure, only one of these two latent abilities is used and is developed in each individual; in a complex structure, based upon a hierarchy of simple ones, many individuals have to use both abilities alternately.

What is the nature of a multitude of power structures united into a hierarchy? Every power structure is a concrete system, in the sense explained above (chap. II, § 1). Systems united by hierarchy form a new system, a complex system, a system of systems. In a hierarchy of power structures the separate existence of each unit structure does not disappear, but all of them taken together form a new unit with domination-submission as the link between the central system and its satellites. The continuity is primarily related to the active centers: every hierarchy of power structures is, first of all, a hierarchy of active centers.

Complex systems are very common in organic structures. Returning to a previous example, we may say that the solar system is complex: the earth and the moon, Jupiter and its satellites, et cetera form so many concrete systems united by gravitation. But the central members of each of these systems are subject to a larger system with the sun at its center. The complexity of the structure does not even stop here: the sun is a member of a larger unit formed by a system of stars.

In every system of power structures one of the structures appears to be not only relatively, but absolutely superior: it is the system forming the top of the structure, the active center of which is not submitted to any other. A generalized (not specialized) system with an independent, "supreme" active center is the State.[6]

A complex system can be efficient only if there is a certain order establishing the function of every member in corporate activity.

[6] Several power structures of a second class, if they belong to the category of generalized ones and if they have formed independent structures in the past, are, perhaps improperly, also called States.

If the power system is transpersonal, the principle of domination may decide which will be the order prevailing in the hierarchical system of powers. Therefore several scientists have concluded that power systems of a higher standard, which are always hierarchical, are necessarily based upon law.

This opinion should be rejected. Law is only one of the possible principles of domination which can furnish a basis for hierarchical order. In a society imbued with religion the hierarchical order may be based upon the latter; such was the case in some ancient theocracies, among others in that of the early Hebrews. But an order, as a complex of efficient rules, may, even in our days, be not at all an order of law. Efficient rules of domination (general commands of the rulers) determining the character of the power hierarchy may be nonethical, merely technical rules. In such a case a hierarchical system of powers may remain outside the realm of law. This is the case within the despotic State. These remarks refer, of course, only to exceptional cases; in general a hierarchical system of powers is an order of law. But they are sufficient to indicate that the equation of "hierarchy of powers" and "legal order" is only natural, not necessary.

More correct would be the following formulation of the relation between power systems and legal order. Well-developed power systems are much more frequent in societies with advanced differentiation than in primitive societies. Complex power systems are able to carry on higher social functions. One of them is to secure the efficacy of law and to help it develop in accordance with changing social needs. A power system endowed with such a function is legal domination, and it could be shown that law actually exists, i.e., is in force, only insofar as it is supported by power structures. There is no necessary antagonism between power and law and he who wants to improve law should never forget that an efficient power structure is a necessary condition of it.

BIBLIOGRAPHICAL NOTE

The general problem of differentiation and integration of power is scientifically *terra incognita*. Of course, very much has been done in constitutional law in the exploration of the problems of state sovereignty and of federal structure. On the other hand, material concerning the structuralization of active power centers is to be found in every textbook on "Government." An attempt to give a general classification of power structures in their interrelation has been made by Merriam (48); this author recognizes the "fundamental similarity between political and all other forms" of power (*ibid.*, 20).

Nobody has expressed better than James Bryce the idea that democracy does not abolish leadership (domination in our terminology), but merely creates a formal technique for the selection of leaders. Kelsen's theory of democracy is contained in his book *Vom Wesen und Werte der Democratie* (*h*). The common view on the majority-minority relationship in democracies is described by MacIver (*a*, 225) and Adams (139). The relationship people-parliament is discussed by Jellinek (*d*, 571 *ff.*), Kelsen (*a*, 525–7), Duguit (*a*, I, 345–6), Hauriou (*a*) and many others.

Ideas expressed in the text as regards personal and transpersonal, legal and illegal domination correspond to the problem generally studied in sociology and social psychology under the rubric of "Institutional Behavior." *Cf.* Allport (*b*), Judd, LaPiere (383–402), Hamilton, Hart, Chapin. The text differs from the customary descriptions in the following points: (1) institutionalization is described as a species of the genus of coördination, (2) institutionalization is brought into correlation with power, and (3) a distinction between transpersonalization and legalization is made.

About the general tendency to abstraction and personification: Wundt (*a*, 219–310), Robinson (123–5) and Meyerson.

An excellent study of "rigid stratification" is given in Sorokin's *Social Mobility* (*d*, 533–6). The peculiarities of behavior within transpersonal power structures are studied by Pigors (67). The possibility of misusing transpersonalized power is discussed by Tufts (351 *ff.*).

Kelsen's theory of the identity of State and law received a definite form in his *Allgemeine Staatslehre* (*g*). He is followed by Morgenthau (74). Horvath (201) seems to follow Kelsen, but later on (211–12) says: "Not every power presupposes law. This must be asserted only of the highest social power which is the source of law." This is a State theory of law incompatible with Kelsen's doctrine.

Descriptions of despotic government may be found in Maine (*c*, 381–2), Westermarck (I, 93–8; II, 89, 130 *ff.*), Post (*a*), Makariewicz, Thomas. Concerning revolutionary expediency in Soviet Russia *cf.* Timasheff (*c*, 130–153).

"Sociological" definitions of the State are given by Horvath and Max Weber (*c*, 19): "The State exists if the staff of a political union successfully displays the monopoly of a legitimate physical compulsion." *Cf.* MacIver (*a*, 122).

The problem of federalism was painstakingly studied in German sciences after the creation of the German Empire. *Cf.* Laband (I, 129 *ff.*), Jellinek (*c*), Gierke (*a*, 61–72). Of later authors, Triepel should be mentioned. Kelsen (*c*, 55 *ff.*) marked the failure of all attempts to define the State without applying the notion of sovereignty (supremacy). Gierke (*c*, 96) and Gurvitch (*a*, 140) consider that within a federal state sovereignty belongs to the concrete system it forms together with the members of the Union (not to the federal State alone).

CHAPTER X

CHANGES IN POWER

§ 1. The Temporal Identity of Power Structures

If we observe a certain social field at two different moments, sufficiently distant from each other, we discover that the distribution of power structures has changed. Some of the power structures observed the first time have vanished, new ones have been created; others have been transformed, both from the quantitative and qualitative viewpoints: they have increased or decreased in dimension or passed from one class to another. Their interrelation has also changed: power systems have been disbanded, new ones created, older ones transformed as regards the intensity of hierarchization.

Concrete power structures have a kind of "natural history": they are created, develop and eventually decline. According to their "social age," power structures have different traits, which constitute their variable elements, whereas the power relationship itself, i.e., the existence of an active center and a passive periphery, is the constant element. It is obvious that, in order to study this natural history, some agreement concerning the temporal identity of power structures is necessary.

The identity of the subjective elements of power structures (individuals endowed with the function of command or having to obey) is not required for the continuous existence of the structure; this is not a peculiarity of power structures, but true as regards social groups in general. Therefore it must be the objective elements (links or chains of power) which provide the continuity. These links correspond to systems of acquired tendencies of behavior, similar in different group-members and interrelated in such a way that the obvious existence of such systems in one individual means a reinforcement of the system created in another, or *vice versa*. Destruction of the totality or of very large parts of these similar and interrelated systems means therefore a breach of continuity, destruction of identity; but on the contrary, so long as such systems continue in large part to exist there is continuity or identity. The death of a monarch, or of a large number of citizens (through epidemic, famine, war, et cetera) does not destroy the power structure represented by the State; but a "total" revolution, breaking the large majority of links, does. From the juridical point of view it is dubious whether the Soviet State continues that of Czarist Russia. But it is sociologically undeniable that the power structure of modern Russia is different from that of pre-revolutionary Russia: for the tendencies of submission existing now are in no sense derivatives of those which existed before.

On the contrary, internal transformations of power-structures, their gradual shifting from class to class (chap. IX), do not destroy their continuity or identity. Groups united by uninterrupted imperative coördination must be considered as units when studying changes in power.

§ 2. The Growth of Power Structures

There is in the history of every power structure a period when polarization is not yet a definite state, but is rather in process of becoming such. During this period, the polarization is "natural," i.e., corresponds completely to the contrast between individuals of high and low dominance feeling. Of course, the appropriate conditions for the birth of a new power structure must be present. These conditions are (1) the existence of an objective need for imperative coördination, (2) the lack in this particular part of the social field, of an adequate power structure and (3) the coexistence of elements which, if joined, would be capable of forming a power structure, with its active center and passive periphery.

It must be emphasized that there is a certain element of chance in the creation of power relationships. Chemical elements with a specific affinity, i.e., with the property of combining to form a new compound, may exist for centuries without displaying this affinity. A chance event bringing them together is all that is necessary to call into being their latent properties. In a similar way dispositions of dominance and obedience may remain latent, and chance events result in bringing such dispositions together, thus creating a new concrete power structure.

The existence of appropriate conditions, especially of the face-to-face contact of individuals with polarized tendencies, may be called a "power situation." The transformation of power situations into power relationships and structures may be observed within social groups of the most diverse types.

In a group of parents and children the parents are, for a certain length of time, relatively superior or more active as compared with the children; their bodily strength and their powers of persuasion are incomparably greater. But this situation does not always last for a long time: if parents are weak or passive, and the child active, the situation is suddenly reversed, and the child becomes the tyrant of the house. Sometimes the rise of a "filiarchic" family is foreshadowed by the half-conscious tyranny of small children (crying to be taken up at the age of three to six months).

The domination of husbands over wives, quite general in primitive society, is chiefly based upon the rôles played by men and women in the sex relation. But if the wife is of higher dominance feeling than her husband, a complete reversal of the primitive relation is possible and happens not only among cultivated people, but also among primitive tribes.

If a certain number of children are invited to play together or happen to meet in the street, within five minutes they will have a leader or even several leaders, if the group is large, and the selection will have taken place quite unconsciously, without the children being aware that several of them have become "rulers" and the others the "ruled."

Suggestive are also situations when people have to work together without any previous preparation. The most obvious case of this sort is that of an accident taking place on the highway, the railway, et cetera. People have to help the victims, pull them out of the wreckage and transport them to the nearest hospital. From the outset certain individuals are selected as leaders, and it is they who organize the work of the others; generally they are willingly obeyed.

A similar polarization takes place when, because of the collapse of normal economic organization, long queues or bread lines are formed: individuals are sure to appear who try to create order, while the other people comply with their commands.

In many cases individuals of the leader type try to find and organize potential followers of the subject type. This is the ordinary way of creating a political party or a league with a definite aim; but in the same way a resolute criminal brings together a gang of associates. The origin of the State seems to have been along similar lines. In the beginning the State was an organization cutting across traditional divisions of a tribal character based upon blood relationship. Bold young men formed groups of armed followers and went in search of their fortunes in unknown countries; if they were successful in fighting neighboring tribes, whose leaders were of course less active, they became dominators and the vanquished tribes became their subjects.

Of course, the power relationships forming a new State do not generally make such a break in the continuity as those mentioned above. The State gradually destroys the domination of the tribes, but tribal discipline forms the basis for the new order. When, during the later Middle Ages, absolute monarchy struggled with feudalism, feudal symbols were incorporated into the new power structure.

The military origin of the State continues, even today, to exert an influence on the distribution of power structures within the "total" social field. "The civilized nations," says Pareto, "are occupying territories by force, and no other principle can be thought of to justify our present-day territorial divisions" (962).

§ 3. The Growth of Power Structures (*continued*)

Like every other social process, the establishment of a concrete power structure must be based upon social interaction, upon individuals' influencing others and being influenced by others. In our case the interaction is an unequal, but correlative one: authoritative suggestions emanating from some must be received by others, and their behavior must be modified correspondingly. The first impulse may emanate from the active as well as from the passive side.

It is characteristic for an individual of high dominance feeling to behave as if a power structure in which he stood in the active center were already established; this is his natural response to various stimuli, and this natural response is reinforced by experience corroborating its effectiveness. A command given with an air of finality, or a gesture of the same sort, interrupts the normal psychic current in the consciousness of the receivers; the imperative motive introduced by this command becomes the only motive present in consciousness, the influence of the more constant motives forming the character of the receiver being temporarily canceled. From the behavioristic viewpoint, imperative words or gestures become stimuli to which the response will be the performance of the imposed action. The first time this occurs it is not a manifestation of a true power relationship, for the imperative motive (stimulus) does not become decisive as a direct result of its origin: it is merely a power situation. But when two individuals, one of high and the other of low dominance feeling, once came into contact, expressing their natures freely, the tendency to command on the one hand, to obey on the other, easily arises. A power situation thus becomes a power relationship. Let us call this method of establishing a power relationship "direct attack."

Sometimes the action initiating a power structure takes still more dramatic forms: after a conflict the individual who is to become a "subject" is physically dominated by the individual who becomes the ruler. In modern times surrender in war means only that one has become prisoner; in ancient times it meant slavery, which established the most complete relationship of dominance-submission. The moment of bodily domination was only a short one: its motivating force, however, endured a long time, possibly for the whole life of the subject. In the first few years after the establishment of the relationship, the slave would remember the deathly fear he had felt when overcome by his present master; later on the inclination to obey would become a fixed tendency.

Sometimes it is even unnecessary to establish actual bodily domination over the subject; the fact that others have been subdued by a masterful individual suffices. It is related that among the Eskimos men of great courage established power by killing everyone who opposed them (Thomas, 419). In other words, force applied to a few reduced the rest to obedience. Mass surrender in war is based upon the same psychology.

Establishing power by struggle for supremacy is a phenomenon we are able to observe in the animal kingdom. The same happens in groups of children. The domination of a boy within a group very often arises after a fight, during which the relative strength of the various members is disclosed and the true situation of bodily domination established.

Direct attack or the struggle for supremacy are not the only means used by future leaders to create a power structure. Threats of the evil consequences of disobedience and promises of recompense in case of obedience are two further closely correlated means. Whereas the methods previously studied are based upon an actual show of force, the last two are based upon the creation of an impression of power which may not correspond to the truth. During the early stages of social development the belief in curses and their potency played an important part. The method of promises is applied already in the early stages of social development. Among the Eskimos, dominators make particular efforts to supply their followers with an abundance of food or to give them presents at festivals (*cf.* Thomas *ibid.*). The "spoils system" still existing in this country is an example of the same method in a highly developed civilization. If applied to larger masses it is called demagogy. Demagogic persuasion on a large scale is propaganda, which, of course, is not only an instrument for creating power, but also for reinforcing and enlarging power already gained.

The technique is not confined to political groups. For instance, when a leader founds a "gang" he awakens the sentiment of cupidity in his future followers by promising them large rewards if they give him power.

The first step toward the establishment of power structures is sometimes made not by the active, but by the passive side. Very often individuals of a passive nature feel the absence of leadership as the lack of something necessary. "For many persons life is heavy with fatigue. I do not know what to do with myself, is the cry . . . of the adult on many occasions" (Merriam, 111). Such people wish to be liberated from the task of deciding their behavior themselves. If they have the feeling that there is someone "superior," they readily abdicate their will in favor of his.[1]

In other cases fear and expectations, used sometimes by individuals of active nature in order to create power structures, arise spontaneously within the consciousnesses of the more passive individuals; the corresponding excitement is relaxed only when they have found leaders whose protection would give them a sense of security and even the hope of an improvement in their lot. Typical was the origin of the feudal order in Europe. Weak individuals, finding no security in troublous times, were on the lookout for protectors and gave over into their hands a portion of their personal freedom and of their estates; in return for which they received the promise to be protected against robbers, adventurers or other strong men.

Motives of a higher sort may play their part in establishing power structures which originate from the passive side. Men may be convinced that acting together, in a corporate way, is expedient for the general welfare; feeling no special vocation for leadership, they look around for leaders and, after having found persons who, they believe, possess the necessary qualifications, begin to obey them. Such was the beginning of many patriotic movements in different countries invaded by foreign armies or ruled by governments despised by their peoples. One of the most suggestive historical examples of this kind is that of the leadership of Joan of Arc. The "miracle of Joan of Arc" consisted, actually, in a strong trend toward national leadership felt by a large number of French patriots and in their simultaneous decision to incarnate their vision in the person of the shepherdess of Domrémy.

Finally, imitation plays an important part in the formation of power structures. A concrete power structure springs up; many

[1] Rougier says (80): "The man of the new, post-war epoch is, above all, an anguished man, living in the uncertainty of to-morrow, demanding to be relieved from the effort of thinking and of making decisions for himself, in whom physiological misery and profound demoralization have developed a latent instinct of servitude, a need for being regimented and commanded."

people already obey the new leader; this small group is surrounded by others who are still neutral, not polarized from the viewpoint of the new power structure, or standing outside it. Among these "outsiders" individuals of passive nature will, of course, prevail in number; observing that many individuals already obey the new leader, some of this neutral group will feel inclined to act in the same way. Gradually, without being able to say when and how it happened, they will be incorporated in the new power structure, and their behavior will act contagiously on that of other individuals not yet attracted by the new center. It is, of course, this tendency to follow suit which explains the quick spread of dominance and sometimes makes a power structure grow as swiftly as a rolling snowball.

It would be wrong to suppose that every concrete power structure arises by means of only one of the above described processes on the active or on the passive side. In practice these processes act at the same time in various combinations. Establishing a new power structure, the future leader may combine the method of direct attack (by word, or gesture) with intimidation or demagogic promises. Awe, inspired by men recognized as superiors, may often act at the same time as the tendency toward imitation: the sentiment of superiority may be induced by imitation as well as by fear or by expectation of improvement to be achieved with the help of the new ruler. The correlative character of the processes within the active center and the passive periphery of a concrete power structure often results in parallel currents on both sides—an active behavior which tends to inspire fear and, on the passive side, mass behavior expressing fear; a direct attack within an atmosphere of awe or an attempt to influence by demagogical promises may take place within groups which are already on the lookout for leadership.

§ 4. Tendencies in the Development of Power Structures

Transformations within power structures consist of manifold fluctuations of concrete structures from one type to another. Monarchies are transformed into oligarchies or democracies or *vice versa*. Personal power structures are transpersonalized, or transpersonal personalized. Despotic structures become imbued with ethics or legalized, legal power structures return to a state of despotism. Disintegrated power structures are united into hierarchies, but hierarchies are, in turn, sometimes disintegrated.

There is indeed a certain prior tendency in the development toward transpersonalization, legalization and hierarchization of power structures, whereas the opposite transformations are rather symptoms of decay. Much more unpredictable are transformations between the forms monarchy, oligarchy and democracy. The belief prevailed twenty-five years ago that democracy was definitely gaining the upper hand; later political development effectively demonstrated that the line of development was more complex than had been anticipated. Concrete transformations of power structures from this viewpoint have been thoroughly studied by historians of constitutional law.[2]

Transpersonalization seems to be the rule in every large and durable power structure. Within transpersonalized structures further changes are possible, depending upon changes in the "principle of domination." The earliest principle of domination seems to have been that of "God's will": dominators were considered to rule not in their own name, but in the name of God or of gods, as His or their representatives: *rex vicar dei*. This is the origin and the essence of the theocratic State, which played such a large part in human history, in ancient times as well as in the Middle Ages, until the seventeenth or eighteenth centuries. At present many sociologists contest the theory of F. de Coulanges (131) and Sir Henry Maine (*b*, 26–49) that primitive society was dominated by the religious idea and A. Comte's theory of a "theological stage" of mentality corresponding to the dawn of human thought. But nevertheless the enormous part played by religious ideas during the early stages of social development is an irrefutable fact corroborated by ethnological studies (*cf.* Thomas, 436 *ff.*, 485 *ff.*); and it was because of religious ideas that power structures were first ascribed a transpersonal existence.

In the principle of "God's will" in its higher forms, the idea of justice is included: for God is just. This opens the way for uniting

[2] Fluctuations between legal and despotic rule will be studied in Chapter XII.

power with ethics. Later on, the idea of God's will is replaced by that of "the people's will," to which a trend toward justice and the common welfare are ascribed: *vox populi vox dei.* The last idea is one of the most powerful. It can be submitted to manifold variations. The opposition between Jeffersonians representing the idea of individual rights and Hamiltonians representing the idea of group interest forms a good example.

Marxism introduced the shibboleth of "class will." On the one hand, this doctrine alleges that the principle of domination within the modern State is that of the "class interests of the bourgeoisie." On the other hand, the idea of interests of the proletariat is stressed, and a providential destiny ascribed to it: the liberation of humanity from the bonds of class structure and the creation of a true structure of justice and common welfare, devoid of State compulsion.

Anticommunist movements of our times have introduced still other "principles of domination"; the domination as such is ascribed to the nation (as the unit of past, present and future generations) in Italy and to the race (as a sort of biological Leviathan) in Germany. The welfare of the corresponding transpersonal entities (nation or race) is considered to form the principle of domination; the actual leaders are merely representatives of the superindividual entities whose function it is to achieve the objective aims.

§ 5. The Hierarchization of Power Structures

The other well-determined process within power structures is that of hierarchization.

Sometimes the integration of power into a hierarchy is given from, or almost from, the beginning of the polarization. The best example of this kind is the rise of feudal society. In a social field where power structures were almost nonexistent, new active centers of domination arose simultaneously in many places; the sphere of action of every center was, at the beginning, indeterminate, and conflicts among them seemed inevitable. But among these centers the intensity of the irradiating power, as well as the attraction exerted by them, were unequal; there were some centers with a strong capacity of irradiation, the attraction of which was felt at a great distance; there were centers of weak irradiation, the influence of which did not reach further than the neighboring villages; and there were centers of an intermediate class, with an irradiation and attraction of medium intensity. Struggles among these centers often took place; but the general tendency was towards coördination. A hierarchy of power structures was created, and the position of every power center within this hierarchy was determined by special titles: barons and viscounts for the lower degrees, princes and dukes for the middle ones, kings and emperors for the superior ones.

In other cases a hierarchy of power structures is intentionally created from above: this is the case when a State is divided into provinces, or an army into corps, divisions, et cetera.

Finally, a hierarchy of powers is often created by means of superimposition of a new, central power over already existing ones. Such for instance was the history of the hierarchy in the Oecumenical Church. Christian parishes were created in different towns and villages of the Roman Empire; at the beginning each one of them was independent. Later neighboring parishes recognized the authority of a leader called a bishop; doing so, they did not abdicate their separate existence as parishes, but continued to form well-expressed power structures. The further steps were those of creating metropolitan dioceses, then patriarchal ones (there were five of them) and finally the Oecumenical Church. This was, of course, the most highly developed hierarchy of powers in universal history; the general term *hierarchy* has been derived from this structure.

Another creation of hierarchies in the same manner was the formation of the United States of America. At the beginning the thirteen States, becoming independent of England, were "sovereign" powers, building no hierarchy. But the common feeling was that they formed a unity and that they should be put under a common authority. The result was the creation of a new political body called the United States: the States had not lost their existence as States, i.e., as generalized power structures, but had simply been combined into a higher unit: in other words, they formed a hierarchy of powers.

Large organizations, insofar as they include parts of the population selected according to a specific characteristic, are often created in a similar way. A political party or a national trade union is nothing but a federation of primary organizations, with, eventually, intermediary structures between the top and the bottom.

The Soviet system, in its ideal structure,[3] was based upon the same sort of hierarchy: superior authorities were created by means of delegation on the part of inferior ones. Correspondingly the Russian Soviet Republic was officially called a federation even before the formation of national autonomies within its limits.

§ 6. The Limit of the Processes

Transpersonalization and hierarchization are processes tending in a definite direction. Therefore the question may be asked whether they have advanced to their logical limit. In addition to this the question of the degree of automatization may also be raised. Our questions might be formulated as follows: Can obedience become completely automatic? Can domination become completely transpersonal? Can power hierarchy become definite?

A concrete power structure in which obedience had become merely automatic would be doomed to destruction because acquired tendencies of submission must occasionally be revivified by voluntary obedience. On the other hand, a concrete power structure in which domination had become entirely "abstract" would also be doomed to destruction: such a domination would be completely defenseless against attacks on the part of inborn dominators, who would like to create new power structures of a personal type for their own profit.

A certain optimum of automatism in obedience and of transpersonalization in domination must be sought for in order to secure a durable power structure. The long-term existence of a concrete power structure testifies that such an optimum has somehow unconsciously been attained.

As regards the process of combining power structures by means of hierarchy, the optimum coincides with the maximum: a power

[3] Definitely destroyed by the Constitution of December 5, 1936.

system is the more durable the more it is submitted to the principle of hierarchy; if the hierarchy of concrete power structures, within a given social field, is not entirely secured, each of the (generalized) structures is endangered.

This does not, of course, mean that, from the viewpoint of securing the stability of power structures, all possible power structures should become merely branches of the State system: hierarchy does not necessarily mean unification; it means merely creating a precise order, with a definite place for every part in the whole. The existence of different (although hierarchized) powers prevents obedience from becoming completely automatic and therefore is rather useful from the viewpoint of power stability.

§ 7. The Decay of Power Structures

A power structure is naturally durable, if the processes of automatizing obedience, of transpersonalizing domination and of transforming the whole system into a hierarchical one have attained their optimum. If nothing happens, such a structure continues to exist. New forces have to begin acting in order to destroy it. Such forces may be internal or external.

External forces are generally represented by other power structures tending toward expansion. Struggle among power structures seems to be a kind of natural law. Political history is, to a great extent, the history of struggles between the strongest power structures, or States. In our times economic organizations have become true power structures; and the struggle for life, for expansion, for absorbing competitors, is one of the main features of their activity.

In this struggle the dimensions of the contending systems, the number of their members and their material means are of great importance. But the relative structures of the competitors also play an important part. Other things being equal, the structures which are nearer to the optimal state (see above, § 6) have the greatest chances of victory. The situation is similar to that studied with regard to ethics: a natural selection must secure victory in the struggle for existence for those groups in which the power structure is better organized, just as it secures victory for the groups in which the efficacy of ethical rules is stronger and the rules themselves more adequate to the true needs of the community.

Numerous, on the other hand, are the power structures which were destroyed by inner forces which may arise both in the active center and in the passive periphery of a power structure. The active center of every power structure is exposed to a specific danger, that of decrepitude. As far as the power structure remains a personal one, the decrease of forces and of energy on the part of the leader or of the principal leaders means a decrease of the relative force of the active center.

If the power structure is transpersonal, there arises the danger of an inadequate selection of individuals for the active center. If this selection is artificial and not natural, it is not always possible to furnish the active center with individuals of active nature in the requisite number. In a monarchy the heir designated to become the future ruler may be a weak man. In an oligarchy the coöptation of new members results sometimes in filling the ruling clique with nobodies. The same may happen in democracies if the process of selecting leaders fails to fulfill its proper function (*cf.* chap. IX, § 4).

There is only one way to prevent decrepitude in transpersonal power structures, and this is to prevent stratification of the given group from becoming too rigid, thereby allowing fresh elements to ascend from the passive periphery and take their places among the dominators. When this condition is fulfilled no sign of decrepitude appears. This seems to be the secret of the amazing vigor of the British political and social organization.

But very often this method of preventing decrepitude in a power structure is not applied, a failure which is quite comprehensible. To open the doors to new elements is to act against the immediate egoistic interests of the elements already belonging to the active center and of their progeny. Preventing members of the passive periphery from climbing in the social scale is a policy which very often prevails.

If the process of decrepitude is far advanced, the active center is composed of persons who are in the main unsuited for their positions. In their characters the inborn tendency of submission is stronger than that of dominance; of course, they may have acquired a multitude of tendencies of dominance, and the tendencies of submission may not be very well developed. But the intensity of their tendency to dominate is not strong enough; they do not possess the necessary power of suggestion, which is one of the principle means of creating and reinforcing acquired tendencies of submission in the subjects. Those who have to dominate perform their functions indeed, but in a lazy, desultory way, like priests of an obsolete religion who celebrate the ancient rites, in the efficacy of which they no longer believe.

They may reasonably be accused of backwardness, of lack of insight, of indecision and weakness. A combination of pride, stubbornness and stupidity is not infrequent among the "Epigones," and this exposes them to terrible blunders in managing the affairs of the group. Since the subjects become increasingly aware of these blunders, the tendency to obey gradually decreases; social inertia finally becomes the sole support of the system, and the system is bound to be destroyed.

Another cause of destruction is just the opposite of decrepitude. This is the mistake of over-activity, frequently made by revolutionary governments and in general by new dominators — not only political, but also in other power structures. An attempt to transform the whole social structure "overnight," to change the habits, the customs, and even the mentality of group members, usually encounters a strong resistance. Circumstances sometimes favor it. If the same indignation, the same resentment is felt by many people simultaneously, disobedience becomes more frequent, and disobedience is just as contagious as obedience; the tendency towards imitation plays the same part in both cases.

Much depends upon the social age of the power structure. If over-activity is displayed within one well established, the limits of possible reforms are greatly extended. The activity of Peter the Great in Russia, on the eve of the eighteenth century, was, from the point of view of transforming a society, a true revolution; however, it did not result in weakening the power structure of the Russian State. But many revolutionary governments, especially in France, lost their power by introducing reforms too quickly. Historians often assert that a reaction always follows a revolution. In any case the often recurring sequence, revolution-reaction, may well be explained from the point of view of the laws of dominance-submission.

Internal destructive forces may arise on the passive periphery of the power structure. If the latter is transpersonal, and if, at the same time, the general social structure is too rigid, hindering the ascent of active elements arising within the passive periphery, a tendency asserts itself toward the creation of secondary power centers, which are at first merely potential. Individuals endowed with strong tendencies to dominate and weak tendencies of submission, when kept back within the passive periphery, protest against the rule of the dominators. They might find and declare reasons for their disgust, but the main one generally remains unacknowledged, namely that they themselves have no share in power. They have to obey, but their obedience is not of the automatic variety; they obey "voluntarily," because they understand that disobedience would have unpleasant consequences — so long as others continue to obey; but they miss no opportunity of disobeying and of spreading their protest, their contempt, their hatred of the dominators and of their rule. "Assailants of the social order, the better to destroy it, try to take advantage of the forces engendered by that order and therefore make every effort to show that acts which are undoubtedly acts of revolt are legal and therefore ought not to and cannot be punished by the defenders of the order" (Pareto, 1879). On the other hand, they try to convince people that the abstract principles of domination are no longer followed by the dominators. Given certain conditions, they may be followed by other individuals: the tendency to imitate again plays an important rôle. People of active nature become heads of small power structures, revolutionary societies or bands, or strong parties of opposition, which try to emancipate themselves from the general hierarchy of power headed by the State. A part of the general energy of the State structure has to be used in combating these new power centers; the force of the main power structure is consequently decreased and the chances of destroying the system increased.

Destructive processes in the active center and in the passive periphery generally run parallel; more than this — they generate each other by induction. It is improbable that concrete power structures can be destroyed from "within" if faults of the above-mentioned types have not been made by the dominators. One of the greatest chess players of the nineteenth century, Dr. Tarrasch, used to say that it was impossible to win a game of chess if one's opponent made no errors. The same seems to be true for power structures: revolutionaries win out only if governments make mistakes. But the right way for a government to act is sometimes so difficult to discover that revolutionaries have a good chance of success.

§ 8. The Struggle for Power

It rarely happens that destructive forces endowed with sufficient strength to overthrow the dominators arise without any warning. More frequent is the case of a struggle for power between the existing active center and one or several of the new potential ones. If the active center is not bound by any considerations excepting those concerning the continuity of the structure, it may use its position to prevent the rise of such potential centers by nipping them in the bud. Such is, of course, the practice of despotic governments. Censorship and terrorism are their means of combat.

If the power structure has been transpersonalized, difficulties in the problem of suppressing State enemies may arise. Especially in a democratic State based upon the principles of justice and common consent, a ruthless destruction of potential rival active centers is impossible: it is one of the aspects of a democratic State that the rulers have to destroy competing centers of domination not by force but by persuasion. Of course there is a limit in democracies also on the sort of activity permitted the potential active centers; they too have to act by means of persuasion and not by means of violent destruction of the existing structure. The limits on action set by the principles of democracy are sometimes not very clear for the dominators, or, for that matter, for the subjects trying to form new centers of domination. Sometimes the dominators become too lenient (a symptom of decrepitude within a democracy) and allow the newly arisen potential centers to display activities wholly incompatible with subjection, and hence resulting in the destruction of the conditioned reflexes of submission. This was the way in which the establishment of dictatorial governments was prepared in a number of more or less democratic states: in Russia, Italy, Germany, Poland, et cetera.

The means which can be successfully employed in order to destroy a potential power center vary immensely. Sometimes ridicule, a weapon frequently applied by revolutionaries against the government, can be brought to bear on the revolutionaries themselves. In the year 1908 a kind of revolution threatened to develop in Southern France; the revolutionary leader was a certain Marcelin Albert. He came to Paris in order to negotiate with the premier as one power with another. After an interview M. Albert noticed that he was temporarily out of cash and borrowed a hundred francs from the premier. The latter let this fact be published and the revolution was over.

If the dominators, for some reason, have not succeeded in destroying the potential power centers opposed to them, the destructive process goes on. Relatively unorganized murmuring and grumbling (*malaise*) becomes organized "non-violent" resistance (sabotage, passive resistance, "sit-down strike") and still later organized resistance reinforced by violence, accidental or deliberate. Within a "community which is keenly dissatisfied with its government, a preacher arises and gives distinct and exact form to the residue, concentrating the manifestations upon one point" (Pareto, 1453). In primitive society dominators are suddenly deserted by their followers (*cf.* Thomas, 434–5). In modern society, in analogous cases, nobody is any longer there who is able and at the same time willing to combat the revolution.

In this struggle for power, the situation of the actual active center seems in general to be favorable, for the process of liberating minds of the "illusion" of objective power never advances with the same speed in different parts of the social field. Protagonists of "liberty" arise not simultaneously but at different times. At first chains of obedience are broken only by isolated rebels; they try to act in conformity with their newly acquired mentality but are hindered by the apparent "objectivity" of power: the chains and links continue to have meaning for others, and their corporate action is, for a certain time, strong enough to overcome the first efforts of the "liberated" rebels. The first of these are always doomed to defeat; the meaning of their behavior is only to set an example, to reinforce the movement of resistance. Very often the activity of the dominators in struggling against their first adversaries results in "opening the eyes" of other individuals; the first victims of revolutionary struggles become martyrs and exert the same influence on public opinion as martyrs do in religious conflicts.

It has often been noted that technical developments have reinforced still more the relative power of existing active centers as compared with that of their adversaries. Some hundred years ago conspiracies were often crowned with success: a dozen conspirators, armed with swords, or later with pistols able to fire only a few yards, frequently gained the upper hand over guards armed in the same way and overthrew the dominator or the dominators: the conditioned reflexes of submission seemed, to a large degree, to be dependent on the traditional place of origin of commands. It is noteworthy that for a long time the success of an upheaval or revolution in France depended on capturing the *Hôtel de Ville* in Paris; this objective won, a new government seemed to be established and henceforth began to be obeyed.

Quite different is the present situation. With the exception of military upheavals, governments have command over a wealth of technical means, and this in a somewhat monopolistic way. Only the governmental forces — but not those of revolutionaries — are supplied with long-range artillery, machine guns, tanks, et cetera, if only the government does not become so weak as to give up its natural monopoly. The transportation system is largely in the hands of the government, as are also the means of communication: post, telegraph, telephone and radio; therefore the government may concentrate its efforts in subduing one revolt before new upheavals can take place.

The situation of governments seems to have become impregnable. Nevertheless, cases of a revolutionary overthrow of governments, of destroying power structures of the highest degree are today no less frequent than they were earlier. The technical aids to the governmental position have been counterbalanced by the development of such forms of power structures which are rather favorable to antagonists of established powers. Furthermore, it is necessary to keep in mind that political power structures are not the only ones. In other kinds of power structures technical progress plays only a minor part, and revolutions, i.e., violent destructions of established power structures, happen just as frequently as in earlier times.

Power structures, when transformed into transpersonal and hierarchical ones, seem to have become immortal, everlasting. They have "social inertia." But up to now no power structure has proved to be eternal. A power structure is a combination of human wills. This combination may be transmitted from generation to generation; but, when transmitted, the wills have to adjust themselves to the needs and ideas of new generations. Sometimes they succeed in doing so for centuries; but in every power structure sooner or later a moment arrives when destructive forces get the upper hand and cause a social explosion.

Therefore, whenever we analyze and describe a concrete power structure, we have to indicate not only the positive forces which create and maintain it and aid in its development, but also the lack or the insufficiency of opposite tendencies: in the sociology of power, statics are never complete without dynamics.

BIBLIOGRAPHICAL NOTE

Power situations in general are mentioned by Vierkandt (52), Pigors (144) and Merriam (15–46).

Elements of dominance in family, as regards primitive society, are discussed by Westermarck (I, 597–600), and as regards civilized society by Tarde (*b*, 25–31), Bogardus (63), and Sorokin (*h*, III, chap. 1–4). Many works of fiction illustrate how crude familistic dominance has often been until our days in lower social layers: *cf.* Russian novelists and Zola's *L'Assomoir*.

The rise of dominance in groups of children is studied by Chevaleva, Pigors (24–41, 164–191, with large bibliography) and by Murphy (397–404); of dominance (leadership) in casual groups by Pigors (37). As regards the military origin of the State see, among recent authors, Holsti (116, 132, 265).

The method of direct attack in establishing domination is mentioned by Pigors (21) and LaPiere (292); that of struggle by Merriam (36). For the general sociology of combat: Steinmetz (*b*). Concerning combat between animals: Craig.

The curse as an instrument of domination is studied by Westermarck (I, 562–5, 621–7; II, 622–4, 687–90, 703, 732) and Thomas (590–8, 765–9). A good survey of the factors playing a part on the passive side of the power structure and helping its creation is that of Merriam (12, 113, 126).

The study of "the principles of domination" is one of the principal topics in the history of legal philosophy: *cf.* R. W. Carlyle; a short survey by MacIver (*a*). Some specifications of modern principles of domination in Ross (78–9, 85).

The general idea of the hierarchy of powers is expressed by Tarde (*b*, 199 *ff.*). The soviet system as a hierarchy created from below is described by Timasheff (*c*).

Concerning ruling dynasties and their decay: Sorokin (*c*). A kind of "natural law" of decrepitude of bourgeois dynasties forms the backbone of the eighteen volumes of E. Zola's *Les Rougon-Macquart*.

The question of the decay of political domination is amply studied by Merriam; *cf.* Chapin and Bogardus (268). The sociology of revolutions has been twice studied by Sorokin (*a* and *h*, III, chap. 12–14). For the *coup d'état:* Malaparte.

PART IV

LAW

CHAPTER XI

LEGAL EQUILIBRIUM

§ 1. The Relationship of Ethics and Power

Ethics and power are two social phenomena which may exist independently of each other. It is possible to conceive a social field in which coördination would be either of the ethical type, without any participation of power, or of the imperative type, without any element of ethics. Ethics may be efficient without any relation to power; power may exist without any relation to ethics. Both are based upon primary phenomena: the efficacy of ethics — upon group-conviction and the resulting socio-ethical pressure; the efficacy of power — upon polarization, i.e., the creation of large systems of interrelated inborn and acquired tendencies of dominance and submission.

This is the chief result of the analysis of ethics (Part II) and of power (Part III). The power phenomenon could be described without having recourse to any conception belonging to ethics. Sometimes analogies showed a certain parallelism between the two phenomena, but never the dependency of power on ethics or *vice versa.*

The same men act both in securing the efficacy of ethics and in ruling or obeying in a power structure. Within the same social field ethical rules are born and upheld by social pressure, and power structures created, reinforced and combatted. Necessarily the two social phenomena come into contact. A certain relation between them has thus to be established.

This relation may be either antagonistic, neutral or friendly; repulsion, indifference or affinity may express these several relations, each of which has actually occurred many times.

1. When conquerors of a primitive type, after having formed a social group of the pure power type, imposed their rule on foreign tribes or nations, they commonly began by exterminating the ethical coördination already existing in the conquered area.

In this endeavor they might be more or less successful; but in any case, as long as a struggle of this kind lasted, there would be an antagonistic relationship between imperative and ethical coördination.

The antagonistic relationship between ethics and power may be more complex. An active center of domination may become (or may have coincided from the beginning) with a social group possessing a certain group-conviction; to enforce the corresponding rules throughout a large social field might seem obligatory to members of this group. If they are not interested in gaining the allegiance of other individuals present in the larger field, or if they encounter an insuperable obstacle (in other words, if there is a conflict of ethical group-convictions), the elements of the central group-conviction are imposed upon the passive periphery in an imperative manner, and are enforced by means of power.

2. Cases of neutrality are more frequent. A system of ethical coördination of human behavior and another system of imperative coördination may coexist in the same social field without being conjoined: ethical rules (the objects of ethical group-conviction) are enforced only by means of socio-ethical pressure without any injection of power, while commands of the active center are carried out because of the specific relationship between the rulers and the subjects, without any support of ethical group-conviction. This is a frequent situation in primitive society.

The idea may suggest itself that the independence of power structures from ethics might in general be only ephemeral. For the existence of a durable power structure creates the habit of obedience; there is also the "normative tendency of actuality" (chap. VI, § 5), which tends to transform every habit into custom. This seems to mean, therefore, that long-lasting obedience should necessarily create a group-conviction that obedience to the established power "ought to be."

This is, to be sure, the usual sequence of events, but not a necessary one. In certain cases the active centers of power structures hinder such an evolution, for example, by giving contradictory commands. As ethical principles are always expressed in general rules of behavior, in such cases no conceptual image appears which might become the object of ethical group-conviction.

Furthermore, the content of consciousness of the ruled may be of such a kind as to hinder the process of combining power with ethics. If the commanded acts are such that they are considered by the ruled as acts which "ought not to be," or if prohibited acts are of such a kind as to be considered by the ruled as acts which "ought to be," the corresponding acts may be carried out (in other words, the power relationship may be completely actualized) without engendering ethical group-conviction.

Therefore, sometimes even well-established power structures may remain unconnected with ethics. On the other hand, it is obvious that many ethical structures remain unconnected with power; the group supporting moral or customary rules may not be at all interested in seeing these rules enforced by power. Furthermore, there is sometimes no power structure with interest in enforcing this or that element of socio-ethical conviction; this is generally the case with respect to rules of decency and politeness.

3. Historical experience as well as everyday observation show that it is affinity and not repulsion or neutrality that generally prevails in the relationship between ethics and power.

The study of social ethics and of power has revealed their affinity. The efficacy, the very existence of social ethics, is partly based upon the ethical leadership of prominent persons; and leadership in a more intensive form is dominance, the very essence of power. The efficacy of ethics is secured by means of socio-ethical pressure; this pressure may present different degrees, and it is obvious that pressure organized by the active power center is the strongest of these. On the other hand, power structures tend to become transpersonal, and the ethical principle of justice plays an important part in this development. Another process within power structures is that of transforming simple structures into hierarchical systems; the order needed in every hierarchy may be (but also may not be) an ethical order. In other words, affinities between ethics and power are manifold, and the union of ethics and power to form a higher complex is something quite natural. The probability of combining ethics and power is a high one, though varying through time and space. Generally imperative coördination through power display tends to become simultaneously ethical coördination through a display of balanced social pressure. Rules of behavior are created which are simultaneously ethical rules and general commands of an established power structure. They form a system of human behavior in society presenting simultaneously the features of efficient ethics and efficient power, of *law*, the object of this study.

Ethics and power are not two coördinated or subordinated phenomena. They may be thought of as two circles which cross one another. Their overlapping section is law. These propositions may be considered as a restatement of the basic working hypothesis (chap. I, § 5). Yet the situation here is somewhat different. *Phenomena* corresponding to the *concepts* of ethical and imperative coördination have been studied since the hypothesis was expounded. In order to verify the hypothesis, the question must be investigated whether certain more concrete propositions are valid (correspond to facts).

The propositions to be verified are the following: (1) legal rules are recognized by group-members; (2) legal rules are obeyed by group-members; (3) legal rules are recognized by the members of active power centers; (4) legal rules are supported by them. In these propositions the essence of the basic hypothesis is condensed. If they prove to be correct, the basic hypothesis is also correct.[1]

§ 2. First Proposition: Legal Rules are Recognized by Group-Members

Legal rules are recognized by group-members. This recognition of legal rules must contain all that the recognition of ethical rules

[1] These propositions can be deduced from the statements made in Parts II and III when taking into consideration the following: if law is a combination of ethics and power, every proposition suitable for ethics in general may be applied to law. (But it would be scientifically incorrect to ascribe to law in particular that which pertains to the whole domain of ethics: for law is only a part of it.) On the other hand, every proposition pertaining to the power phenomenon in general may also be applied to law. (But, as in the former case, it would be scientifically incorrect to ascribe to law alone that which pertains to the social phenomenon of power in its entirety, for power may appear in the form of law, as well as in other forms not connected with it.)

does. Therefore, recognition must signify: (1) the disposition to follow the rule in one's own conduct and (2) the disposition to help the rule be enforced in the conduct of others.

1. The recognition of legal rules as obligatory patterns of behavior by the large majority of citizens, of course, dominates the situation termed "legal order"; evidence of this fact has been given at the very beginning of this study (chap. I, § 1).

Now it must be added that the recognition of legal rules may be direct or indirect. Some individuals recognize a certain number of legal rules directly, i.e., they know these rules either in abstract form or in the form of concrete examples, and combine with this knowledge the will to act in accordance with them. This will is not necessarily based upon the conviction that these rules are excellent ones or at least better than any others which might replace them; relevant is only the existence of the general readiness to obey them.

Much more frequent is the indirect recognition of legal rules. Such a recognition is always based upon the fact that other people recognize the rule. Typical for law is the recognition, by an average group-member, of rules recognized by the power or the powers he obeys. This recognition is generally an indirect one; therefore, it pertains to rules which, in a concrete situation, are unknown to a given individual; he does not know every rule recognized by power or powers, but is ready to follow them at the moment they would enter his consciousness. Such an attitude is, of course, very natural; there is, in the relationship of subjects to rulers, something of the nature of an inferiority complex, and imitating superiors is, despite the denials of many social psychologists, one of the most frequent determinations of human behavior.

Two further problems must be analyzed at this point. The first concerns the behavior of the members of certain subgroups which form a part of the larger social field ruled by law, yet do not help but rather counteract law; for instance, groups of revolutionaries or criminal gangs, or groups of ill-educated youths. This is a phenomenon closely related to the existence within a given social field of various different active power centers — those actually dominating and those in actual or latent revolt. For members of the subgroups surrounding these potential centers law is no longer truly law, but merely a complex of generalized commands of an overwhelming power. Therefore, they do not exert pressure tending to enforce law, but, on the contrary, use their influence in order to undermine law. Sociologically speaking, the individuals belonging to these peripheral subgroups are, first of all, members of the larger group to which a certain legal order is related. From this viewpoint certain rules are legal rules even for them; they are under the common patterns of behavior. But they are also members of the revolutionary or, generally, antisocial subgroup; within such subgroups the corresponding rules are no longer objects of ethical group-conviction; they are, potentially, no longer "binding" for them. The behavior of such individuals is determined by two contradictory tendencies and is, therefore, disorganized.

The second problem could be put in the following way: Is it true that all legal rules are recognized at least indirectly? There are authors who doubt this. In the opinion of Ehrlich, "the entire military system and the entire tax system of the modern State . . . could not exist for a single moment without coercion exercised by the State" (*a*, 74).

But what is coercion exercised by the State? It is the sum total of the sanctions imposed by law against the transgressors of rules, including those related to military service and the tax system. These sanctions are regulated by rules which, surely, are legal rules. Are these rules, at least indirectly, recognized by the people? Of course they are; with few exceptions nobody opposes as being unjust the infliction of sanctions on others according to these rules; occasionally people help to discover violators whose successful activity actually results in increasing the burden weighing upon the others.[2] The recognition and support of State activity against the transgressors of rules is the cultural sublimation of primitive hostile attitudes. The existence of this cultural

[2] Even as regards unpopular laws there is almost no opposition to the application of sanctions on violators. If there is actual and strong opposition, the further existence of the legal rule becomes dubious; it is a case of legal disequilibrium to be studied below (chap. XV).

sublimation in itself constitutes the recognition of the transgressed rules, in our case those regulating military service and the tax system.

Another author, Fehr (29), stresses the point that the legal conviction of the people pertains only to major problems and that minor problems, for instance, such as to whether a joint-stock company is created by agreement or by registration, et cetera, is absolutely nonpertinent for them. Therefore, he is inclined to subdivide law into truly legal and technical rules.[3] Such a construction would mean that recognition is not essential for law; yet there is no necessity to argue in this way, if the concept of "indirect recognition" is introduced: people recognize, indirectly, rules dealing with the technicalities of law, because these rules are directly recognized by the active power center.

2. As regards the second part of the recognition, the disposition to help impose rules on the behavior of others forms a distinct element in the ethico-imperative coördination of behavior. Violations of legal rules are prevented not only by specific activity of active power centers, but also by a continuous — but not very obvious — activity of social groups in general. A child is taught to abstain from violating not only moral or customary rules, but legal rules as well; ethical education in the family is always complex and deals simultaneously with ethical rules of all types. External symbols of law (policemen, courts, et cetera) are introduced into the consciousness of younger group-members as "mental objects" associated with the specific ethical idea of "ought to be" or "ought not to be." That, in most cases, obedience to law "ought to be" is one of the essential elements of the ethical tradition inculcated by the older generation in the younger; in other words, socio-ethical pressure is exerted in order to mold the behavior of younger persons so as to accord with legal patterns.

This activity is, of course, not limited to the family. Almost every social group has its existence within "legal space"; that is, it is related in a specific way to certain complexes of legal rules;

[3] His concept of technical rules differs from the one analyzed in chap. IV, § 6. Fehr's subdivision of law recalls Duguit's (*a*, I, 36, 41) distinction between "normative" and "constructive" rules, or Freund's distinction between "declaratory" and "regulative" rules (7).

younger group-members in any group whatsoever are subject to the same process of molding as children in a family; respect for law is thus reinforced, and the probability of legal behavior increased by means of socio-ethical pressure.

This pressure is exerted as regards group-members who are tempted to violate the law. Families and other social groups do their best to prevent illegal behavior; they proceed by means of persuasion, but also by threatening with intragroup sanctions, going even as far as expulsion from the group.

The preventive pressure of social groups plays a more important part in enforcing law than repressive pressure. The reason for this is the existence of another stronger pressure exerted by power. But sometimes intragroup sanctions are added to those imposed by power; in certain cases they even possess a stronger force of motivation than the official sanctions, especially from the viewpoint of reinforcing the ethical group-conviction and of preventing further transgressions.

The existence of official sanctions or, more exactly, the knowledge that such sanctions exist and will be applied, results sometimes in inhibiting the transformation of retributive dispositions into retributive emotions, when the violated rule is a legal one, for the natural current of sentiments and the corresponding sequence of acts have been sidetracked by creating social retribution. The retributive disposition is actualized in sentiments of confidence and support as regards the official action. This deviation of the natural retributive sentiment is always precarious; just as a river for which a new bed has been created by means of a dam may under certain circumstances overcome the dam and return to its natural bed, so also with retributive dispositions and emotions. These are only exceptional cases; but public resentment, disapproval and indignation accompanying crimes certainly form one of the elements in the recognition of legal rules by group-members.

§ 3. Second Proposition: Legal Rules are Obeyed by Group-Members

Legal rules are not only rules recognized and followed by group-members and forming the object of the ethical group conviction.

They have also to be obeyed as the generalized commands of the rulers within certain power structures. This is, in a somewhat expanded form, the second of the four propositions to be verified.

That legal rules are "obeyed" seems to belong to the most trivial and undoubted propositions. Yet, in modern jurisprudence, this proposition is more and more frequently denied. Its antagonists reason as follows: if legal rules are obeyed, they are necessarily commands; but, in their opinion, it is obvious that a large number of legal rules are not commands (permissive rules in contrast to imperative rules). A legal rule, says Robson (305), may be a direction of conduct. It may be a mere declaration of the consequence of particular acts — a legal signpost indicating where the various roads lead.

If legal rules were really merely "directions," how could we distinguish them from friendly advice? In order to make this distinction a reference to power structures seems to be necessary: legal rules always express dominance and, therefore, they are commands. But the commands are not always directed to the totality of the group-members. In the majority of cases only a subgroup is bound by the command in correlation with the if-clause essential to every ethical rule (chap. IV, § 5). This subgroup may be (1) a class of common citizens characterized by certain properties (young men having reached the age of 21 . . . bachelors . . . persons having an income above $2,000, et cetera); (2) a class of public officers (administrative or judicial) on which a certain function is imposed. The command-character of the rule addressed to authorities makes its realization very probable indeed; and the knowledge of this fact induces the members of the corresponding subgroup to act in a certain manner. Their behavior is not "obedience to a command"; yet it is determined by the fact that other individuals obey legal rules. This happens in the following situations: (1) when the behavior of individuals is determined by their conviction that they are "backed up" by law (direct attributive motivation by law); (2) or when it is determined by their "concern with law" (indirect motivation by law). These behavior types are added to the basic type of direct imperative motivation by law.

1. The roots, instruments and forms of the direct imperative motivation by law are exactly the same as the roots, instruments and forms of obedience within power structures in general, especially when the almost irresistible force of automatic obedience, based upon acquired tendencies of submission, is added to the general tendency to follow ethical rules.

Within an established power structure a number of words, gestures or symbols related to dominance (in other words, expressing the will of the dominators) have become stimuli in tendencies in which the performance of "indicated acts" is the response. Ethical rules, already existing or newly created, might be introduced into this system. Sometimes a solemn act of some outstanding individual may be applied as a means of creating new tendencies of this type. For instance, in a proclamation, "It is the command of the ruler that rule N should be carried out," the words "it is the command of the ruler" form the stimulus of a preëstablished tendency of submission. The substance of the new ethical rule, proclaimed simultaneously with the solemn words, becomes a new stimulus to act. Generally such proclamations are addressed to many; then for every single member of the populace the obedience of others becomes an additional stimulus, reinforcing the principal one.

Ceremonies or solemnities are not always necessary. The words "law," "statute," "court" and a thousand others have gradually become stimuli of submission. Introducing new rules under the aegis of such terms means, therefore, the creation of new tendencies of submission.

When rules exist which people obey automatically, a number of further tendencies to obey are created by means of their concrete application. The stopping gesture of a policeman, red lights, the seal of an official body, the document embellished with such a seal or with the appropriate signatures, et cetera, have become accustomed symbols which automatically produce submission to the positive or negative orders embodied in them.

The effect of direct imperative motivation by law is that, in many cases, individuals abstain from the behavior which naturally (i.e., without the existence of law) they would have preferred, for law prohibits this behavior and demands an opposite mode of action. The individual pays his debts or taxes, or destroys in his shop the commodities which were illegally produced, or allows another to walk through his estate, or abstains from building an edifice which would damage the prospects of another, or does not pronounce insulting words which he had already prepared, et cetera. In all these cases he knows and feels that he has law against him.

The behavior imposed on men by law may be described positively or negatively. Positive patterns determine behavior with much greater precision than negative ones. When the requirements of a positive pattern are fulfilled, every act, with the exception of the commanded one, will be contrary to law: you have to pay your debts or, in a country with compulsory military service, you have to join the army at a certain date. On the other hand, if you are subjected to a negative rule, designating behavior which "ought *not* to be," you may freely perform every act except the forbidden one.

2. The direct attributive motivation by law is based on the fact that the patterns of behavior imposed by law upon certain classes of individuals very often enable them to carry out acts which they could not have been able to undertake had they to reckon only upon their "natural" forces; law backs them, endows them with additional power. For instance, property may be left unprotected by the owner, because law protects it, or service on the part of an individual superior in force may be claimed, for law demands this service, or an intruder may be ejected from one's house, or abuses of other people in spite of their social power may be openly denounced.

The behavior of individuals endowed with "rights" or, in other words, of the individuals appearing to be the beneficiaries of the direct attributive motivation is not "obedience." But the very possibility of such a behavior can be reduced to the direct imperative motivation of other individuals on whom "duties" or obligations are imposed. In normal cases the obligation between the debtor A and the creditor B is fulfilled half automatically: for A, the act of paying is nothing more than a case of automatic obedience to law (generalized commands); for *B*, being paid is the actualization of everyone's expectation that automatic obedience to law will take place.

The situation changes or, more exactly, becomes clearer in conflict cases. When *B* is demanding that he be paid by *A*, who refuses, *B* knows that he has the law behind him. This means that conditions are given for applying a number of legal rules addressed especially to minor representatives of power; either by means of voluntary obedience, or by the mechanism of the acquired tendencies of submission, they will help *B*, who, under these circumstances, has so mighty an ally as the power structure of the State.

One of the most typical examples of the direct attributive motivation by law is the one effected by the ascription to men of the right of property. How is this right secured? By imposing on others (i.e., on everyone) a negative pattern of behavior, enforced by both the instruments of legal efficacy — social pressure and official force. The increase of power on the part of the owner is based upon the fact that this pattern, in the concrete situation, is not imposed upon him. His natural force is freely expressed; the forces of others are curtailed by the force of law. The freedom of the owner prevails, becomes a social force quite distinct from his natural one.

Another example would be the ascription by law of the right of dominance (for instance, of parental rights): dominance, being the creator of law, can also be created by law in that, in certain relations, obedience is imposed on all but one whose situation consequently becomes dominant.

3. Finally, there is "indirect motivation by law": the behavior of individuals is determined by their concern with law; a precise conduct is not imposed by law, but the individual knows that his acts will be interpreted from the legal viewpoint and chooses, among different possibilities, a mode of conduct which will better secure the realization of his purpose. For instance, law commands authorities to distribute heritage according to the principle of intestacy, if no testament was left. The nature of the rule addressed to authorities makes its realization very probable indeed,

and the knowledge of this fact induces citizens to make testamentary dispositions, if they are unwilling to see these conditional rules applied to their estates. When settling a contract, parties introduce certain clauses in order to avoid the application of "dispositive" [4] legal rules, i.e., of such rules which would apply in the case if the parties had not settled the corresponding elements of their relation (for instance, the rate of interest, or the liability for defects in sold commodities).

Private autonomy preserved by "dispositive law" is only one of the possible aspects of indirect motivation. In other cases, law permits the individuals to choose. For instance, when law makes railway companies liable for the cattle killed on their right of way in the absence of adequate fencing, it creates for the managers of railway companies the following alternatives: either to fence their right of way against cattle or to pay for the cattle killed. Whatever the choice is, the behavior of the managers will be indirectly determined by law.

Again another type of indirect motivation is that of creating rewards for the behavior considered beneficial; of such a type is the technique of preferential tariffs, subsidies, et cetera. Sometimes rather artificial means are used; for instance, in order to create uniformity in spelling, law can impose the application of a certain spelling in public schools, at official examinations, and make a corresponding certificate the necessary condition for entering civil service. The British school law of 1843, by permitting children to work in factories only in case they continued to attend school, made the parents eager to keep their children in school (Gunton, 299).

In the cases of the described type a determinate behavior is imposed on officials (they have to grant subsidies or certificates only if certain conditions have been fulfilled); yet indirectly the behavior of large masses of individuals is motivated by law.[5]

[4] This is a term used in continental European jurisprudence; Rheinstein (*b*) translates it as "stopgap rules." The term "yielding law" (contrasted to "absolute law") is inadequate in many cases.

[5] Studying the phenomenon of indirect motivation, Ward (*b*, 306) applied the concept of "attractive legislation" and expressed the opinion that such noncompulsory legislation could gradually supersede the compulsory legislation inherited from olden times. He did not realize that the actualization of "attractive legisla-

Avoidance of law forms a somewhat special example of this behavior type in which the individual acts in a certain manner in order to escape a situation in which a precise legal pattern of conduct would be imposed on him or would be used for interpreting his conduct.[6]

In these cases, as in the preceding ones, the behavior of individuals cannot be interpreted as obedience to legal rules, but can and must be reduced to the fact that other individuals are regulated in their conduct by the direct imperative motivation by law.

Within a social field, the concatenation of individuals by means of direct imperative motivation forms for others "stimulus situations" (Sherif, 104). In some cases these others react to this situation by means of voluntary actions, in which the existence and the specific peculiarities of the concrete stimulus situation play a decisive part. In the majority of cases, the stimulus situation plays the part of a stimulus in a fixed tendency of behavior — the response is carried on automatically or half-automatically.

It appears that the fact that men obey law explains in full the process of the legal determination of human behavior, either directly, or indirectly through specific "stimulus situations." In this way the validity of the general proposition N2 (§ 1) seems to have been demonstrated.

On the other hand, the existence and the rôle of indirect motivation makes dubious the very existence of "anomy" asserted by Durkheim (*a*), anomy being a legally free space. Economic activity within a legal order characterized by the freedom of competition is perhaps the best example of the situation studied by Durkheim. Of course, such activity is determined neither by imperative nor by direct attributive motivation; yet it is obvious that this activity is possible and is displayed only because of the existence of a complex legal regulation of the behavior of the part-

tion" depended on compulsory directives addressed to certain social groups (those of officials, et cetera).

[6] Striking examples were mentioned by the Secretary of the Treasury Morgenthau concerning the means of avoiding the integral payment of income tax (*New York Times*, June 2, 1937, p. 17). *Cf.* Angell. Another example is "fictitious adultery" in order to get divorce in countries with rigid divorce laws (Cruet, 131).

ners, of the "freely acting individuals" as well as of that of the courts and administrative boards.

§ 4. Third Proposition: Legal Rules Are Recognized by Rulers

Legal rules are recognized not only by subjects, but also by rulers. This is the third proposition to be verified. If it is correct, then within a social field, where legal coördination of behavior is present, at least some of the general commands of the rulers must be simultaneously ethical (legal) rules. Conversely, in such fields at least some of the ethical rules must be simultaneously general commands of the dominators; in other words, the active power center must recognize and support at least a part of the rules forming the object of the socio-ethical conviction.

To recognize an ethical rule means, first of all, to determine one's own behavior in accordance with it. If a power center recognizes certain ethical rules, it loses part of its "natural" independence, for concrete decisions are to be made with a regard for the recognized rules. This is self-limitation of power.

Self-limitation is first of all a fact; the ethical "ought" is added to this fact, according to the tendency by which lasting states of affairs are transformed into objects of group-conviction (chap. VI, § 4). If the fact of self-limitation disappears, the legal structure is broken either in its entirety, if the power center has emancipated itself completely from the bonds of ethics, or in part, if it did so only in respect to a certain group of rules, or if the emancipation took place not at the highest, but at one of the inferior power levels.

Cases of self-limitation and of departure therefrom are frequent in legal history. Every time a constitution is granted by an absolute monarch there is self-limitation. This likewise occurs if he introduces independent courts in the decisions of which he does not interfere. Other examples are if an individual economic enterprise is transformed into a joint-stock company, or if the general rules for dividing the booty among the members of a gang have been recognized by their chief (*cf.* Thomas, 425–6, 430–1).

On the contrary, so-called *coups d'état* repealing or curtailing already existing constitutions are instances of violating self-limitation of power, as are also cases when industrialists impose their will in transgressing the statutes of their own companies, or when leaders of criminal gangs break their promises and appropriate the whole booty. There are, of course, many hindrances in the way of dominators who would like to violate an already established self-limitation; every breach means dislocating the union of ethics and power. The attitude of subjects resulting from such breaches cannot be accurately foreseen. If purely ethical motivation prevails over the purely imperative one, then the breach may result in destroying the power structure. Therefore dominators, before carrying out a *coup d'état,* study the situation carefully and prepare to combat resistance. The very necessity of such preparations and the hazard of such breaches constitute the major guarantee against illegal activities on the part of supreme dominators.

On the other hand, truly legal guarantees which would secure legal order in its totality are impossible, for all legal means cease to exist if the power center has violated the situation created by self-limitation. There is then no longer legal order, but only a number of struggling groups, some of which would like to restore legal order (after having created a new power structure), while others seek illegal domination.

This means that the constitutional order in a country exists as long as it is recognized by the active power center. In other words, a realistic explanation of the constitutional order is possible if the basic hypothesis is accepted that law is ethico-imperative coördination.

The same is true as regards international law. Many systems of legal thought have broken down because of the impossibility of accounting for international law in their terms. This was the case with the system of John Austin, for whom international law was a kind of positive morality.

It is, on the other hand, impossible to consider international law as a complex of legal norms ruling sovereign States from above, since this would mean postulating a power structure dominating over all States, which is obviously not the case. It is equally impossible to postulate that international law is "valid" because it is engendered by the unorganized communion of civilized nations, this community being "superior" to the national States (Gurvitch, *d*). The international communion engenders, of course, ethical values and ethical conviction. Many rules are created in this way, but only those rules which have been selected and fixed by States have become rules of international law. Who else could formulate the obligatory rules of international law? Is it science? And who would be the arbiter in the case of controversy within science?

The only possible construction of international law is the following. International law is formed by similar legal rules of different States, insofar as they refer to interstate relations. The active power center in every State recognizes a number of rules which are binding and supports these rules. The majority of such rules refer to internal situations. But nothing prevents the State from doing the same with respect to its international relations. The State, which could behave quite freely in these relations, limits itself; the power holders declare that they will act in a certain way, if one or another condition presents itself. As long as there is proper recognition and support, the corresponding rules are in force and constitute actual international law; if this recognition is withdrawn, the rule ceases to exist as a legal one. What is left in the latter case is nothing more than a sum of desires (of the subjects of the State which broke the self-limitation by international law, or of other States, or of their subjects) tending toward the restoration of the situation which existed before the break.

International law is self-limitation of the States and, therefore, complete legal guarantees of its execution are impossible. There are, however, strong actual guarantees; they consist of the existence of ethical conviction concerning international relations and of the interdependence of the interests of particular States. This does not prevent the rules of international law from being violated, in fact. A violation of a rule of international law on the part of a State does not necessarily mean its repudiation — just as a crime committed by a nonpersistent offender does not mean its internal "liberation" from law. Japan transgressed the basic rule *pacta sunt servanda*, but she did not repudiate the rule as such, for she continues to "serve" other pacts and to consider other States bound by pacts concluded with her.

The chief peculiarity of international law is the necessary similarity or identity of the rules recognized by different States. This similarity is consciously striven for, the reason being the same as that which induces individuals in groups to recognize similar rules; there is nothing to be gained in recognizing rules not recognized by others. The primary tendency towards reciprocity (chap. V, § 6) plays a part even in these high spheres of coördination of human behavior.

The technique by means of which the similarity is attained is varied. The unorganized interaction of States creates a number of customary rules, some of which are selected and elevated to the rank of legal rules. States conclude conventions in order to assimilate each other's international law, but only subsequent internal acts (ordinarily acts of legislation or decrees) give to the corresponding rules the force of law. Finally, States sometimes enact (by different means) rules already recognized by other States or rules that seem likely to be introduced by other States.

The common opinion declaring international law to be a kind of superstate law belongs to the class of natural law theories — it is based upon wishful thinking, not upon facts. A cursory survey of the international law of every State shows that there is no such thing as superstate law; almost every rule, while recognized by one group, is not recognized by another group of States. The basic hypothesis and its application to international law are in complete accordance with these facts.

Another problem remains to be solved. It might seem that in many cases the recognition of legal rules, insofar as it pertains to one's own behavior, cannot be ascribed to active power centers. There are some rules which seem to bind only those ruled, to impose specific duties of obedience. A more careful analysis of the situation permits us to formulate it in somewhat different terms.

Legal rules to be understood must not be taken separately.

The precise sense of every separate rule can be elucidated only after a comparison with other rules, for all rules have to act in unison; all of them have to determine human conduct and they have to do it in a consistent way (chap. XIII). Therefore, the sense of every separate unit, even if it seems quite clear at first sight, must be verified in order to make it compatible with the sense of the neighboring units in the system.

Let us take a rule which seems to bind only the subjects, as for instance, that people have to obey the commands of a traffic policeman. A detailed analysis shows that these commands are themselves subjected to numerous modifications which vary from town to town, from year to year, et cetera. Subjects are considered to transgress such commands only if they have transgressed the conditions stipulated. Transgression results in definite sanctions and in these precise sanctions alone. These facts do not permit the interpretation and application of the rule without taking into consideration that it forms only one link in a chain. Its precise meaning may be discovered only in connection with the other links; and these other links bind the dominators — they can act only if precise conditions are given and their action is limited only to certain measures.

§ 5. Fourth Proposition: Legal Rules Are Supported by the Rulers

Legal rules are not only recognized, but also reinforced and supported by the active centers of power structures. This is the fourth and last proposition to be verified.

Observation shows that display of power in order to prevent violation of legal rules or to restore the situation after a violation — either actually or theoretically — occurs frequently. The causes of the phenomenon are obvious. The recognition of legal rules by active power centers, like any recognition of ethical rules, includes a tendency to impose the recognized rules upon the behavior of others. If this tendency is displayed by individuals who form the active center of a power structure, it necessarily becomes a support. On the other hand, as recognized rules are simultaneously general commands of the active centers, all the considerations which commonly influence an active center to carry out prestige policy are applicable: the power center must insist upon legal rules being followed by everyone, because their nonobservance would mean disobedience, and disobedience undermines power structures.

The display of force called "reënforcement of legal rules" may be (1) unlimited — of the same type as in the defense systems of illegal power structures, or (2) limited, i.e., fixed in advance by rules forming a sublimation of the primitive power-defense system. These rules determine what "ought to be" in case a violation of a legal rule is threatening or has taken place; these rules are, moreover, recognized and supported by power; they belong to the class of rules determining the organization of authorities and their functions. Therefore, they are necessarily legal rules.

Of course, rules of second degree may, in their turn, be transgressed: the officers who apply them are sometimes lazy, sometimes partial. Tertiary rules must be provided in order to secure the efficacy of secondary ones, et cetera. This idea of a never-ending series is used by Petrazhitsky in order to combat the idea that sanctions form a necessary element within the legal structure. According to him, the assertion that sanctions belong to the essential elements of law represents, first of all, a *regressus ad infinitum*, for, in order to secure the efficacy of a rule of the nth degree, a rule of the $n + 1$ degree is necessary. Secondly, it must then be recognized that law could never consist of a small number of rules, but must necessarily, from the very beginning, be a large system of rules — a statement contrary to legal history (*b*, 273–85).

The arguments of Petrazhitsky [7] may be shown, however, to be invalid. As observation proves, the probability that a legal rule will be violated is never very high. This improbability is based upon the twofold nature of legal rules: their transgression is prevented not only by potential power display, but also by socio-ethical pressure. Let us designate the probability of violating a primary legal rule by 1:v, where v is a rather large number.

[7] Repeated, without knowing it, by Stoop (207).

Then, according to the theory of probability, the probability of both the primary and secondary rules being successively violated, must be expressed by the formula $1:v^2$; the probability that three rules would be successively violated by the formula $1:v^3$, etc. The quantity $1:v^3$, still more $1:v^4$ is negligible, and law might not need to make any provision to prevent the occurrence of phenomena of so high an improbability and yet retain its character of being bound in chains of concatenated rules endowed with sanctions.

Furthermore, the sanctions imposed by power are not the only ones in the system. It belongs to the essence of law that socio-ethical pressure is also present, and the higher the order of legal rules, the greater is its part. There is one other sanction also: violating legal rules of the highest order means breaking the self-limitation of power; and it has already been noted that many motives check a tendency of active power centers to do this.

The more highly developed a society is, the greater is the importance of purely legal sanctions in the system in securing the efficacy of law; even on highest levels of social development extralegal elements continue to exist (Petrazhitsky is right in his assertion that it is impossible to secure the efficacy of law by purely legal means); on lower levels these extralegal elements prevail, and, therefore, underdeveloped legal systems consisting of only a few rules are possible — on this point Petrazhitsky is wrong.

The system of legal sanctions seems to be limited by human nature. Punishment is the central point in the system of sanctions. It is nothing more than organized and developed social retribution. Acts which have become stimuli producing hostile attitudes have also been molded into stimuli within a complex behavior system on the part of individuals who have to act as officials, or executors of the corporate will. These sequences of acts are regulated by legal rules; generally they result in inflicting on the offender that degree of pain which, according to socio-ethical conviction, has been "merited" by him.

To inflict punishment means to restore the ideal order defined by law. Legal power shows its force and the socio-ethical conviction is reinforced. Other sanctions restore the material order.

They are of two kinds: (1) compulsory execution of acts which, though commanded, were not performed (a sum of money equivalent to an unpaid tax is exacted by authorities; a house built in violation of legal rules is torn down by workers hired by the authorities; a young man who is required to join the army is compelled to do so; people sentenced to prison who have not appeared at the indicated time are arrested and delivered to jailers); (2) compulsory execution of acts which are regarded as "compensations" for a transgression. Today such compensations are possibly only in monetary form; the usual case is that of sentencing an individual to pay a certain sum corresponding to the damage caused by him; sometimes compensations for violations of primarily nonpecuniary types are expressed in money, for instance, in cases of "breach of promise" in Anglo-American law, or of *choc moral*, according to French practice. In ancient times compensation was applicable also in nonmonetary form: in old German and Russian law an individual who had insulted another was coerced to beg his pardon by means of humiliating formalities.

In addition to this there are sanctions of minor importance. One of them is that of nullity. In order to make an act valid or to create a right of obligation, prescribed conditions must exist or prescribed formal requirements must be observed, or both. Without these, the intended legal act is defective and the purpose of the partners, which is to obtain legal protection, fails (Freund, 345). The display of power is in advance denied for cases when certain legal rules are not obeyed; thus in modern States it is impossible to buy real estate or to marry (in the legal sense of the word) otherwise than strictly in accordance with certain prescriptions. These prescriptions are not rigidly imposed by law; the law does not command one to buy real estate or to marry; it only declares that "If you intend to buy real estate or to marry, you must do so according to the prescribed forms, or I shall not recognize your acts."

Another closely related sanction is the deprivation of special rights granted by law (a license or a concession may be cancelled), or even the deprivation of expected gain. For instance, in Sweden the restaurants are ordered to limit their sales of alcohol; their owners are not directly forbidden to sell more than the allowed quota, but every incentive to do so is removed, for profits on the surplus have to be paid in full into the state treasury (*cf.* Childs, 107–8).

Self-redress, which plays a larger part in primitive society, but which is also recognized by law in developed social conditions, is still another form. Finally, there is the "immediate sanction" of force, which may by physical compulsion prevent the perpetration of a crime (police activity).

§ 6. Law as a Social Force

Law is a social force. The structure of law as a social force has been studied in former sections. The result of our study was to reduce this social force to the specific interaction of individual group-members. This is an interaction in which both the socio-ethical coördination and the imperative coördination are joined. Both types of interaction, when combined, form a genuinely new and higher social structure, endowed with new specific qualities, just as a combination of two chemical elements forms a new compound with new properties.

In the first place, if ethico-imperative coördination is present, patterns of behavior are imposed, first of all, by a minority (the active center of a power structure); but in contrast to purely imperative coördination this minority is not "outside," but "within" the larger group of individuals on whom the pattern is imposed, because legal rules, like ethical rules in general, are obligatory not only for "others," but also for those who impose them. Moreover, the imposition of patterns is only primarily the function of a minority; the minority may be and very often is really "inspired" and supported by the totality of the group or, at least, by its majority.

Secondly, if ethico-imperative coördination is present, every group-member (with the exception of those who belong to the revolutionary or to the asocial subgroups) takes part in the general socio-ethical pressure backing up legal rules. The individuals who belong to the active center exert, in addition to this, the pressure peculiar to power structures. Every group-member is influenced by a corporate pressure which is equal to the sums of the second parts of individual recognition. This pressure is increased by the pressure of power, which is felt, first of all, by the subjects but, secondly, also by individuals who form the active center.

Thirdly, if ethico-imperative coördination is present, all the strong motives which incite people to serve justice and to insist upon its fulfillment in social life become secondary motives of submission, for a power center which is acting (displaying power) according to ethical rules serves justice — the main ethical idea. A power which serves justice, or at least appears to serve justice, is considered by the subjects to be not a personal domination, but the domination of an abstract idea. Therefore, it may be said that law is possible only within a social field dominated by a power center of the transpersonal type, which has chosen justice for at least one of its principles of domination.

Finally, if ethico-imperative coördination is present, obedience becomes not only a response in a series of fixed tendencies of behavior, but also an element in the ethical group-conviction. The social pressure exerted by group-members in order to secure the efficacy of ethics becomes a second root of submission and, simultaneously, of the efficacy of power. But, on the other hand, the support of power forms the second basis of law, which is added to the main basis of all ethics, social pressure.

The double nature of law as ethico-imperative coördination is clearly expressed, when the insidious question is raised as to whether men obey the law because of conviction or because of the evil consequences which threaten if law is transgressed. Both possible answers are given with equal confidence, but both are false insofar as it is asserted that people obey law exclusively for the first *or* for the second reason. In actuality both motivations are closely associated, and it depends on the individual character and the concrete circumstance whether the first or the second element of legal coördination plays the primary rôle. Lawfulness is never *merely* fear of punishment or *merely* respect for the aims pursued by law.

§ 7. THE TYPES OF BEHAVIOR DETERMINED BY LAW

A social group in which both instruments of legal motivation (§ 6) are strong and closely correlated with each other necessarily tends to restore its initial or normal situation. This tendency might be called legal equilibrium. This restorative activity is legal pressure. The similarity of the conduct of group-members, based both upon the recognition of legal rules and upon legal pressure and, in its main outlines, corresponding to the definitions of legal rules, is legal order.

The legal order is expressed in human activities of different kinds. Three layers can be observed in advanced society.[8]

1. There are individuals who form "the active centres of power structures" and who impose on men patterns of behavior commonly called legal rules. Yet the imposition is not at all necessarily a creative one, for the content of the imposed rules can be borrowed from those created by unorganized groups for their members. In this case the imposition by power centers means (1) either merely the reënforcement of rules for individuals who were already submitted to them,[9] or (2) the expansion to larger social fields of rules created for smaller groups.

2. There are individuals whose behavior is commonly interpreted as the activity of social institutions, the function of which, exclusively or in addition to other functions, is to apply the abstract rules of N 1 to concrete cases. Such institutions are commonly called courts and administrative boards.[10] The behavior of the mentioned individuals is, at least partly, deter-

[8] "Three very different things," says Dean Pound, "namely, the legal order, the authoritative methods in which to find the ground of judicial and administrative determinations, and the judicial process, have gone by the name of law" (*q*, XXXI).

[9] This happens when a customary rule becomes a rule of customary law (*cf.* chap. XII).

[10] The addition of the words "administrative boards" is necessary, for in many countries the application of law by such boards is definite, and there is no recourse to tribunals. Courts and administrative bodies belong, of course, to the "active centres of power;" but in advanced societies these centers are structuralized, and certain parts (in our case, courts and administrative boards) may be contrasted to their "nuclei" where the impulses originate, in which "domination" is expressed. The imposition of patterns belongs obviously to the number of such impulses.

mined by law. On the other hand, this behavior determines, directly or indirectly, the behavior of average men.

3. There are individuals who, performing economic, cultural or simply "vital" acts, adjust their behavior to the patterns imposed as stated in 1 and applied as stated in 2. They form the large majority of every social group; only persistent offenders and professional revolutionaries are outside it, although, as a matter of fact, every member of this majority, under certain circumstances, may be induced to commit a transgression.

This enumeration of the cases, when in modern society human behavior is molded by its relation to law, is merely indicatory of the vast range of such situations. The efficacy of law is secured not only through tribunals and administrative boards, but also through the unorganized pressure of citizens in favor of legal order, regardless of the system of official sanctions. The application of the technicalities of law has become the object of professional activity for a special social group — that of lawyers. Teaching law has become another vocation. Furthermore, men, both lawyers and laymen, frequently act in order to produce changes in law. Insofar as they apply legal means, they are reformists, but sometimes their animosity to the existing legal order grows so great that they become revolutionaries and act in order to overthrow law.

Even with these additions it is likely that the description of the "X" called law is not an exhaustive one. But some of its more important parts have been set forth.

Three problems are to be solved in order to complete the knowledge already gained. The first is the problem of the limits within which the facts observed can be generalized (chap. XII, § 3). The second is the problem of the identity of law within the three layers described (chap. XIII). The third is the problem of the disturbances in legal equilibrium which, when accumulated, are capable of producing the phenomenon of legal disintegration (chap. XV).

BIBLIOGRAPHICAL NOTE

The theory of law as the overlapping part of ethics and power originates with the author of this book, but its fundamental elements are very common. For instance, Tassitch says: "Law is the integration of the idea of justice and of peace with that of efficient force" (185). The ethical character of law is denied by Schein, Gumplowicz (*a, b*) and Laun (*b*); partly by Rolin (17) and some American neorealists. The character of law as a display of power is rejected by authors who deny that compulsory sanctions belong to the essential elements of law (*cf.* the bibliographical note to chap. VII). Sometimes the idea is advanced that "law is a specific type of existence and its specific nature cannot be deduced from anything else" (M. Cohen, *a*, 196–7). Older sociologists were satisfied with very imprecise statements of the kind of those of Ward: "Law . . . is merely a sentiment like religion; it may be called the sense of order in society" (*d*, 187). The statements in text form an attempt to *analyze* and no longer simply to *mention* the socio-psychological basis of law.

The double root of law is recognized by Pareto (89), Vinogradoff (*a*, 52) and many others. Excellent are the statements of Tönnies (*c*, 204).

The best study of "behavior according to law" is that of Petrazhitsky (*b*, 143–61). Interesting concrete material has been collected by Britt (*b*). The question of the recipients of legal rules has been amply studied in German jurisprudence. The outstanding work is that of Binding. Of further studies those of M. E. Mayer and of Binder are important.

The rôle of symbolic elements in legal behavior is studied by Arnold, Burrow (691), Le Henaff (41–5). Concerning speech habits in law, see J. Frank (26).

Law among outlaws is studied by Merriam (86–101). The attitude of criminals toward law is brilliantly described in Dostoievsky's *House of the Dead* (part II, chap. I).

Jellinek is the author who created the classic theory of the self-limitation of power (*d*, 331–7). For the further development of the theory *cf.* O. Mayer and Anschütz. For a criticism, see Duguit (*d*).

Opinion considering international law to be a rule over States from above: Martens (I, 1–2), Triepel, Hyde (1–13), Pound. The latter author says: "International law is in a sense a superior body of rules, not depending on the will of any particular State, but imposed on all States . . . by natural law, or by the moral sentiment and public opinion (*a*, 394). Morgenthau (191, 2–16, 252–3) tries to explain that international law is independent of national States by an artificial construction, according to which international law imposes itself on national States through "internal sanctions," i.e., through the sanctions of state law concerning violations of international law. Yet in the imposition of sanctions, the recognition of particular rules of international law by particular States is clearly expressed. The text reflects the ideas of Liszt (*b*, 9–12). A recent attempt to transfer the "primary norm" of Kelsen to the sphere of international law was made by Gurvitch (*b*, *d*). Austin's theory on international law was stated in his *Lectures* (173, 183–4). An excellent study of the idea of *civitas maxima* (legal order standing above States) is that of Kelsen (*e*, 204–74, 319–30). Among recent statements see those of Decencière-Ferrandière.

The most complete studies of the system of legal sanctions, based upon large comparative investigations, are those of Tagantseff (I, 59–110) and Zhizhilenko (70–111, 248–572). *Cf.* Ehrlich (*a*, 22–3), Hippel (27–8, 34–6), Pound (*l*, *m*). Brilliant studies concerning separate parts of the system are those of Jellinek (*d*) and Goldschmidt. The necessity of extra-legal sanctions in order to secure the efficacy of law is stressed by Ferneck (86 *ff.*), Brodmann (30–1, 41–3), Morgenthau (26 *ff.*, 78 *ff.*).

The concept of legal equilibrium applied in the text is a formal one; in the literature a material concept is more usual — for instance, understanding legal equilibrium as a distribution of rights corresponding to a just distribution of duties (Duprat, 465).

CHAPTER XII

CHANGES IN LAW

§ 1. INTRODUCTION

LAW is not a necessary form of human existence, not a necessary category of human thought, as several legal philosophers seem to think. Law is a historical phenomenon, a product of cultural development.[1] It appears only at a certain level of this development, after a certain degree of advance has been reached both in ethics and in power, i.e., in the phenomena out of which law is created. Even today many primitive groups do not know what law is.[2]

As a historical phenomenon, law is dynamic. Changes in law are effected slowly. Whenever law is altered, resistance, or a sort of social inertia, has to be overcome. One may, of course, record large numbers of rules changed within one year in this or that country or State, but the changed rules form only a small percentage of those which continue to exist. The slow changes in law are a striking contrast to the fast changes in fashion or to the ceaseless fluctuation of public opinion. In a generalized form changes in law can be studied from the following viewpoints: (1) how ethico-imperative coördination arose historically and gained its present place within the system of social coördination; [3] (2) how the objective elements of a legal system, i.e., legal rules, are changed.[4]

[1] Therefore, I cannot subscribe to statements such as the following: "Social life without law is just as impossible as biological life without air" (Hippel, 7) or "Society cannot exist without law or exist without producing it" (Carter, 120).

[2] The statements below should not be considered a revival of unilinearism. No predetermined stages of evolution are assumed. Yet the similarity of human nature produces law everywhere and every time when the universal phenomenon of ethics is combined with the equally universal phenomenon of power.

[3] Such a study seems to be a "false quest of origins," criticized by MacIver (293, 423 *ff.*). In my opinion, MacIver's criticism does not pertain to the complex and relatively late social institutions, to which law belongs.

[4] Changes in the legal behavior of individuals have been partly studied in chapter XI (in connection with the problem of the legal molding of individuals by

The first question is, of course, amply studied in historical and, still more, in comparative jurisprudence. Therefore only a schematic description of the process will be given here (§§ 2–6), to stress the purely relative character of modern legal structures and the impossibility of deducing the essence of law from a study of these structures alone.

The second question forms one of the objects of study of analytical, partly of historical jurisprudence. Only very general statements will therefore be in order in the sociology of law (§§ 7–8).

§ 2. Pre-legal Social Fields

Pre-legal social fields present the following aspect. Human behavior is already being determined by ethical coördination. This is undifferentiated ethics; in other words, there are as yet no distinctions between what we now designate as the three ethical branches; all ethical rules are of one category and correspond rather to custom than to morals (in the contemporary senses of both words). There is indeed a certain relationship of socio-ethical coördination with religious representations; but religion is commonly rather crude, containing far more of magic than of mysticism. Hence the connection with religion cannot give to this undifferentiated ethics, even in part, that character which we now call "moral."

At the stage we are studying, the first step of ethical evolution, i.e., the substitution of social retribution for individual revenge even of most rudimentary degree, has already been achieved. Certain rules already exist limiting and organizing the blood feud, rules which are enforced by means of socio-ethical pressure.

Within a system of undifferentiated ethics the chief method of creating new rules of behavior (as well as changing rules already in existence) is conscious or unconscious adaptation to circumstances. Selection of new methods primarily creates habits (not yet custom, or ethical rules). In this selection process individual acts play the part of "offers," and of these offers those are chosen

groups), and will be partly studied in chapter XV (in correlation with the problem of legal disequilibrium); the problem of the causes of the changes in law is studied in chapter XIV.

which are emotionally more compatible with the existing habit system. Later on the element of "oughtness" is added by the "normative tendency of the actual" (*cf.* chap VI, § 4).

In undifferentiated ethics there is only one type of sanction, the punitive; even in mature society extra-legal branches of ethics employ sanctions of this type almost exclusively. The original punitive sanction is of a type which is commonly called "private punishment:" it depends upon the will of the injured individual whether a sanction will or will not be inflicted; the interference of social groups (later on of group leaders as well) only limits and moderates this will.

Power, superior to the rudimentary power within the family and small kinship groups, does not exist at the lowest cultural levels. "Of course, authority does not lack completely; yet it is not concentrated in the hands of 'rulers' but is comprised in tradition safeguarded by old men who feel themselves subjected to it" (Thurnwald, *b*, 4). A comparatively high level of cultural development is sometimes attained without producing the rise of power and its interference in ethical affairs; such was the case with the Arabs before Mohammed (Nöldecke, Wellhausen).

But even if there is a type of power somewhat superior to a primary family or kinship organization, the designated leaders do not necessarily consider the enforcement of ethical rules as constituting one of their functions. This is for instance true as regards the Indians of Labrador, the Ibani on Borneo, the Samoans or the Caribs. The Germans of Tacitus and the Icelanders of the sagas seem to have been on the same level, whereas Homeric Greece was already inclining toward a combination of ethics with power.

§ 3. Primitive Law

The propositions expounded above are far from being uncontested. Both the religious root of ethics and the descent of law from undifferentiated ethics are now frequently denied. Thus, for instance, the religious origin of ethics has been contested by Westermarck. Diamond's book is especially devoted to the purpose of destroying the *communis opinio*.

The question of the religious roots and interconnections of

primitive ethics depends very much on what religion is considered to be and on what sort of connection is asserted. The formula used above in the text is an attempt to reinterpret the older *communis opinio* in such a manner as to bring it into conformity with more recent investigations.

But how is it with the general theory of differentiation? Diamond, who denies differentiation as the form in which law was created, tries to discover law at the earliest stages of social development. "Among the tribes which have not yet evolved courts . . . we may observe . . . settled rules of conduct as to marriage and inheritance and perhaps property, and these . . . might well be described as law." Why? Because these rules "are in the direct line of the history of law." On the other hand, the legal character of other rules, which were enforced together with the above-named, but which later disappeared, is denied (191–9, 213). In other words, the author separates early rules into two classes from the viewpoint of their later destiny. The lack of any satisfactory *differentia specifica* for legal rules is obvious.[5]

Modern ethnologists try to create such a concept of law which would permit them to find it in very early stages of social development. According to Malinowski,[6] (*a*) "there must be in all societies a class of rules too practical to be backed by religious sanctions, too burdensome to be left to the mere goodwill, too personally vital to individuals to be enforced by any abstract agency. This is the domain of legal rules" (67–8). "The positive law governing all the phases of tribal life consists of a body of binding obligations, regarded as a right by one party and acknowledged as a duty by the other and kept in force by a specific mechanism of reciprocity and publicity inherent in the structure of their society" (58). Such rules "are sanctioned not by a mere psychological motive, but by a definite social machinery of binding force based upon mutual dependence" (55).

[5] Diamond had a predecessor in the person of Mazzarella, who proceeded by distinguishing ten orders of legal phenomena in modern society (such as family, succession, contract, et cetera) and applied the concept thus gained to primitive society, despite the fact that he knew that "in primitive society there is no separation of law" from other ethical forces (*a*, 46).

[6] Pound sees in Malinowski's statements "a fruitful idea from the sociological viewpoint" (*q*, XXXIV).

Malinowski's statements seem to be completely endorsed by Robson, according to whom primitive societies may have clearly discernible laws, and those laws may be followed with a high degree of loyalty (303). We cannot "believe that law is the exclusive possession of societies who have acquired the mature apparatus of thought and action which we term civilization. . . . Whenever men have managed to live together, there shall we find the rudiments of law" (15).

Every scientific theory must be tested by confronting it with facts. Malinowski's theory is that law is equal to the sum of rules of conduct which create corresponding rights and duties of parties and are sanctioned by a social machinery. Let us apply this concept to some phenomena which can be observed in advanced societies. Within such societies there are (or recently were) groups whose members considered that the acceptance of a challenge was a duty to which a "right" of the challenger corresponded; in addition to this, there was "a social machinery" which, almost without exceptions, applied sanctions to people who rejected challenges. Were, therefore, rules regulating duels legal rules?

There are many "rules of politeness" creating "duties" for certain individuals and "rightful claims" for others; these rules regulate greeting, sitting down at table, address in speech and letters, congratulation or expression of sympathy, et cetera (chap. VII). If they are transgressed, a certain reaction on the part of the "victim" (the person to whom a "rightful claim" is ascribed) is expected and is commonly supported by other group-members, for the transgressor is considered to have violated a "duty." Are such rules legal rules? It is obvious that the somewhat vague theory of Malinowski, when applied to later social configurations, does not work.[7] It covers not only law, but also large parts of nonlegal social regulation endowed with comparatively strong sanctions.[8]

A theory which would cover both: (1) that part of primitive

[7] This is correctly recognized by Cairns, 18. *Cf.* Pound (*q*, XXXIV).

[8] The merit of Malinowski's work is to have shown that there are many layers in the non-legal regulation of life in primitive society; such layers are commonly discussed in sociology (as regards advanced society) under the rather vague terms of folkways, custom, mores, etiquette, fashion, et cetera (*cf.* chap. VII).

social regulation which is endowed with relatively strong sanctions imposed not by organized power but by "society" as such, and (2) that part of modern social regulation which is commonly called law, but not those modern rules which are sanctioned just in the same way as those mentioned in (1) seems to be logically impossible. One has to make one's choice, when applying the term law. Out of the two possibilities the second should be chosen, and this is the theory of law based primarily on the observation of what law is in advanced society. There are two arguments in favor of this procedure.

1. It is in conformity with the rule that the unknown (the past) should be explained by the known (the present), and not the known by the unknown, which almost necessarily happens if the search for uniformities begins with studying "primary" aspects of the problems.

2. A theory based on the analysis of law in advanced societies stands in no contradiction to facts observed in primitive societies which can be interpreted as follows: though there is a social regulation of behavior in primitive society, this is not yet legal regulation. On the contrary, a general theory of law based on statements of the type of Malinowski introduces great confusion into the analysis of modern society.

It is impossible to trace a definite line which would separate legal and pre-legal stages in the development of society. The imposition of patterns by active power centers is essential for the legal stage, and therefore also the very existence of such centers, although an intermediary stage perhaps existed just after law originated. Its aspect could be understood by an adequate interpretation of what was called by Sir Henry Maine "the period of Themistes" (*a*, 7 *ff.*), which, in his opinion, was the earliest stage of legal development. Themistes were judicial decisions of kings or priests based on inspiration or intuition of right and wrong. They did not necessarily follow each other in any orderly sequence. This means that they did not correspond to any general rule which would be present in the mind of the judges.

But there are, in the works of Sir Henry Maine, other statements which seem to be incompatible with such ideas. The books of Manu, in Maine's opinion, "are chiefly called law-books because they contain rules of conduct stated with the utmost precision" (*b*, 36). Furthermore, he called "inconsistent" the theory which "assumed" that adjudged cases and precedents existed antecedently to rules, principles and distinctions (*a*, 8). In actuality, the Themistes could have been of two kinds: arbitrary decisions based on a momentary mood and naked power, but, in other cases, almost unconscious expressions of generalized ideas on right and wrong conduct. Only in the latter case could they belong to the realm of ethics and especially to that of law; and insofar as they belonged, they were already based on preëstablished rules.

The main aspect of the transitory period was therefore not that judicial decisions were not based on rules, but that the interference of active power centers in the settlement of conflicts and in the enforcement of social rules of conduct was merely a sporadic one. Gradually this interference became habitual; a new rule endowing chiefs and others with the corresponding function was created. This was the beginning of the period which Sir Henry Maine called the period of custom. Actually it was the period of customary law, when active power centers regularly reënforced by their authority the patterns of conduct created by other social forces.

Such statements can help us to answer one of the questions posed toward the end of chapter XI: whether the description of human behavior given there is appliable to every human society. Of the three layers the first one, the imposition of abstract rules by active power centers, must be necessarily lacking in societies where no developed power structures have yet evolved, as well as in societies where power structures do not care or do not regularly care for the imposition of behavior patterns (possibly, with the exception of the pattern commanding the obedience to power).

Such social structures do not belong to the number of myths of the kind of "the state of nature." German and Slavic tribes, before the development of the system of compositions had, of course, social rules of behavior, but they were imposed and enforced by small social groups of the familistic type and not by organized power (private revenge, blood feud). Though Arab society before Mohammed was advanced in many directions, there was no organized power which would have imposed rules for behavior. Many African tribes already possess consolidated power structures, but power is not considered to be the instrument of imposing and enforcing rules of behavior; this continues to be the task of unorganized groups. These instances substantiate the fact that law as a system of authoritatively imposed patterns is the result of cultural evolution.

Much older seems to be the application of rules of conduct by special institutions. But necessarily so long as the behavior of the type No. 1 did not yet exist, the behavior of the type No. 2 was somewhat different from that described above, in that rules which were applied by courts were not rules imposed by active power centers. Here the question arises whether every court, i.e., as umpire settling a conflict, is to be considered as a court of law, or whether courts of other categories are also possible. Observation shows that even in advanced societies there are courts which are not courts of law ("courts of honor" settling conflicts in which the honor of parties is involved; private arbitration of business conflicts insofar as it is not related to the mechanism of law). It is conclusive that courts are possible only if a certain social regulation of behavior exists, but this regulation is not and was not necessarily a legal one.

The behavior type No. 3 (adjustment of behavior to certain preëstablished and compulsory patterns imposed at least by means of socio-ethical pressure) is of course as old as social life, for social life consists very largely of such adjustment. But the question remains intact whether, in a given situation (in this or that primitive society, at this or that stage of the development of societies which later on became "advanced" ones) the patterns to which the behavior was adjusted were legal ones or belonged to other forms of social control.

The result of our historical verification can be summed up in the following way. Observation concerning modern legal life cannot be absolutely generalized. It corresponds only to certain (later) stages of social evolution. It is adequate to the mechanism of law, as it appears after it has surpassed the *status nascendi.* On the other hand, every time the mechanism of law exists, human behavior of the types described in chapter XI, § 6 may be observed. Their study forms, therefore, a sufficient basis for a sociological theory of law.

§ 4. Power as the Factor of Differentiation

Power was the agency which led to the differentiation of ethics, or putting it more exactly, to the separation of the legal branch; for other forces were responsible for the separation of morals. Both ethics and power may coexist without there being any connection between them, just as may chemical elements endowed with mutual affinity. Then circumstances may arise which accentuate this affinity and transform potential affinity into actual union, just as certain natural events, for example, the rise of temperature, may promote the formation of chemical compounds.

In the growth of power it was a decisive moment when power structures first surpassed in size the social groups which served as "supporters of ethical patterns" and displayed socio-ethical pressure.

As long as power structures were very small, these latter groups were superior in size. Power was in general rather familistic, whereas ethical conviction was common to a number of familistic groups. This conviction, obviously, could not be influenced or supported by power. Sometimes the "elders" of various families formed a kind of council which represented the socio-ethical attitudes of all group-members.

It is of the nature of many power structures to grow. In every developing social field, at one time or another, power structures become equal in strength and size to the groups supporting ethics, or even surpass them. The possibility of influence and of mutual support is then given, which in larger power structures is very soon utilized to unify the ethical convictions of different groups subjected to the same active power center. Concomitant with the gradual growth of power, it gradually becomes a recognized function of the chiefs to hear and decide disputes between individuals. We do not know who was the first chief who ever interfered in ethical affairs by settling conflicts or creating new rules, just as we do not know the names of early inventors. Invention plays in law the same part as in technology. "The lack of a legal institution," says M. Weber, "cannot always be explained by the lack of the corresponding economic need. Rational legal institutions have to be invented, just like technical instruments. Economic situations do not automatically beget legal forms; they merely increase the chances that an adequate legal invention will be adopted" (*c*, 427).

The intervention of chiefs in disputes (i.e., the support of ethics by power, forming the essence of law) is reported as regards many primitive tribes. A society just making this transition (the second decisive step toward modern social coördination) is reflected in the Hittite Code, in the Hebrew Code expressed in the *Book of Exodus*, in the Twelve Tables of the Romans and in the earlier Germanic and Slavic Codes; on the other hand, the Code of Hammurabi refers to an epoch when this step already belonged to ancient history.

In the beginning this interference was, we may assume, accidental. Single conflicts were settled by chiefs who were able to impose both their interference and their decisions. Law was created on a basis of precedents, when this interference became institutionalized. A certain number of ethical rules forming the object of ethical group-conviction were selected by organized social power and sanctioned with its support, thus combining the selected rules with organized sanctions. The formerly weak and indefinite link between transgression and punishment became strong and realistic; social retribution was partly transformed into legal pressure.

The rules which were primarily selected were those determining the limits of blood revenge, or indicating the fine by paying which the offender could atone for his offense. The catalogue of offenses (and, correspondingly, of ethical rules) with which power had to deal in the beginning was almost identical in different legal systems: homicide, assault, robbery, certain forms of theft, rape, et cetera. These were surely the main cases which provoked blood revenge, and political power (not necessarily of the State type), which was then just at the beginning of its development, was interested in limiting and replacing the ancient custom of blood revenge, which weakened the social group and decreased its relative strength in the struggle with competitive groups.

The form of selection was sometimes determined by the stipulation that experts of some kind were to declare what was right and just. Thus the assessors of Frankish tribes had to "find" the law for the parties who challenged them by a solemn formula to do so. *Lagmen* in the Scandinavian countries held the position of juridical authorities "declaring" the law. In Iceland we find a kind of juridical professor who delivered courses of instruction in the law before the general assembly (*cf.* Vinogradoff, *a*, 165–6).

Of the numerous ethical rules in force in primitive society only a few ever acquired the support of power. Most of them remained what they were before: ethical rules unsupported by power or customary rules. This is the reason we are able to say that the birth of law was at the same time a step in the differentiation of primitive ethics.

Not very much had been changed at this early stage. The Roman kings and early magistrates only applied existing rules, and created no new laws; the early German and Slavic rulers acted in a similar manner. Courts had not yet become organs of power. The declaration of what was right or wrong in any concrete case remained a function of the tribe, acting just as it had before the creation of law. The power organization demanded only the convocation of a tribal assembly and the appearance of the plaintiff and defendant before it, and then secured the execution of the sentence. It continued to depend on the will of the injured parties whether the offense would or would not be prosecuted. Side by side with the emerging order, the primitive power-defense system continued to exist. At this stage power was still unlimited.

Many authors would disagree with the ideas formulated above, because in their opinion not every kind of power, but only political power, is able to convert ethical rules into law. They tend to designate the State as the agency which differentiated ethics and created law.

The State theory of law seems to be an illegitimate universalization of considerations valid for modern society alone. Within this society the enforcement of law is a governmental concern; the State monopoly of coercion is often proclaimed as one of the basic principles of modern social organization. The existence of this monopoly may in itself be disputed, for in many cases the State does not itself employ coercion: for instance, in cases of self-redress or of disciplinary punishment inflicted by private bodies (say, in a private school). In such cases the State merely regulates coercion. But be that as it may, the State theory of law is relevant only for the later stages of social development. Throughout legal history cases of interdependence between law and power structures other than the State frequently appear: tribal chieftains, feudal lords, ecclesiastical potentates, et cetera, may enforce the law as much as kings. Therefore, the State theory of law describes only one of several possible cases. As this case is that of our present social order, the theory might be used, as a simplification, in analytical jurisprudence; but it cannot be fruitfully applied in the general sociology of law.

§ 5. From Primitive to Mature Law

After the possibility of using power in the service of ethics was discovered, law gradually came to constitute the everyday framework of social life, with ethics unsupported by power and power not limited by ethics as phenomena of secondary importance. This gradual development consisted of a number of parallel and interrelated processes: (1) power gradually gained a monopoly in inflicting legal sanctions; (2) these sanctions were differentiated; (3) the primitive penal sanction was submitted to a thoroughgoing transformation; (4) power added new forms of selection to the primitive practice in this regard; (5) power was submitted to the process of legalization; (6) law became technicalized, and a new professional class — lawyers — arose.[9]

[9] Once more the statements below should not be considered as a revival of unilinerism. Two ideal types of legal order are compared: primitive law and mature law. It is not assumed that primitive law *had* to evolve toward the configuration of mature law; yet the historical process has not, until now, created any other superior type than that termed "mature law."

1. The first steps of the power (State) monopoly in inflicting legal sanctions were very modest: primarily, a parallel action on the part of power was introduced, whereas the dependence of the punishment on the will of the plaintiff was not abolished.

We do not possess sufficient knowledge concerning this aspect of the evolution of Oriental law; for Roman law our information refers only to the later stages of the process. But there exists a wealth of information concerning this change in the history of Christian Europe. Very important were some of the innovations effected under Charlemagne's reign which is considered by some historians as the First Renaissance (i.e., revival of the institutions and cultural trends of the Ancient World).

A certain number of high officials (*missi domici*, generally earls and bishops) received commissions from the Emperor to visit certain territories of the State, to convoke in each place several of the men of best repute and to exact from them an oath to answer questions, concealing nothing (*nec propter amorem, nec propter timorem, nec propter praemium, nec propter parentelam*). One of the principal questions they had to answer concerned the crimes committed in the corresponding area but left without just atonement because of the absence of a plaintiff. The convocation was also required to give the names of persons whom they might suspect. These persons were compelled to take a purgatorial oath.[10]

Gradually the interference of power came to prevail and private punishment was almost totally replaced by public (State) punishment. This was the third decisive step in the development of the social coördination of behavior. Today it seems "natural" that the State should be the arbiter in conflicts, but this is only a result of historical development, not rooted in the nature of things.

2. When power began to dominate in the administration of justice, a split within the originally uniform legal sanction took place: in addition to the punitive sanction, the purely restorative

[10] This was the beginning of a development which eventually resulted in trial by jury, constituting the basis of judicial procedure in England and in this country (*cf.* Brunner, *b*).

sanctions of compulsory execution and of assessing damages (civil sanctions) developed; these latter sanctions continued to depend entirely on the will of the injured person, whereas punitive sanctions began to be used both by the State and by private individuals.

Self-redress was known from the remotest times; but in the beginning it could hardly be distinguished from punishment. Its specific rôle was created, when power replaced private individuals as the agency for inflicting legal sanctions (*cf.* Stephen, I, 62–4). With the development of legal technicalities the sanction of nullity was added, as well as other minor forms (chap. XI, § 5).

The general tendency of legal sanctions is of course to become more and more precise; it would, however, be erroneous to introduce the element of determinateness into the notion of legal sanctions. For centuries the penal sanctions were almost indeterminate; the punishment, in concrete cases, depended on the arbitrary will of the Judge, the Law Faculty [11] or the Monarch. After a short period of completely determinate sanctions, as in the French Revolutionary Codes, sanctions have again begun to be only relatively determinate. Today, in criminal law there is a tendency toward making them again indeterminate, though not arbitrary.

3. Punitive sanctions, which in the beginning were based on the principle of *material retaliation* and did not depend on the "evil intent" of the offender, were gradually transformed: *ideal retaliation* according to the degree of guilt is the principle of later criminal law. This was an evolution common to all the branches of ethics; therefore it has already been treated in the chapter concerning changes in ethics (chap. VI, § 2).

4. The selection, by power, of rules forming the object of socio-ethical conviction and their "elevation" to the rank of legal rules, continued and still continues to exist. In addition to the "primary selection" mentioned above, other rules of behavior, long since acknowledged within the social group, also acquired the support of organized power. On the other hand, the ethical group-convic-

[11] In Germany, in the sixteenth and seventeenth centuries, the law faculties of Halle, Greifswald and Jena possessed a *jus respondendi* in criminal trials (Vinogradoff, *a*, 203).

tion itself underwent a development and very often new elements of this conviction were "selected" by power. Finally, a certain number of rules, once selected, have later on been excluded, either because they were no longer included in the ethical group-conviction, or because the political power was no longer interested in supporting them.

For instance, large categories of rules were excluded as a result of the trend toward secularization during the sixteenth, seventeenth and eighteenth centuries. Rules concerning the relationship of human beings to supernatural forces (apostasy, heresy or witchcraft) or rules of sexual morality introduced by the Church (sodomy or concubinage), ceased to be punishable. Later on a reaction took place and part of the abolished rules were reënacted.

The elevation of custom to the dignity of law continues until our days. For instance, in France the law of February 6, 1893, enacted the old custom of a wife taking her husband's name. In this country, courts continue to transfer into judge-made law the content of customary rules. Thus, for instance, the Supreme Court recognized the existence of a custom, according to which, in uninclosed and uninhabited places, it is customary to wander, shoot and fish at will until the owner sees fit to prohibit it (*McKee et al* v. *Gratz*, 260 U. S. 127–36).

Eventually this passive attitude of power toward the content of rules was supplemented by an active attitude, by the creation and imposition of new rules. This was *creative selection* or legislation.

A curious intermediary stage can be observed. Legal experts, mentioned above, began to create new rules instead of those already existing. This was, of course, continuing the old tradition. But the place of individuals who made the "offer" at random was taken by the power itself or by individuals specially designated by the power. Unconsciously they were guided by the principle of emotional compatibility so essential in the development of habit systems. The change consisted in replacing the slow and uncertain process of "normalizing the actual" by a formal, sometimes even ceremonial declaration concerning what conduct "ought to be."

True legislation was known in many advanced legal systems of the Ancient World. Thus, for instance, the Code of Hammurabi seems to be a codification of earlier statutes. The Romans legislated both under the Republic and under the Empire. It seems that the idea of legislation grew up on the ability of power structures to enforce special commands (Jung, *b*, 59). But legislation is one of the human inventions, and in many cultural areas this invention was either not made or not applied. For instance, it was unknown in Indian society and is now entirely due to importation from outside (Allen, 36).

True legislation (the creation of new rules, not the enforcement of those already existing) was almost unknown in the German States which grew up in the territory of the Roman Empire. Alfred's law contains an illuminating statement: "I durst not set down much of my own" (quoted by Pound, *c*, 761). The first revival of ancient civilization, during the reign of Charlemagne, produced a certain amount of true legislation in the form of *capitularia;* similar phenomena can be observed in English legal history. During the next centuries legislation was at a standstill. A new revival occurred in northern Italian towns in the eleventh century. However, until recent times, the idea that legislation could be used as a means of rationalizing social life remained quite unfamiliar. Thus, according to Dicey, the British Reform Act, 1832, conveyed to the amazed public that venerable institutions could be reformed by legal means.

In no legal system did creative legislation wholly replace the older form of creating legal rules. It only formed a supplementary method, and for many centuries the older method survived; it is only since the eighteenth century that men have become fully aware of the enormous potentialities of legislation, i.e., the power of creating new ethical rules by acts of authority.

Legislation, considered as creative selection, underwent an internal development. In the early stages legislators proceeded in a quite intuitive way: only common sense arguments were used. The stage of intuitive legislation seems to have never been outlived in the Ancient World.

Since the period of the enlightenment, a new type of legislation was added: rational legislation based upon general concepts. This new type first appeared in a metaphysical form: the legislation of the French Revolution and of the first half of the nineteenth century was in general based upon abstract theories and doctrines ("rights of men," liberty, equality and fraternity, "psychic coercion" in criminal law, *raison d'état*, et cetera). With the second half of the century a new form of rational legislation appeared: scientifically grounded legislation. A glance at the parliamentary papers of our own time reveals numerous statistical data, quotations from scientific authorities, studies in comparative legislation accompanying draft laws of major importance (civil and criminal codes, codes of social insurance, et cetera). "Expert legislative draftsmen are commonly attached to legislators" (Landis, 232). The idea of "social engineering" is gradually gaining the upper hand.

5. Power was the instrument which led to the differentiation of ethics. But having decisively influenced the ethical development, power itself was deeply transformed by the contact. Arbitrary power became, at least in part, legal power; especially the primitive power defense system was assimilated to the ethical defense system and formed together the legal defense system consisting of legal sanctions.

This process may be discovered in the history of ancient Oriental, Roman, German and Slavic law, but nowhere was the evolution so obvious as in Roman law.

In the beginning the Roman magistrates who had replaced the kings had practically unlimited coercive powers. According to Mommsen (*a*, *b*), the situation was one of legal arbitrariness: the magistrates considered it to be their duty to prosecute every citizen thought to have damaged the interests of the State. Historical evidence shows that this generally happened in cases of treason and of theft of sacrificial goods (because of the fear of divine anger). There were no fixed forms for beginning or ending judicial proceedings. Every citizen was compelled to answer every question put by the investigating magistrate, whose arbitrary will decided the issue of whether the defendant was to be punished and, if so, what punishment was to be inflicted. This was obviously an arbitrary régime, a primitive power defense system not related to law.

Later on the unorganized coercion exercised by the magistrates was submitted to more complicated rules. First of all, an individual convicted by the magistrates received the right to appeal to the people, convoked in *comitiae*. But the people did not want to condemn or to absolve the appellants without knowing the case in its totality; they demanded proofs of guilt or innocence. Finally, proceedings before the magistrate came to be merely preliminary and the real trial took place before the *comitiae*, i.e., before an organ of the ethical defense system. The unification of the power defense system with the ethical defense system into the legal defense system was in this way fulfilled.

The study of the development in one cultural area, may it be as important as the Roman, cannot be considered as a proof of the validity of a generalization; this would mean repeating the common fallacy of the illustration method. Students of early power (especially M. Weber, *c*, 645 *ff.;* Thurnwald, *b*, 180 *ff.*) consider that, primarily, the function of power structures were extremely modest; in any case it cannot be asserted that securing internal order belonged to the number of its functions.[12] Yet, if two propositions are correct: (1) that early power does not care for the efficacy of ethical rules (for the social order) and (2) that power in advanced societies does care for it, then the conclusion must be drawn that, historically, power gradually became connected with ethics. Decisions in conflicts, from case to case (Themistes, see above, § 3), and the enforcement of the sanctions of popular courts were ordinarily the first steps in that direction; the regular organization of justice was the second and the introduction of legislation into the number of the functions of power centers the third.

Gradually, precise limits of power were created in many legal systems: relationships between subjects were exempted from arbitrary interference by power and therefore became the exclusive domain of law; but in relations between power and sub-

[12] For instance, in West Africa, despite the existence of political power, the police function is carried out by men's clubs.

jects, as well as in the internal structure of power, the interference of the power defense system remained possible. This was the stage of semi-arbitrary rule. Such was, for instance, the situation in continental Europe during the period of absolute, and especially enlightened monarchy, or in England up the Revolution of 1688. Nowhere was it better expressed than in Prussia under Frederick II or in Russia between 1864 (when independent courts of law were created), and 1905 (when the autocracy was transformed into a constitutional monarchy).

The succeeding stage is that of the "rule of law." Every relation between power and subjects is supposed to be regulated by legal rules; in other words: arbitrary commands of power to subjects are no longer possible; the last remnants of the primitive power defense system, if any indeed have survived, are to be sought for within the organization of power itself. This is a stage reached in a few societies only and has been threatened by the political developments of recent years.

6. With the gradual penetration of the various domains of life by law a special technique arises: law, in contrast to other ethical forces, is no longer a result of intuition attainable by every group-member; in its higher ramifications it is attainable only by specialists, but it remains obligatory for everyone (i.e., it has to determine the behavior of every group-member insofar as he comes into contact with a problem regulated by law). Therefore the development of the ethico-imperative or legal system of coördination of human behavior is combined with the rise and development of a special profession, that of lawyers, whose rôle is that of helping individuals and courts to apply the technical parts of the law.

§ 6. Mature Law

The development of courts and boards, the amplification of the system of sanctions and the creation of a class of lawyers or specialists in law gave to ethico-imperative coördination its modern aspect, which marks it off so clearly from the other branches of ethics. These *differentia* are not, however, characteristic of law as such but merely of its present historical form.

It must be emphasized that the gradual addition of new elements to the system of legal coördination did not necessarily mean the abolition of the older ones: the process is rather one of accumulation than of a successive destruction which would leave only one method in force, namely, the youngest. Thus, for instance, in modern legislation we are able to distinguish metaphysical elements (such as a great part of the laws in contemporary ideocratic dictatorships in Russia, Germany and Italy), intuitive elements (laws based upon common sense, such as minor laws concerning many different branches of human activity) and finally elements based on scientific data.

Unscientific elements continue to prevail. According to Planiol (I, 43–4) modern codes can be considered fabrics of contradictions and of juridical heresies. The unscientific manner of legislation in both aspects (common sense and metaphysical) is frequently misused, perhaps in this country more than anywhere else. "Because of the habit of turning to legislation in all occasions, two sets of lawmaking have become very common despite their notorious futility: (1) lawmaking which has nothing behind it but the sovereign imperative; (2) lawmaking intended to educate" (Pound, *m*, 67).

Different historial layers may be discovered even in modern law (which we are inclined, without any very good reason, to call "mature"). There are in every system of legal rules such as are to be understood as reinforcements of the socio-ethical conviction.[13] The totality of legal rules of this type may be called "the socio-ethical minimum within law." This is a term falsely applied by Jellinek (*a*) to law in its totality. In doing so he overlooked the other parts of the legal system.

There are also rules which may be understood as derivations from the command to obey legal authorities; such are, first of all, the rules creating governmental offices and bodies and regulating their functions; the main legal effect of the existence of such rules is the imposition, on the subjects, of the duty to obey the directions of such bodies and agencies. Rules of this type may be called

[13] The conviction reinforced by law may be that of today or of yesterday: in many countries statutes are still "in force" which reflect the ethical views of the early nineteenth century or even of more remote times (for instance, statutes punishing blasphemy).

"the political complex within law." Its existence is generally expressed in the following incorrect form: legal rules only partly correspond to ethical rules; a certain number of them are neutral from the ethical point of view and in extreme cases they even run counter to ethical rules. This formula is incorrect, for legal rules *are* ethical rules.

There is an intermediary type, namely, behavior indifferent from the ethical viewpoint and not related to power defense, imposed upon subjects with a view toward the common welfare. This complex of legal rules which belongs neither to the socio-ethical minimum nor to the political complex might be called "the cultural complex in law."

§ 7. The Legality of Legal Changes

"Mature law" is the product of a gradual transformation to which the entire system of the legal coördination of human behavior has been submitted. As a part of this general transformation the objective elements of the system, the legal rules, were gradually altered. With advances of the process of the penetration of law throughout all walks of social life, these changes became "legalized:" it is usual, in "mature law," to have these changes take place in certain formal patterns established in advance by (constitutional) law.

The legal formalization of the process of changing the content of law means a new reinforcement of the legal system. If a new legal rule is created in forms foreseen by law, it is easily introduced into the behavior system forming law. Every time conditions are given which correspond to the if clause of the new rule, the response foreseen by law is effected almost automatically. These conditions form the "stimulus situation" within a new tendency of behavior built up on already existing ones. The relative efficiency of the creation of new rules in legal form and the facilitation of their introduction into the already existing legal coördination of behavior is so obvious that, as regards mature law, the proposition may be formulated: "legal rules are created only in legal form." This proposition raises the problem of the validity of legal rules.

This is, first of all, a practical question. Before applying law one asks the question: What are the external symptoms which distinguish a legal rule "in force" (to be applied by courts and administrative bodies and to be taken into consideration for scientific construction and for practical behavior in life) from other similar things, i.e., from moral and customary rules; from individual and collective legal conviction (ideas of what law ought to be); from legal rules of the past (rules which are no longer valid); from future law (juridical drafts, official or private), et cetera? The answer is: a rule is "in force" (valid) if it has been created under the conditions *a*, *b*, *c*, foreseen by actual law for the creation of future law (in other words, for the introduction of changes into the contents of law).[14]

In such terms, for instance, can be described the activity of the Supreme Court of the United States when it solves the problem of the constitutionality of a statute passed by the Congress. The constitution settles certain conditions concerning both the procedure in which federal statutes are to be enacted and their possible content (more exactly, the limits of federal regulation). The court examines the conformity of a given statute with these prescriptions and declares the statute constitutional (valid law) or unconstitutional (non-law, something which, in the mind of the authors, was to become law, but could not because of the transgression of the necessary conditions).[15] The same situation is present when courts investigate the validity of bylaws, or of collective contracts, or of the statutes of corporations, et cetera. Lawyers and laymen solve identical problems when they try to foresee how the question of the validity of certain rules will be

[14] This rather juridical proposition expresses the fact (which is relevant from the viewpoint of sociology) that, if certain conditions have been observed, a newly created rule will commonly be endowed with the power to determine the behavior of group-members.

[15] In the United States the first decision concerning the constitutionality of a law was made in 1780 in New Jersey. A practice similar to that of the United States is applied in Canada. For instance, on March 4, 1938, Canada's supreme court overruled three Alberta bills concerning the Social Credit Plan. At the outset of his judgment, the chief justice wrote: "It is no part of our duty to consider the wisdom of these measures. We have only to ascertain whether or not they come within the ambit or the authority entrusted by the constitutional statutes to the legislature of Alberta and our responsibility is rigorously confined to the determina-

answered by courts. Analytical jurisprudence helps courts, lawyers and laymen to solve such problems.

The reference to the legal form of the creation of a rule is certainly a formalistic approach to the problem of the validity of law; yet it is an approach which completely suffices for practical purposes. It cannot, however, pretend to explain scientifically the validity of law.

The validity of a rule is determined by means of a reference to law. The basic formula indicates the symptoms which permit us to classify a new rule within the system of legal rules which already exists; the legal character of these rules could be ascertained by a reference to some older configurations of law, et cetera. It is a *regressus ad infinitum*, which is the more unsatisfactory as we know that earlier configurations of law were not submitted to the principle of legitimacy (*cf.* below, § 8).

Furthermore, the basic proposition could be transformed into a legal rule: you shall consider legal every rule created under the conditions *a*, *b*, *c*. The question arises: How is the validity of this rule to be explained? Commonly some "ultimate principles" are referred to. The school of the natural law based the validity of legal rules (belonging to the system of natural law) on their conformity with reason, the historical school on their conformity with the demands of the national spirit. In our days the idea of social solidarity is commonly invoked. Such is, for instance, the doctrine of Duguit (*b*, *c*), whereas Gurvitch (*c*, *e*) stresses the basic value of the community and of all that is derived from it. Such "ultimate principles" obviously introduce into the doctrine of the validity of law quite heterogeneous elements. Sometimes they are meant by their authors (especially by Duguit) to give individuals the right of insurrection against positive law which would not conform to them. They obviously express merely the scientific conviction of certain individuals, and not a social fact (the fact that rules are applied by courts and administrative boards, et cetera). They can neither be corroborated nor refuted

tion of that issue. As judges we do not and cannot intimate any opinion upon the merits of the legislative proposals embodied in them, as to their practicability or in any other aspect" (*New York Times*, March 5, 1938).

by the observation of facts: they are beyond science and belong to the province of the philosophy of law.

A modification of the reference to "ultimate principles" can be seen in Kelsen's reference to a "primary norm." According to Kelsen, every legal rule is valid if it has been created in a form established by a legal rule of a higher degree: a general command of an authority is legal if it has been issued according to the higher rule represented by statute law; a rule of statute law is legal if it has been established according to the constitution, or the supreme law. But how is the validity of the constitution to be defended? Kelsen has to postulate the existence of a "primary rule" giving legal validity to the constitution. This primary rule, however, can be validated only by appeal to something standing outside the law. The unity of Kelsen's system is therefore broken and in the last analysis no valid explanation of the validity of law is given.

§ 8. Extralegal Forms of Changes in Law

The basic proposition, "legal are rules created in a form foreseen by law," is only an approximation which is invalid (1) as regards the earlier stages in the development of law and (2) in certain situations within mature law, namely (a) in the situation termed "obsolete law" and (b) in the situation termed "revolutionary law."

1. It is obvious that at the earlier stages of social development the principle of "legal" creation of law was quite unknown. Power proclaimed new rules to be supported by it and followed by the subjects — in any form at all. One of these forms was the tacit recognition of rules "offered" or suggested by legal experts. The best example is that of the *Sachsenspiegel*, which was the common law of Germany during the thirteenth and fourteenth centuries. This "source" was created as a private book by a private individual, but was later employed by tribunals as a code of obligatory rules! "The *Schwabenspiegel*," says Ehrlich, " . . . arose in the same way. In France the same thing occurred in the case of several books of law, especially the *Grand Coutumier de Normandie*, the *Etablissements de Saint Louis*, the *Somme rurale*

and the *Beaumanoir;* in England, in the case of Bracton, much more so in the case of Littleton and Coke.[16] The same may be said of the records of feudal law, the Assizes of Jerusalem, etc." (*a*, 252–3).

2a. The second situation regards not so much the basic proposition as a corollary drawn from it. If every rule created in a form foreseen by law is legal, then every rule created in this form should remain in force until it has been repealed in the same form. In order to make the doctrine consistent with facts, the students of "Modern Roman law" introduced the proposition that customary law might sometimes repeal statute law; a long-lasting nonapplication of statute law was considered as an application of a contrary rule of customary law. Yet the possibility of repealing a statute in this way is contested by many, and the very existence of a contrary customary rule is sometimes dubious.

2b. The last situation is that of revolutionary law. Let us assume that a new constitution has been established in a manner incompatible with the rules of the former constitution. For Kelsen and other formalists the new order of things is simply inconceivable. In actuality there is no difficulty at all. If a revolution occurs, a violent change takes place in the power system which supports law. One system is replaced by another. The new power system continues supporting the great majority of ethical rules which have been supported by the older power system: the rules of civil law, of criminal law, et cetera. But, in some instances, the support of the new power system is transferred to newly created rules. These new rules possess, therefore, sociologically, just the same support as the former ones.

If the revolution was a *total* one, such as the Communist Revolution in Russia, every rule of the former legal system becomes obsolete. The support of the new power system is given only to the newly created rules, to the rules of "revolutionary law." It may even happen that the new power system will lose every trace of a connection with ethics; in this case revolution means not a violent change in ethical rules recognized and supported by power,

[16] It must be left on the responsibility of Ehrlich whether the English instances are actually analogous to the continental ones.

i.e., of legal rules, but rather a violent suppression of legal order altogether, which is replaced by arbitrary rule.

The relationship between the legal and the extralegal forms of creating law is the following. The legal form of creation is weighty evidence that both elements of law — support of the ethical group-conviction and support of power — are united in the corresponding rules. This is only a high probability, not a certainty: cases may occur when either one or both elements are lacking; a rule created in the legal form does not, in such cases, become an objective element in the legal coördination of behavior.

The extralegal form is devoid of external symptoms. If a new rule of behavior is created outside the bounds of legal forms, and if support of the ethical group-conviction and of power are both proved, then we are in the presence of a new legal rule; if only one element is present, but attempts are made to create the other, we are in the presence of a projected legal rule.

Summing up we may say: The results of the study of mature law at normal times should not be generalized; propositions based on such a study cannot be given the force of "natural laws;" they are merely empiric propositions which accurately express facts related to certain social structures; beyond such limits their validity is nil.

BIBLIOGRAPHICAL NOTE

The best modern study of the origin and development of law is that of Thurnwald (*c*). Of the earlier literature: Maine (*a*, *b*), Kohler (*a*, *b*), Vinogradoff (*b*, *c*, *d*), Pound (*h*). Many excellent remarks are to be found in Ehrlich's book (*a*, especially 31, 37, 139–40, 143, 146, 214–15, 249, 252–3, 255, 272). Concrete material concerning law in primitive society is given by Diamond and Thomas; the first of the works mentioned must be used with caution. A good study of pre-legal society is that of Kulischer. The books of Diamond and Robson are useful for the study of the early stages of the development of law among historical nations. More specialized studies are: (1) concerning Greek law, Lipsius, Calhoun and Ranulf; (2) concerning Roman law, Jhering (*a*) and Mommsen (*a*, *b*); (3) concerning early German law, Brunner, His, Heusler, Amira; (4) concerning early Slavic law, Vladimirsky-Budanoff, Sergeevitch, Taranovsky (*b*); (5) concerning early Semitic law, Merz, Nöldecke, Wellhausen; (6) concerning the Ossets, Kovalevsky; (7) concerning Islamitic law, Tabbah, 657 *ff*.

The classic statement concerning the idea of differentiation of law from ethics is that of Maine (*a*, 14–16; *b*, 5). Among the new authors: Schmoller, Tönnies (*a*), Tourtoulon (179 *ff.*), Horvath, Gierke (*c*, 193), Gény (*a*, I, 457, n. 2), Ginsberg (150 *ff.*), Morgenthau (25–7). Evidence for the connection of primitive ethics and of religion has been collected by Robson (16–56 and 108–39) and by Gutmann. For the theory of the differentiation of law from a "primordial undifferentiated plasm" (an expression of Ward, *d*, 134, 185): Post (*b*, 46), Trimborn (417), Allen (28) and especially Hubert, with evidence from Chinese, Indian, Hebrew, Greek and Roman law.

The primary independence of power and law is stressed by Duguit (*b*, especially 19, 56, 246, 261, 350, 672), Kistiakovsky (594 *ff.*) and Kotliarevsky (27, 32). That power was the force which led to the separation of the legal branch, is recognized by Rolin (96), Vaccaro (446), Rogge, Max Weber (*d*, 42). According to Rogge, legal order originated when the retributive order (of ethics) and the political power defense system were combined into a unity (216–22). According to Max Weber, there can be no differentiation between custom and customary law as long as there is no authoritative agency recognizing certain rules.

The evolution of legal (especially penal) sanctions toward modern ideal retribution is studied by Löffler, Makariewicz (358–438), Hentig; *cf.* Lewin. The general evolution of legislation has been studied by Robson (161 *ff.*). For the evolution of legislation in medieval Europe: Jenks. Statements in the text differ from those of Jenks because he does not distinguish between creative legislation and the mere enforcement of earlier rules. That creative legislation appears only in a late period in the course of development is stressed by Sumner and Pound (*f*, 722). The idea of scientific legislation is one of the favorite ideas of Ward (*a*, II, 395–8; *b*, 309; *c*, 188–271). The idea that legislation is a series of inventions was expressed by Ward (*b*, 309) and Tarde (*c*, 169). Concerning the continuity in the development of law and the predictability of future changes see Timasheff (*a*).

Concerning the half-arbitrary rule in Prussia under Frederick II: Stölzel; in Russia, Gradovsky (I, 50–101).

The idea of law as the socio-ethical minimum was expressed by Jellinek (*a*). *Cf.* Soloview, Tönnies (*a*) and Schmoller; the latter calls law "the socio-ethical maximum" because of the intensity and the certitude of legal sanctions. The fluctuations of this minimum are treated in detail by Sorokin, in coöperation with the author (*h*, II, 538–618).

An excellent study of the validity and the efficacy of legal rules in their mutual correlation is that of Morgenthau (30–4, 39, 47–8, 227).

His conclusion is that validity is the abstract ability of a rule to determine the behavior of the subjects and that efficacy is the corresponding concrete faculty. *Cf.* Bierling, Ferneck (I, 79), Duguit (*a*, I, 43), Huber (388), who confuse validity and efficacy.

Kelsen's theory of the "primary norm" is expressed in *a* (83–9) and *k* (14–15 and 198). *Cf.* Janzen and Wilson. Correct statements concerning revolutionary law may be found in the book of Cruet: "a triumphant revolution abolishes *de plano* the constitution; this is a principle of law recognized in France, Spain and in Latin America" (102–3). *Cf.* Bieberstein (88) and Fehr (26).

CHAPTER XIII

DIFFERENTIATION AND INTEGRATION OF LAW

§ 1. Introduction

The differentiation and integration of law is necessarily a function of the differentiation and integration of ethics and power. Ethics are differentiated only, but not integrated: there exists no judge who could definitely adjudicate a conflict among the ethical divisions, and law forms one of the products of the differentiation of ethics.

Power is manifoldly differentiated. Among various differentiations, that into legal and extralegal (arbitrary, despotic) power is the most important from the standpoint of law. This differentiation is closely related to that into personal and transpersonal power with the intermediate class of charismatic: legal power is always transpersonal or charismatic (of course, the converse would not be correct: transpersonal or charismatic power *may* be extralegal).

Law is almost independent of the differentiation of power into general and special: generalized power structures (especially the State) are generally legal; specialized power structures may easily exist without being legal. For instance, insofar as the modern family is a power structure (very commonly it is not), the familistic power is extralegal (arbitrary): family law is not law applied within the family but law imposed upon the family by other power structures.

Law is also almost independent of the differentiation of power into monarchy, oligarchy and democracy. Even true monarchy (the rule of One) can be a legal power (autocracy in opposition to despotism). On the contrary, democracy may present the aspect of extralegal power: many ancient democracies degenerated in this way and became ochlocracies.

In contrast to ethics, power is not only differentiated, but is also integrated by means of hierarchy. The tendency of power structures to form larger, complex systems is rooted in their very essence. Systems of domination which remained independent of one another and, at the same time, claimed obedience within the same social field, from the same individuals, would encounter conflicts. Conflicts among power structures result either in the destruction of all the conflicting units or in a combination of them into hierarchies.

Law is closely related to social power. To every power structure a system of legal rules may correspond, namely those recognized and supported by the active center. Therefore the hierarchy of power structures has its replica in a hierarchy of legal orders; the legal rules recognized and supported by power structures of lower degree have to yield precedence before legal rules related to power structures of a higher degree.

The State is the highest of all power structures. Therefore legal rules emanating directly from the State or directly recognized by it form the upper layer of law. But other social groups have their legal rules as well, which form the lower layer of law. Let us call the upper level *State law*, and the lower level *social law*. As a result of the hierarchy of powers, social law can be "in force" only insofar as it is recognized by the State. This recognition is commonly indirect, as when the State recognizes large masses of legal rules created and supported by other power centers. On the other hand, the State gives its recognition and support to many rules created by unorganized social interaction and not supported by any power structure whatsoever. Such rules also belong to the category of social law.

The relationship between the two categories of law may be expressed in the following formula: State law determines the limits of the validity of social law. For instance, the State law may order administrative officials and tribunals to recognize the customary rules in force in a certain branch of trade. If a conflict then arises between two merchants, the tribunal will have to investigate what customs are recognized in the corresponding social field and apply these customary rules to the case in the same manner as if they had been directly created by State authorities. Another instance: State authority may declare that it recognizes, in matrimonial questions, the rules issued by the church, which is somewhat the case in Fascist Italy. Then, if a matrimonial conflict arises, the tribunals will have to investigate the rules in force according to church tradition and apply them to the concrete case. The recognition is not necessarily expressed in explicit formulas, but often rests merely on actual tolerance which, according to "the normative tendency of actuality," later on becomes endowed with the sentiments and reactions expressed in the formula "ought to be."

§ 2. State Law

State law is law directly created by the State. It depends upon the degree of complexity of a State whether State law forms one or more levels. In the primitive State there is only one promulgating organ: the monarch personally or the monarch acting with the help of his court. There is no room for further distinctions.

In the modern State the active center is generally complex and highly structuralized (chap. IX, § 4). This complex structure begets a corresponding hierarchy of legal rules: it is "natural" to recognize that the rules created by minor units within the power center must yield precedence before rules created by major ones. If a minor unit has created a rule which is incompatible with a rule created by a major one, this rule is from the start devoid of legal force. If a major unit has created a new rule with which certain already existing rules of power systems are incompatible, these rules cease to have force. The chief task is to discover the hierarchy within the active power center.

In States of a truly monarchic type (where power belongs to One, be he called Monarch or Leader) a rule created by this One or with his immediate participation belongs, because of its origin, to the higher level, and every rule created outside this privileged source to the lower level. In autocratic monarchies of ancient times the situation was expressed by the formula: *quod principi placuit legis habet vigorem.* The term *lex*, law, was especially applied to rules created by the monarch. Today the same formula may be applied to the creative activity of dictators in the legal domain. In modern Germany a true law is one that has been sanctioned by Hitler. In modern Russia, where the dictator stands outside the official State apparatus, his name nevertheless appears under the most important of the newly created rules, together with the signature of the "legal" authority.

In modern democracies the term *lex*, law, as in the phrase statute law, is reserved to acts of creating new legal rules in which parliament (the people's "representatives") take part. Sometimes a further subdivision may be discovered within this higher level. Out of the mass of legal rules created with the help of the people's representatives, one complex is kept apart, sublimated, endowed with superiority. This is the constitution, the complex of rules expressing the hierarchy within the active center and the relative positions of its members. A constitution forms a truly superior level of legal rules if (1) a special procedure has been created in order to revise it, or (2) if every law which does not form a part of the constitution is considered to be valid only insofar it is compatible with the constitution, or (3) if both conditions are united, as in this country (*cf.* above, chap. XII).

The term constitution is often applied in nondemocratic States as well as others. Practical evidence shows that it is only a misuse of the term. Older constitutions are still "in force" in Italy and Germany; but have they not lost all meaning in actuality, since they are no longer supported by the supreme State power? And the constitution of the Soviet State deals with the organization of a secondary set of authorities only (the soviets), whereas the structure and the functions of the primary authorities (party organization) are determined by rules existing outside the constitution.

The lower level of State law can be very complex. Minor members of the active power center may be empowered to create legal rules by means of delegation by the main legislative body (the One; or the people's representatives). The number of rules to be created in a modern State is so large that one corporate body is unable to carry out the corresponding task in a rational manner, i.e., after some deliberation. Therefore definite bodies (frequently administrative boards) are empowered with the right to create legal rules which are to be in force throughout the entire territory of the State, or in single divisions of it. Normally, it is administrative bodies who are granted this power; but sometimes special bodies are created within the judicial system. Thus, for instance, in Great Britain, "rules of procedure were codified by the Judicature Act, 1873; under a flexible system they have been and can now be altered from time to time by a statutory Rule Committee" (Durley, 77).

Generally this "subordinate legislation" is limited to special subjects (for instance, epidemics, highway traffic, public school curricula). Recent times,[1] characterized by unprecedented economic troubles, have produced a new type of delegation of general emergency powers to governments (in Belgium, Czechoslovakia and France).

The meaning of the delegation (or devolution) of powers is as follows. It is declared in advance that a legal rule created by the agent or administrative board will be recognized and supported by the total power structure in the same manner as if it had been created by normal legislative means. This support is naturally given only as regards rules created within the limits of delegation; if a local police board, empowered to create rules concerning traffic, should decide to introduce confiscation of newspapers carried by automobiles, such rules would not be recognized and supported by the central power structure; on the contrary, measures would be taken by higher authorities of this structure to stop the misuse of the delegated power.

Within this type of situation, subdelegation is possible: an authority empowered with the right to create legal rules is generally allowed to cede a part of this function to subordinate authorities. This produces new complications in the lower level of state law.

This lower level usually contains also another set of rules: those created by practice and precedent (judicial or administrative, in a certain degree also parliamentary). In the Anglo-American cultural area, where the right of tribunals to create legal rules seems never to have been contested, this possibility is generally considered as quite natural. In actuality it is not so; comparative

[1] C. Schmitt (403) argues that the "Kommissarische Diktatur" is an old type.

legal history shows structures where the creation of new rules in this manner was replaced by special judicial reports to the central authorities (the "first-hand legislators"), who then decided the concrete question and simultaneously stated a new rule (authentic interpretation).[2]

The very possibility of creating new rules by means of practice and precedent is the result of the following situation:

1. It is impossible to create rules which foresee every possible future situation and give completely clear directions for acting.

2. Insofar as completely new or confusing situations arise, someone must be empowered to find the solution. This agent might be either "the first-hand legislator" or the courts or boards generally dealing with analogous situations insofar as they are clear and not unforeseen. But this second possibility is really based upon delegation by the first-hand legislators; this delegation may be explicit (Russian Codes of Civil and of Criminal Procedure, 1864; Swiss Civil Code, 1907) or based upon tacit consent. This consent is expressed by giving to the concrete decisions of tribunals or administrative boards the same support as to those which represent merely the application of already existing rules.

The decision of a new or confused case is first of all a concrete decision. It states how the interests in conflict are to be adjusted. Such a decision is made by a tribunal or an administrative body with a regard for existing legal rules; it must be the solution which is most compatible with them.[3] If a similar case, therefore, is judged by the same tribunal or board, or by another tribunal or board, the same solution should be chosen: this is the way a judicial or administrative decision becomes a precedent: a rule ("prin-

[2] The Code of Justinian forbade any interpretation of law (Const. Deo Auctore, § 2; Const. Tanta, § 29. C.7.45.13). The philosophy of the Enlightenment generally demanded and obtained an analogous prohibition. *Cf.* the Saxon law of January 10, 1724, the Prussian law of April 14, 1790 (and the *Allgemeines Landrecht, Einleitung*, § 6), the French law of August 24, 1790, the Bavarian decree of October 19, 1813, which prohibited the publication of any commentary concerning the new Criminal Code (elaborated by Anselm Feuerbach).

[3] This proposition should not be confused with a theory which confines the judicial function to the mere application of a rule formulated in advance. Pound (*c*, 756) is right when he says that such a theory "proceeds upon an eighteenth-century conception which we cannot accept to-day."

ciple") is discovered (invented) in one case, and then this rule (and not the concrete decision) is applied in later similar cases.

Insofar as there are many tribunals or boards of different degrees of importance within the State, the obligatory character of "precedents" is variable. The decisions of lower tribunals or boards may remain unknown to other bodies or may be modified by higher tribunals or boards; the probability that any concrete decision of a new or confused case may "set a precedent" is rather slight. This probability increases with the ascent on the hierarchical scale of tribunals or boards and becomes about 100 per cent on the highest level, for the decisions of the highest tribunals are published. Different degrees of trust are ascribed to the judgments of courts of different degrees (Cardozo, *a*, 148). Even in countries where the decision of a higher court in a particular case binds lower courts only insofar as they continue to try the same case, the decisions of supreme courts create "great currents of juridical consciousness" (Aillet, 467). Furthermore, the certainty of practice and its predictability increase with the number of the decided cases (Moore and Sussman).

Similar instances take place in regard to administration. The acts of the highest administrative bodies become well known in interested circles; therefore, very probably, the rule contained in such decisions immediately becomes adopted as part of State law.

But if this is the case, it is incorporated only in the lower level of law, since sometimes the "first-hand legislator" immediately undertakes steps to reverse the situation. For instance, after the Supreme Court of Germany decided that the tapping of electrical power lines was not a theft and could not be punished, a law was enacted expressly in order to make such acts punishable. When the Supreme Court of Belgium declared that public provocation to murder was not punishable because of the lack of a corresponding law, a law punishing such a provocation was immediately enacted both in Belgium and in Germany. This practice corresponds in the United States to overrule, by constitutional amendments, the decisions of supreme courts invalidating ordinary laws because of their anti-constitutionality. This shows that rules created by means of judicial or administrative practice may at any time be repealed by legislation, whereas tribunals and boards, in their decisions, have to conform with legislation.[4]

§ 3. Autonomous Law

Social law is non-State law. It is law created by other social groups, but recognized and supported by the State; and the recognition on the part of the active power center is indirect.

The objects of this recognition may be of two kinds: rules recognized and supported by the active centers of other power structures, or rules not so recognized and supported. In the first case the recognition by the State is superimposed on the recognition by other power structures as a consequence of the hierarchical principle and the dominating position of the State in the hierarchy of powers. In the second case it is superimposed on the "social recognition," on the recognition, that is, by members of a group not organized by power. Autonomous law and customary law would be appropriate names for these two classes of social law.

[4] From the sociological viewpoint the question is important whether the propositions in the text refer to mature law in general, or merely to continental European law in contrast to Anglo-American common law. If the second alternative is correct, the propositions are of minor sociological value. Therefore a short discussion of the relation between the two forms of mature law seems necessary.

Of course, Anglo-American judges apply common law (judge-made law) much more than statutes. Yet this quantitative viewpoint is not decisive. Decisive is the fact that a rule of common law has to yield before statute law. Cardozo says: "If the rule that fits the case can be supplied by the constitution, or by statute, the judge looks no further" (*a*, 14). Allen (185) says that judges make law only in a derivative or secondary sense. The basic peculiarity of common law as compared with European continental law (wrongly called civil law) consists in the strict interpretation of statutes by common law judges in case the statutes conflict with common law (Stone, 130–3; Allen, 269). "Judges," says Pound (*a*), "not only refuse to reason from (new law) by analogy and apply it directly only, but also give to it a strict and narrow interpretation, holding it down rigidly to those cases it covers expressly. (This) represents the orthodox common law attitude toward legislation" (385).

Frequently distinctions between "common law" and "civil law" are made which cannot stand the test of verification. "Under the common law system the judge has to find his rule from the cases, digests, and statutes, whereas the judge using the code finds it or assumes to find it ready to his hand" (Durley, 77). Yet the judges, applying the codes, use precedents and digests as amply as the common law judge.

In any case the difference between common law and civil law is not so great as it is frequently assumed; it pertains more to the technicalities than to the content of the legal regulation of human behavior; it is not large enough to let us subdivide the "ideal type" of "mature law" into two subtypes.

Autonomous law appears in many varieties. It may be based upon: (1) one-sided declarations; (2) two-sided agreements or conventions; or (3) corporate acts of groups endowed with power.

1. One-sided declarations are capable of creating law only if the declaring individual is recognized as an active power center within a certain group; this recognition must give him a place within the power system headed by the State. For example, the owner of a private art gallery enacts rules for visitors, such as that the gallery is open from 9 to 5, that coats and umbrellas are to be left in the cloakroom, that no noise is allowed. Or, the owner of a factory enacts rules for his employees, such as the forty-hour week, certain standards of production, obedience to superiors, et cetera. In both cases rules might be supported by private sanctions which may be drastic (dismissal, in the second case). Insofar as the corresponding power structure is a part of the general hierarchy of powers, to that extent its rules are indirectly recognized and supported by the State; the power of the State may then be called in if the disciplinary mechanism of the "local" power structure proves insufficient.

2. Agreements or conventions may create autonomous law, if the rules created by social interaction mutually obliging the partners are indirectly recognized by the State. The most obvious case, in modern times, is of course that of collective contracts; such contracts create rules of behavior binding the partners (such as owners and employees), and behavior conforming to these rules is enforceable by the courts and administrative bodies (if not, there is no true collective contract). In this case, large social groups come into contact and create rules of conduct which are considered as obligatory by the corresponding "private" power centers. State recognition is superimposed thereon.

But there would be no creation of legal rules in a contract between two individuals, as, for instance, in a contract according to which one of the partners became obliged to work at the command of the other. There is here no new law, for no power centers are involved in the situation: it is merely an application of already existing law.

3. The corporate activity of social groups produces new laws of

the autonomous type if it creates rules of behavior enforced, first of all, by their own means and further by State means. Both private and public corporations can do this. Thus a private school or a club may issue rules of conduct to be followed by its instructors and pupils or by its members; or public bodies with self-governmental structures may do the same: a municipal council enacting a bylaw, or an "agricultural marketing board" in England, or a guild in Italy or Germany, or a Church creating rules of conduct (not dogmatical objects of belief) for its followers. Here, as well as in other cases, rules are valid only if created within the special competence of the body. This refers also to sanctions: only if they are in conformity with the legal rules defining the scope of autonomy are such sanctions applicable, if need be, by the agents of the State. Insofar as their application by the State is impossible, there is no autonomous law: for display of coercion is, within a hierarchical system, a monopoly of the higher power structures, mitigated by partial delegation of this function in favor of the lower structures.[5]

§ 4. Customary Law

The other main type of social law is customary law. Rules of this type are created like all purely ethical (customary or moral) rules; later on, however, they are recognized by the State and enforced by its tribunals and administrative bodies, though without ever having been promulgated as parts of statute law.

This is a very important point. If a rule created by unorganized social interaction is later incorporated in statute law (earlier legislation was generally of this kind, *cf.* chap. XII, § 5), the basis of the validity of the rule changes; if, by chance, such a rule later ceases to be directly supported by the group, it does not cease to be a legal rule, provided the indirect recognition by group members of all rules recognized by the authorities persists; true rules of customary law, on the contrary, do lose their validity if

[5] In order to see the situation clearly one must not forget that social groups constantly create not only autonomous law, but also customary rules, which are equipped with sanctions, but for the most part unorganized and applicable without a display of force.

it is proved that they are no longer supported by the corresponding social group.

Let us assume, for instance, a case in which parties are invoking a certain rule; for instance, that the sale of a landed estate breaks every leisure contract concerning it (*Kauf bricht Miete;* this was the case in certain parts of Germany). Insofar as customary law is to be applied, the plaintiff has to prove that such a rule is included in the group-conviction prevailing at that time (say: among the inhabitants of a certain rural district). But if the rule was first created by unorganized interaction but later embodied in a statute, the validity of the statute (rather than the disappearance of the group-conviction) could be contested in order to bring a decision in favor of the defendant.

The historical school of jurisprudence exalted customary law. Its principal idea was that legislation is only a secondary means of determining social conduct; the chief means is custom — an instinctive, empirical manner of finding out the best way for human beings to get along, a manner based on the activity of the "national spirit." Customary law is therefore, in this view, the best form of law: for, within customary law, conflicts with public opinion (or, in their terminology, with the national spirit) are impossible. The aim of legislation should be to describe already existing rules in such a way as to make them clear and unambiguous. In other words: legislation should be in the main conservative, not progressive.

Today such ideas cannot be accepted. Legislation, in its creative branch, is one of the most marvelous of human inventions. It would be unwise to leave the course of social life to the irrational vagaries of custom when the possibility of influencing it in a conscious and enlightened manner is given. But here the question arises: What are the limits to such influence? For it has been proved time and again (and here the historical school was quite right) that rash attempts to transform social life by means of legislation alone frequently resulted in failures and even catastrophes.

In the second place, the historical school tried to discover "natural conditions," the existence of which would permit one to distinguish obligatory customary law from merely "recommended" customs and habits. This was indeed a hopeless undertaking and, moreover, incompatible with the principles of the school: natural conditions would form something like that "natural law," the existence of which it so insistently challenged.

Customary law can be distinguished from customs and habits only by answering the question whether this or that rule is recognized by power (especially the power of the State) or not. Sometimes State law or autonomous law gives clear specifications as to which groups of customary rules should be recognized, supported and thus elevated to the dignity of legal ones. In other cases tribunals and administrative boards are left without such specifications; then they use customary rules whenever they have to create rules, instead of creating them "freely." Here lies the root of the intimate connection between customary law and the rules created by judicial practice, a connection which in Anglo-American countries produces the mixed notion of common law. "Today we recognize that the custom is a custom of judicial decisions, not of popular custom" (Pound, *a*, 383).

Customary law is not limited to the first stages of legal development, but continues to play a part even in "mature law." Pareto is right when he says: "Customary law is not merely primitive; it goes hand in hand with positive law, creeps into jurisprudence and modifies it. Then the day comes when the theory of such modifications is formulated and positive law opens a new chapter" (176). Yet so long as statute law has not been changed, "customs can never be set up" (Allen, 89). Of course, in practice sometimes they are (chap. XV).[6]

[6] Where is, in our classification, the place for such structures as the law of jurists and canon law?

When the ideas of jurists are regarded as binding for tribunals (the *responsa prudentium* in ancient Rome), such jurists become, by means of delegation, "subordinate legislators." If tribunals, in creating rules, freely accept doctrines professed by jurists, there is no *law* of jurists, but judge-made law. This is the actual meaning of the fact, stressed by Ehrlich (*b*, 135) that in many places the law of jurists displaced all other law.

If a Church is not yet organized in the general framework of the State, it may promulgate law just as the State does: there is church legislation (primary and subordinate), church decrees, canon customary law (insofar as certain rules created by unorganized interaction are recognized by the church authorities). If Churches

§ 5. The Correlation of Legal Orders

It may seem that the facts discussed in the preceding sections are of no sociological value. Yet they are. They can be expressed in the following proposition: the relative force of a legal rule (i.e., its ability to determine human behavior) is the higher the nearer is its point of origin to the kernel of the power center.[7] The sociological importance of the proposition is obvious; it forms certainly additional evidence for the proposition that, sociologically, law is the overlapping part of ethics and of power, for, if this basic proposition is correct, the relative force of legal rules must be proportional to the distance of their point of origin from the highest power center.

Let us now continue the study of the differentiation and integration of law. Different legal orders are superimposed each over another. Taken together, they are all imposed upon men. This is, of course, a heavy burden. The behavior of everyone is determined by the totality of the orders: one moment one has to act with a regard for a rule of statute law, the next moment according to a rule of customary law and then possibly according to a collective contract recognized by the group to which one belongs. This multitude of legal orders is generally not consciously realized and not felt by individuals. The interweaving of the different grades and types of law is such that it permits individuals to behave as if there were only one order. This interrelation of rules derive from the principle of the hierarchy of legal orders, which prevents and adjusts conflicts within the system.

How are true conflicts avoided and adjusted? The key to the problem is to be sought for in the specific relationship between rules belonging to higher and lower levels of law. This is the relationship of concretization: rules of higher and of lower levels, insofar as they refer to similar subjects, are likewise more abstract and more concrete rules respectively. For instance, a rule of

form parts of a power hierarchy, the rules of conduct created by them form a part of autonomous law. It should not be assumed that canon law is a peculiarity of the Roman Catholic Church. The Church of England possesses its ecclesiastical law (Allen, 318 *ff.*) as well as the Greek Orthodox Church.

[7] Of course, the term "relative force" must be interpreted qualitatively, not quantitatively.

statute law may enunciate the principle that every damage voluntarily caused shall be made good by the perpetrator. A number of rules belonging to the level of judge-made law (judicial precedents) determines what kind of damage is to be considered as reparable with the help of tribunals: whether "breach of promise" is such a damage (positive answer in Anglo-American law, negative in many continental European systems); or whether the "shock" received by a pedestrian or bicyclist knocked down by a vehicle (without causing bodily damage) is to be judged sufficient ground for claiming damages; or how cases are to be judged when the injured person was himself not entirely without fault. "In Common Law, if a plaintiff in an action for tortious negligence has shown to have been himself negligent, this either bars his right to reparation altogether, or leaves his right intact. In Civil Law . . . the principle is that when both parties are shown to have been in fault, the damage is apportioned between them" (Amos, 52).

As regards the rules belonging to the same order, an important principle may be derived from the fact that legal rules are recognized by active power centers: the special commands of these centers are to conform with their general commands, for these latter are ethical rules, recognized by the active power center. To recognize rules means to follow them in one's own activity. If the active center transgresses its own general commands, giving special orders not to conform with the general commands, the recognition would be only fictitious. The power structure would then belong to the type of arbitrary dominations — law would therefore not exist. This means a breach of self-limitation followed by the above-described consequences. Such is the sociological basis of the maintenance of the principle of legality in the activity of administrative boards.

§ 6. The Identity of Law

Now the problem of the identity of law can be discussed, more exactly, the problem of whether the term law is identical in the three layers of behavior to which people generally apply it (chap. XI, § 7).

The problem of identity is studied intensively by the modern sociology of law. American neo-realists deny the identity of law as the sum of abstract rules (X') and as the practice of tribunals (X''); the outstanding German sociologist of law, Ehrlich, denies the identity between this practice (X'') and the average behavior of law-obedient people (X'''). He asserts that the rules of conduct in force in social groups never exactly coincide with the rules of decision applied by tribunals. According to the doctrine of the American neo-realists, the decisions of tribunals depend not only upon abstract rules called "law," but also upon a number of considerations which cannot be foreseen in advance in any concrete case.[8] Not only the political, social, racial and other convictions and prejudices of the judge play a part in his decision, but also his state of health, his state of mind (which sometimes depends upon his recent domestic troubles), et cetera. This produces an element of unpredictability as regards law; jurists generally deny its existence, but laymen feel it and accuse jurists of being insincere and of unnecessarily complicating law. Furthermore, laymen have not yet relinquished the childish need for an authoritative father and unconsciously have tried to find in the law a "substitute." This produces a "basic myth of law certainty." It is a myth, for "until a court has passed on these facts, no law on that subject is yet in existence." [9]

For Ehrlich, a certain discrepancy between rules of conduct and rules of decision is quite natural: ". . . for a relation as to which there is dispute is something different from the same relation at peace" (*a*, 123). Rules of decision, the sanctions of which are punishment and compulsory execution, are "merely the extreme means of combat against those that have been excluded from their associations."

These opinions are, however, erroneous; they are based upon a failure to apply the notion of probability to the problem. It is

[8] Extreme realists deny any efficacy of rules!

[9] J. Frank, 21, 41 and 46. American neo-realists have as predecessor Pareto. "It is a serious error," he says, "to assume that court decisions in a country . . . are made in accord with written laws." In the decisions by jury not only written law, but political influence, humanitarian sentiment, emotional, social, political and other inclinations play a part (278–81).

only to be expected that a concrete judicial decision is the result of a number of factors, among which are those indicated by Pareto and American neo-realists. But we should distinguish between constant and variable factors. The constant factor is perhaps only a single one, but it is decisive: this is the tendency of judges to apply the same abstract rules. This tendency is inculcated in judges by "a taught tradition of ideals, methods, doctrines and principles, continuous as long as the course of teaching remains unbroken" (Pound, *r*, 8–9).[10] On the other hand, "the courts are creatures of the State and of its power, and while their life as courts continues they must obey the law of their creator" (Cardozo, *b*, 49).

The personal opinions of judges and their actual state of mind belong to the group of variable factors and their concrete value changes from case to case. But there are no reasons to expect that these variable factors tend systematically in any one direction.[11] Opinions of judges vary from day to day around some center of gravity. According to the theory of probability, the influence of these factors is mutually neutralized, and an average judicial decision must hence be determined by the constant factor, the abstract rules.

It is frequently said that a judge first finds the solution of the case and then justifies it from the legal viewpoint.[12] Yet this does not prevent the decision from being in the line of the pre-established statutory and judge-made rules; the subconscious activity resulting in the decision is guided by the reference to the value system embodied in these rules (*cf.* Isay, 56–7, 64, 98, 189; Haesart, 82).

This happens not only on an average, but also in the large majority of concrete cases: only "difficult" cases are more influenced by considerations of the kind indicated by the neo-realists; in ordinary cases routine methods prevail [13] as a result of the

[10] Hicks (23–32) draws a fine distinction between certainty of law for lawyers and certainty of law for laymen.

[11] If they do, a new rule of "judge-made law" is created which replaces written law.

[12] This is analogous to the manner of proceeding of many excellent physicians, who first state the diagnosis and then justify it by logical reasoning.

[13] This is stressed by Rolin (53–4), Tarde (*c*, 183) and Haesart (82).

principle of economy of energy unconsciously applied by judges in dealing with simple cases. "Lawyers and courts . . . get their law mainly from the standard textbooks" (S. E. Baldwin, 59).

Furthermore, within the legal order many technical means are applied in order to facilitate the victory of the constant factor over the variable ones. This tendency is expressed more in continental European law than in Anglo-American law. In continental Europe, courts are generally composed of many judges (at least three), and recourse to higher courts is much easier. This is generally explained in continental jurisprudence by the necessity of eliminating in each concrete case the influence of variable factors on the decision.

Is this dependence of judicial decisions on preëstablished rules constant? Are there no legal configurations and could no new legal configurations arise in which judges would decide cases without any reference to preëstablished rules and base their decision only on their sentiment of justice? Historical evidence seems to suggest a positive answer: pretorial law in Rome, equity in England, kadi-justice in the Islamitic world are perhaps significant examples. The "free law school" in Germany (and partly in France) and such a case as the "*phénomène Magnaud*," in which the revolt against the existing order of settling juridical conflicts became apparent and the vague idea of "*le bon juge*" was embodied,[14] can be considered as symptoms of a future development of the mentioned type. Careful analysis, however, leads to a diagnosis of the same kind as that concerning Maine's Themistes (chap. XII, § 3). Decisions, which seem to be absolutely free, are unconsciously based on value systems expressed in positive law or in custom approaching the stage of transformation into law.[15] "The judge, even when he is free, is not wholly free. He is not to innovate at pleasure" (Cardozo, *a*, 141).

Abstract legal rules are of course somewhat modified by courts and administrative bodies, but the relationship between abstract

[14] Magnaud was the president of the court of Château-Thierry (France) from 1889 to 1904. He simply disregarded legal propositions which seemed to him unjust. *Cf.* Leyet and Cornil (78–9).

[15] "Procedure presupposes an already existing law," says Carter (31), "or something in the place of law, which is to be administered by it."

rules and concrete judicial decisions is not that of discrepancy, but that of concretization. Writers who speak of discrepancy themselves involuntarily concretize the abstract rules in a broader manner than do the tribunals and then compare the two concretizations. They will very likely appear to be divergent, but the discrepancy is between the scientific opinion and the legal rules of the judge-made type, not between two legal rules.

Therefore, there is a norm to which individual behavior can and should be adjusted. The relationship between "rules of decision" and "rules of conduct" (Ehrlich) is just the same as that studied above. When acting within the domain of law (i.e., within the domain where certain rules of conduct can be imposed on individuals by tribunals and administrative bodies), the individual is influenced by both constant and variable factors. The constant is that of the existence of a certain judicial and administrative practice; the variable factors are represented by changeable social situations [16] and by the concrete mentality of the acting individual. The same causes which result in harmonizing average judicial decisions with preëstablished abstract rules create conformity between individual acts and the demands expressed in average judicial decisions. According to the theory of probability, the variable factors neutralize each other, and the actual behavior of individuals is, on the average, determined by the constant one, namely, the imposition of behavior patterns by tribunals and administrative bodies; the relationship between rules of decision and rules of conduct is not that of discrepancy, but, again, that of concretization.

Every concretization can be understood as an approximation toward the aim to be attained. Therefore, X''' is an approximation to X'', X'' an approximation to X'. Such statements are to be explained and corroborated.

When a statute is enacted, a goal is set for human activity — that of realizing the pattern of behavior expressed in the statute — and by this means a tendency toward uniformity is created in human behavior. To state this goal is the very sense of every

[16] Sometimes social situations play the part of constant factors; this happens, for instance, if durable changes in economic conditions are not reflected in law.

act of legislation. Of course, it is never its true end: one or another uniformity in human behavior is considered by the legislator as a means to a certain end (a high or modest, generalized or specialized social ideal). It is another question whether this end is attained; experience shows that commonly it is not or is attained only incompletely: objective results differ from ideals. In no human activity is the adjustment of actual behavior to goals perfect. Even a perfect team in sport does not make the goal every time. A brilliant business man is not always successful in his operations. The discrepancy between X' and X'', between X'' and X''' is nothing more than this necessary maladjustment between actual behavior and the goals it pursues.[17]

Up to this point we have analyzed the efficacy of statute law. The analysis requires little modification as regards customary law. In customary law the goal is to mold human behavior in accordance with preëxisting patterns; social pressure is displayed in order to attain this, and the pressure of the organized social machinery (courts and administrative boards) is only added to it. The difference from the case previously studied is that ends generally do not exist: everyone has to act in this and not in another way *because* fathers and forefathers did so; the motivation is much more causal than teleological. Even within customary law the goal of making conduct absolutely uniform and completely adjusted to the pattern is never completely attained, as disturbances play their part here too, and the actual behavior both of the members of tribunals and of average citizens forms only an approximation to what was demanded.

The fact that X''' and X'' are gradual approximations to X' does not prevent us from understanding X' as an approximation to X'' and X'''. This again is to be explained. X''' and X'' are approximations to an order in which actual behavior would completely conform to a system of authoritative patterns of behavior.

[17] It is probable that the cases of maladjustment are distributed around the pattern in accordance with the "normal curve" established by the theory of statistics; cases in which the deviation is relatively small are much more frequent than those characterized by large deviation. If the distribution is different, this testifies to the existence of certain disturbances which create a general maladjustment between the configuration of law (in the sense of abstract rules and of judicial and administrative decisions) and changing social needs.

X' is an approximation to an order in which these patterns of behavior would be completely realized in the activity of institutions and in the behavior of group members; it is merely an approximation, for every concretization is necessarily somewhat different from the abstract pattern.[18]

It is obvious that behind X', as well as behind X'' and X''', there is something that we designate by X. This X is an ideal order, in which authoritative patterns of behavior would be completely realized — in other words, a perfect coördination of human behavior. Such a coördination would probably exist under the following conditions: (1) if the system of legal rules would have been absolutely consistent, so that one response and only one would be indicated for every life situation, and (2) if the system of legal rules would be completely adequate to the forces, interests and needs of the social groups to be molded by law.

Law, in the sense of X', is always far distant from this perfect stage. In modern law, with well-developed technique, the first aim is probably better attained than it was in rudimentary legal configurations. But the increasing complexity of social life makes the achievement of the second aim more and more difficult. As perfect coördination cannot be attained, courts and administrative bodies are established in order to secure the best possible approximation to it, and the distance between the approximation and the goal certainly depends on the excellency of the machinery of courts and administrative bodies.[19]

Summing up, we may say that law is the common goal of manifold activities which are displayed in every advanced society and

[18] Let an abstract pattern be expressed by $abc + N$, where a, b and c are the aspects of behavior determined by the pattern and N is the indetermined field to be concretized. Every concrete act can be expressed by the formula $abc + pqr$, or $abc + pqt$, or $abc + tuv$, et cetera. It is obvious that none of the concrete acts is simply equal to $abc + N$ (for pqr, pqs and every over combination $< N$), and it cannot even be proved that one of the concrete acts corresponds better to $abc + N$, insofar as p, q, r, s, t, u and v are within the field designated by N.

[19] The situation can be expressed in the formulas:

$$X' = f(X) \qquad X'' = f(X) \qquad X''' = f(X).$$

The detailed study of these functional relations belongs to the most interesting special tasks of the sociology of law to be monographically studied. The study should tend toward the discovery of the factors influencing the differences between X and its functions and the approximate evaluation of their relative importance in different legal configurations.

which tend toward the realization of a perfect coördination of human behavior. This goal is never completely realized, and we use the term law when keeping in mind the behavior, the meaning of which is a certain approximation to it. Insofar as approximations are many, there are as many derived significations of the term law. They do not correspond to "three different things" (Pound),[20] but express one basic social phenomenon, that of the coördination of human behavior by authoritative patterns.

§ 7. The Rôle of Jurists

The coördination of human behavior by law can be more or less perfect. The degree of perfection attained in a concrete society depends on the number and the intensity of frictions which almost necessarily accompany the process of concretization. In advanced society, this process is helped by the activity of specialists, the technicians of law, or lawyers, to whom laymen appeal when they do not know the exact rules to be applied in a certain situation, or when their opinions concerning such rules are in disharmony.

The social rôle of these specialists is a complex one. Besides the function mentioned, they ordinarily, in more advanced countries, form a human reservoir from which future judges are chosen; they play a part in the conscious creation of law (legislation) as members of legislative bodies or as the technical advisers of legislators; they often play a large part in politics. But their principal social function is that related to legal conflicts.

These conflicts are pseudo-conflicts: for it is known in advance that only one solution can be compatible with the principle of the hierarchy of legal orders. The aim is to discover the exact legal rule or the exact legal rules which should be applied in the concrete case. But every concrete case must be adjudged in a manner compatible with past, present and future judgments in other similar cases; the solution must fall within a unified logical system, not outside it.

[20] The text refers to later statements of Pound (*cf.* above, the footnote 8 to chap. XI). In earlier works the trichotomy was somewhat different, for instance (1) a body of legal precepts, (2) a traditional technique of finding the grounds of decision and (3) a body of received ideals of the social and legal order (*m*, 37) were mentioned.

Lawyers have to help find such solutions. Their technique seems to have been once and for all completely developed during the first period of the blossoming of law, in ancient Rome; this was one of the decisive legal "inventions." Interpretation and extrapolation are the two means applied. Interpretation may be literal, logical, historical or teleological. Extrapolation is to be applied only in cases in which there is no rule to be discovered in statutes, in precedents or in custom (Cardozo, *a*, 22).[21] Extrapolation may be by analogy or free creation. The technique of both means in their finer ramifications is studied in jurisprudence.[22] In the sociology of law the social function of the activity of lawyers should be emphasized: to unify conflicting opinions as regards law, to find solutions in conformity with the total system of legal rules and not with single rules only.[23]

This is the soil on which misunderstanding between lawyers and laymen often arises. Laymen form their opinion of the law to be applied, basing it upon two or three rules they happen to know and consider to be very clear. Lawyers have to take into consideration the totality of rules. Often they have to explain to laymen that their interpretation is incompatible with one or another legal rule; laymen generally do not understand and begin to feel that the lawyers are intentionally complicating the situation. The same kind of conflict, which is unfortunate but inevi-

[21] Examples of completely new cases in American practice have been collected by Allen (182–3). The first post-war years created an extremely difficult "new case" to be solved by courts of many countries; it concerned the legal status of the foreign branches of Russian corporations nationalized by the Soviet government. *Cf.* Timasheff (*i*).

[22] The statements of Rheinstein (*b*) concerning the various possibilities in deciding new cases are excellent. Three answers are possible: (1) the rule for the new case is assumed to be logically implied in the existing rules; (2) the new rule is to be derived from the value systems expressed in legal rules; (3) the rule is to be derived from "living law," i.e., from the observation of actual relations between men.

[23] The function of lawyers, like any social function, may be missed: casuistry and the help to "laymen" in evading law are the main elements of social pathology as regards lawyers. On the other hand, they form an agency both of persistence and of development of law. Thus, for instance, in medieval France they maintained, in contracts, the obsolete formulas of Roman law concerning ceremonious stipulations (Cruet, 32). In modern France notaries included into wedding contracts a clause to ensure for the wife the usufructus of the husband's estate in the case of his death and prepared a change of the most unsatisfactory part of the "code civil" (Cruet, 159–60).

table, occurs in many other branches of human activity, when laymen and technicians come into contact: for instance, when the owner of a piece of real estate approaches an architect with certain ideas concerning the construction of a building without taking into consideration the nature of the soil, the size and style of neighboring buildings, et cetera; or when laymen do not believe physicians who disapprove of their homely "precepts" which, the laymen assert, worked as well "in quite similar cases." The trouble is that *cases* — in law as well as in medicine — are never "quite similar." Under such circumstances it is regrettable when scholars accuse lawyers of having such attitudes as a "priesthood with prestige" (Robinson, 28), or call the desire of laymen for legal security a myth based upon childish representations (J. Frank, 41, 161, 194).

Conflicts between laymen and lawyers are constantly retarding and hindering that unification of conduct which is the prime objective function of a complex legal order. But laymen approach the problem from varying viewpoints, lawyers from the more constant viewpoint of law. The random interventions of laymen tend to neutralize each other; the constant efforts of the lawyers tend to triumph. This is still another aspect of the phenomenon of the triumph of law, which is our basic object of observation in the study of law as an actual social phenomenon.

Other things being equal, in the struggle between power structures acting upon different masses of individuals, as well as in the struggle between the existing power centers and potential centers emerging from within the passive periphery, those systems get the upper hand which are endowed with a well-functioning mechanism for coördinating legal rules. Such a mechanism conserves strength and permits its application for more fruitful ends than intragroup struggle. This mechanism is represented by courts of law, practicing lawyers and students of jurisprudence. Such, from the sociological viewpoint, is the contribution of lawyers toward social stability.

BIBLIOGRAPHICAL NOTE

Petrazhitsky (*b*) showed how to reconstruct the rather fruitless juridical theory of the "sources of law" into a vivid sociological doctrine concerning the multiformity of legal order. His exaggerations were corrected by Taranowsky (*a*, 157–61). Gurvitch (*e*, 138–52) is continuing the analysis. More conservative statements on the same subject are those of Sternberg, Lambert (*a*) and, in older literature, of Austin (526) and Bierling (vol. III). A very stimulating study of the sources of law has been given by Hicks (9 *ff.*); however it is difficult to consider law as a *function* of legislation, judicial decisions, and administrative ruling; in another place (27) he calls legislation and the like *manifestations* of law which seems to be more correct.

Concerning the notion of constitutional law in its opposition to ordinary law see MacIver (*a*); concerning the devolution of power see Allen and Freund.

The prohibition of judge-made law and of creative decisions of administrative bodies was highly developed in Russia before 1864; *cf.* Gradovsky (I, 76–84). The authentic interpretation is studied by Gény (*a*). An attempt to construct a code which could be applied without creative effort on the part of judges was the Indian penal code; *cf.* Philips. Concerning the explicit acknowledgment of judge-made law in Russian statutes since 1864 see Foinitsky (I, 126–87). Concerning German and Belgian legislation directed against the decisions of supreme courts see Liszt (*a*, 599–600).

The best analysis of the difference between common law and civil law is that of Pound (*r*, 15–8).

The theory of discretionary power is especially developed in France. *Cf.* Jèze. The modern theory of executive power is stated by Jellinek (*d*, 564–72).

The notion of social law was studied by Gurvitch (*c*, 15–46); his views, however, differ from that expressed in text. In his opinion social law is the complex of rules determining the relation between the members and the "totality" within a concrete system. *Cf.* Renard and Hauriou (*c*). An antagonist of the very idea of social law is Bonnecasse (52 and 174).

The ideas of the historical school of jurisprudence concerning customary law were brilliantly expressed and criticized by Ehrlich (*a*, 443–63). Other statements on the same subject: Schuppe and Réglade. A modern review of the problem is that of Mokre. An interesting (but incomplete) study of the possible relationship between State and non-state law is that of Morgenthau (107 *ff.*). In his opinion, the relation can be (1) passive (non-interference), (2) positive (reinforcement by

State sanctions) and (3) negative (intervention aiming at some change in the contents of non-state law).

The honor of having correctly formulated the relationship of different legal levels as phenomena of concretization belongs to Kelsen (*g*).

The principal works of American neo-realists are those of Robinson, Arnold, J. Frank, Llewelyn, Yntema. Criticism by M. Cohen (*a*), Kantorowicz (*d*), Goodhart and Mechem. Ehrlich's statements concerning "rules of conduct" and "rules of decision" were made in (*a*); *cf.* Pound (*k*). In American literature ideas similar to those of Ehrlich were expressed by Carter; in his opinion, "human conduct follows its own inherent laws uncontrolled, except in minor cases, even by the deliberate judgments of courts" (12–13).

The rôle of jurists is brilliantly treated by Petrazhitsky (*b*, 171–84) and Ehrlich (*a*, 341–66). The means applied in continental Europe in order to prevent the influence of personal factors in judicial decisions are studied in every textbook on procedure; for instance, Birkmeyer (210–2, 686–7) and Garraud (V, 1 *ff.*). The multitude of imposed orders is duly appreciated by Commons (147).

The technique of the interpretation of legal rules is described in every textbook on jurisprudence; *cf.* Bentham, Austin (II, 348–70), Stephen (II, 347–67), Salmond, Wharton, Ehrlich (*c*), Allen (155 *ff.*), Mallieux, del Vecchio (*a*).

CHAPTER XIV

THE INTEGRATION OF LAW IN CULTURE

§ 1. Introduction

Law, as a product of historical development, is integrated in culture; in other words: interrelated with its other elements.[1] The correlation between law and the other elements of culture may be either (1) an "external association," based on the fact that certain causes produced simultaneously this aspect of law and that cultural formation; or (2) "causal-functional integration" based on a direct causal connection between law and certain elements of culture; or (3) internal or "logico-meaningful" integration, based upon the submission of law and of other cultural elements to higher values determining the style of the culture; or (4) mixed, composed of elements considered under headings (1) to (3) (Sorokin, *loc. cit.*, 10–53).

There are surely many elements in the correlation of law and culture which belong to the first category. He would be a god, who could explain, from the causal-functional or the logico-meaningful viewpoint, *every* trait in *every* culture. Explanation is always schematization, elimination of what is accidental. Therefore this first type of correlation must be put aside. The only question which should be asked would be how extensive are the accidental elements in a given legal system? But this question can be answered only after the causally or meaningfully related elements have been measured; and today science is very far from such an achievement.

Efforts have been made to describe the causal-functional correlation in a general way and to show the specific configuration of a society where legal coördination (determination) of behavior exists, as compared with a hypothetical society where such a determination is lacking (§§ 3–4). Much less advanced, because of

[1] The term element of "culture" is used in the same meaning as by Sorokin (*h*, I, 10, footnote 13).

methodological aberrations and erroneous opinions concerning law as a social phenomenon, is the study of special correlations between the configurations of law and those of other elements in culture (§§ 5–6). This study of causal-functional integration (in both its aspects) should be preceded by a short survey of the doctrines concerning this relationship (§ 2).

The last form of integration of law in culture is the internal or logico-meaningful. A logical relationship is, of course, possible only between terms and propositions, not between real things or phenomena. Not phenomena as such are to be compared and brought into correlation, but their meaning, expressed in judgments. If a culture is completely integrated, all judgments acknowledging or rejecting values, or organizing them into a hierarchy (of values) form a perfectly balanced system. In a completely disintegrated culture, judgments of the described type form a chaotic conglomeration. Both these extreme cases correspond rather to "ideal types" than to reality. Actually there is always a certain degree of integration, but it is only partial. The possibility of partial cultural disintegration, insofar as law is concerned, the conditions of such disintegration and the mechanism of the restoration of balance are to bestudied in the sociology of law. For practical reasons the study should be united with that of legal disintegration (chap. XV, § 5).

§ 2. The Basic Theories

Insofar as the causal-functional correlation between law and other elements of culture is concerned, the following theories are *a priori* possible: (1) Law is one of the factors determining the social process in its totality, without being (for the most part) determined by it; or even more: law is *the* moving spring of social development. (2) Law is determined by other factors, without helping (for the most part) to determine the social process; in other words: law is completely determined by other elements of culture. (3) Law determines other cultural elements and is determined by them.

1. A theory which considers the social process from the viewpoint of "legal monism" never existed. Nobody, in science or

philosophy, ever maintained that law was the only factor determining the configuration of culture and society, but a mentality congenial to such an idea is not rare; this is the idea of the law of nature. The doctrine of "natural law" should not be confused with legal monism; its essence is that there exist eternal, immutable elements and configurations in law, based upon the nature of things, or reason (God's or Abstract), and that men should incorporate these eternal principles in their positive codes if they want to exist in a rationally constructed society.

There are two varieties of this doctrine: the conservative and the progressive. The first (Roman and Christian doctrine) assumes that natural law *is* embodied in positive law, forming its essential part. The second (Enlightenment, modern doctrine) opposes the ideal natural law to the real positive law, which by this juxtaposition is necessarily depreciated.

This second doctrine is easily vulgarized, especially in revolutionary periods. The French revolutionaries believed that, possessing unlimited powers of legislation, they would be able to completely transform society; this belief was based upon the idea that society was a function of law. Introduce changes in law, they thought, and society will be correspondingly transformed. The Russian (Communist) revolutionaries believe that they are able to transform human nature and with it society by means of legislation or quasi-legislation (they are not very firm concerning this point). Law is for them only a secondary factor in the social process, since they are Marxists, i.e., economic monists (*cf.* below, under 2). But a direct correlation between the law imposed on society and the subsequent aspect of society is nevertheless asserted; a monistic causal-functional relationship between law and other elements of culture is therefore implicitly recognized by them.

The fallacy of legal monism was *experimentally* proved by the French and now again by the Russian Revolution; in both cases it proved impossible to transform culture in complete accord with revolutionary law. This means that other factors than law determine the configuration of a given society.

In a modified form one could assert that law played more of an active than passive part in the determination of culture. Such a doctrine would belong to the category of verbally quantitative theories, which can generally be neither proved nor refuted. In still more moderated form such a doctrine is transformed into the dualistic theory (3).

2. In contrast with the case just studied, doctrines considering law to be completely determined by other social factors are many. Every "monistic" theory in sociology (with the exception of the rather hypothetical legal monism) must come to the conclusion that if there is only one factor which determines the social process and if this factor is not law, then law must depend wholly on this factor. This is the idea of the "geographical," "biological" or "idealistic" monists; but only economic monism, known under the name of historical materialism or the materialistic interpretation of history, gives a well-developed doctrine of this kind. According to it, law is a part of the "superstructure," which is completely determined by the "basis," i.e., by the "mode of production." To every phase in the development of the basis a particular configuration of law must correspond. A great zoologist once said that he would be able to reconstruct the skeleton of an animal given only one of its bones. Marxists should theoretically be able to reconstruct the entire social organization, including law, given only the basic economic structure.

The doctrine of economic materialism has been described and refuted so often that it would be superfluous to do so here. One of the all too few statements on which all modern sociologists agree is the impossibility of explaining the social process by the development of any one factor, which would thus play the part of a moving spring within the complex machinery of social advance (or regression). If this is so, then law cannot be entirely determined by any one of the social factors, including the economic.

The monistic doctrine might be asserted with qualifications: law plays a passive rather than an active part in the determination of culture; in other words, the influence of other factors on law is stronger than the influence of law on the other factors. This is again a verbally quantitative theory which can be neither proved nor refuted. A further modification means again a transformation into the dualistic theory, now to be considered.

3. This third theory is the prevalent one, though it is seldom stated explicitly. According to this doctrine, in the interplay of various social factors law plays simultaneously an active and a passive rôle. This means that (1) the configuration of law depends on the configuration of the coexisting (or preceding) elements of culture; in other words, law is a function of social factors; (2) the configuration of law influences these other elements; in other words, law possesses social functions; (3) the relative strength of these two influences cannot be measured.

§ 3. The Social Functions of Law: the Viewpoint of the Individual

The correlation between the very existence of law and sociocultural configuration should be studied first. This study (or, more exactly, conjectures in this direction) was undertaken long before the sociology of law began to exist. A great number of "definitions" of law are nothing more than attempts to discover the social functions of law (ordinarily: *the* social function; for the majority of authors believe that this function is only one). A brief survey of the ideas expressed on the subject gives a valuable perspective.

The social functions of law may be regarded from two points of view: (1) that of individuals as group-members and (2) that of social groups consisting of a number of members whose natural drives are to be socialized.

From the individual's viewpoint, the most general function of law is the redistribution of forces within society. Law might aim at equality or at inequality; in either case it introduces changes in the respective positions of individuals, in their endowment with potential social force.

The individual who has the law on his side in any concrete case is much more "mighty" than he would have been without it; for to the individual's strength the corporate strength of the power structure is thereby added, perhaps not in its entirety, but in the amount available for such cases. This is what is technically called a "right."

On the contrary, the individual whose natural drives are checked by legal dispositions is much less powerful than he would have been otherwise: from his strength the corresponding amount of corporate strength must be subtracted; such an operation usually leaves nothing, or less than nothing (a negative quantity); only in exceptional cases is anything left, and even this only temporarily (rebellion followed by coercion and repression). The situation of having to act under actual or potential coercion (of law) is technically called legal "duty."

This redistribution of forces can be expressed in terms of freedom (will), of interests and of values. Both the first and the second expressions have been used in the history of legal philosophy in order to discover the essence of law; proponents of both views have frequently argued over the matter. The third expression belongs to recent acquisitions of human thought.

According to the freedom (will) theory, the essential function of law is to create precisely delimited fields for the activity of every individual and to protect these fields by insuperable barriers; within his own field the individual is sovereign and can freely display his will; but every attempt to overcome the barrier is checked by law.

According to the theory of interests, the function of law is to protect and to delimit human interests. The reflexion of interests in human mind (the ends) appears to be the moving spring in the struggle for law and the decisive factor in giving law this or that configuration. This is the essence of Jhering's brilliant theory, which stressed the teleological element in law. It became the "credo" of the progressive branch of the historical school in jurisprudence, another representative of which, Sir P. Vinogradoff, said: "More, perhaps, than any other part of human activity, law is directed towards aims; it receives its orientation not only from the past but from the future too" (*b*, I, 135).

The birth of this current in jurisprudence coincided with the dominance of utilitarianism in social philosophy. Therefore, the basic theorem of utilitarianism was, implicitly or explicitly, introduced into the doctrine that the struggle of individuals for the best expression of their interests in law secured the realization of social interests in law also. This realization was considered to be attained rather unconsciously, whereas the struggle for individual interests was explained in terms of conscious activity.

The value theory is characterized by the denial of the basic theorem of utilitarianism; it lays stress on unconscious or half-conscious actions guided by sentiments or emotions, and expresses the interdependence of law and other elements in culture in terms of values. Law is the recognition and the protection of values both by the active power center and the unorganized mass of group-members. The "requirement of uniformity" (Pareto, 1166) creates a situation whereby the recognition of certain values by someone is simultaneously a demand of their recognition by others; and how could general recognition be better ensured than by introducing the value into the number of those protected by law? Yet, within a given social field, there are many systems of values which are in competition, and positive law is the expression of a compromise between social forces supporting one or another value. In this way not intellectual, but emotional factors are given the first place (for the recognition of a value is an essentially emotional attitude) — both in the struggle for law and in legal statics. Pareto's fine remarks concerning lawmaking (1453, note 1) as well as Mannheim's basic proposition concerning the correlation between social situation and human thought (to which law certainly belongs) can be interpreted in this way.

It may seem that the will and interest theories are incompatible with each other and that therefore only one should be retained and the other rejected. Actually it is not so, insofar as the problem is studied from the viewpoint of what is and not from that of what ought to be.[2] Potential force based upon law means both increased "freedom" of the individual and increased protection of his interests. Potential force limited by law means both limited or denied freedom and curtailed or denied protection of interests.

[2] How near actually both theories of the active social function of law are, may be illustrated by the fact that Jellinek in two consecutive editions of his monograph devoted to the question (*b*) used both in the following combinations. "Right is an interest protected by power (1st edition). . . . Right is recognized will directed towards interests" (2d edition).

Are conflicts between "will-spheres" and "interest-spheres" possible? If they are, the dispute between the will theory and the interest theory is sociologically relevant; if not, it remains in the realm of verbal disputes which are so frequent in the history of jurisprudence and the existence and the frequency of which (but not their contents) form a sociological problem. In jurisprudence it is often stressed that sometimes protected freedom is beyond interest and that, on the other hand, interests are sometimes protected which are not backed by the individual will, which is the central point of every sphere of protected (or limited) freedom. Instances of abuse of rights (an owner destroying a valuable picture, a rich creditor pursuing a poor debtor, without needing the money), or of protecting interests of persons devoid of will (minors or the insane), or impersonal interests (corporate bodies), take a large part in such arguments.

Cases are conceivable when the redistribution of potential forces in society, effectuated by law, is more accurately expressed in terms of freedom than of interests, and there are other cases where the opposite is true. But this is a quantitative rather than a qualitative distinction. In cases of the first type, there is possibly no "objective" interest; in other words, an average man judging the situation would not feel any interest in using the corresponding rights. But there is still a "subjective" interest: if an individual is abusing a right he shows that he has some interest in doing so, perhaps a peculiar or even a morbid one; therefore the interest theory remains appliable. In cases of the second type a too strict interpretation of the terms *will* or *freedom* is the cause of the difficulty, for freedom as security against intervention on the part of "others," as the guaranteed support of social power in case of a conflict, is always present; therefore the situation can be always expressed in the term of the will theory. In addition to this, both types of cases are rather exceptional; usually both freedom and interest are clearly expressed within the legal redistribution of potential forces.

The true meaning of the antagonism between the two theories refers to problems *de lege ferenda*. The will theory favors a system of legal rules based upon the principle of nonintervention: the freedom of one is limited only if it is necessary to protect the freedom of another; the volume of the redistribution of potential forces in society by means of law is constantly tending toward zero. The interest theory favors a system of legal rules based upon the principle of intervention: interests are compared and evaluated from a social (super-individual) viewpoint, and the results of the evaluation are expressed in legal terms in order to protect the higher interests at the expense of the lower ones. The volume of the redistribution of potential forces in society by means of law tends towards the maximum.

Summing up, it may be said that the fluctuation of jurisprudence between both theories is, sociologically, a sympton of much more important fluctuations between individualism and collectivism as social ideals and patterns of social structure.

As regards the interest theory and the value theory, it appears that there is no great difference between them. The works of Heck, who, probably, is the most important among the followers of Jhering, amply testify to this fact. His chief work is entitled *Interessenjurisprudenz;* yet he uses the concept of value widely and applies it to the theory of interpretation of law and of the creation of law by judges.

§ 4. The Social Functions of Law: the Viewpoint of the Community

From the collective viewpoint the most general function of law is to create "order;" individual activities, which, without law, would interfere with each other, are transformed according to patterns which make them mutually compatible. This function of law may be expressed in terms of "peace," of "security" or of "organization," all epitomized in the common phrase "law and order."

1. Law produces *peace*. The opposite of peace is conflict. Law either (1) prevents conflicts or (2) gives simple and (from the viewpoint of energy to be displayed) inexpensive methods of settling conflicts.

Conflict situations of different kinds arise daily, in every social field, in large numbers. They arise from both the similarity of individuals (many simultaneously want to have something which can reasonably be used by only one) or from their dissimilarity (some are not inclined to behave in a manner corresponding to the desires of the others). Conflicts may be as many, within a certain social field, as there are possible relations among groups and subgroups. One of the possible conflicts which is more serious than others is the one between the specific interests and values of the active power center and those of the "mass." [3]

The very existence of law often prevents conflict situations from developing into actual conflicts. The persons involved in a conflict situation know that a mechanism exists which will impose a definite solution; generally this knowledge is sufficient to make the mutual behavior of partners conform to the pattern. Conflict situations develop into actual conflicts only in exceptional cases: (1) when there is hope, at least for one of the partners, to evade the hand of the law (a pickpocket always acts on this supposition); (2) when there are doubts as regards the law to be applied (most cases of conflict to be adjudged by Civil Courts); (3) when the "temptation" becomes too acute (for instance, inflicting bodily injury on an individual who had insulted the offender).

If, in spite of the general tendency of law to prevent active conflicts, a conflict actually arises, the law is there to restore "peace." The chains of concatenated rules are put into force: an actual conflict means generally that a primary rule of law has been disregarded; a secondary rule or, more exactly, a set of secondary rules are applied; they limit the conflict, show directions in which a solution should be sought for and finally enforce the concrete solution, backed by the total force of power.

2. Law produces *security*. At least, it increases security already created by other ethical forces or, in certain situations, restores security, if, for some reason, the efficacy of these forces has been shaken. Security (in society) is the probability that everyone will act in a manner compatible with the ways of others.

[3] Sometimes the specific interests and values of the active power center are not egoistic (i.e., useful for the persistence of the power structure), but social. An example of a conflict between social values recognized by active power centers and the values recognized by masses concerns the treatment of criminals (*cf.* my article *h*).

Within a legal order every subject is sure that the totality of rules forming the order will be carried out; he knows that he has the right to act up to the very limit of acts prohibited by general rules or by special commands based upon such rules; he knows that an intervention of the rulers, before this limit is reached, will not take place, and that he only risks the definite reactions of the rulers stated in the "secondary rules," but no other reactions. From this viewpoint, law is sometimes called the Magna Charta of criminals; of all actual or potential offenders would be a more adequate expression.

Legal security is an advantage not only for subjects. It works for the advantage of power. The support of ethics gives new force to every power structure and the struggle against potential power centers springing up on the periphery is largely effectuated by the mechanism of ethics, by the social pressure tending to secure its triumph. Even within the power structure new motives of obedience arise or older ones are reinforced. For instance, the motive of social solidarity, which may play a certain part in enforcing obedience, is newly awakened if the idea prevails that the concrete power structure tends toward justice. Finally the difficulty arising when the persons exerting domination change (as result of death or of other circumstances), is greatly diminished when the order of domination coincides with the ethical order.

The legalization of power results also in hemming in the arbitrary will of the rulers. Therefore sometimes rulers prefer to remain outside ethical systems, to rule "from case to case." But it is always through a mistaken calculation or a mistaken conception of ethics that rulers are led to act in this way. In a power structure supported by ethics the rulers have to adjust their conduct to the ethical rules in force. But in such a structure the rulers play an important part in developing ethics, or, more precisely, its main branch, law. The loss in freedom is more than compensated by the gain in efficacy.

Limiting power by ethics is therefore the best policy of domination. Power structures imbued with ethics are, everything else being equal, stronger than structures of the arbitrary type. Social development tends to make the combination of ethics and power in law the commonly accepted form of human existence in society. Arbitrary power structures are either elements of primitive social development or, in modern times, atavistic backslidings to older patterns.

3. Law creates and enforces *organization*. Organization assures to every group-member his relative position in the group and his function (Ehrlich, *a*, 40). Organization produces and enhances the social division of labor, and division increases labor's efficiency. Large-scale industrial enterprises, or great educational institutions cannot be imagined without a set of legal rules ascribing to every individual involved in the system a certain function and securing the noiseless and frictionless running of human machinery.

Keeping the peace, granting security and creating social organization are sometimes considered to be successive stages in the development of law (Pound, *e*). It is true that keeping the peace was the outstanding element in primitive law (replacing blood feud by "composition" or organized and limited revenge); but this social function of law did not lose its importance in later epochs either. Security seems to have been added during the period of "strict law," when legal rules and procedures received a formalistic aspect: the material tangibility of the external form of the bodily movements of the participants seems to have been the first technical method of introducing security or regularity into human conduct. But neither has this function lost its importance with the later development. Finally organization, which plays a large part in modern law, especially in the form of social organization (beginning with English labor laws and the Bismarckian laws of social security), was already present in former times: early laws for keeping the peace often took the form of organizing social defense against attacks (as in the laws of criminal procedure).

Stress may sometimes be laid on keeping the peace, sometimes upon guaranteeing security, sometimes upon the development of organization. Nevertheless these are not three different social functions of law, but merely different expressions for *law as order*.

Three great problems arise when we try to analyze this order as an actual social phenomenon: (a) whether this order necessarily expresses a "principle" or might represent a compromise; (b) whether this order is conservative or progressive; (c) whether this order (and its elements) tend toward immutable social ends.

(*a*) Every legal order is possible only on the basis of a transpersonalized power structure; every transpersonalized power structure is based on one or more principles of domination (chap. IX, § 4). This does not hinder law to commonly express compromises, and this for two reasons. Being a regulation of political, economic and other elements in culture (*cf.* below, §§ 5 and 6), law (as well as other ethical forces) is correlated to each of them. It may be said that the integration of different factors into a more or less consistent culture is effected by law (and other ethical forces). Integration is always a compromise; therefore law must be a compromise too. There is an additional reason for this. Not only have political and economic, economic and ethical, political and vital, interests and values to be integrated into one system, but the same must take place with respect to various and divergent interests and values within every particular field (political, economic, et cetera). In law compromises are expressed (1) between different factors in culture and (2) within every particular element in culture.

(*b*) Is legal order mainly conservative or progressive? Revolutionaries [4] are wont to accuse law of being a reactionary force hindering progress; law is praised by conservatives as a bulwark against too rapid social change. Revolutionaries use law as a weapon to uproot conservatism and create "a new order"; conservatives use law as an instrument to reinforce the traditional structure.[5]

This well-known divergence of views testifies that it is inaccurate to ascribe to law either a conservative or progressive tendency. Law can be the instrument of stability as well as the instrument of change. The choice depends first of all on the attitude of

[4] And some American neo-realists (*cf.* Robinson, 36).

[5] Pound says: "Legal precepts are almost certain to lag behind public opinion, whenever the latter is active and growing" (*m*, 43). This means an implicit recognition of the possibility of cases when public opinion lags behind law. *Cf.* Ward (*a*, II, 399).

the holders of power. If they are in a conservative mood, they will support already existing rules of behavior and carry out only minor changes, which will tend to reinforce the system in its main lines. If they are in a progressive mood,[6] they will deny their support to a large number of traditional rules and try to introduce, within the ethical group-conviction, a number of new rules. Very often they will be unsuccessful, as will also their conservative antagonists: the first, if the socio-ethical conviction will not follow them, the second, if this conviction excludes from its objects of attachment certain traditional rules which, according to the desires of the active power center, should continue to exist. The conservative or progressive character of law is therefore not a primary, but a secondary social phenomenon. It reflects the organization of society, the interplay of social forces at any given moment.

(*c*) The problem of the ends of the legal order may be analyzed "in general" as regards the sum total of legal dispositions; for instance, the question might be asked whether "the purpose of (legal) rules is the influencing of human behavior toward socially desirable ends" (Hall, *b*, 4). Hall assumes that the positive answer to the question is one of the basic hypotheses of the sociology of law. It is hardly so; a favorable influence is *ascribed* to legal rules by lawmakers and by people interested in the maintenance of one or another rule; the mass *belief* that a favorable influence actually exists belongs to the factors of the efficacy of law. But there is no reason to assume that serving socially desirable ends actually belongs to the essence of law or that this is actually believed by lawmakers, et cetera. Of course, law is a part of ethics; yet ethical rules may express any kind of socially imposed behavior, and it is only one of the possibilities that imposed behavior is (or seems to be) socially desirable behavior. In any case the sociology of law does not depend on the accuracy of the proposition; on the contrary, the proposition is one of the objects for analysis in the sociology of law.

Secondly, the problem could be reduced to an attempt to

[6] The term "progressive" is used in the same sense as by Sorokin: progress is equalized to change; rulers in progressive mood are those who are *rerum novarum cupidi*.

classify the ends of particular legal dispositions. Because of the compromise character of law it would be a futile task. All human concerns have had their part in creating law and will continue to do so in the future; a study of all the considerations would amount to a study of human motives and aims in general. But human aims are one thing, achievements another. The concrete ends of legislators are only rarely attained; *ad hoc* laws are always, from this viewpoint, partial or even complete failures. Moreover, they frequently produce unexpected effects, sometimes favorable, sometimes unfavorable. Nowhere are discrepancies more obvious than in the domain of criminal law and revolutionary legislation. In creating prisons, legislators hoped to reform the men submitted for treatment in them; but statistics have shown that, unfortunately, cases are much more frequent when prisons definitely disorganize human behavior, increase the probability of recidivism.

Revolutionary legislation always aims at a complete transformation of life in accordance with new patterns. Experience shows that generally, after a certain time, the old patterns are restored, at least in part; definitive are generally only such revolutionary changes as were already being prepared by the earlier development. Such was the fate of the French Revolution, and such is also the fate of the Communist Revolution, from both of which utopian dreamers expected the regeneration of humanity.

§ 5. The Quest for Imaginary Correlations

We have now to pass to the second aspect of the problem of the causal-functional integration of law in culture, and study the concrete correlation between the configurations of law and those of other elements of culture. This seems to be an easy task. For instance, in order to prove the correlation between law and economic activity we could study a certain economic formation, say, the system of free competition, and then study the legal rules concerning it. The study should result in formulating the empirical "law:" whenever the economic formation *A* is present, a legal system *B* will be found to prevail.

This appears to be a kind of scientific discovery. In actuality it is nothing but a tautology; for the economic and the legal description of the same social field are nothing but two different abstractions derived from the same set of concrete phenomena. To have free competition (from the economic viewpoint) *is* just the same as to have unlimited private property and freedom of contracts (from the legal). On the contrary, to have an economic system of the collectivistic-monopolistic type *is* just the same as to have private property abolished and contracts replaced by orders of administrative bodies. The correlation is a causal-functional one, but an *a priori* correlation, of the same type as the correlation between the angles of a triangle. Scholars who spent time searching for evidence of such correlations could well be considered to rival people who, by thousands of exact measurements, "proved" that the sum of the angles of a triangle is equal to two right angles. This is a very important question and should be examined in some detail.

When we search for correlations between law and other elements in culture, we seek to compare legal order with orders of other kinds: for we are able to compare only similar objects. What is, let us ask, economic order? It is a set of natural or imitative uniformities organized around a common social function (we do not have to investigate what this function is). What is familistic or religious order? Each is a set of natural or imitative uniformities plus uniformities of the "imposed" type, applications of morals or custom, all of them being organized around a certain social function. What is legal order, in its aspects which we relate to economic, religious or familistic order? It is, in each case, *the same order plus* the element of determination of a specific kind.

Law is not something that could exist independently, in addition to the other elements of culture. Law only structuralizes them, gives them a more definite and stable form. There are no acts which are legal acts only: every legal act is simultaneously either an economic act (to buy something means likewise to conclude and carry out a legal transaction), or a political act (display of power, voting, et cetera), or a "vital" act (founding a family by means of legal marriage), or a cultural act in the narrow sense of the word (giving university an endowment).

An objection to this view might urge that there are sometimes discrepancies or lags in the development of law as compared with other social factors. For instance, law continues to protect the indissolubility of marriage, whereas the mores have changed and correspond rather to a system of free love; or law continues to protect economic individualism, whereas real economic relations have become dominated by a régime of private monopolies. In both cases (and in thousands like them) law has been subsequently changed and readjusted to meet the changes in social life.

In actuality there cannot be any discrepancy between legal order and the elements of culture structuralized by it. The alleged discrepancies, lags, et cetera, are always imaginary. In our examples, sexual *liaisons* continue not to be legally recognized, and conflicts arising in connection with them (concerning children, alimony, inheritance, et cetera) are adjudged in the old manner;[7] or, in the other case, illegal trusts are mercilessly disbanded. As long as this lasts, the subjects have to act at least with a regard for this behavior of the authorities; the law is often evaded, but the behavior, while evading law, is still partly determined by law; if the law were changed, the behavior would become different.[8]

[7] Cruet (129, 131) seems to give good evidence in support of the contrary opinion, when he says: "In modern French law the legal marriage is being moulded according to the pattern of the free union; the pressure of mores has almost annihilated the prescriptions of the laws concerning divorce." Yet he has in mind (1) a gradual, but slow change in legislation and (2) a gradual, but much quicker change in judge-made law. The lag between law and the mores concerning marriage would be stated only by naïve observers for whom law is equal to the sections and paragraphs in the *code civil.*

[8] The correlation between the legal determination of behavior and the contents of the determined acts can also be represented in the following manner. Let us study a set of acts, which, legally, are cases of carrying out a precise contract *M* and, from the economic viewpoint, pursue a particular aim *E*. Single acts belonging to the set might be represented in the following way: a b c d e f g; a b c d e g h; a b c d e h i; a b c d e f j, etc., where the elements *abc* correspond both to the legal form and to the general economic purpose of this contract, *d* to the element of legal determination (the existence of the legal sanction and its influence on behavior), *e* is the element which is particularly relevant from the economic standpoint, and elements *fghij* are legally "free" and irrelevant from the economic standpoint. The legal study will take into consideration only the elements *abc* and *d*, whereas elements *efghij* will be declared "irrelevant" and dropped when constructing the legal abstraction. The economic study will take into consideration the elements *abc* and *e*, whereas both the element *d* (as being related to the social imposition of behavior and not to its

The ideas developed above are not new. In summary form they have been frequently stated. "Law is the totality of life," said Savigny, "but seen from a specific viewpoint." "Law is not a particular order of phenomena, as economic, domestic, moral or religious orders are. Law is the manner in which all these phenomena must be carried out. One could think of courts; yet their activity always tends to regulate economic, domestic, etc., situations" (Worms, *b*, III, 200–1). "We always look upon the same pieces from different angles," said Commons, "always seeing the same outlines, but under different shapes, colors and shadows" (8). "Law contains men in totality, in their relations to other men" (del Vecchio, *b*, 22).

For many authors the correlation between law and culture is that of form and matter (Stammler) or shell and content (Sorokin). Nothing can be urged against such formulas as long as they are considered to be only metaphors. But it is impossible, if we accept such formulas, to speak of a maladjustment between form and contents, for their correlation is given *a priori*.

A somewhat better approach to the problem of correlation is the search for immutable connections between different parts of legal systems or between certain parts of such systems, *P*, and social factors not regulated by *P* alone. Attempts of this kind may appear in the shape of assertions like these: civil law consecrating unlimited ownership is the satellite of democracy in constitutional law; or: to the same civil law there corresponds a definite familistic organization (monogamy with divorce prohibited); or: Roman civil law was revived in Italy and Germany during later Middle Ages, because of the fact that similar economic conditions recurred.

No one has yet been able to proceed far in this direction.[9] For

contents) and the elements *fghij* (as being variable) will be dropped when constructing the economic abstraction. The economists will proclaim that within a certain social field the juridical form *M* is used to make possible the economic purpose *E*, whereas other economic aims might be, but are not pursued in spite of the possibility of so doing within this legal framework. The lawyer will say that, within the same social field, the behavior *abc* (completely corresponding to the legal pattern *M*) is required.

[9] Especially studies in primitive laws show a disappointing variation in legal institutions of tribes belonging to the same economic level (directly opposed matrimonial systems and governmental organization varying from arbitrary rule to rudimentary democracy, with feudal structures in between).

instance, the system of unlimited ownership and free contracts has existed and continues to exist in connection with the most varied configurations of constitutional law. Liberal economics are now replaced by managed economics in autocracies (Germany and Italy) as well as in democracies (the New Deal in the United States, Agricultural Marketing Boards and semi-compulsory organization of key industries in Great Britain). The monogamic family with practically no divorce was established in Europe long before capitalism arose, despite the assertions of Marxists that this type of family is merely an expression in sex relationships of the principle of unlimited private ownership. Finally the revival of Roman law in Italy and Germany took place under economic conditions totally different from those of ancient Rome; Roman society was slave-holding, but there was no longer any slavery, and serfdom was on the decline, when this revival took place.

Researches of this type are based upon a mistaken attitude with regard to the aims of causal research in the abstract sciences; instead of correlations between the abstract elements of social phenomena, concrete causation of single phenomena is investigated. This is the attitude common in daily life (we try to discover the cause of illness or of the failure of some particular enterprise) and in history (e.g., the causes of Napoleon's failure to conquer Spain and Russia).

But even when attempts are made to discover correlations between abstract configurations, they result in nothing, as long as the *content* of legal change is considered as a variable. Let us analyze this assertion in some detail.

Changes in technique produce changes in law. Can such a correlation be denied? It is obvious that the invention of the automobile necessitated the enactment of many legal rules concerning the traffic on highways,[10] or that the invention of photography resulted in creating a new "right to dispose of one's own photographic portrait" (protected against unjustified publication).

[10] Before new rules had been created, inadequate rules of older law were applied. In France the pedestrian had to prove the fault of the driver (Cruet, 244). In the United States "drivers have been prosecuted for assault and battery, assault out of specific intention, and many convictions are found for manslaughter and even for second-degree murder" (Harper, *b*, 321–2).

The invention of the phonograph forced the German Supreme Court to assimilate the right concerning records to the exclusive rights of authors or inventors. The development of electrical power stations using waterfalls engendered a large series of new legal rules, et cetera.

But are such statements sufficient to justify a "natural law" to the effect that whenever a technical invention is made, a change in the configuration of law follows? Of course not; this would be an erroneous induction, for in the great majority of cases inventions do not produce any change in law. If one is inclined to doubt this one should analyze the list of patents in a given country; the percentage of items within it correlated with new laws would be infinitesimal.

Therefore our hypothetical generalization must be restated in the following way: "Sometimes, when a technical invention is made, changes in law follow." The task then arises to discover the circumstances under which technical inventions are followed by changes in law.

The following working hypothesis could be offered for testing: whenever a technical invention is made, and this results in creating conflicts of a type not yet regulated by law, changes in law follow. The invention of the automobile created new conflicts on the basis of the similarity of human desires: two or more individuals began to desire to occupy, simultaneously, the same space on the highway, which was impossible. The invention of photography created new conflicts on the basis of the dissimilarity of human desires: the desire of a publisher to sell photographs of a woman in a bathing suit conflicted with the desire of the woman not to have her portrait in this form exposed for sale (this was the essence of a German case which led to the creation of a new "right").

But now the question arises whether the first element in our hypothetical generalization, that concerning inventions, is necessary? Conflicts of new types arise without changes in technology, and this also produces changes in law. For instance, the increase of population or the decrease of crops (as a result of the exhaustion of the soil) may create conflicts of the scarcity type where they did not exist before. New legal rules may become indispensable.

Therefore, our hypothetical law is to be transformed accordingly: "Whenever conflicts of a type not yet regulated by law arise, changes in law follow." This is a highly probable proposition as it stands, but further observations would be needed in order to decide whether some additional qualifications (such as the frequency of conflicts, their relation to higher values, their relation to the problem of the stability of power, et cetera) are not necessary.[11] The striking fact is that the "obvious" correlation between technical inventions and changes in law proves to be a fallacy.

Identical results are attained when studying the correlation between law and religion or scientific ideas. Such studies [12] show that in periods when belief was common and strong, law was "sacral" and strongly protected the manifestations of religious sentiments; that in periods of skepticism, law was secularized; that scientific discoveries (for instance, in the domain of psychiatry) were incorporated in law; that law, sooner or later, begins protecting the new interests created by the advance of science. But these are obvious things; the contrary would have been almost impossible, for a certain style of culture (and every concrete degree attained within this style) is expressed (1) in specific contents of behavior (attitudes towards religion, science, et cetera) and (2) in a specific regulation of this behavior. The correlation between both is a necessary, *a priori* one.

[11] Haesart, the author of a recent work on the subject, concludes that the legal regulation of a new type of conflicts depends very much on the novelty of the case, on the particular interests involved, on the interest provoked by the case in jurisprudence, on the good pleasure of the rulers, on historical incidents, et cetera. According to him, the process of the legal regulation of new conflict situations might be compared with the impredictable sequence of the objects by which the attention of an individual is attracted (20–2). An attempt to study, from the same viewpoint, the development of defamation in common law (Harper, *b*) clearly shows that the changes in the attitude of the group-members are manifested by changes in law; yet no technique is indicated by the author (and for good reason) which would permit us to study the change in social attitudes independently of those in law.

[12] The most recent is that of Robson. The author was certainly unaware of the character of the correlation he studied, but was forced to study the development of culture and of the legal regulation of culture as an entity; the pattern "variable-function" was not and could not have been applied by him.

§ 6. The Volume and the Intensity of Legal Regulation

A correct approach to the problem of the causal-functional correlation of law and culture can be reached only when we remember that law is a complex instrumentality for the determination or coördination of human behavior in society and that the sociology of law is the study of this instrumentality. Therefore, when searching for correlations, one has to bear in mind the different forms of this determination (not the variations of the determined behavior) and to compare their variations with the variations of other cultural elements.

Legal coördination of behavior can be (1) of greater or lesser extensity or (2) of a higher or lower intensity. From the first viewpoint life can be *more* or *less* regulated by law. From the second viewpoint life may be legally regulated by means of (1) direct or (2) indirect motivation, in both cases with the use of (1) stronger or (2) milder sanctions. The problem to be investigated is therefore: What are the principal variations within social structures related to the increase or decrease of the extensity or intensity of legal coördination (determination)?

In this study we shall use an "indicator" varying from zero, when legal coördination does not exist, to one, when there is a complete regulation of the corresponding activity. The objects coördinated by law will be classified as political, economic, "purely ethical," aesthetic and intellectual elements in culture.[13]

1. The political factors in social life consist of the display of two social forces: political (or State) power, and public opinion. Power has been especially studied in Part III of this work. As

[13] There is no consensus among scientists as regards the classification of the vital factors regulated by law. Stammler and Croce call everything regulated by law economics. Kraft (*a*, 5–6) assumes that the primary objects regulated by law are economics and education (?). Schinkler (44) contrasts economics to politics and stresses, within the latter, the national sentiment.

What follows is only a preliminary and superficial study. An attempt to discuss the fluctuations of the volume and of the intensity of legal regulation is made in Sorokin's *Social and Cultural Dynamics* (chap. XV of vol. II), a chapter written in coöperation with N. S. Timasheff. A definitive study of this correlation depends on a continuation of this investigation (1) in other domains than that of criminal law, (2) in other cultural areas and (3) with regard to a larger number of periods. Many years of work by a large staff of skilled investigators would be necessary to carry out such a task.

regards public opinion it is formed by the summation of all efforts of persuasion (not coercion) emanating from the subjects and addressed to the active power center; of course their summation must be understood in the mechanical sense, as a sort of "vector." Strong "waves" of persuasion divided into two currents of equal force but of opposite direction produce the vector zero; whereas the vector produced by a number of weak waves, but of identical direction, can be very large.

Public opinion is an important social force. A member of the passive periphery, having personal opinions contrary to those expressed by rulers, feels powerless; but if he is aware that he is supported by public opinion, his confidence and strength are greatly increased. This feeling is one of the conditions inhibiting the acquired tendencies of submission.

What is the relationship between law and these political factors? Law, in the first place, is a link between the political and the ethical elements in culture. The relationship is not a necessary one; the legalization of power, i.e., the regulation of the first political factor, may be equal to zero, or be somewhat larger, or nearly equal to one. This maximum figure cannot be attained, for reasons already explained (chap. X, § 6).

In the second place, law forms a link between the two political factors: their relationship may be more or less regulated by law and this regulation may be of different kinds:

(a) If the relationship is not at all regulated, power displays its natural force, while public opinion is disregarded or suppressed.[14] This is autocracy.

(b) If the relationship is strictly regulated, power may depend on public opinion, i.e., may be structuralized in a manner making it necessary to conform to it. This is democracy, possible only in transpersonalized power structures with the people's will as one of the principles of domination.

[14] The opinion is sometimes expressed that the exercise of authority is always based on public opinion and that there can be no rule in opposition to public opinion (Ortega, 138, 140). This author admits that sometimes public opinion does not exist and that "the empty space is filled by brute power." He overlooks the fact that sometimes "brute power" suppresses public opinion and then fills the "empty space."

In a democracy, governmental policy has to conform to public opinion.[15] But even in democracies it is not always possible to apply this principle. Public opinion may be divided, as was the case in post-war Germany, where the situation resulted in abolishing democracy. Sometimes public opinion is set on carrying through an impracticable policy. This was the case in Great Britain towards the end of 1935, when public opinion insisted simultaneously on stopping the Italian aggressors and avoiding war. As the situation was only a transitory one, it did not seriously endanger British democracy.

(c) If the relationship is partly regulated, power and public opinion form two forces with no intermediate authority to settle their conflicts. This results in deadlocks. Therefore this is necessarily only a transitional, unstable structure. The constitutional (in contradistinction to parliamentary) monarchies of Germany, Austro-Hungary and Russia before the War were typical examples; Japan seems to be in an analogous situation today. Such systems generally destroy themselves, though this rule is not without exceptions. An example of how a power structure overcame a long and sharp conflict with public opinion within the framework of a constitutional monarchy is presented in the history of Prussia in the 1860's. King William and Bismarck strengthened the army against the opposition of public opinion. When, one after another, three wars ended in victory, the opposition was replaced by an enthusiastic acceptance of the governmental policy.

2. As regards economics, variations in the volume and intensity of legal regulation correspond to the different styles of economic order. If the indicator is equal or near zero, we have a "free" or liberal economy (regulation concerns only direct damages to the interests of others, with a rather narrow interpretation of this notion). If the indicator approaches the number one, we have collectivism (complete regulation, enforced by severe sanctions, with no individual initiative left, since economic activity becomes a collective monopoly). Between the two extremes are

[15] Even in democracies public opinion may be managed and manufactured (*cf.* Tufts, 363). If such processes reach a certain degree of intensity, democracy is virtually abolished and replaced by ideocracy.

different types of regulated economies (the feudal economic system; economics partly regulated by guilds; economics regulated by the State, in accordance with the doctrines of Mercantilism; the planned or managed economics of our days, i.e., partial regimentation, indicating for every economic subject his place in the collective activity, from the viewpoint of national solidarity).

3. The correlation of law with purely ethical factors in culture is based upon the fact that law is the link between ethics and power. This correlation is not a necessary one: there may be social order where ethical currents have nothing to do with power (primitive societies; arbitrary rule). Generally, however, the "indicator" lies somewhere between the two extremes. It never reaches the maximum, for in no society has purely ethical coordination of behavior been wholly nonexistent and failed to determine behavior in the sphere "free" from law. The totalitarian State merely *tends* to push the indicator toward unity.

Insofar as purely ethical coördination of behavior is effective, legal regimentation is either nonexistent or feeble (small in volume, low in intensity). Law is, to a certain degree, a substitute for a weakening code of pure ethics. There was no necessity for law within a truly Christian community. But in pseudo-Christian communities and in other hypocritically "moral" communities (for instance, in "Utopian" communities of different denominations) legal enforcement of behavior proved to be unavoidable. Revolutions (political, ethical, but also economic) disintegrate traditional social groups and simultaneously undermine their codes of ethics. Therefore they have to rely upon an intense legal regimentation enforced by severe sanctions.

4. The regulation of the aesthetic and intellectual elements in culture by law may vary from zero to one.

(a) If there is no legal regulation at all (with the same exception as was made with regard to a liberal economy), we are in the presence of a system of "free culture," which normally accompanies democracy.

(b) The regulation can be primarily negative: law (power through law) may not interfere in the development of culture, but only hinder developments which might create a danger for political stability, or which would be emotionally incompatible with the principle or principles of domination: atheistic literature is legally prohibited in a theocratic State, which has thus a negatively managed culture. Censorship is the main instrument of this negative control.

(c) The regulation can be positive. Law (power through law) may determine the content of cultural development. This is positively managed or totalitarian culture. A certain sort of official culture exists everywhere. At all times rulers and members of the social élite try to maintain this culture by speeches and pamphlets, or simply by exemplary conduct. But the official culture is not considered to enjoy or to merit a monopoly. The propaganda of official culture encounters other cultural influences issued by other centers than the official one: by political parties, economic or racial groups, religious societies, et cetera.

Quite different is the situation in a totalitarian State. Here the official culture is supposed to cover all realms of life. The cultural movement is not a result of numerous and varied impulses issued by an indeterminate number of cultural centers, collective or individual, but the result of only one impulse, that of the State, acting directly or through subordinated centers closely controlled by the State.

BIBLIOGRAPHICAL NOTE

Methodological questions concerning the correlation between law and culture have been studied by Kelsen (*b*, 612–4 and *c*, 875–6), and by Kraft (*a*, 1–6). According to the latter, the study of the social functions of law does not belong to the task of the sociology of law. A competent study of the integration of law in culture is that of Guins (*b*).

According to Sorokin (*c*), Petrazhitsky, Stammler and Commons could be considered as legal monists, but there is no necessity to interpret their theories in this manner. Commons indicates as legal monists authors in the tradition of Hobbes, Bentham and Austin (299). Cruet (241) mentions Schmoller. The idea that legal monism frequently accompanies radicalism in politics is expressed by Schinkler (67).

Sociological monism denying any place to law in the social process is described by Sorokin (*e*, 224 *ff*., 314 *ff*., 439 *ff*., 523 *ff*.). Marx's decisive statements on law are contained in his *Kritik* (*b*). Later studies of the same trend are those of Kautsky and Bukharin. Among the immense critical literature *cf.* Masaryk, Novgorodtseff, Gentile, Hook, Strachey,

Stammler (*d*) and Max Weber (*b*). Attempts to discover concrete correlations between the configurations of law and of economics are made by Loria.

As representative of the passive theory Carter should be named; according to him, law is merely a recording of habits.

The literature concerning the social functions of law virtually coincides with the general literature of theoretical jurisprudence: almost every author has his own view. Vinogradoff's statement concerning law as a redistribution of social energy is one of the best from the sociological viewpoint (*a*, 46–52). Not very different are the opinions of Merkel and Hippel; for the latter a legal rule is a help for one who acts within its limits, a barrier for one who tries to transgress it. Law as the delimitation of the spheres of freedom is Kant's theory. In later literature the work of Windscheid is the most representative. That law is the delimitation of interests is Jhering's theory. Long before him the German literature treated the term of "legal values" as objects of protection; the first statement is that of Birnbaum; *cf.* Oppenheim. The legal doctrine of Marxism can be considered a variation of the interest theory. Among recent American statements concerning interests, the following ones should be mentioned: Harper (*a*, 308–10) and Pound (*c*, 763–6; *m*, 3 and 5–9; *o*, 368–70). Very important are the statements of Petrazhitsky (*b*) who discusses the distributory, the organizing and the educative functions of law; *cf.* Babb (*b*). For the correlation of values and of interests see Perry (27).

A very suggestive discussion concerning the meaning of the term "right and duty" has taken place in American literature since 1913. The outstanding works are those of Hohfeld, Corbin, and Kocourek (*b*). An attempt to apply the conclusions of this controversy to the sociological study of law was made by Commons (86–115). In European literature the most important works concerning the subject are those of Bierling (I, 175–274) and Petrazhitsky (*b*, 371 *ff.*).

The best study of law as an instrument of order is that of Pound (*e*); he considers keeping the peace, security and organization as historical stages in the general evolution of law.

The relationship of law to conservative or progressive order is mentioned by Vinogradoff (*b*, I, 146). *Cf.* Schinkler (63).

The problem of the ends of law (especially that of common welfare as its end) has been amply discussed at the third session of the International Institute of the Philosophy of Law and of the Sociology of Law (*cf.* Annuaire III, published in 1938).

The frequently recurring discrepancy between the ends of social actions and their results has been studied by Merton. As regards law, excellent statements have been made by Pareto (453, note 1).

The compromise character of legal evolution has been stressed by Jhering (*c*) and Jellinek (*e*).

Public opinion and its influence in social life (especially in law) are studied by Ross (352), Bauer, Michels and Young. Democracy as the rule of public opinion is studied by Bryce (I, 151–62).

Philosophical studies of the correlation between law and economics are those of Stammler (*c*) and Croce. Stammler's viewpoint has been criticized by Max Weber (*a*). *Cf.* Ehrlich (*a*, 241). More sociological are the works of Darmstaedter (*b*), Navratil, Renner, Voigt, del Vecchio (*b*) and Véniamin.

The correlation between the development of law and of culture is studied by Robson. Concerning cultural lags *cf.* Cairns (166 *ff.*) and Britt (*a*, 696).

CHAPTER XV

LEGAL DISEQUILIBRIUM AND LEGAL DISINTEGRATION

§ 1. Introduction

It is now possible to study some questions which were postponed during the previous discussion, questions concerning legal disequilibrium and legal disintegration.

The probability that law will be obeyed seems to be so high that the question naturally arises, how it is possible that in certain cases law may remain ineffective. In other words, how it is possible that legal equilibrium would be disturbed. The possibility of crime or of other abnormal acts does not present a great difficulty. Crime as a regularly repeated anomaly is provided for in the legal structure. Yet this question must be studied: How could the recurrence of such anomalies be interpreted without destroying the concept of legal uniformity of behavior (§ 2)?

More difficulty is presented by the familiar case when a discrepancy takes place between the demands of the verbal formula in which law is expressed and the actual behavior of the individuals submitted to law, i.e., when average human behavior is somewhat different from what it ought to be according to formulated law (§§ 3–4).

Finally, when accumulated, cases of "legal disequilibrium" may be interpreted as a partial disintegration of culture, with law as one of the disintegrated elements. The question arises whether such an interpretation is consistent with the basic proposition stated in chapter XIV, according to which the configuration of law (in its totality, not in its sometimes deceptive "written" part) is merely another expression of the configuration of extra-legal elements in culture (§ 5).

§ 2. Legal Uniformities and Crime

No legal rule is carried out in every case to which it should be applied; every rule is sometimes transgressed. Does this not destroy the very concept of legal uniformities of behavior? Are not such uniformities something completely different from those expressed by scientific laws?

Law is a social force which acts on the behavior of individuals. Like every force, this action should be expressed quantitatively; unfortunately, there is no unit of measurement available, and there is no technique existing which would help to measure this action in separate cases. Nevertheless, the action of law can be compared with the action of other forces; it can be larger or smaller than their influence; it can vary from case to case, be larger at one time and smaller at another. In order to describe the efficacy of law in a concrete case we can use the concept of the resultant in the composition of forces. In a given case, we may say, the force of law was encountered by other forces (for instance, by asocial drives of the individuals, or by their moral conviction incompatible with the demands of law), and proved to be weaker than the latter. In another case the force of law, when also encountered by other forces, proved to be the stronger. In still another case the force of law was helped by other forces and the resultant was a series of energetic acts in the direction pointed out by law.

Cases in which law does not gain the upper hand do not mean that law had not displayed its force; they testify only that law is not the only force determining human behavior. The situation is somewhat identical with the one in the physical world. According to the law of gravitation every body is attracted by the earth, but an air-balloon rises, as does also an aeroplane. This does not mean that a balloon or an aeroplane is not submitted to the law of gravitation; it means only that, in the concrete case, the force of gravitation was smaller than other forces acting in the same field. For a superficial observer, the corresponding bodies behaved as if they were not submitted to the law of gravitation. Careful observation, however, will show that the force of gravitation was completely represented in the resultant.

Summing up, we may say that crimes and other cases of abnormal behavior do not invalidate the proposition that to legal rules in force correspond legal uniformities of behavior, the sum of which forms legal order.

§ 3. Legal Disequilibrium

Observation shows that in some cases the prediction of behavior based on the interpretation of legal rules is not completely corroborated by facts. Actual behavior forms a uniformity which does not completely coincide with that demanded by the verbal formula of law. Law in books and law in action are two different things (Pound, *m*, 120). How can this be explained?

Every individual's behavior lies somewhere between complete determination by law and complete freedom from such determination. The position of an individual on this scale is variable: he can advance or regress on it. So long as individual movements are casual they tend to neutralize each other and do not produce uniformities. But the majority of the causes of deviation are of a kind that makes probable simultaneous and similar changes in the attitudes of a large number of individuals. Added together, individual deviations produce disturbances in the total system.

The correlation between legal and extralegal uniformities may be that of the identity of trends: the imposition of legal patterns of behavior acts on the behavior of men in the same direction as the imposition of other patterns (purely ethical or purely imperative), or as the tendency of imitation, or as the resultant of the forces contained in "similar conditions." Such identity may be the result of a simultaneous and parallel development within law and of other factors in culture — this is probably a rather rare case. Ordinarily, identity is created by means of the superimposition of one uniformity on another of a different type; this happens, for instance, in all cases of "conservative legislation," when a customary rule is selected and elevated to the rank of a legal rule.

If the legal determination of behavior is superimposed on nonlegal uniformities, it helps to make "atypical acts" less frequent. If a legal rule reinforces a customary rule which, in its turn, is thoroughly adapted to the economic (and other) conditions of existence in the given social field, then to the legal pattern *A* a set of acts *a*, *a*, *a*, . . . *a* (where *a* is an act conformable with *A*) will correspond with almost no interference.

The same happens if nonlegal (customary, moral, purely imperative) coördination of behavior is superimposed on a legal one; for instance, a philosophical theory may be created which initiates a new system of social morals; these new morals reinforce weak points in the framework of law.[1]

The identity of trends is not at all necessarily present. It is entirely possible that legal and nonlegal uniformities *tend* to become divergent: legal patterns are imposed which are incompatible with extralegal (moral or customary) patterns — this gives rise to ethical conflicts (*cf.* chap. VII, § 8), or legal patterns are imposed which are incompatible with existing imitative or "natural" uniformities of behavior. Conversely, imitative or natural tendencies may arise or extralegal patterns of behavior be imposed which would be incompatible with legal patterns in force.

1. In many cases newly imposed legal patterns succeed in molding human behavior; no legal disequilibrium arises. In other cases the realization of new legal rules encounters resistance on the part of the subjects.

The causes of such resistance are various. Resistance very often depends on the fact that social groups endowed with distinct ethical convictions and social groups endowed with power structures do not coincide. On a map representing a social field the boundaries dividing the two kinds of groups cross each other a hundred times. Legal coördination is often an attempt at unification of behavior within different groups, and as long as such an attempt persists, cases of maladjustment and resistance may be frequent.[2]

Resistance is to be observed especially in cases when the law-

[1] Hegel's *apologia* for the Prussian State reinforced the legal rules commanding obedience to authorities; this philosophy was perhaps one of the factors promoting the proverbial law-abiding character of pre-war Germany.

[2] Before the war Austria-Hungary gave a number of excellent instances based on the heterogeneity of her population and on the difference of the historical fate of her provinces. Some of them (concerning the practical nonapplication of many parts of the Austrian Civil Code in Bukowina) were fully treated by Ehrlich (*a*) who probably unduly generalized such facts when creating his basic theory in the field of the sociology of law.

maker commands acts which, according to the ethical group-conviction, "ought not to be" or prohibits acts which, according to this conviction, "ought to be," — as for instance, if the law orders everyone to denounce attempted offenses, even those committed by one's relatives. When an active power center imposes total abstinence, though custom demands drinking, and there is no general moral disapproval of a moderate consumption of alcohol; when an active power center prohibits all private trade, whereas public opinion (one of the expressions of ethical group-conviction) considers it natural; when fugitive slaves have to be extradited to their owners; when the obligatory declaration of venereal diseases is introduced by law, whereas it is customary to conceal them; when all sexual intercourse outside marriage is prohibited (as in the legislation of Louis IX in France in the thirteenth century or in that of the Empress Maria Theresa of Austria in the third quarter of the eighteenth century); when the customary burning of widows or the "sitting dharna custom" (*cf.* chap. I, § 3) is combated by law, or in many other similar cases, deep conflicts are introduced into the human behavior which ought to be regulated by law.[3]

Another group of cases may be described under the title of misuse of legislation.[4] Insofar as power selects rules which belong to the socio-ethical conviction and makes them law there is no danger of misuse. The possibility of misuse begins when we enter the domain of the political and of the cultural complexes in law. The Sherman Anti-Trust Law or the laws prohibiting the teaching of Darwinism can be cited as instances.

When the political or cultural complex in law is created or enlarged, political power reckons upon a peculiar extension of retributive dispositions. "In the view of the legislator, the prefatory *be*

[3] Inadequate terms chosen by legislators and applied by courts may create conflicts of minor size. For instance, according to § 833 of the German Civil Code, a physician was sentenced to pay damages for the injuries received by an old woman whom he had, at her own request, taken into his carriage, and this when he was not at fault in the accident that had occurred (Jung, *b*, 124). This caused a largely diffused sentiment of injustice, and later on the law was modified.

[4] According to Rheinstein (*b*), the misuse is engendered by the imposition of rules by conquerors, or by the tendency to transform legislation into benevolent education, or by the influence of the value judgments of a particular social class.

it enacted justifies what follows" (Pound, *a*, 785). He hopes that the ordinary association between reprehensible deeds and group disapproval will be inverted and acts directed against political power and its institutions will be backed up by social pressure; in other words, he hopes that the punishment which is ordinarily a consequence of social disapproval will become a cause of social disapproval. Success of such an enterprise is possible, but not inevitable, because the relation of the political or cultural complex to the ethical conviction is not direct, but indirect. The affective tone associated with rules belonging to these complexes and with their transgression is, of course, much weaker than with rules belonging to the "socio-ethical minimum in law." Power display must at least in part replace the weak, uncertain and precarious social pressure. In some cases, therefore, the assimilation of new rules by socio-ethical conviction never takes place at all, and the introduction of new rules consequently results only in disorganizing legal behavior.

In all the above-stated situations the normal effect of the creation of a new legal rule cannot take place. The legal form of the governmental act should create new concrete tendencies of submission among subjects, yet here this is inhibited by the existence of strong tendencies of behavior with opposite responses. The structure of the social field will be determined by two forces — the drive to ingrain new tendencies represented by the activity of the agencies of law enforcement and the resistance of many. Consequently, these agencies will soon recognize that they lack the ordinary support of the socio-ethical pressure. Some individuals, certainly, will obey, but they may not be numerous, and, therefore, the additional stimulus of obedience for *A* which consists in the fact that *B*, *C*, *D*, et cetera, obey, will be lacking.

2. The other main case of growing disequilibrium is present when changes in the ethical group-conviction or in the objective conditions of existence (in the political or socio-economic framework of society) are not followed by changes in *written* law.[5] This case may appear in various aspects.

[5] As has been explained above (chap. XIV, § 5) changes in the objective conditions of existence almost necessarily produce changes in unwritten law; otherwise these changes would remain changes in human minds.

The first variety is in evidence when an ethical revolution is brewing or has already taken place. For instance, if the changing ethical group conviction ceases to support the principle of religious homogeneity of the population which is still recognized by the law of a theocratic State, there arises a kind of emotional incompatibility between the extralegal and the legal rules. Legal behavior, at least in part, loses its socio-ethical root and derives its support almost exclusively from imperative coördination, and legal rules become merely "general commands" of the active power center.

The second variety arises when the process of destroying power structures is far advanced, as, for instance, if the sentiment of awe and reverence for traditional political power has been lost; in other words, if the recognition of and the obedience to a power center ceases to be one of the demands of social ethics. If a political revolution succeeds (i.e., if a power structure is overthrown), legal rules may continue to be obeyed, but as moral or customary rules only, for the imperative root gradually or suddenly disappears.

Summing up, we may say: law is a social force which must be expressed in verbal formulas. Yet words may be misused; verbal statements continue to be repeated after the configuration of forces has changed. Furthermore, verbal statements can be made which do not correspond to the actual distribution of forces.[6] The disharmony between real forces and verbal formulas is the deepest cause of legal disequilibrium.

§ 4. The Incomplete Validity of Law

In the life of a legal rule the period when it still struggles for complete recognition as well as the period when its enforcement becomes inhibited because of subsequent changes in the ethical group-conviction may be called periods of indecision. During such periods the validity of a legal rule is incomplete — a concept almost impossible from the viewpoint of formalistic jurisprudence, but which expresses the social fact that, under certain

[6] Thus, for instance, the Kellogg Pact never expressed anything else but the will of peaceful nations to avoid war; for them the statement was superfluous, whereas concerning other nations it was fallacious.

conditions, the predictability of behavior conforming to law is decreased. This is a fact not too rarely recurring in legal history. Unduly generalizing it, some American realists have asserted that the realization of law was always unpredictable.

Sociologically, the existence of the state of incomplete validity cannot be denied, but so long as a legal rule determines the behavior at least of authorities (as long as they continue trying to model the behavior of subjects in accordance with legal patterns), it truly remains in force, and the frequency and importance of deviations cannot increase too intensely.

The issue of a period of indecision depends on the correlation of forces involved in each concrete case. It might be threefold.

1. The agencies of law enforcement gain the upper hand (ingrain new tendencies in the behavior systems of the citizens, or destroy a newly created antilegal tendency); this means that the legal equilibrium has been restored at the initial point.

2. There are certain natural limits to the struggle of power for the efficacy of law. Careful studies of criminal legislation show that the more atrocious punishments are, the more difficult is their application.[7] On the other hand, very few power structures are so strong that they are able to enforce every general command, and commonly the active power center has to make a certain choice in displaying its energy. If the prestige question is not openly raised in the concrete case, the power center may give up the struggle for the enforcement of a concrete rule. Officials may grow tired of enforcing the law against very strong opposition and finally abandon it altogether. The active power center recognizes its failure and, implicitly or explicitly, changes the law.

3. The most frequent case is probably the third. Individuals submitted to a new legal rule which they do not yet accept or to an old rule which they no longer accept do not resist directly, but try to evade law, to find a middle course between law and the values they recognize. According to the (scientific) laws ruling the formation of habits and customs (chap. VI, § 4) the responses of the individuals will converge and vary in certain limits around a certain average. On the other hand, the agencies of law en-

[7] Good examples are given by Szende.

forcement (especially if there is overproduction of law) will display their force half-reluctantly, and will easily recognize as being in conformity with law the practice created in order to avoid it. In this way these practices will be fixed by the mechanism of learning: to the stimulus situation created by the new legal rule will be linked not the response foreseen by the verbal formula of law, but another one which deviates from it. After a certain time the actual behavior of group-members gets the support of the socio-ethical pressure (by the application of the "normative tendency of the actual") and the support of power which would permit deviation from the ideal pattern to the limits posed by actual behavior, but not further.

In this way law is implicitly changed. If the legal rule in question is a statute, jurists will apply the concept of "the derogatory force of the custom" which must be applied by judges (Reichel, 13, Fehr, 26, 171); sociologists will use the concept of folkways of disobedience which nullifies law (Sumner, 195).

Sometimes the lawmaker will consider it worth while to introduce corresponding changes in written law. Thus, for instance, custom actually abolished Emperor Augustus's interdiction of the receiving of gifts by local advisers, and this custom, which had nullified law, was enacted by Claudius (Haesart, 26). In France, the prohibition of betting on the prices of the stock market was nullified by custom since 1848, and this was recognized by statute law in 1885 (Cruet, 140–1). In such cases there is no change in the content, but only in the form of law: a customary law is elevated to the rank of a statute law. The change in content occurred much earlier, when power abandoned its resistance to commonly accepted deviations, so that the restoration of older statutes and bylaws nullified by custom would have meant an actual revolution (Cruet, 255).

Adepts of formalistic theories of law would contest the majority of the statements made above. They assert that theory cannot make distinctions where legislators did not make them, and that it is vain to deny, merely because of its inefficacy, the legal character of a rule enacted according to the accepted technique of legislation.

But such a doctrine is incorrect in that "being in force" is essential to any law which is a social force, for "what is not practiced is not law" (Jhering). Contrary to their theory, the acts of legislators, et cetera, form only one of the conditions of the existence of law; another is acceptance (willing or reluctant) by the subjects on which depends the capacity of the rule to determine their behavior — a new argument in favor of the concept of law as ethico-imperative coördination.

This self-adaptation of ethico-imperative coördination to changing conditions is a kind of social mechanism parallel and additional to legal pressure (imposition of sanctions). It limits the number of cases when legal pressure must be actualized and facilitates the interplay of forces forming legal equilibrium.

§ 5. Legal Disintegration

The accumulation of periods of indecision concerning many legal rules produces a phenomenon which might be termed "legal disintegration." Law seems to be no longer integrated in culture, but to be opposed to its other elements, to form an obstacle to social change. Its symptom is that judgments in which the attitudes of power and those of subjects are expressed cannot be united into an uncontradictory system.

Another case, closely related to the first, is when there may be a lack of integration between some extralegal elements in culture, and this disintegration (for instance, between political organization and the socio-economic order) almost necessarily produces a certain disintegration within law. Before this disharmony appears, the judgments regarding legal, customary and economic evaluation are mutually consistent. With the advance of disharmony the judgments concerning legal determination and those concerning the "principles" of conduct in which economic and other vital values are expressed can no longer be brought into conformity. Tension in the social field is the expression of this disintegration.

We do not yet know all the causes which produce cultural integration or disintegration. It is very probable that these causes are "immanent," i.e., belong to the essence of culture, just as decrepitude is contained in the very nature of an individual organism and in the structure of many social groups (for instance of power structures). In any case it seems that they appear more frequently during periods when a culture is changing its basic type. These general changes, which are sometimes part of long-time, sometimes of short-time cycles, and which in either case are submitted to the principle of limits (Sorokin,*f*), are to be regarded as the "final causes" of the fluctuations in the relationship between different elements of culture.

It is obvious that disintegration in the elements in culture must be reflected in law, insofar as the legal determination of behavior is added to the social uniformities related to these elements. As this disintegration never has law for its source, it must be studied rather in general sociology than in the sociology of law. Thus far Kelsen (*c*) was right when he tried to prove a much more ambitious — and, of course, erroneous — idea: that every sociology of law would necessarily become general sociology.

Even an individual disintegration of behavior, if it is not wholly negligible, produces a certain degree of tension in the social field where the individual is. Still more important are tensions which arise simultaneously in many individuals and cover larger parts of social fields. If the tension increases, especially if it lasts (power being unable to force individuals to act "normally," but nevertheless not allowing the legal pattern to be tacitly transformed and adjusted to the actual behavior), and if one of the elements causing the tension is law (and this is generally so), a discrepancy between positive law and public opinion as to what law should be (legal conviction) arises. As a result of such an objective situation, the doctrine of "natural law" of the "progressive" type (*cf.* chap. XIV, § 2) gains the upper hand in jurisprudence and legal philosophy. The contents of the collective opinion are submitted to the process of objectivization: what "should" be is declared to exist already. This is just the reverse of the "normative tendency of the actual."

As social tensions (especially if law is involved because of the connection of law with power) produce "prerevolutionary situations," a rather necessary connection exists between the appearance of the doctrine of natural law and prerevolutionary situations. Natural law of the progressive type flourished in legal doctrine in the seventeenth and eighteenth centuries, before the English and the French revolutions. A revival of natural law was to be observed in continental European jurisprudence about the beginning of the twentieth century, before the outbreak of the Communist and Fascist revolutions. A flourishing natural law of the second type is, therefore, a symptom of disintegration in culture. Integrated culture does not feel any need for it.

Periods of disintegration in culture, which in the realm of law are expressed in the phenomenon of legal disintegration, necessarily come to an end. This end is either disruption of society ("total" revolution) or peaceful integration according to a new pattern, commonly with the help of law which is an important factor of integration. In law such integration is commonly expressed by large codification. The incorporation of Roman law by Theodosius and Justinian signified the definite coördination of pagan and Christian elements in Roman culture. The codification of Napoleon took place when the problems asked by the French Revolution were definitely settled. The great codification in Russia (achieved in 1832) meant the consolidation of the order based on the unification of national tradition with the western elements imported by Peter the Great and his successors. The German codification of 1900 followed the definite stabilization of the German Empire. The lack of great codifications in the post-war period corresponds to the fact that a period of tremendous disintegration in culture has not yet come to an end.

Codification commonly testifies to the beginning of an "organic period" in social development. The first years after codification are commonly characterized by strict interpretation of law on the part of courts (Haesart, 33). Yet this never lasts: processes producing legal disequilibrium and legal disintegration start up again, and a new critical period is once more in preparation; the cycle of legal fluctuation never stops.

BIBLIOGRAPHICAL NOTE

Jhering is the author who showed that "being in force" is the very essence of law (*a*, I, 49 *ff.*). Heck (*a*) correlated the validity of law with the idea of its real existence. Out of recent studies the following statement should be mentioned: "Law without effect approaches zero in its meaning" (Llewellyn). A general study of the discrepancies between written law and actuality is that of Sinzheimer (*a*). Stressing this discrepancy forms the essence of the book of Ehrlich (*a*) who, I believe, exaggerates it (*cf.* chap. XIII). The struggle for the efficacy of law was especially investigated by Spiegel, Cruet (224–38) and Merriam (102–32). The difficulties of law when it runs counter to socio-ethical conviction are studied by Adams (117, 129) and Tufts (310–311). Concerning the classic example of prohibition *cf.* Colvin. A good concrete study of changing interpretation of verbal formulas is that of Hall (*a*, 68 *ff.*).

The causes of the low respect for law in the United States are discussed by Adams (11–13). One of his arguments is the relative frequency of insurrections and riots in this country (110–14). After Sorokin's study of the frequency of social disturbances in Europe (*h*, vol. III, chaps. 12–14) the American "inferiority complex" concerning obedience to law should be overcome; violent breaches of legal order are much more frequent than is commonly assumed.

As regards the revival of natural law, *cf.* Cathrein, Stammler (*d*), Jung (*a*), Charmont (*a*), Tourtoulon, Cassirer, Orton, Kelsen (*j*), Haines, Keller, Piot, Ripert and M. Cohen (*b*).

Legal disintegration is amply studied by Petrazhitsky (*b*, 615 *ff.*) from the standpoint of the interrelation of intuitive and positive law.

CHAPTER XVI

THE VINDICATION OF LAW

§ 1. Introduction

Sociology is a nomographic, not normative science. It is not the task of sociology to tell us whether one or another social institution is rational, just, useful, and the like.

The sociology of law deals with law as a social phenomenon. Law is related to the world of values. In law (as in ethics in general) certain values are embodied in and act on human behavior. Legal order would be impossible without the recognition of certain values by men.

This recognition must be widespread, or else the legal coördination of behavior is replaced either by a purely imperative coordination or by a total lack of any coördination (chaos). Exceptional cases of nonrecognition of law do not affect its efficacy; for even nonrecognizing individuals are commonly forced to *act* with regard to law. But what if there are *social* tendencies to nonrecognition?

The nonrecognition of law may be in the concrete or in the abstract. In the first case the contents of law is submitted to criticism. The existing legal order, it is felt, should be destroyed and replaced by another. This is the usual form of revolutionary propaganda. It may be successful, but even success would not destroy law; only its content would be changed.

In the second case, law as an institution is criticized. Not only should the existing legal order be destroyed, but it should be replaced by another nonlegal order. The triumph of such propaganda would mean the end of law as such, and since law is a cultural, historical phenomenon, the possibility of its abolition cannot be denied *a priori*.

The abolition of law is the focal point of anarchistic doctrine (in the broad sense of the term). The theoretical system of the sociology of law would be incomplete if it did not deal with the objections of anarchists to law as such and with their plans for displacing legal order once and for all. The recurrence of the total negation of law is a sociologically relevant fact. It is an example of the broader phenomenon of the persistent misrepresentation of actual social phenomena, of misrepresentation which, time and again, becomes a more or less important factor in social development. Of course, the point at issue, in argument with the anarchists, should not be the contention that legal order is more rational, just or useful than the proposed anarchic "order," but that the theory of anarchism is based on false sociological conceptions of what law is and of what its social functions are.

This demonstration cannot be made at once, for anarchism is far from being a consolidated movement of human thought. Extreme contrasts are combined in its theoretical framework. Three main trends may be distinguished: (1) anarchism in the narrow or pure sense of the term, (2) orthodox Marxism in its extreme form, and (3) anarcho-syndicalism.

§ 2. The Negation of Law: Pure Anarchism

The basis of pure anarchism is its intense aversion to violence; not only illegal force, but even force displayed in the name of the law seems repugnant to it. The State is the chief enemy of the anarchists. Generally they accept the State theory of law and deny law because it is a necessary function of the State. If they do not accept this theory, their hatred of law is only decreased by a little, for law is coercion, and this is what they want to abolish.

Anarchism as an *apologia* for stateless society is one of the oldest trends in human thought. Zeno (IVth century B.C.) and Carpocrates (IId century B.C.) were its representatives in ancient Greece. A certain anarchistic trend was present in many Christian sects, beginning in the thirteenth century, with P. Chelcicky (XVth century) as its outstanding proponent during the period of religious conflicts. Three hundred years later Diderot, with his famous words, "*Je ne veux ni donner ni recevoir de lois,*" expressed the anarchic trend among the Philosophers of the Enlightenment. W. Godwin (1756–1835) created the first systematic exposition of anarchism and is the first of the seven thinkers who, according to a widely accepted opinion among the students of anarchism, were its apostles during the last one hundred and fifty years. The other six are: Max Stirner, Proudhon, Bakunin, Prince Kropotkin, B. J. Tucker and Count Leo Tolstoi. Among the secondary figures only a few can be mentioned: J. H. Mackay, as the follower of Stirner; Johannes Most, P. Brousse and E. Réclus as followers of Kropotkin; Gandhi as a follower of Tolstoi; anarcho-syndicalists (see § 4) as upholders of the tradition of Proudhon.

The attitude of anarchists with regard to State and law is primarily an emotional one: they hate force, which seems to them of necessity to be a species of oppression, and they hence deduce all the miseries of mankind from the existence of political power and of law as its instrument. They do not, however, advocate anarchy in the vulgar sense of the word, i.e., chaos; they recognize the necessity of social order. But in the descriptions of the social order they would like to create in place of the existing one they differ greatly.

1. First of all, there is divergence of opinion as regards the possibility and usefulness of a detailed description of this projected order. From this viewpoint, Bakunin and Kropotkin stand at opposite poles. Bakunin repudiates any detailed speculation concerning the future as being reactionary; Kropotkin, on the contrary, gives a detailed description of this future state of society, which was to be based upon the ideal of mutual aid (solidarity).

2. As regards the character of the order to be created after the abolition of the State and law, two main ideas are expressed. For Stirner, Proudhon, Bakunin and Kropotkin this order will be a "natural" one, based on the natural drives and tendencies of mankind. "The sphere of activity of every citizen will be determined by the natural division of labor and his free choice of the field of occupation," wrote Proudhon. "As social functions are correlated in a manner that produces their harmony, the new order is created by the free activity of everyone. There is no government. He who touches me in order to rule over me, is a

usurper: I declare him to be my enemy" (*a*, 6). For Bakunin the coming of the new order is to be attested by the law of evolution; it is nothing other than that stage of evolution which naturally follows the legal. For Kropotkin the progress from lesser to greater happiness is the supreme law; for Stirner, the interest of the individual.

On the contrary, for Godwin and Tolstoi the new society should be based upon "moral law." According to Godwin, reason and justice should rule (objectivization of metaphysical abstractions). For Tolstoi, the supreme law of love, which is implanted by God in human nature but is inhibited by positive law, will govern human relationships in this Kingdom of God on earth. "My primary idea is that love induces love in others. God awakened in you awakens God in others" (XIV, 21). Self-perfection is therefore simultaneously the perfectioning of society (XX, 77).

3. The degree to which law should be destroyed seems to be another matter on which the different systems disagree. Godwin, Stirner and Tolstoi are radical: no particle of legal order can be carried over into the new society. Others agree that the State should be altogether abolished, but recognize the necessity for retaining at least one legal rule, *pacta sunt servanda:* for a contract is a law which one imposes on oneself, so that to follow it is not to be coerced. This norm is, moreover, necessary in order to stabilize the free associations which are to replace the State. Tucker agrees that a certain number of legal rules must be retained.

How are rules to be enforced? "He who has not promised to keep his agreements," wrote Proudhon, "is a savage. He has retired from society. He is not protected by anything. Because of the smallest offense anyone can kill him, and the only objection against such an act would be that it were too cruel" (*a*, 342–3). According to Kropotkin, law in the anarchistic society of the future would be customary law only, and its enforcement would be based on everyone's need for coöperation and help and sympathy (*a*, 24), and by the fear of being excluded from society (*b*, 202), but sometimes by individual or collective intervention (*b*, 109, *d*, 30). In Tucker's opinion, keeping contracts can be enforced by violence, which may be individual, or collective, if other people agree to help the injured party; but such a decision must remain entirely voluntary.

It may seem that anarchists of this trend are not pure anarchists: for they recognize law of a certain quantity and quality; but this supposed recognition of law is nothing more than a misunderstanding of the nature of law. The legal rules of anarchist Utopias are not legal, but customary rules, enforced either by "natural forces" or by socio-ethical pressure without any help of power, which is supposed no longer to exist. This misunderstanding induced Eltzbacher (246–9) to say that anarchism is a negation of the State only, not necessarily of law. The contrary, more correct opinion was expressed by Stammler (*b*, 2, 4) and Diehl (*b*).

On the other hand, it is noteworthy that anarchists of this school tend to retain the norm in which the basic tendency toward reciprocity or retribution is expressed (chap. V, § 6). They invite Humanity to return to one of the earliest stages of the development of social coördination. The appearance of the new order might be completely different from that of the primitive one, being based on the accumulation of material and cultural riches; but the form in which social processes would be determined in an anarchic society would mirror those of the epoch of undifferentiated ethics.

Finally, the ideal of government by one single legal rule (this is Proudhon's favorite ideal) is self-contradictory. Correctly interpreted, this would mean that the basic rule is to be the only one supported by social pressure, or in other words the only customary rule, whereas all other human relationships would be determined case by case. When one understands, however, what socio-ethical pressure is (see chap. V, § 8), one cannot but express the opinion that a limited pressure of this sort would be no pressure at all. Only a well-developed system of customary rules supported by group-members works; a single rule, taken by itself, would be unthinkable.

§ 3. The Negation of Law: Extreme Marxism

The assertion that orthodox Marxism in its extreme forms approaches the ideas of anarchism may seem a paradox. The contrary opinion is often expressed: that socialism (of which Marxism is only one variety) is no less opposed to anarchism than the tendency to increase the regimentation of life is opposed to the tendency to abolish it. It is the merit of Novgorodtseff to have definitely shown (193–232) that within the works of Marx and Engels both extreme étatistic and anarchistic-Utopian ideas are present. This indicates the futility of the polemics between the German Social-Democrats, who accepted and developed the étatistic trend in Marx, and the Russian Bolsheviks, who accepted and developed, at least in theory, the anarchistic trend.

In contradistinction to the pure anarchists, the basic motive of Marxism is not the hatred of violence, but the hatred of exploitation. The State is, according to Marx, the organized exploitation of one class by another, and law is one of the instruments of exploitation. The society of the future will be a classless society; therefore the State and the law, which belong to the "superstructure" based upon the economics of exploitation, will lose their material foundation and disappear.

Statements of an anarchistic sort, prophecies of a "definitive political emancipation of Humanity," were made in the earliest works of the creators of Marxism; such statements are rather infrequent in the middle years of their activity, but again crop out towards the end of their activity.

Already in 1844 Marx declared that the final aim of the historical process was not the victory of the State over society (as had been proclaimed by Hegel), but rather the victory of society over the State, which would be swallowed up in it (*a*). In the *Communist Manifesto* (1848) the idea was expressed that after the Socialist Revolution the State would lose its political (coercive) functions.

Of the later statements the following, by Engels, is the most famous: "The first act of the new State in which it really acts as the representative of the whole of society, will also be its last independent act as a State. The interference of the authority of the State with social relations will become superfluous in one field after another and will finally cease of itself. The authority of the government over persons will be replaced by the administration of things and the direction of the processes of production. The State will not be abolished; it will wither away" (*a*, 301–2). In another place Engels asserts: "The whole State machine will be banished to a place which will be the most proper one for it: the museum of antiquities, side by side with the spinning-wheel and the bronze axe" (*b*, 179–80). The abolition of the State forms the phenomenon which Engels metaphorically calls "a leap from the realm of necessity into that of freedom" (*a*, 305).

In one of Marx's latest works (*c*) there are assertions indicating the same trend of thought. Every law, he writes, is a law of inequality; law will continue existing during the first period after the socialist revolution, the period of collectivism, when the leading principle will be: to everyone according to his merits. Only in the second, definitive, truly communist stage, when the principle, "To everyone according to his needs," will and must dominate, can law be abolished.[1]

There is a certain inner contradiction between the political anarchism of radical Marxism and its economic doctrine which demands a degree of organization and centralization possible only on the basis of imperative (or at least legal) coördination. This inner contradiction is stressed by Kelsen (*i*, 90–113). Novgorodtseff (229) tries to explain the contradiction in the following way. In the economic doctrine of Marxism, the economic system is transformed into an impersonal productive process; in the political doctrine, stateless society becomes impersonal and automatic. There will be no power and no coercion, because there will be no individual freedom or individual will. This is the triumph of an objective order, a complete rationalization of life. This is, as Kelsen puts it (*i*, 105), "an abstraction condensed into a fictitious reality."

The ideas of Marx and Engels, concerning the later, communist phase of socialism were developed by Lenin in one of his later works. To the ideas of Marx and Engels he added the assumption that, in the future stateless society, the behavior of individuals would necessarily conform to the social plan; for, during the

[1] It is probable that this return of Marx and Engels to the ideas of their youth was an effort to steal the thunder of Bakunin, whose anarchistic propaganda was at that time very successful.

transitory period of collectivism, the appropriate behavior patterns would be elicited by means of coercion (96). The political functions of the State should be replaced by registration and verification (44–6); these functions should be carried out by all citizens in turn (71).[2]

The anarchism within orthodox Marxism is parallel to that trend in pure anarchism which hopes to replace the legal coördination of behavior by natural regularities: everyone will act in a similar way, just as bees and ants do, because everyone's nature, be he man or ant, will compel him to behave so.

§ 4. The Negation of Law: Anarcho-Syndicalism

It is very difficult, almost impossible, to describe in precise terms the attitude of anarcho-syndicalism toward the State and law. This movement is a continuation of Proudhon's doctrine. Headed by G. Sorel, it was developed by Lagardelle, Berth, Griffuhels and Labriola.

Violence is an object of hatred for pure anarchists; violence is an object of worship for anarcho-syndicalists. Pure anarchists disapprove legal order, for in their opinion it is violence. Anarcho-syndicalists disapprove legal order, for it hinders violence. "Violence must save the world," — this is Sorel's famous dictum.[3] The general strike is proclaimed as the best instrument for destroying the State and creating the new society to have neither state nor law.

Why is the State to be destroyed? It is to be destroyed because all changes in political form have failed to change its nature. The State as such destroys the natural economic structure. Producers (members of economic society) are transformed into abstract citizens. Destroy the State, and the reverse process will take place: the "natural" economic order will reappear, within which citizens will occupy definite positions as producers.

[2] The tremendous increase of coercion in the Soviet State has been persistently "explained" by its rulers by the fact that this State corresponds only to the collectivist stage of socialist evolution, when the State and coercion cannot be abolished. However, it seems rather futile to attempt to prepare for habitual social behavior, to be no longer based on coercion, by an exceptional display of imperative coördination.

[3] In his later years Sorel renounced his earlier doctrine. *Cf.* his latest book. (*b*).

This will be an order without preëstablished rules and coercion, a free federation of free associations of producers. But how will the scale of production be assured in the new society? The decisive rôle, in the eyes of the anarcho-syndicalists, belongs to the new morality which will be embraced by group-members; it will be a morality of heroism, and of accuracy and precision in labor.

In contradistinction to the majority of pure anarchists and to the orthodox Marxists, the anarcho-syndicalists imagine the new order as based not on natural regularities, but, like Tolstoi, on ethical, especially moral coördination. But, unlike Tolstoi, it is not the Christian law of love, but the heroic morals of Nietzsche which will be cultivated in the new society, the instinct of superiority, of audacity, of struggle. This new morality must be created and inculcated in the working class during the period of revolutionary struggle and general strikes. In this point anarcho-syndicalists, from the viewpoint of lack of logic, are rivals of Lenin: he hoped that coercion might inculcate in men the ability to conform freely to social patterns; the anarcho-syndicalists hope that the violence of the revolutionary period will prepare men for a peaceful existence under the aegis of self-discipline.

Heroic morality is foreseen not only for the transitional period, but also for the future society in its definitive form. Leadership and a certain degree of hierarchy is unavoidable even in that society. But the selection of leaders will be carried out without preestablished rules, i.e., it will be based on factual superiority, testified by competition within the producers' associations. This will supposedly be the same kind of authority as that displayed within trade unions in a capitalist order.

Many of the ideas of the anarcho-syndicalists were shared and accepted by scholars and politicians who did not object to the State as an institution. A federation of classes is considered by Duguit (*c*) to be the best pattern for the new State. Mussolini also did not renounce the creed of his younger years when he transformed Italy into a corporative State; he merely "adapted" syndicalism to fit the ideology of the authoritative State.

§ 5. The Affirmation of Law

Anarcho-syndicalism seems to have had a momentary period of brilliant success; but today, the doctrine has no more followers, whereas representatives of orthodox Marxism rule over a sixth part of the earth's surface, though it is true they give little regard to the political anarchism of their masters. Pure anarchism has today only isolated adherents scattered throughout the world.

The defensive war waged by the ideas of State and law against their wholesale negation by anarchism seems to have been won. Won for ever? That is another question. The periodic reappearance of anarchistic doctrines warns against too much confidence. It is yet another question as to whether anarchism could ever get the upper hand, especially for a longer period of time. In the light of the sociological study of law a positive answer seems very improbable.

In destroying the legal coördination of behavior, anarchism does not aim at producing chaos. Social order is recognized as a value which must be maintained. Two main solutions are proposed by anarchism. This new social order will be either a "natural" one (based on the fact that men, who are similar by nature, will behave similarly when placed in similar conditions), or a purely ethical one (moral rather than customary). Two facts make either solution very improbable. The first is that there exists a kind of principle of compensation between legal and purely ethical coördination. The second is that the urge to domination is widespread throughout humankind.

1. The first principle was pointed out in studying the internal differentiation of ethics (chap. VII, § 7). The legal form of coördination is generally used when the others are either too weak or are completely lacking. For instance, the rise of capitalism meant the destruction of many rules which had previously regulated production and trade. How was this possible? Because the new order possessed an automatic mechanism of coördination (the so-called price mechanism) which would function only with a social field exempt from legal determination. As long as this mechanism was efficient, law did not interfere. But when exter-

nal and internal causes created many complications, and new conflicts appeared which could no longer be settled by the automatic price mechanism, new legal rules were created in order to combat the supposed causes of the conflicts (antitrust legislation; prohibition of strikes; restriction of imports): legal coördination had to fill the place left by the failure of another instrument of social coördination. Today the point at issue is whether or not legal coördination should take the place of the obsolete mechanism of liberal economics?

This law of compensation is fatal for the anarchistic argument. Even supposing that it could succeed in establishing a new order in one country or throughout humanity, this order would be an imperfect one (for the hope of perfection is utopian as long as the men composing society remain imperfect), and within this imperfect society law would be restored as an instrument of coördination in those domains of life where the extralegal coördination had proven to be a failure.

2. Still more important is the second point. The abolition of law would not mean that the phenomenon of polarization within social groups had also been abolished, and that the tendency of certain individuals to seek positions of domination had also been extirpated. It is unfortunately less difficult to destroy ethical than imperative coördination.

After the abolition of law all the tendencies favoring the development of power structures would be displayed. In order to prevent them from causing a kind of restoration of the abolished social structure, the use of force would be necessary, since simple persuasion is ineffectual when addressed to potential dominators (e.g., Kerensky *versus* Lenin). This use of force would result in civil war. The fulfillment of anarchistic ideals seems to be possible only as a provisional state of affairs; a new domination *has* to arise after legal order has been destroyed. This domination may be again limited by law or it may employ arbitrary rule.

This is just the point overlooked by the anarchists. To the one side of legal order stands anarchy, in the sense of purely ethical coördination or of the precarious coördination based on natural regularities in human behavior (chap. I, § 2); but to the other side stands despotism.

The war of anarchists of all schools against law and social power, embodied in our time, in the State, is based on a false conception of law and political domination. They assume that political power is always exerted by the privileged classes in order to oppress and rob the masses. To be sure, such a use or rather abuse, of law is possible; oppression of the masses by means of law is not a wholly exceptional situation. But this is not essential to law; law *may* be used as an instrument of oppression, but also as an instrument of common welfare. And it is obvious that in our days as well as in many other historical periods [4] this second use prevails or prevailed over the first.

Therefore the struggle against law as an institution (not against the concrete contents of law within a certain social field) is to be regarded as an aberration; it is a kind of counterpart to the workers' revolt against and destruction of the machines which, they imagine, deprive them of labor and plunge them into misery. People of good will should fight not against the legal order, but for the transformation of this order in a manner calculated to secure the realization of the noblest human ideals in political, economic and moral affairs, and in general culture.

BIBLIOGRAPHICAL NOTE

The importance of utopias from the standpoint of the sociology of law is shown by Guins (*b*, 196 *ff.*). The list of the basic works of the principal anarchists has been published so often that it seems superfluous to repeat it here. The best (not the longest) bibliography of this kind is that of Eltzbacher. See some additions, concerning recent works, in Diehl (*b*). Generally overlooked is the interesting work of E. de Girardin, who insisted on the necessity of replacing all legal sanctions by "a book of the life," in which all transgressions against the established order should be mentioned and which should be at the disposal of every member of the society.

The best works on anarchism are those of Zoccoli, Eltzbacher, Stammler (*b*), Nettlau and Douglas. Concerning especially Proudhon:

[4] For instance, in despotisms of the "enlightened" type (in the eighteenth and in part early nineteenth centuries); during the best periods of the Greek and Roman democracies; during certain periods in the history of the Hebrews, et cetera.

see Diehl (*a*) and Gurvitch (*c*, 327–406); concerning Bakunin: Huch; concerning Stirner: Mackay. The eclipse of anarchism and the reasons for it are discussed by Yarros.

The works of Marx, Engels and Lenin in which political anarchism is expressed are quoted in the text. The most brilliant analysis of this trend in Marxism is that of Novgorodtseff; that of Kelsen (*i*) is not on the same level, but is useful because of its many polemical digressions on recent Marxian literature, especially of that in German. The later development of the orthodox Marxist approach to law in Soviet Russia has been described by Timasheff (*j*), Paschukanis and Gsovsky. The negation of law by later Marxists outside Russia has been discussed by Zürcher.

The best analysis of anarcho-syndicalism is that of Guy Grand.

GENERAL BIBLIOGRAPHY

Adams, J. T., "Our Business Civilization" (New York, 1929).
Aillet, G., "Droit et sociologie," *Revue de métaphysique et de morale* 30 (1923).
Alexander, F., and Staub, H., "The Criminal, the Judge and the Public." A psychological analysis (trans. from German) (New York, 1931).
Allen, C. K., "Law in the Making" (Oxford, 1927).
Allport, F. H., (*a*) "Social Psychology" (New York, 1924).
(*b*) "Institutional Behavior" (Chapel Hill, 1933).
Amira, K. v., "Die germanischen Todesstrafen" (München, 1922).
Amos, Sir M., "The Common Law and the Civil Law in the British Commonwealth of Nations." In: "The Future of Common Law." *Harvard Tercentenary Publications* (Cambridge, Mass., 1937).
Angell, M. B., "Tax Evasion and Tax Avoidance," *Col. Law Rev.* 38 (1938).
Anschütz, G., "Die gegenwärtigen Theorien über den Begriff der gesetzgebenden Gewalt," 2te Aufl. (Tübingen, 1900).
Anzilotti, D., "La filosofia del diritto e la sociologia" (Firenze, 1892).
Arensberg, C. M., "The Irish Countryman. An anthropological study" (New York, 1937).
Arnold, Th., (*a*) "The Law Enforcement," *Yale Law Journ.* 42 (1932).
(*b*) "The Symbols of Government" (New Haven, 1935).
Aronson, M., "Cardozo's Doctrine of Sociological Jurisprudence," *J. Soc. Phil.* 4 (1938).
Atkinson, J. J., and Lang, F. A., "The Primal Law" (London and New York, 1903).
Auburtin, A., "Amerikanische Rechtsauffassung," *Zeitschrift für ausländisches öffentliches Recht und Völkerrecht*, 3 (1932).
Austin, John, "Lectures on Jurisprudence, or the Philosophy of Positive Law," 5th edition (London, 1911).
Babb, H., (*a*) Petrazhitsky: "Science of Legal Policy," *Boston University Law Review*, 17 (1937).
(*b*) Petrazhitsky: "Theory of Law," *Ibid.* 18 (1938).
Bagehot, W., "Physics and Politics. Thoughts on the application of the principle of natural selection and inheritance to political society." 5th edition (London, 1879).
Bakunin, M., "Dieu et l'État" (Paris, 1871–95).
Baldwin, J. M., "Social and Ethical Interpretations in Mental Development" (London, 1897).
Baldwin, S. E., "The American Judiciary" (New York, 1905).

Barnard, Ch. I., "Mind in Everyday Affairs." The Guide of Brackett Lecturers (Princeton, 1936).

Barnes, H. E., and Becker, H., "Social Thought from Lore to Science" (New York, 1938).

Barr, E. de Y., "A Psychological Analysis of Fashion Motivation," *Archives of Psychology* (New York, 1934).

Bass, M. J., "Differentiation of the Hypnotic Trance from Natural Sleep," *Journ. Experim. Psychology*, 14 (1931).

Bauer, W., "Public Opinion," *Enc. Soc. Sciences*, XII (1934).

Baumgarten, A., "Die Wissenschaft vom Recht und ihre Methode" (Tübingen, 1920).

Bayet, A., "La science des faits moraux" (Paris, 1931).

Beling, E., "Die Vergeltung und ihre Bedeutung für das Strafrecht" (Leipzig 1908).

Below, G., "Das Duell und der germanische Ehrbegriff" (Cassel, 1896).

Bentham, J., "An Introduction to the Principles of Morals and Legislation" (London, 1789).

Bergson, H., "Les deux sources de la morale et de la religion" (Paris, 1934).

Berth, E., "Les nouveaus aspects du socialisme" (Paris, 1906).

Beseler, G., "Volksrecht und Juristenrecht" (Leipzig, 1843).

Bieberstein, M. v., "Vom Kampf des Rechts gegen die Gesetze" (1927).

Bierling, E. K., "Juristische Prinzipienlehre," 5 vols. (Freiburg und Leipzig, 1894–1917).

Binder, J., "Rechtsnorm und Rechtspflicht," (Leipzig, 1912).

Binding, K., "Die Normen und ihre Übertretungen," I. 2te Aufl. (Leipzig, 1890).

Binet, P., "La femme dans le ménage" (Paris, 1902).

Birkmeyer, K., "Deutsches Strafprocessrecht" (Berlin, 1898).

Birnbaum, I. M. F., "Über das Erforderniss einer Rechtsverletzung zum Begriff des Verbrechens," *Neues Archiv des Criminalrechts*, 15 (1834).

Bluntschli, J. C., "Allgemeine Staatslehre" (München, 1852).

Bobrzynski, M., "Dzieje Polski," 3d ed. (Krakow, 1890).

Bogardus, E. S., "Leaders and Leadership" (New York, 1934).

Boldyreff, W. N., "Two New Laws of Cerebral Functions" (Battle Creek, 1929).

Bonnecasse, J., "Le romantisme juridique" (Paris, 1928).

Bradley, F. H., "Ethical Studies," 2d edition (Oxford, 1927).

Britt, S. H., (*a*) "Blood-grouping Tests and the Law. The Problem of Cultural Lag," *Minnesota Law Review* (May, 1937).
(*b*) "The Significance of the Last Will and Testament," *Journ. Soc. Psychol.*, 8 (1937).

Brodmann, S., "Recht und Gewalt" (Berlin, 1921).

Brown, J. F., "Psychology and Social Order" (New York, 1936).
Brugeilles, R., "Le droit et la sociologie" (Paris, 1910).
Brunner, H., (*a*) "Deutsche Rechtsgeschichte," 2 vols. (Berlin, 1887–92).
(*b*) "Die Entstehung der Schwurgerichte" (Berlin, 1871).
Bryce, J., "Modern Democracy," 2 vols. (London, 1888).
Bukharin, N. I., "Theory of Historical Materialism" (in Russian), 2d ed. (Moscow, 1922).
Bunge, C. E., "Il Derecho" (in Spanish) (Buenos Aires, 1915).
Burrow, T., "Crime and the Social Reaction of Right and Wrong," *Journ. Crim. Law*, 24 (1933).
Cairns, H., "Law and the Social Sciences" (New York, 1935).
Calhoun, G. M., "The Growth of Criminal Law in Ancient Greece" (Berkeley, 1927).
Cannon, W. B., "Bodily Changes in Pain, Hunger, Fear and Rage" (New York, 1915).
Cardozo, B. N., (*a*) "The Nature of the Judicial Process" (New York, 1921).
(*b*) "The Growth of the Law," 5th ed. (New Haven, 1924).
Carlyle, R. W., and A. J., "History of the Medieval Political Theory in the West," 3 vols. (New York, 1903–16).
Carr, H. A., "The Survival Values of Play" (Boulder, Colorado, 1902).
Carter, J. C., "Law. Its Origin, Growth, and Function" (New York, 1907).
Caruso, I., "La notion de la responsabilité et de la justice immanente chez l'enfant" (Louvain, 1937).
Cassirer, E., "Natur- und Völkerrecht im Lichte der Geschichte und der systematischen Philosophie" (Berlin, 1919).
Cathrein, V., "Recht, Naturrecht und positives Recht," 2te Aufl. (Freiburg Br., 1909).
Chadbourn, J. H., "Lynching and the Law" (Chapel Hill, 1933).
Chapin, F. S., "Leadership and Group Activity," *Journ. Appl. Sociol.*, 8 (1923–4).
Charmont, J., "La renaissance du droit naturel" (Montpellier, 1910).
Chevaleva-Janovskaya, E., "Les groupements spontanés d'enfants à l'âge prescolaire," *Arch. de psychologie*, 20 (1927).
Childs, Marq. W. "Sweden, The Middle Way" (New Haven, 1936).
Chironi, G. P., "Sociologia e diritto cicile" (Torino, 1886).
Cohen, H., "Die Logik der reinen Erkenntniss" (Berlin, 1902).
Cohen, M. R., (*a*) "Law and the Social Order" (New York, 1933).
(*b*) "Jus naturale redivivum," *Phil. Review*, 25 (1916).
Coker, F. W., "Lynching," *Enc. Soc. Sciences*, IX (1933).
Colvin, H. L., "Prohibition" (New York, 1926).

Commons, J. R., "Legal Foundations of Capitalism" (New York, 1924).
Comte, Aug., (*a*) "Cours de philosophie positive," 6 vols. (Paris, 1830–42).
(*b*) "Système de philosophie positive," I (Paris, 1851).
Cooley, C., (*a*) "Humane Nature and Legal Order" (New York, 1902).
(*b*) "Social Process" (New York, 1918).
Corbin, A. L., "Legal Analysis and Terminology," *Yale Law Journ.* 29 (1919).
Cornil, G., "Le droit privé. Essai de sociologie juridique simplifiée" (Paris, 1924).
Craig, W., "Why do Animals Fight?" *Int. Journ. Ethics*, 31 (1921).
Cress, R., "Die soziologischen Gedanken Kant's" (Berlin, 1929).
Croce, B., "Reduzione della filosofia del diritto alla filosofia del' economia" (Napoli, 1907).
Cruet, J., "La vie du droit et l'impuissance des lois" (Paris, 1914).
Darmstaedter, F., (*a*) "Recht und Gewalt," *Archiv für civil. Praxis*, 125 (1926).
(*b*) "Das Wirtschaftsrecht in seiner soziologischen Struktur" (Berlin, 1927).
Davy, G., (*a*) "La foi jurée" (Paris, 1922).
(*b*) "Le droit, l'idéalisme et l'expérience" (Paris, 1922).
Decencière-Ferrandière, A., "Essai critique sur la justice internationale," *Revue générale de droit international* (1934).
Delos, J. T., "Le problème du rapport du droit et de la morale," *Archives de philosophie du droit et de sociologie juridique*, I (1931).
Diamond, A. S., "Primitive Law" (London and New York, 1935).
Dicey, A. V., "Lectures on the Relation between Law and Public Opinion in England in the 19th Century" (London, 1905).
Diehl, K., (*a*) "Proudhon: Seine Lehre und sein Leben," 3 vols. (Jena, 1886–96).
(*b*) "Anarchismus": *Handwörterbuch der Staatswissenschaften*, I (Jena, 1923).
Douglas, P. H., "Proletarian Political Theory," in Merriam, Ch., and Barne, H., "History of the Political Theory" (*Recent Times*) (New York, 1924).
Drabovitch, V., "Fragilité de la liberté et séduction des dictatures" (Paris, 1934).
Drake, D., "New Morality" (New York, 1928).
Drost, H., "Das Ermessen des Richters" (Berlin, 1930).
Duguit, L., (*a*) "Traité de droit constitutionel," 5 vols. (Paris, 1922–28).
(*b*) "L'État, le droit objectif et la loi positive" (Paris, 1901).

(c) "Le droit social, le droit individuel et la transformation de l'État" (Paris, 1911).
(d) "The Law and the State," *Harv. Law Review*, 31 (1917).
(e) "La doctrine allemande de l'auto-limitation de l'État" (Paris, 1919).

Dunan, Ch., "Principes moraux du droit," *Revue de métaphysique et de morale* (1901).

Duprat, G. L., "Introduction à l'étude des équilibres sociaux," *Revue intern. de sociologie* (1936).

Durkheim, E., (a) "De la division du travail social," 6me ed. (Paris, 1932).
(b) "L'education morale," Nouvelle édition (Paris, 1934).
(c) "Jugements de valeur et jugements de réalité" (Paris, 1911).

Durley, Lord Wright of, "The Common Law in Its Old Home." "The Future of Common Law," *Harvard Tercentenary Publications* (Cambridge, Mass., 1937).

Ehrlich, E., (a) "Grundlegung einer Soziologie des Rechts" (München, 1913). English translation (Cambridge, Mass., 1936).
(b) "The Sociology of Law," *Harvard Law Review*, 36 (1922–3).
(c) "Die juristische Logik" (Tübingen, 1918).
(d) "Replik" (to Kelsen's criticism), *Arch. für Sozialwissenschaft und Sozialpolitik*, 41 (1916).

Ellis, Havelock, (a) "Studies in the Psychology of Sex" (Philadelphia, 1902).
(b) "Study of the British Geniuses" (London, 1904).

Ellwood, C., "Sociology and Modern Social Problems" (New York, 1924).

Eltzbacher, P., "Der Anarchismus" (Berlin, 1900).

Engels, F., (a) "Herrn E. Dühring's Umwälzung der Wissenschaft," 11te Aufl. (Stuttgart, 1900).
(b) "Der Ursprung der Familie, des Privateigentums und des Staates," 8te Aufl. (Stuttgart, 1900).

Ewing, A. C., "The Morality of Punishment" (London, 1929).

Fehr, G., "Recht und Wirklichkeit" (Zürich, 1928).

Ferneck, H. v., "Die Rechtswidrigkeit" (Jena, 1903).

Ferri, E., "Sociologia Criminale" (Torino, 1884).

Foinitsky, I., "Russian Criminal Procedure" (in Russian), 2d edition (St. Petersburg, 1896).

Folsom, J. K., "Changing Values in Sex and Family Relation," *Am. Sociol. Review*, 2 (1937).

Förster, F. W., "Schuld und Sühne, Einige psychologische und pädagogische Grundfragen." 3te Aufl. (München, 1920).

Frank, J., "Law and the Modern Mind" (New York, 1931).

Frank, S., "The Problem of Power" (in Russian), in *Philosophy and Life* (St. Petersburg, 1905).

Frankfurter, F., "Justice Holmes and the Supreme Court" (Cambridge, Mass., 1938).

Freund, E., "Legislative Regulation" (New York, 1932).

Friedländer, L., "Darstellungen aus der Sittengeschichte Roms." 9te Aufl. 4 vols. (Leipzig, 1919–21).

Fürth, J. H., "Praktische Aufgaben der Rechtssoziologie," Zeitschr. öffenfl. Rechts, 17 (1935–6).

Fustel de Coulanges, N. D., "La cité antique. Etude sur le culte, le droit et les institutions de la Grèce et de Rome," 3d ed. (Paris, 1870).

Garraud, R., "Traité de l'instruction criminelle" (Paris, 1928).

Gentile, G., "La filosofia di Marx" (Pisa, 1899).

Gény, F., (*a*) "Science et technique du droit privé positif." 4 vols. (Paris, 1914–22).
(*b*) "Méthodes d'interprétation et sources du droit positif," 2me ed. (Paris, 1919).

Gerber, C. F. V., "Grundzüge eines Systems des deutschen Staatsrechts" (Leipzig, 1865).

Giddings, F. H., (*a*) "Principles of Sociology" (New York, 1906).
(*b*) "Studies in the Theory of Human Society" (New York, 1922).

Gierke, O. v., (*a*) "Laband's Staatsrecht und die deutsche Rechtswissenschaft" (*Schmoller's Jahrbuch*, 1883).
(*b*) "Das deutsche Genossenschaftsrecht," 4 vols. (Berlin, 1868–1913).
(*c*) "Die Grundbegriffe des Staatsrechts und die neueste Staatsrechtstheorie," 2te Aufl. (Tübingen, 1915).
(*d*) "Recht und Sittlichkeit," Logos 6 (1916–7).

Ginsberg, M., "Sociology" (London, 1934).

Girardin, E. de, "Du droit de punir" (Paris, 1871).

Glueck, Sh., (*a*) "Principles of a Rational Penal Code," *Harv. Law Review*, 41 (1927–8).
(*b*) "Mental Disorder and the Criminal Law" (Boston, 1925).
(*c*) "One Thousand Juvenile Offenders" (New York, 1934).

Gnaeus Flavius, "Der Kampf um die Rechtswissenschaft" (Heidelberg, 1906).

Godwin, W., "An Enquiry Concerning Political Justice and Its Influence on General Virtue and Happiness" (London, 1793).
Goldschmidt, J., "Verwaltungsstrafrecht" (Berlin, 1902).
Goodhart, D. C. L., "Some American Interpretations of Law," in *Modern Theories of Law*.
Gradovsky, A. D., "Principles of Russian Constitutional Law" (in Russian) (St. Petersburg, 1875).
Grasserie, R. de la, (*a*) "Les principes sociologiques du droit civil" (Paris, 1906).
(*b*) "Les principes sociologiques du droit public" (Paris, 1911).
Gray, J. C., "The Nature and Sources of Law" (New York, 1909).
Greef, G. de, "Introduction à la sociologie" (Bruxelles, 1886).
Griffuelhes, V., "L'action syndicaliste" (Paris, 1908).
Gross, K., "The Play of Men." Transl. from German (New York, 1908).
Gruhle, H. W., "Kriminalpsychologie." In *Handwörterbuch der Kriminologie*, edit. by Elster, A., and Lingemann, H. (Berlin, 1933-6).
Gsovsky, V., "The Soviet Concept of Law," *Fordham Law Review* (1938).
Guins, G., (*a*) "Petrazhitsky" (in Russian) (Harbin, 1931).
(*b*) "Law and Culture" (in Russian) (Harbin, 1938).
Gumplowicz, L., (*a*) "Der Rassenkampf" (Innsbruck, 1925).
(*b*) "Individuum, Gruppe und Umwelt," in "Soziologische Essays" (Innsbruck, 1899).
Gunton, G., "Wealth and Progress" (New York, 1887).
Günther, L., "Die Idee der Widervergeltung," I (Altenburg, 1889).
Gurvitch, G., (*a*) "O. v. Gierke als Rechtsphilosoph." Logos XI (1922-3), und erweiterter Separatabdruck (Tübingen, 1922).
(*b*) "Introduction to the General Theory of International Law" (in Russian) (Prague, 1923).
(*c*) "L'idée du droit social" (Paris, 1932).
(*d*) "Le temps présent et l'idée du droit social" (Paris, 1932).
(*e*) "L'expérience juridique et la philosophie pluraliste du droit" (Paris, 1935).
(*f*) "Morale théorique et science des moeurs" (Paris, 1937).
(*g*) "Essai d'une classification pluraliste des formes de la sociabilité," *Annales sociologiques*, A 3 (1938).
Gutmann, B., "Das Recht der Dschagga" (München, 1926).
Guy Grand G., "La philosophie syndicaliste," 2me éd. (Paris, 1911).
Haff, K., (*a*) "Rechtspsychologie" (Berlin, 1924).

(b) "Rechtsgeschiche une Soziologie," *Vierteljahresschriften für Sozial und Wirtschaftsgeschichte*, 22 (1929).

Haesart, J. P., "Contingences et regularités du droit positif" (Paris, 1933).

Haines, Ch. G., "The Revival of the Natural Law Concepts" (Cambridge, Mass., 1930).

Hall, J., (a) "Theft, Law and Society" (Boston, 1935).
(b) "Criminology and a Modern Penal Code," *Journ. Crim. Law*, 27 (1935-6).

Hamilton, W. H., "Institutions," *Enc. Soc. Sciences*, I (1930).

Harper, F. V., (a) "Law in Action and Social Theory," *Int. Jour. Ethics*, 40 (1929).
(b) "The Pragmatic Process in Law," *Ibid.* 41 (1930-1).

Hart, J., "Social Life and Institutions" (New York, 1924).

Hartmann, N., "Ethik" (Berlin, 1926).

Hauriou, M., (a) "Précis de droit public," 2me éd. (Paris, 1916).
(b) "La théorie de l'institution et de la fondation," *Cahiers de la nouvelle journée* (1923).

Healy, W., "The Individual Delinquent" (Boston, 1914).

Healy, W. and Bronner, A., "New Light on Delinquency and Its Treatment" (Boston, 1936).

Heck, Ph., (a) "Gesetzesauslegung und Interessenjurisprudenz" (Tübingen, 1914).
(b) "Die reine Rechtslehre und die jungösterreichische Schule der Rechtswissenschaft," *Arch. für civil. Praxis*, 122 (1924).

Heindl, R., "Der Berufsverbrecher" (Berlin, 1929).

Henderson, L. J., (a) "An Approximate Definition of Fact," *University of California Studies in Philosophy* (1932).
(b) "Pareto's General Sociology. A Physiologist's Interpretation" (Cambridge, Mass., 1935).

Hentig, H. v., "Die Strafe. Ursprung, Zweck, Psychologie" (Stuttgart, 1932).

Hessen, S., "Die Philosophie der Strafe," Logos 5 (1914).

Heusler, A., "Das Strafrecht der Isländersagas" (Leipzig, 1911).

Hicks, F. C., "Material and Method of Legal Research" (Rochester, 1933).

Hippel, R. v., "Deutsches Strafrecht, Vol. I (Berlin, 1925).

His, R., "Geschichte des deutschen Strafrechts im Mittelalter," 2 vols. (München, 1927-37).

Hobhouse, L., (a) "Morals in Evolution" (London, 1906-7).
(b) "Mind in Evolution," 2d edit. (London, 1918).

Hoche, A. E., "Das Rechtsgefühl in Justiz und Politik" (Berlin, 1932).

Hohfeld, W. N., "Some Fundamental Legal Conceptions as Applied in Judicial Reasoning," *Yale Law Journ.* 16 (1913).
Holmes, O. W., "Collected Legal Papers" (New York, 1921).
Holsti, R., "The Relation of War to the Origin of State" (Helsingfors, 1913).
Holt, E. B., "Animal Drive and Learning Process," I (New York, 1931).
Hook, S., "Towards the Understanding of K. Marx" (New York, 1923).
Horvath, B., "Rechtssoziologie" (Berlin, 1934).
House, F. N., "Pareto in the Development of Modern Sociology," *Journ. Soc. Phil.*, I (1935).
Huber, E., "Recht und Rechtsverwirklichung" (Basel, 1921).
Hubert, R., "Sur quelques faits caractéristiques de differenciation juridique," *Arch. de philosophie de droit et de sociologie juridique* (1936).
Huch, M.O., "M. Bakunin und die Anarchie" (Leipzig, 1923).
Hull, C. L., "Learning. The Factor of Conditioned Reflex," in *A Handbook of General Experimental Psychology* (1934).
Humphrey, G., "The Conditioned Reflex and the Elementary Social Reaction," *Amer. Journ. of Abnormal Psychology and Social Psychology*, 17 (1922).
Hyde, Ch., "International Law, Chiefly as Interpreted and Applied by the United States" (Boston, 1922).
Isay, H., "Rechtsnorm und Entscheidung" (Berlin, 1929).
James, W., "Habit" (New York, 1890).
Jankélévitch, V., "La mauvaise conscience" (Paris, 1933).
Janzen, H., "Kelsen's Theory of Law," *Amer. Polit. Science Review* (1937).
Jellinek, G., (*a*) "Sozialethische Bedeutung von Recht, Unrecht und Strafe" (Wien, 1879).
(*b*) "System der subjectiven öffentlichen Rechte," 1te Aufl. (Freiburg, 1891); 21te Aufl. (Berlin, 1905).
(*c*) "Die Lehre von den Staatenverbindungen" (Berlin, 1882).
(*d*) "Das Recht des modernen Staates" (Berlin, 1900).
(*e*) "Der Kampf des alten mit dem neuen Rechte" (Heidelberg, 1900).
Jenks, E., "Law and Politics in Middle Ages" (New York, 1898).
Jerusalem, F. W., "Soziologie des Rechts" (Jena, 1925).
Jèze, G., "Les principes généraux du droit administratif," 3ed. (Paris, 1935–6).
Jhering, R. v., (*a*) "Geist des römischen Rechts auf den verschiedenen Stufen seiner Entwickelung," 3 vols. 2te Aufl. (Leipzig, 1866).

(*b*) "Der Zweck im Recht," 2 vols. (Leipzig, 1877–83).
(*c*) "Kampf ums Recht" (Wien, 1872). 19te Aufl. (Wien, 1919).

Judd, C. H., "The Psychology of Social Institutions" (New York, 1926).

Jung, E., (*a*) "Das Problem des natürlichen Rechts" (Leipzig, 1912).
(*b*) "Rechtsregel und Rechtsgewissen," *Arch. für civil. Praxis*, 118 (1920).

Kantorowicz, H. U., (*a*) "Rechtswissenschaft und Soziologie. Verhandlungen des ersten deutschen Soziologentages" (Tübingen, 1911).
(*b*) "Die Aufgabe der Soziologie. Erinnerungsgabe für Max Weber," I (München-Leipzig, 1923).
(*c*) "Aus der Vorgeschichte der Freirechtslehre" (Mannheim, 1925).
(*d*) "Some Rationalism about Realism," *Yale Law Journal*, 43 (1933–4).

Kantorowicz, H., and Patterson, E. W., "Legal Science," *Columbia Law Review*, 28 (1928).

Kautsky, K., "Ethik und materialistische Geschichtsauffassung" (Stuttgart, 1906).

Keller, H., "Droit naturel et droit positif en droit international public" (Paris, 1931).

Kellett, E. E., "Fashion in Literature" (London, 1931).

Kelsen, H., (*a*) "Hauptprobleme der Staatsrechtslehre entwickelt aus der Lehre vom Rechtssatze" (Tübingen, 1911).
(*b*) "Zur Soziologie des Rechts," *Arch. für Sozialwissenschaft und Sozialpolitik*, 34 (1912).
(*c*) "Eine Grundlegung der Rechtssoziologie," *Ibid.* 39 (1915).
(*d*) "Erwiderung" (to Ehrlich). *Ibid.* 41 (1915).
(*e*) "Das Problem der Souveränität und die Theorie des Völkerrechts" (Tübingen, 1920).
(*f*) "Der juristische und der soziologische Staatsbegriff" (Tübingen, 1922).
(*g*) "Allgemeine Staatslehre" (Berlin, 1925).
(*h*) "Vom Wesen und Werte der Demokratie," 2te Aufl. (Tübingen, 1929).
(*i*) "Sozialismus und Staat," 2te Aufl. (Leipzig, 1923).
(*j*) "Reine Rechtslehre" (Leipzig and Wien, 1934).
(*k*) "Die Idee des Naturrechts," *Zeitschr. öffentl. Recht*, 7 (1928)
(*l*) "L'âme et le droit," *Annuaire de l'institut international de philosophie de droit et de sociologie juridique* (1935).

Kistiakovsky, Th., "Social Sciences and Law" (in Russian) (Moscow, 1915).

Kocourek, A., (*a*) "An Introduction to the Science of Law" (Boston, 1930).

(*b*) "The Hohfeld System of Fundamental Legal Concepts," *Ill. Law Quart.* 15 (1920).

Kocourek, A., and Wigmore, H., "Evolution of Law. Select Readings on the Origin and Development of Legal Institutions." 3 vols. (Boston, 1915).

Kohler, J. D., (*a*) "Die Anfänge des Rechts und das Recht der primitiven Völker" *Kultur der Gegenwart*, VII, I (Leipzig, 1914).

(*b*) "Das Recht der Halbkulturvölker," *Ibid.*

(*c*) "Orientalisches Recht und Recht der Griechen und Römer," *Ibid.*

Kohlrausch, J., "Zweikampf," *Vergleichende Darstellung des deutschen und ausländischen Strafrechts*, *Besonderer Teil*, III, (Berlin, 1906).

Korkunoff, N. M., (*a*) "Russian Constitutional Law" (in Russian), 4th ed. (St. Petersburg, 1893–1901).

(*b*) "General Theory of Law" (in Russian) English translation (Boston, 1909).

Kornfeld, I., (*a*) "Soziale Machtverhältnisse. Grundlegung einer allgemeinen Lehre vom positiven Rechte auf soziologischer Grundlage" (Wien, 1911).

(*b*) "Das Rechtsgefühl," *Zeitschrift für Rechtsphilosophie*, I (1931).

Kotliarevsky, S., "Power and Law" (in Russian) (Moscow, 1915).

Kovalevsky, M. M., "Modern Custom and Ancient Law" (in Russian) 2 vols. (Moscow, 1886), French translation (Paris, 1893).

Krabbe, H., "Die Lehre von der Rechtssouveränität" (Groningen, 1906).

Krafft-Ebbing, R. v., "Lehrbuch der gerichtlichen Psychopathologie," 3te Aufl. (Stuttgart, 1900).

Kraft, J., (*a*) "Vorfragen der Rechtssoziologie." *Zeitschr. für vergl. Rechtswiss.* 45 (1930).

(*b*) "Rechtssoziologie." *Handwörterbuch der Soziologie* (ed. Vierkandt) (Stuttgart, 1931).

Kropotkin, P., (*a*) "Anarchism-Communism; Its Basis and Principles," 2 vols. (London, 1895).

(*b*) "La conquête du pain," 5me ed. (Paris, 1895).

(*c*) "Paroles d'un révolté" (Paris, no date).

(*d*) "Revolutionary Studies" (London, 1892).

Kulischer, E., "Das Strafrecht der Giliaken," *Zeitschr. für die ges. Strafrechtswissenschaft*, 30 (1910).

Laband, P., "Das Staatsrecht des deutschen Reichs," 3 vols. 5te Aufl. (Tübingen, 1911–4).
Lagardelle, H., "Le socialisme ouvrier" (Paris, 1911).
Lambert, E., (*a*) "Le droit coûtumier contemporain" (Paris, 1893).
(*b*) "La fonction du droit civil comparé," I (Paris, 1903).
LaPiere, R. T., and Farnsworth, P. R., "Social Psychology" (New York, 1936).
Landis, J. M., "Statutes and the Sources of Law," *Harvard Legal Essays* (Cambridge, Mass., 1934).
Lashley, K. S., "Brain Mechanisms and Intelligence" (Chicago, 1929).
Laski, H., "Authority in Modern State" (New Haven, 1919).
Laun, R. v., (*a*) "Recht und Sittlichkeit" (Hamburg, 1927).
(*b*) "Der Wandel der Ideen Staat und Volk als Ausserung des Weltgewissens" (Barcelona, 1933).
Le Henaff, A., "Le droit et les forces" (Paris, 1926).
Leist, B. W., "Die realen Grundlagen und die Stoffe des Rechts" (Jena, 1877).
Lenin, W., "The State and the Revolution" (in Russian) (Petrograd, 1918).
Leopold, L., "Prestige" (London, 1913).
Le Senne, R., "Le devoir" (Paris, 1930).
Lévy-Bruhl, L., "La morale et la science des moeurs" (Paris, 1903).
Lewin, K., "Wille, Vorsatz und Bedürfniss" (Berlin, 1925).
Leyet, H., "Les jugements du président Magnaud" (Paris, 1900).
Lindesmith, A., and Levin, Y., "The Lombrosian Myth in Criminology," *Am. Journ. Sociology*, 42 (1937).
Lindemann, E., "Social Discovery" (New York, 1924).
Linton, R., "Study of Man" (New York, 1936).
Lipsius, J. H., "Attisches Recht und Rechtsverfahren," 3 vols. (Leipzig, 1905–15).
Lisle, J., "The Justification of Punishment," *Intern. Journ. Ethics*, 25 (1914–5).
Liszt, F. v., (*a*) "Lehrbuch des deutschen Strafrechts," 24te Aufl. (Berlin, 1922).
(*b*) "Das Völkerrecht systematisch dargestellt," 12te Aufl. (Berlin, 1925).
Llewellyn, K. N., "Some Realism about Realism," *Harv. Law Review*, 44 (1930–1).
Löffler, A., "Die Schuldformen des Strafrechts in vergleichender historischer und dogmatischer Darstellung," I (Leipzig, 1895).
Lombroso, C., "L'uomo delinquente" (Torino, 1876).
Loria, A., "The Economic Foundations of Society" (transl. from Italian) (New York, 1899).
Lumley, F. E., "Means of Social Control" (New York, 1925).

Luriia, A. B., "The Nature of Human Conflicts" (transl. from Russian) (New York, 1932).
MacDougall, W., "An Introduction to Social Psychology," 10th ed. (Boston, 1916).
MacIver, R. M., (*a*) "The Modern State" (Oxford, 1926).
(*b*) "Society" (New York, 1926).
Mackay, J. H., "Max Stirner. Sein Leben und seine Werke" (Berlin, 1898).
Maine, Sir H., (*a*) "Ancient Law. Its Connection with the Early History of Society and Its Relation to Modern Ideas" (London, 1861).
(*b*) "Early History of Institutions" (New York, 1875).
(*c*) "Dissertation on Early Law and Custom" (London, 1883).
Makariewicz, J., "Einleitung in die Philosophie des Strafrechts auf entwickelungsgeschichtlicher Grundlage" (Stuttgart, 1906).
Malan, G. H. T., "The Behavioristic Aspect of the Science of Law," *Amer. Bar Assoc. Journ.* 8–9 (1922–3).
Malaparte, C., "Technique du coup d'État" (Paris, 1931).
Malinowsky, B., (*a*) "Crime and Custom in Savage Society" (London, 1926).
(*b*) "Introduction to Ian Hogbin's Law and Order in Polynesia" (London, 1934).
Mallieux, F., "L'exégèse des codes et la nature du raisonnement juridique" (Paris, 1908).
Mannheim, K., "Ideology and Utopia" (transl. from German) (New York, 1936).
Margolin, A., "The Element of Vengeance in Punishment," *Amer. Journ. Crim. Law*, 24 (1933–4).
Martens, F. v., "International Law" (in Russian). French translation (Paris, 1883–7). German translation (Berlin, 1883–6).
Marx, K., (*a*) "Zur Judenfrage. Neue Ausgabe" (Berlin, 1919).
(*b*) "Zur Kritik der politischen Ökonomie" (Basel, 1859).
(*c*) "Zur Kritik des sozialdemokratischen Parteiprogramm." *Neue Zeit* I.
Marx, K., und Engels, F., "Das Kommunistische Manifesto" (1848).
Masaryk, Th. G., "Die philosophischen und soziologischen Grundlagen des Marxismus" (Wien, 1899).
Maslov, A. H., "Dominance Feeling, Behavior and Status," *Psychol. Review*, 44 (1937).
Mayer, M. E., "Rechtsnormen und Kulturnormen" (Breslau, 1903).
Mayer, O., "Deutsches Verwaltungsrecht" (Leipzig, 1895).
Mazzarella, G., (*a*) "Les types sociaux et le droit" (Paris, 1908).

(*b*) "Studi di etnologia guiridica," 15 vols. (Catania, 1903–37).

Mead, G. H., "The Psychology of Punitive Justice," *Amer. Journ. Sociol.* 23 (1917–8).

Mechem, Ph., "The Jurisprudence of Despair," *Iowa Law Review* (May, 1936).

Meinong, A., "Psychologisch-ethische Untersuchungen zur Werttheorie" (Graz, 1894).

Merkel, A., "Juristischen Enzylopädie," 7te Aufl. (Leipzig, 1922).

Merriam, Ch., "Political Power" (New York, 1934).

Merton, R., "The Unanticipated Consequences of the Purposive Social Activities," *Amer. Sociol. Review*, 1, (1936).

Merz, E., "Blutrache bei den Israeliten" (Leipzig, 1916).

Meyendorf, A., "The Theory of Petrazhitsky." In *Modern Theories of Law.*

Meyerson, E., "Identité et réalité" (Paris, 1927).

Mezger, E., "Strafrecht" (München und Leipzig, 1933).

Michael, J., and Adler, M., "Crime, Law, and Social Science" (New York, 1933).

Michels, R., "Zur Soziologie des Parteiwesens in der modernen Demokratie," 2te Aufl. (Leipzig, 1925).

Mira, E., "A New Conception of Moral Behavior," *Am. Journ. Crim. Law*, 24 (1933–4).

"Modern Theories of Law," London School of Econ. and Polit. Science (London, 1933).

Mokre, H., "Theorie des Gewohnheitsrechts" (Wien, 1932).

Mommsen, Th., (*a*) "Römisches Staatsrecht" (Leipzig, 1887–8).
(*b*) "Römisches Strafrecht" (Leipzig, 1899).
(*c*) "Zum ältesten Strafrecht der Kulturvölker. Fragen zur Rechtsvergleichung" (Leipzig, 1905).

Moore, U., and Sussman, G., "Das Gesetz des Juristen." Soziologus, 8 (1932).

Morgenthau, H., "La réalité des normes" (Paris, 1934).

Müller-Freienfels, R., "The Evolution of Modern Psychology." (New Haven, 1935).

Mumford, E., "The Origin of Leadership," *Amer. Journ. Sociol.* (1906).

Muromtseff, S., "Definition and Division of Law" (in Russian) (Moscow, 1879).

Murphy, G., Murphy, L., and Newcomb, Th., "Experimental Social Psychology" (New York, 1937).

Nagler, J., "Die Strafe," I (Leipzig, 1918).

Nardi-Greco, C., "La sociologia giuridica" (Torino, 1907).

Navratil, A., "Wirtschaft und Recht." *Zeitschr. für ungarisches öffentliches und Privatrecht* (Budapest, 1906).

Nettlau, M., "Der Anarchismus von Proudhon zu Kropotkin" (Berlin, 1927).
Nicolai, H., "Die rassengesetzliche Rechtslehre" (München, 1932).
Nöldecke, Th., "Arabisch" in Mommsen (c).
Novgorodtseff, P., "Social Ideals" (in Russian), 5th ed. (Berlin, 1922).
Odum, H. W., "Notes on the Technicways in Contemporary Society," *Am. Sociol. Rev.* 2 (1937).
Oppenheim, L., "Die Objecte des Verbrechens" (Basel, 1894).
Ortega y Gasset, "The Revolt of the Masses." Transl. from Spanish (New York, 1932).
Orton, W., "The Sources of Natural Law," *Intern. Journ. Ethics*, 36 (1925–6).
Pareto, V., "Mind and Society." Transl. from Italian. 4 vols. (New York, 1935).
Parsons, T., (*a*) "The Place of Ultimate Values in Sociological Theory," *Intern. Journ. Ethics*, 45 (1935).
(*b*) "The Structure of Social Action" (New York, 1937).
Paschukanis, E., "Allgemeine Rechtslehre und Marxismus" (Wien, 1929).
Pavlov, I., (*a*) "Twenty-Five Years of Objective Study of the Highest Nervous Activity of Animals" (in Russian) (Leningrad, 1925), English transl. (London, 1928).
(*b*) "Conditioned Reflexes" (in Russian) (Lenigrad, 1927), English transl. (London, 1927).
(*c*) "Essai de l'interprétation physiologique de l'hystérie" (Encéphale, 1933).
Perry, R. B., "General Theory of Values" (New York, 1926).
Petrazhitsky, L., (*a*) "Introduction to the Study of Law and Morals" (in Russian), 3d ed. (St. Petersburg, 1908).
(*b*) "Theory of Law and State" (in Russian), 2d ed. (St. Petersburg, 1909).
Pew, Maj. Gen. W. A., "Making a Soldier" (Boston, 1917).
Philips, H. A. D., "The Indian Penal Code" (Calcutta, 1899).
Piaget, J., "Le jugement moral des enfants" (Paris, 1931).
Piéron, H., "Psychologie experimentelle" (Paris, 1930).
Pigors, P., "Leadership and Domination" (Boston, 1935).
Piot, A., "Droit naturel et réalisme" (Paris, 1930).
Planiol, M., "Traité élémentaire de droit civil," 2me ed. (Paris, 1901–3).
Platonoff, K. I., "Hypnosis and Suggestion" (in Russian) (Kharkow, 1925).
Post, A. H., (*a*) "Afrikanische Jurisprudenz" (Oldenburg, 1887).
(*b*) "Bausteine für eine Rechtswissenschaft auf vergleichend ethnologischer Grundlage" (Oldenburg, 1880).

(*c*) "Die Grundlagen des Rechts. Leitfaden für den Aufbau einer allgemeinen Rechtswissenschaft auf soziologischer Basis" (Oldenburg, 1884).
(*d*) "Grundriss einer ethnologischen Jurisprudenz," 2 vols. (Oldenburg, 1894–5).

Pound, R., (*a*) "Common Law and Legislation," *Harv. Law Review*, 21 (1907–8).
(*b*) "The Scope and Purpose of Sociological Jurisprudence," *Harv. Law Review*, 24–25 (1911–2).
(*c*) "Legislation as Social Function," *Am. Journ. Sociol.* 18 (1912–3).
(*d*) "Courts and Legislation," *Am. Polit. Sc. Review*, 7 (1913).
(*e*) "The End of Law as Developed in Legal Rules and Doctrines," *Harv. Law Review*, 28 (1914–5).
(*f*) "Juridical Problems of National Progress," *Am. Journ. Sociol.* 22 (1916–7).
(*g*) "Theory of Social Interests," *Publications of Am. Sociol. Soc.* (New York, 1920).
(*h*) "Interpretations of Legal History" (New York, 1923).
(*i*) "Soziologische Jurisprudenz," *Jahrbuch der Soziologie*, I (Karlsruhe, 1925).
(*j*) "Law and Morals" (Chapel Hill, 1926).
(*k*) "Sociology and Law." In *The Social Sciences and Their Interrelation* (Cambridge, Mass., 1927).
(*l*) "Introduction to Sayre's Cases on Criminal Law" (New York, 1927).
(*m*) "Criminal Justice in America" (New York, 1930).
(*n*) "The Call for a Realistic Jurisprudence," *Harv. Law Review*, 44 (1930–1).
(*o*) "Twentieth Century Ideas as to the End of Law," *Harv. Legal Essays* (Cambridge, Mass., 1934).
(*p*) Introduction to Cairn's "Law and the Social Sciences."
(*q*) Introduction to Ehrlich's "Fundamental Principles."
(*r*) "What is Common Law." In "The Future of Common Law." *Harvard Tercentenary Publications* (Cambridge, Mass., 1937).
(*s*) "Fifty Years of Jurisprudence," *Harv. Law Review*, 50–1 (1937–8).

Prescott, W. H., "History of the Reign of Ferdinand and Isabella," I (Boston, 1838).

Preuss, H., "Gemeinde, Staat, Reich als Gebietskörperschaften" (Berlin, 1889).

Proudhon, P. J., (a) "Les confessions d'un révolutionnaire" (Paris, 1849).
(b) "Idée générale de la révolution du 19me siècle" (Paris, 1851).
Puchta, G. F., (a) "Das Gewohnheitsrecht," 2 vols. (Erlangen, 1828–37).
(b) "Cursus der Institutionen," 2 vols. (Leipzig, 1845).
Quetelet, A. J., "Sur l'homme et le développement de ses facultés," 2 vols. (Bruxelles, 1835–6).
Radbruch, G., (a) "Rechtsphilosophie" (Leipzig, 1914).
(b) "La theorie anglo-américaine du droit vue par un juriste du continent," *Arch. de phil. de droit et de sociol. juridique* (1936).
Ranulf, S., "The Jealousy of the Gods and the Criminal Law of Athens" (London, 1934).
Raper, A., "The Tragedy of Lynching" (Chapel Hill, 1933).
Ratto, L., "Sociologia a filosofia del diritto" (Milano, 1894).
Ratzel, F., (a) "Anthropogeographie, oder Grundsätze des Anwendung der Erdkunde auf die Geschichte" (Stuttgart, 1882–91).
(b) "Politische Geographie" (München, 1903).
Réglade, M., "La coutume en droit public interne" (Paris, 1919).
Reichel, H., "Gesetz und Richteramt" (Zürich, 1915).
Renard, G., "La théorie de l'institution" (Paris, 1930).
Renner, K., "Die Rechtsinstitute des Privatrechts und ihre soziale Funktion" (Tübingen, 1929).
Rheinstein, M., (a) "Comparative Law and Conflict of Law in Germany," *University of Chicago Law Review*, 2 (1935).
(b) Apropos Moll's translation of E. Ehrlich's "Grundlegung" . . . *Int. Journ. Ethics*, 48 (1938).
(c) Comment to Timasheff's article (*k*). *Am. Journ. Sociol.* (Sept., 1938).
Riezler, E., "Das Rechtsgefühl" (München, 1921).
Ripert, G., "Droit naturel et positivisme juridique." Annales de la faculté de droit d'Aix. Nouvelle série (1918).
Rippy, F., "Dictators in Spanish America." In Ford, G. S., "Dictatorship in Modern World" (Minneapolis, 1935).
Robinson, E. S., "Law and Lawyers" (New York, 1935).
Robson, W. A., "Civilization and the Growth of Law" (London, 1935).
Rogge, H., "Versuch zur Genealogie des Rechts als eine Grundlage für eine Kritik des Rechts," *Zeitschr. für vergl. Rechtswiss.* 27 (1912).
Rolin, H., "Prolégomènes à la science du droit" (Bruxelles, 1911).

Ross, E. A., "Social Control" (New York, 1901).
Rougier, L., "Les mystiques politiques contemporaines et leurs incidences internationales" (Paris, 1935).
Rudeck, W., "Geschichte der öffentlichen Sittlichkeit in Deutschland," 2te Aufl. (Berlin, 1905).
Rümelin, M., "Rechtsgefühl und Rechtsbewusstsein" (1925).
Rumpf, M., "Was ist Rechtssoziologie," *Arch. für civil. Praxis*, 122 (1924).
Russell, B., "Power" (New York, 1938).
Salmond, G. J. W., "Jurisprudence or the Theory of Law" (London, 1902).
Savigny, F. K. v., (*a*) "System des heutigen römischen Rechts," 8 vols. (Berlin, 1840–9).
(*b*) "Vom Beruf unserer Zeit zur Gesetzgebung und Rechtswissenschaft" (Heidelberg, 1814). Neudruck (Heidelberg, 1892).
Scheler, M., (*a*) "Der Formalismus in der Ethik und die materielle Wertethik. Das normative Sollen" (Halle, 1921).
(*b*) "Formen und Wesen der Sympathie" (Bonn, 1923).
Schein, J., "Unsere Jurisprudenz und Rechtsphilosophie" (Berlin, 1889).
Schjedrupp-Ebbe, T., "Die Despotie im sozialen Leben der Vögel," *Forschungen zur Völkerpsychologie und Soziologie*, 19 (1931).
Schinkler, D., "Verfassungsrecht und soziale Struktur" (Zürich, 1932).
Schmidt, R., "Aufgaben der Strafrechtspflege" (Freiburg, 1895).
Schmitt, K., "Die Diktatur" (München, 1921).
Schmoller, G., "Grundriss der allgemeinen Volkswirtschaftslehre," I (Leipzig, 1900).
Schönfeld, W., "Vom Problem der Rechtsgeschichte." *Schriften der königsberger gelehrten Gesellschaft* (Halle, 1927).
Schuppe, W., "Das Gewohnheitsrecht" (Breslau, 1890).
Schutzenberger, E. F., "Etudes de droit public. De la nature du droit" (Strassbourg, 1837).
Sergeevitch, V. I., "Russian Juridical Antiquities" (in Russian), 2 vols. (St. Petersburg, 1890–3).
Sharp, F., and Otto, M. C., (*a*) "A Study of the Popular Attitudes towards Retributive Punishment," *Intern. Journ. Ethics*, 20 (1909–10).
(*b*) "Retribution and Deterrence in the Moral Judgment of Common Sense," *Ibid.*
Sherif, M., "The Psychology of Social Norms" (New York, 1936).
Sidis, B., "The Psychology of Suggestion" (New York, 1898).

Simmel, G., (*a*) "Soziologie. Untersuchungen über die Formen der Vergesellschaftung" (Leipzig, 1908).
(*b*) "Philosophie der Mode" (Berlin, 1905).
(*c*) "Philosophie des Geldes" 4te Aufl. (Leipzig, 1922).

Sinzheimer, H., (*a*) "Die soziologische Methode in der Privatrechtswissenschaft" (München, 1909).
(*b*) "De Taak der Rechtssoziologie" (in Dutch) (Haarlem, 1935).

Soloview, W., "The Vindication of the Goodness" (in Russian). Coll. works, 7. (St. Petersburg, 1897).

Sorel, G., (*a*) "Réflexions sur la violence," 3me ed. (Paris, 1912).
(*b*) "Matériaux d'une théorie du prolétariat" (Paris, 1919).

Sorokin, P. A., (*a*) "Sociology of Revolution" (Philadelphia, 1925).
(*b*) "American Millionaires and Multimillionaires," *Soc. Forces* (1925).
(*c*) "Monarchs and Rulers. A comparative statistical study," *Soc. Forces* (1925–6).
(*d*) "Social Mobility" (New York, 1927).
(*e*) "Contemporary Sociological Theories" (New York, 1928).
(*f*) "The Principle of Limits Applied to Problems of Relationship and of Direction of Social Processes," *Public. of the Amer. Sociol. Society*, 26 (1932).
(*g*) "Le concept d'équilibre est-il nécessaire aux sciences sociales," *Public. of the Amer. Sociol. Society*, 26 (1936).
(*h*) "Social and Cultural Dynamics," 3 vols. (New York, 1937).

Spencer, H., "Principles of Sociology," 3 vols. (London, 1880–96).

Spiegel, L., "Jurisprudenz und Sozialwissenschaft," *Grünhut's Zeitschr.* 36 (1909).

Stammler, R. v., (*a*) "Recht und Willkür" (Halle, 1895).
(*b*) "Die Theorie des Anarchismus" (Berlin, 1894).
(*c*) "Wirtschaft und Recht nach der materialistischen Geschichtsauffassung," 5te Aufl. (Leipzig, 1924).
(*d*) "Die Lehre vom richtigen Rechte," 2te Aufl. (Halle, 1926).
(*e*) "Die materialistische Geschichtsauffassung" (Gütersloh, 1927).

Stearns, A. W., "The Evolution of Punishment," *Journ. Crim. Law*, 26 (1935–6).

Steinmetz, S. R., (*a*) "Ethnologische Studien zur ersten Entwickelung der Strafe," 2 vols. (Leiden, 1894).
(*b*) "Soziologie des Krieges" (Leipzig, 1929).
Stephen, Sir James, "A History of the Criminal Law in England," 3 vols. (London, 1883).
Stern, W., "System des kritischen Personalismus" (Leipzig, 1924).
Sternberg, Th., "Einführung in die Rechtswissenschaft," 2te Aufl. (Leipzig, 1912).
Stölzel, A., "Fünfzehn Vorträge aus der brandenburgisch-preussischen Rechts- und Staatsgeschichte" (Berlin, 1889).
Störk, F., "Studien zur soziologischen Rechtslehre," *Arch. öffentl. Rechts*, I (1886).
Stone, H. F., "The Common Law in the United States," In: "The Future of Common Law," *Harvard Tercentenary Publicat.* (Cambridge, Mass., 1937).
Stoop, A., "Analyse de la notion du droit" (Haarlem, 1927).
Strachey, G. L., "The Coming Struggle for Power" (New York, 1935).
Sumner, W. G., "Folkways" (Boston, 1906).
Sutherland, R. L., and Woodwarth, J. L., "Introductory Sociology" (Chicago, 1937).
Szende, P., "Sur Soziologie drakonischer Gesetze." *Zeitschr. für soziales Recht* 4 (1931–2).
Tabbah, B., "Du heurt à l'harmonies des droits" (Paris, 1936).
Tagantseff, N. S., "Russian Criminal Law" (in Russian), 2 vols. (St. Petersburg, 1902).
Taranovsky, Th., (*a*) "Legal Encyclopedia" (in Russian), 2d ed. (Berlin, 1923).
(*b*) "History of Serbian Law" (in Serbian), I (Belgrade, 1931).
Tarde, G., (*a*) "Les lois de l'imitation" (Paris, 1890). English transl. (New York, 1903).
(*b*) "Les transformations du pouvoir." 2me éd. (Paris, 1903).
(*c*) "Les transformations du droit" 8me édit. (Paris, 1922).
Tassitch, G., "L'État et le droit." *Archives de philosophie du droit et de sociologie juridique*, 3 (1933).
Thomas, W. I., "Primitive Behavior" (New York, 1937).
Thurnwald, R. C., (*a*) "Banaro Society." *Memoirs of the Amer. Anthrop. Association* (1916).
(*b*) "Werden, Wesen und Gestaltung des Rechts im Lichte der Völkerforschung" (Berlin, 1934).
(*c*) "Cultural Rotation," *Amer. Sociol. Review*, 2 (1937).

Timasheff, N. S., (*a*) "Tendencies in the Development of Law" (in Russian). *Journ. of the Ministry of Justice* (1913).
(*b*) "Law and Social Psychology" (in Russian). Works of Russian Scholars outside Russia, II (Berlin, 1922).
(*c*) "Grundzüge des sovietrussischen Staatsrechts" (Mannheim-Berlin, 1925).
(*d*) "L'evoluzione del diritto penal sovietico. Rivista italiana del diritto penale" (1932).
(*e*) "The Essence of Law" (in Russian). *Law and Courts* (Riga, 1935).
(*f*) "L'éthique, le droit, le pouvoir." *Archives de philosophie de droit et de sociologie juridique*, 6 (1936).
(*g*) "What is the Sociology of Law," *Amer. Journ. Sociol.* 43 (1937).
(*h*) "The Retributive Structure of Punishment," *Journ. Crim. Law*, 28 (1937).
(*i*) "Nationalisierung der Banken in Sovietrussland und ihre rechtliche Wirkungen im Auslande," *Arch. civil. Praxis*, 129 (1928).
(*j*) "Gesetz und gerichtliche Praxis im heutigen Russland," *Arch. civil. Praxis*, 133 (1930–1).
(*k*) "The Sociological Place of Law," *Am. Journ. Sociol.* (Sept., 1938).

Tolman, E. C., "Purposive Behavior in Animals and Men" (New York, 1932).

Tolstoi, L. N., Collected works (in Russian) (Moscow, 1911).

Tönnies, F., (*a*) "Die Sitte" (Frankfurt M., 1909).
(*b*) "Einteilung der Soziologie," *Zeitschr. für die ges. Staatswissenschaften*, 79 (1925).
(*c*) "Thomas Hobbes," 3te Aufl. (Stuttgart, 1925).
(*d*) "Einführung in die Soziologie (Stuttgart, 1931).

Tourtoulon, P., "Les principes philosophiques de l'histoire du droit" (Lausanne, 1919). English translation (New York, 1922).

Triepel, H., "Volkerrecht und Landesrecht" (Leipzig, 1899).

Trimborn, H., "Die Methode der ethnologischen Jurisprudenz," *Zeitschr. vergl. Rechtswissensch.* 43 (1928).

Tripp, E., "Untersuchungen zur Rechtspsychologie des Individuums" (Leipzig, 1931).

Tufts, J. H., "America's Social Morality" (New York, 1933).

Vaccaro, M., "Les bases sociologiques du droit et de l'État" (Paris, 1898).

Vecchio, G. del., (*a*) "Principi generali di diritto" (Modena, 1921).
(*b*) "Droit et économie," *Revue d'économie politique* (1935).
(*c*) "Ethics, Law, and the State," *Intern. Journ. Ethics*, 46 (1937).
(*d*) "The Homo Juridicus and the Inadequacy of Law as a Norm of Life," *Tulane Law Review*, 11 (1937).

Véniamin, V. L., "Essai sur les données économiques dans l'obligation civile" (Paris, 1931).

Vierkandt, A., "Gesellschaftslehre" (Stuttgart, 1928).

Vinogradoff, Sir P., (*a*) "Common Sense in Law" (New York, 1913).
(*b*) "Outlines of Historical Jurisprudence" (London, 1920–2)
(*c*) "Custom and Right" (Cambridge, Mass., 1925).
(*d*) "Customary Law." In Crump, Ch., and Jacob, E. F., "The Legacy of the Middle Ages" (Oxford, 1926).
(*e*) "Comparative Jurisprudence," *Enc. Brit.*, 11th edition, 15.

Vladimirsky-Budanoff, M., "History of Russian Law" (in Russian) (Kiew, 1904).

Voigt, A., "Wirtschaft und Recht." *Zeitschr. für Sozialwiss.* Neue Folge 2 (1911).

Wallas, G., "Great Society" (New York, 1914).

Ward, L., (*a*) "Dynamic Sociology" (New York, 1883).
(*b*) "Psychic Factors of Civilization" (Boston, 1897).
(*c*) "Outlines of Sociology" (London, 1898).
(*d*) "Pure Sociology" (New York, 1903).

Watson, J. B., "Behavior. An Introduction to Comparative Psychology" (New York, 1914).

Waxweiler, E., "Esquisse d'une sociologie" (Bruxelles, 1906).

Weber, M., (*a*) "Stammler's Überwindung der materialistischen Geschichtsauffassung," *Arch. für Sozialwiss. und Sozialpolitik*, 24 (1907).
(*b*) "Gesammelte Aufsätze zur Religionssoziologie" (Tübingen, 1922–3).
(*c*) "Wirtschaft und Gesellschaft." In *Grundriss der Sozialökonomik.* 2te Aufl. (Tübingen, 1925).

Weigelin, E., "Sitte, Recht une Moral" (Berlin, 1919).

Weininger, O., "Geschlecht und Charakter" (Wien, 1904; English transl., New York, 1906).

Wellhausen, J., "Ein Gemeinwesen ohne Obrigkeit" (Göttingen, 1900).

Westermarck, E., "Origin and Development of Moral Ideas," 2 vols. (New York, 1906).
Wharton, F., "Commentaries on Law" (Philadelphia, 1884).
Whitehead, T. H., "Leadership in Free Society" (Cambridge, Mass., 1936).
Wilson, Ch., "The Basis of Kelsen's Theory of Law," *Politica*, I (1934-5).
Windelbandt, W., "Über Willensfreiheit" (Tübingen, 1905).
Windscheid, B., "Lehrbuch des Pandektenrechts," 3 vols. (Düsseldorf, 1875-8).
Worms, R., (*a*) "La sociologie et le droit," *Revue intern. de sociologie* (1895).
(*b*) "Philosophie des sciences sociales" (Paris, 1907).
Wundt, W., (*a*) "Völkerpsychologie," Band IX. Das Recht. (Leipzig, 1918).
(*b*) "Logik der Geisteswissenschaften," 4te Aufl. (1921).
Yarros, V. S., "Philosophical Anarchism. Its Decline and Eclipse," *Amer. Journ. Sociol.* 41 (1935-6).
Yntema, H. E., "The Rational Basis of Legal Sciences," *Col. Law Review*, 31 (1931).
Young, K., "The Nature of Public Opinion." Sourcebook for Soc. Psychology (New York, 1927).
Zhizhilenko, A. A., "Punishment" (in Russian) (St. Petersburg, 1914).
Zitelmann, E., "Irrtum und Rechtsgeschäft" (Leipzig, 1879).
Zoccoli, E., "Anarchia" (Torino, 1907). Germ. transl. (1908).
Zuckerman, S., "The Social Life of Monkeys and Apes" (New York, 1932).
Zürcher, E., "Die Verneinung des Strafrechts," *Schweizer Zeitschrift für Strafrecht*, 32 (1919).

INDEX OF AUTHORS

INDEX OF SUBJECTS